LAW AND CIVILIZATION

The Legal Thought of Roscoe Pound

Edward B. McLean
Eugene N. and Marian C. Beesley Chair
Department of Political Science
Wabash College

UNIVERSITY PRESS OF AMERICA

Lanham • New York • London

University Press of America®, Inc.
4720 Boston Way
Lanham, Maryland 20706

3 Henrietta Street
London WC2E 8LU England

Printed in the United States of America
British Cataloging in Publication Information Available

Library of Congress Cataloging-in-Publication Data

McLean, Edward B.
Law and civilization : the legal thought of Roscoe Pound / by Edward B. McLean.
p. cm.
Includes bibliographical references.
1. Pound, Roscoe, 1870–1964. 2. Sociological jurisprudence.
3. Law—Philosophy. I. Title.
K369.M35 1992 340'.115—dc20 92–2245 CIP

ISBN 0–8191–8698–8 (cloth : alk. paper)

The paper used in this publication meets the minimum requirements of American National Standard for Information Sciences—Permanence of Paper for Printed Library Materials, ANSI Z39.48–1984.

This book is dedicated to the memory of my parents
Mr. & Mrs. Alexander MacDonald McLean

Acknowledgements

The author wishes to acknowledge the following presses which have extended permission for use of materials published by them, which have been quoted in this book.

The Political Science Reviewer, Intercollegiate Studies Institute, Bryn Mawr, Pennsylvania, and *Il Politico*, The University of Pavia, Italy, for their permission to use materials from articles on Roscoe Pound written by the author for these journals.

Permission granted by Alabama State Bar, *The Alabama Lawyer*, Montgomery, Alabama, for use of materials from "The Disappearance of the Law," permission granted by Alabama State Bar, *The Alabama Lawyer*, Montgomery, Alabama.

The American Bar Association for permission to use materials from: "The Limits of Effective Legal Action," "The Problem of Law," "Place of the Judiciary in a Democratic Polity," and "The Challenge of the Administrative Process," reprinted with permission from *ABA Journal*, the Lawyer's Magazine.

Materials from "Political and Economic Interpretation of Jurisprudence," from *Proceedings of the American Political Science Association, Vol. 9*, with permission from the American Political Science Association, Washington, D.C.

Materials from "A Theory of Social Interests," with permission granted the American Sociological Association, for materials appearing in *Papers and Proceedings of the American Sociological Society, Vol. 15*, Washington, D.C.

Materials from "Making Law and Finding Law," which appeared in the *Ohio Law Reporter, Vol. 15*, with permission granted by the Anderson Publishing Company, Cincinnati, Ohio.

Materials from *Interpretations of Legal History*, with permission granted by Cambridge University Press, New York City, New York.

Materials from *Contemporary Juristic Theory*, with permission granted by the Claremont Colleges, Claremont, California.

Materials from "Justice According to Law, Part I," Copyright c. 1913 by the Directors of the Columbia Law Review Association, Inc. All Rights Reserved. This article originally appeared at 13 *Colum. L. Rev.* 696 (1913). Reprinted by permission. "Justice According to Law, Part II," Copyright c. 1914 by the Directors of the Columbia Law Review Association, Inc. All Rights Reserved. This article originally appeared at 14 *Colum. L. Rev.* 1 (1914). Reprinted by permission. "Justice According to Law, Part III," Copyright c. 1914 by the Directors of the Columbia Law Review Association, Inc. All Rights Reserved. This article originally appeared at 14 *Colum. L. Rev.* 103 (1914). Reprinted by permission.

Materials from *The Task of the Law*, Franklin & Marshall College, Lancaster, Pennsylvania.

Materials from Roscoe Pound, *Law and Civilization*, (c) 1960 by the University of Georgia Press. Used by permission.

Materials from *The Harvard Law Review* published by the Harvard Law Review Association, Cambridge, Massachusetts: "The Scope and Purpose of Sociological Jurisprudence, I, II, III" (c) 1911, 1911, & 1912 by the Harvard Law Review Association; "The End of Law as Developed in Legal Rules and Doctrines," (c) 1914 by the Harvard Law Review Association; "The End of Law as Developed in Juristic Thought," (c) 1914 by the Harvard Law Review Association; "Interests of Personality," (c) 1915 by the Harvard Law Review Association; "Juristic Science and Law," (c) 1918 by the Harvard Law Review Association; "the Progress of the Law—Analytical Jurisprudence 1914-1927," (c) 1927 by the Harvard Law Review Association; "The Call for a Realist Jurisprudence," (c) 1931 by the Harvard Law Review Association; "A Comparison of Ideals of Law," (c) 1933 by the Harvard Law Review Association; "The Theory of Judicial Decision," (c) 1923 by the Harvard Law Review Association; "Fifty Years of Jurisprudence I, II, & III," I (c) 1937, II (c) 1938, III (c) 1938 by the Harvard Law Review Association; "A Survey of Social Interests," (c) 1943 by the Harvard Law Review Association.

Materials from *The Spirit of the Common Law*, permission granted The Golden Quill Press and Marshall Jones Company, Francestown, New Hampshire.

Materials from "The Twilight of Liberty," permission granted by *Nation's Business*, Chamber of Commerce of the United States, Washington, D.C.

Materials from "The Future of Common Law," published in the *Nebraska Law Bulletin*, with permission granted by the *Nebraska Law Review*, University of Nebraska Lincoln, Lincoln, Nebraska.

Materials from "What Use Can Be Made of Judicial Statistics," Reprinted by permission of *Oregon Law Review*, Copyright c. 1933 by University of Oregon.

Materials from "Administrative Law: Its Growth, Procedure, and Significance," with permission from *Pittsburgh Law Review*, University of Pittsburgh, Pittsburgh, Pennsylvania.

Materials from "Proposed Legislation as to Federal Administrative Procedures," published in *Indiana Law Journal, Vol. 20*, with permission granted by Fred B. Rothman & Co., Littleton, Colorado.

Materials from "The Recrudescence of Absolutism," with permission from *The Sewanee Review*, Sewanee, Tennessee.

Materials from "The Problem of an Ordered Society," published in *Tennessee Law Review, Vol. 11*, with permission granted by William S. Hein & Co., Buffalo, New York.

Materials from "Sociology of Law and Sociological Jurisprudence," published in the *University of Toronto Law Journal, Vol. 5*, with permission by the University of Toronto Press, Toronto, Ontario, Canada.

Materials from "Modern Administrative Law," published in the *Proceedings of the 50th Annual Meeting of the Virginia Bar Association*, with permission from The Virginia Bar Association, Richmond, Virginia.

Materials from "The American Idea of Government," published by *Vital Speeches, Vol. 10*, with permission from Vital Speeches of the Day, Southold, New York.

Particular acknowledgement is made of the permission of West Publishing Company to utilize materials from Roscoe Pound's monumental Five Volume work *Jurisprudence*, which was published in 1959 by West Publishing Company, St. Paul, Minnesota.

Materials from "The Growth of Administrative Justice," published in the *Proceedings of the Wisconsin Bar Association, Vol. 14*, with permission granted by the State Bar of Wisconsin, Madison, Wisconsin.

Materials from "Liberty of Contract," reprinted by permission of the Yale Law Journal Company and Fred B. Rothman & Company from *The Yale Law Journal, Vol. 18*, pp. 454-87; "Law and Science of Law in Recent Theories," reprinted by permission of the Yale Law Journal Company and Fred B. Rothman and Company from *The Yale Law Journal, Vol. 43*, pp. 525-36; "The Future of the Law" reprinted by permission *The Yale Law Journal* and Fred B. Rothman and Company from *The Yale Law Journal, Vol. 47*, pp. 1-13; "Theories of Law," reprinted by permission of the Yale Law Journal Company and Fred B. Rothman and Company from *The Yale Law Journal, Vol. 22*, pp. 114-150.

Materials from *An Introduction to the Philosophy of Law*, and *Social Control Through Law*, and *The Development of Constitutional Guarantees of Liberty*, all published by the Yale University Press with permission from Yale University Press, New Haven, Connecticut.

Greatful appreciation is expressed to the Earhart Foundation, Ann Arbor, Michigan, whose generous support facilitated much of the research for this book.

The author wishes also to acknowledge with gratitude Wabash College which has encouraged, and facilitated the research and completion of this manuscript, and to Liberty Fund Inc., Indianapolis, Indiana which sponsored two conferences dealing with Roscoe Pound's writing. The insightful discussion at those conferences provided helpful and insightful commentary on Pound's ideas.

Finally, the author wishes to acknowledge, with great love and affection, my wife Maria's constant support and encouragement in pursuing this project.

TABLE OF CONTENTS

INTRODUCTION

Roscoe Pound is considered to be one the foremost theorists of "sociological jurisprudence" in American legal history. Of this school Pound writes:

> The sociological jurist is studying law as a highly specialized social control in the developed state, in this respect following Austin in thinking of matured or developed law as his province. He holds that legal institutions and doctrines are instruments of a specialized form of social control, capable of being improved, with reference to their ends, by conscious, intelligent effort. He thinks of a process of social engineering, which in one way or another is a problem of all the social sciences. In sociological jurisprudence, it is a special problem of achieving this engineering task by means of the legal order, the body of established or recognized norms or precepts, technique of developing and applying them and received ideals in the light of which they are developed and applied, and the judicial and administrative processes. It is treated as a problem of jurisprudence, and yet in its larger aspects is not merely a problem of that science. Law in all its senses is studied as a much specialized phase of what in a larger view is a science of society.[1]

Pound never apologized for his role in founding sociological jurisprudence, which he felt was an important and respectable school of legal philosophy. Indeed, one can properly maintain that the technique and substance of sociological jurisprudence as this was developed by Roscoe Pound, provides both an effective and realistic philosophy directed toward the major objective of law, *i.e.*, the maintenance and furtherance of civilization. Current legal practice—guided by either legal realism in all of its variations, or a jurisprudence of conceptions, is "all sail with no anchor." Law, when employed by persons not directed by a legal philosophy that is consonant with the dictates of a jurisprudence securely anchored in the major tenets of western civilization, becomes a destructive force that will ultimately transform the great liberal traditions of the west and lead to an absolutist system which considers whatever is done by officials to be law. As Pound warns, this absolutism is as real when done in the name of democracy as when it is done by a king or super-man leader. Absolutism is absolutism, however it is cloaked in rhetoric or apology. Pound was bothered by the cooption of sociological jurisprudence by those who confused its principles and purposes with "socialism,"[2] for in his mind sociological jurisprudence provided both an explanation and justification for the uses to which the law had to be put in order to handle the variety and complexity of conditions with which it had to deal in the era of industrialization, urbanization, and technological change, and avoided the emphasis on power and standardlessness which he felt made legal realism and the jurisprudence of conceptions both unacceptable. Pound was convinced that the "rigidities" of nineteenth century legal philosophy were based on abstractions, and did not reflect the type of jurisprudence needed in an age of industrialization, urbanization, and technological change, which had combined to bring about significant social changes. He was not prepared, however, to reject totally what nineteenth century philosophy of law had to say, any more than he would reject as valueless all philosophical thinking of centuries preceding the nineteenth. He greatly respected all legal thinking which had attempted to formulate philosophical conceptions about law to explain its nature, role, and purpose. Because he had such a profound respect for preceding thought, much of his professional career was spent in examining and critiquing this previous philosophy. One cannot understand Pound's own prescriptive statements about the nature, role, and purpose of law, unless one examines and understands his treatment of the development of legal philosophy in the western world, and much of his writing was devoted to this examination. Pound, never felt that his writing on the nature of law, the role of the judiciary, the dangers of administrative absolutism, sprang from a "new vision" of his own creation. He viewed the development of law as a process which tied modernity to the classical era, and felt that our capacity to consider law fruitfully could only come from an historical perspective that took account of the past historical development of law in practice and theory. One can see in his examination of the development of legal philosophy the origins of much of his thought, since Pound adapted various theorists to his own formulation of sociological jurisprudence. The law of the nineteenth century—and indeed the early part of the twentieth century—was for Pound too individualistic. The rigidities that had crept into law and found expression in fairly immutable doctrines of contract and tort, and which were greatly suspicious of attempted legislative reform, Pound felt, thwarted the ability of the law, properly understood, to condition change and accommodation in ways that maintained and furthered civilization. Pound, who was neither a collectivist nor a positivist but a legal practitioner and philosopher, felt that the concepts of strict individual responsibility and individual liberty, which were suited to the strict application of principles of contract and tort law, were ill-equipped to deal with the hazards and problems which were the consequences of industrialization, urbanization, and technological change. He did not wish, however, to see every notion of individual responsibility and liberty removed from the law's concern and protection. Rather, he hoped to fashion a philosophy of law which would, on the one hand, retain the fixity and certainty of previous developments in the law which secured individual liberty and yet would, on the other hand, provide the means to accommodate individual liberty and responsibility to the changed conditions of society. Social engineering, he felt, could preserve individual liberty, responsibility, and a civilized order and yet, could also provide for advancement and change in society. Sociological jurisprudence, therefore, was suited to this end. This volume attempts to sketch the major components of Pound's legal philosophy, which cannot be fully understood without understanding that Pound's entire legal philosophy is tied to his belief that what he wrote is a reflection of a course of developments—in legal practice and legal thought—which reaches back to antiquity.

A brief examination of the bibliographies of Pound's writing reveals the enormous amount of publication which he produced during his long and productive life. Much of what he wrote, however, is of antiquarian interest, since it is directed to specific legal problems of current interest at the time he wrote, but of little enduring significance. However, even in the earliest years of his career Pound wrote much of enduring value which, when considered together, reveals a coherent and developed philosophical statement on the law. No collection of essays could reveal the texture of this philosophy, for no one thoroughly reveals it. Consequently this study divides Pound's writing into nine chapters each of which addresses a topic that is vital to understanding Pound's vision of the law as both the product and conveyor of civilization, which is the major premise of his legal philosophy and the thread that connects his treatment of all dimensions of the law. Pound identifies the symbiotic relationship between law's derivation and its task, and he would never accept the conclusion that the law is a product of will exercised by government. Rather it is, at any given period of time, a reflection of the culmination of centuries of development, which serves as a vital means of accommodating and facilitating ordered and peaceful change.

The first chapter of this study considers Pound's general theory of the law, and describes and identifies what Pound considered to be the necessary elements of the law, the explanation of its origin, and more important, its task. For Pound, law was a specialized form of social control which was complemented by, and based on, a host of other mechanisms of social control—family and church, for example—which served to curb man's selfish, self-aggrandizing, and anti-social tendencies in order to induce cooperation and accommodation that would in turn maintain and further civilization. This task in the modern era could be properly done only if one considered the historical developments in law and legal philosophy which preceded and conditioned the role of law in a developed legal order. Law must not, therefore, be viewed as something made by a sheer act of will, but must be viewed as the consequence of long historical evolution in which precepts and concepts of law emerged and were fashioned by reason and experience. Only this view of law, as historically developed, would enable man to deal with issues and questions of the modern era, in order to maintain and further civilization.

The second chapter deals with Pound's formulation of the pattern and process of legal history. Pound was of the opinion that law follows a fairly predictable pattern in its development which alternates between periods of "fixity" and periods of "innovation and change." It is in the interplay of these two alternating conditions that law is provided the wherewithal to adapt to changing conditions and circumstances. This historical record, Pound felt, revealed the law's growth, alteration, and change in dealing with the problems of social ordering. Such alterations as occur often are the result of changes in the area of legal philosophy. Consequently what men think about the law soon becomes what it is that they do with the law in practice. Pound's theory is suggestive of the growing demand for "fixity" and "certainty" in the law to replace the fluidity and flexibility of the law during the past few decades.

The bulk of Pound's scholarship during the early and middle part of his career was devoted to tracing the historical developments in legal philosophy from the classical to the modern era. Three chapters of this study distill his writing in this area. The value of Pound's scholarship in this field, however, is not confined to a mere recordation of the various schools of thought of which legal philosophy is composed for it is also a careful critique and analysis of the strengths and weaknesses of these schools of thought. Perhaps more important is Pound's identifying the ways in which these schools of legal philosophy influenced the course of the development of law through periods of "fixity" and "innovation and change."

The culmination of these developments in legal philosophy, according to Pound, was to be found in the school of sociological jurisprudence, of which he certainly is the major spokesman. Thus, chapter six provides an analysis of Pound's conception of sociological jurisprudence. Sociological jurisprudence, Pound feels, properly describes the function of law in a developed society as social engineering. Social engineering as Pound understood it was not a concept of engineering men's conduct by means of law to achieve a set of predetermined objectives and social arrangements; to consider this to be Pound's view is to "stand his theory on its head." Pound's concept of social engineering was tied to two anchors which would prevent it from being employed to create a given arrangement or style of social order. On one hand, social engineering was a technique to be employed in reacting to alterations and changes in the society. Newer, emerging interests in a society could assume that law, in responding to the circumstances or conditions which needed redressing or protection, would accommodate such interests by altering certain concepts or precepts of law which were unsuited to providing the redress or protection needed. Thus, a host of protective and regulative measures given over to the protection of an increasing industrial class would replace older theories and practices which held that contract and tort law were sufficient for the task. It was not Pound's view, however, that law should ever seek to create new interests and fashion law to protect them, or to give protection of one interest in a fashion that would destroy or make useless another equally valued interest. Indeed, in his opinion such a view or use of the law would tear "sociological jurisprudence" from its second anchor. This second anchor, was the result of the "...established or recognized norms or precepts, techniques of developing and applying them, and received ideals in the light of which they were developed and applied..."[2] The received ideals occupy the paramount importance in Pound's scheme. Central to these ideals is the preservation and maximization of individual liberty. The law, as Pound considered it, has as its primary objective the preservation and transmission of civilization. Civilization in Pound's view was not a relative term, but a product of western cultural development, which had as two of its major tenets: (1) the belief that law is a means of controlling power, and (2) that law serves to protect the individual in his liberty. Therefore, even though law was to serve emerging interests, it was not, in his view, ever proper to consider that law could be used to ride "roughshod" over other interests. The traditional precepts and norms, as well as judicial technique, would prevent this from happening and would allow for a continuation of a civilized order in which law could be nothing other than a product of experience and reason fashioned in light of the overriding necessity to preserve and transmit civilization.

His development of the theory of interests would provide the means whereby legal institutions could measure and calculate the sacrifices and advantages that must be protected and furthered if law is to serve as the mechanism to maintain and further civilization. It was Pound's belief, which becomes so evident in his critique of nineteenth century legal philosophy, that concepts of contract, strict responsibility, and individualism, all were unsuited to modern society, for the reason that modern society's challenges to individuals were almost beyond their control, and could not be satisfactorily resolved by the application of a theory of abstractions such as freedom of contract. Rather, the legislative bodies, and the courts, must evaluate the interests that would be effected by any decision and the theory of interests was to provide the balancing scale wherein such measuring of interests could be weighed. What is interesting about Pound's theory of interests, however, is that he did not feel that this was some form of pure mechanical calculation. Rather, the weighing of interests would proceed on the basis of applying values of a civilized society against the interests involved and the resolution to be made. Never in the course of his writing about sociological jurisprudence or his theory of interests does he forget that the function of law is the preservation and transmission of a civilized society, which requires that respect be accorded to the individuals involved. Consequently, the decision to evaluate one interest in preference to another would reflect a concern about the impact such a decision would have on the civilized order to be served. What is most frequently ignored by those in the legal or judicial profession, is that Pound's argument of balancing interests was not confined to some type of relative economic condition or strength. Indeed, his theory of interests is far more richly textured and descriptive of the complexity which characterizes modern society. Thus, when Pound speaks of balancing interests he is speaking of interests in the security of institutions, moral life, individual life, general security, and the conservation of social resources. Nothing so prosaic as mere economic interests dominated the structure of his theory of interests. Rather, Pound's theory of interests would require the highest degree of imagination and competence for its proper employment. He would, no doubt, be saddened by the misuse of this theory as it is currently used in legal practice and legal thought.

In the same fashion he argues that social engineering is to be used to maintain and further civilization. Pound's conception of social engineering was not a reflection of a "slide rule" mentality that measured the steps to be taken to achieve a predetermined configuration of society. In his theory, social engineering is used to describe the technique to be employed in reconciling conflict and disagreement as these emerge in society, in order to achieve a reconciliation which could preserve and further civilization intact, not by employing power but by restraining power and preserving the effective operation of the social order. Pound emphasizes again and again that the use of social engineering or the theory of interests must always be given over to restraining power.

Pound felt that his legal philosophy achieved the bridging of the old and the new, and that it embodied what was viable and desirable from the past philosophy of law—from the time of antiquity to the present—and applied it to law's task in the modern era. One cannot fully understand Pound's attraction to sociological jurisprudence, however, without an understanding of the critical role that his theory of interests played in this scheme of legal philosophy, for Pound felt that the "theory of interests," as he developed this concept, provided the tool whereby standards could be created and principles employed which would serve as an effective means to be used to make the adjustments and alterations necessary to meet changing conditions in society, and yet preserve civilization. His "theory of interests" is a highly influential notion in contemporary juristic practice and theory. Unfortunately, Pound's theory is not what is most often employed. Pound's "theory of interests" is the embodiment of balance, and clearly recognizes that while certain interests may need more protection and advancement at a particular point in time, this cannot and should not be done without assuring other interests are considered and protected. His "theory of interests" masterfully explains the balancing that must be at the center of the operation and application of the law, if law is to avoid the dangers of what Pound calls "the jurisprudence of conceptions," *i.e.*, an abstract serving of the "reason" of the law without sufficient regard to the "experience" of the law. Chapter seven is devoted to an examination and explanation of this element of Pound's legal philosophy.

Chapter eight examines what became Pound's major concern in the later years of his life—the growth of unlimited government, and the dissolution of the law. These developments he felt were most clearly reflected in the growth of "administrative law" which could only be considered "law" in the most nominal sense. Pound deplored the decay of the legal order and attributed this decay to the influence of legal positivism and its encouragement of unlimited government. Thus, chapter eight examines Pound's critique of the vast expansion of government through the growth of executive power.

Chapter nine, is devoted to Pound's constructive plea for the restoration and preservation of "judicial justice" as the only means of assuring the preservation and continuation of a civilized order.

Chapter ten is devoted to evaluating Pound's legal philosophy on its own terms and significance. There is no irreparable and unbridgeable gap between Pound's view of law as tradition and historical development and its role as an active agent in the fashioning of means to handle needed adjustments in a changing world.

Pound marks the transition from nineteenth century legal philosophers who viewed law as a static mechanism to serve abstract concepts of property rights and individual liberty, and the modern schools of legal philosophy which consider law purely as a set of policy imperatives designed to bring about whatever results or consequences those wielding the power desire at a given point in time. Pound labored long and hard in the world of the law and much of what he wrote is no longer read. In those portions of his writing which are non-technical and therefore not dated, he is a towering figure in the field of legal philosophy as well as a wise counsellor to the legal profession. He is deserving of attention in terms of his unique legal philosophy which, while it has lost much of its influence, should be restored to a position of careful attention and consideration. Unfortunately, Pound's influence—both personally and philosophically—has waned dramatically in the past four decades. There is a richness in Pound's theory that could provide guidance to our much troubled legal order. Limited recognition of Pound's contributions and stature was achieved in 1976, at a conference based on one of his earliest and most famous pamphlets—Causes of Popular Dissatisfaction with the Administration of Justice.[3]

Unfortunately Pound never fully expressed his ideas in any one work. The closest he came to this was in a set of lectures delivered at Tagore, India in 1956; which has not been published in the United States.[4] It is hoped that this study will contribute to a revival of interest in this wise legal counselor.

CHAPTER ONE

POUND ON THE LAW

Pound argues that law emerges in all societies, because of the common human problems which require the use of law for their solution. He says:

> Apparently there is some common fundamental element in human nature which calls forth the same jural institutions and gives rise to the same judicial puzzles under the most diverse circumstances and in the most distant times. The problems of legal history, then, are recurrent problems. They are perennially recurrent problems.[1]

While it is apparent from his criticisms that he is not a determinist, historicist, or an Hegelian,[2] Pound nonetheless feels that practical necessity compels the emergence of law, and that the historical record verifies that.[3] Man cannot live in society without law: "Every Utopia that has ever been written," observes Pound, has pictured the conditions of full security, order, and justice in that Utopia "as existing without law".[4] Such concepts of ideal states have always been attractive, but they overlook the nature of man and his history which clearly indicate that Utopias are not possible.[5] Therefore, Pound feels that law and all social sciences should have as their starting points of inquiry the concept of civilization that enables men to control their individual anti-social characteristics in order to dominate the external world.[6] Further, Pound argues, that a civilized society needs to protect certain interests and be directed to specific purposes. As he notes:

> Civilized society brings about and its control and progress requires adjusting of human relations and ordering human conduct in order to eliminate or at least minimize friction and waste in satisfying human claims and ends.[7]

If men are to dominate, to any degree, their natural environment, cooperative social effort is needed. To achieve such cooperation, man must control those elements in his character which are destructive of society. Pound believes that man has two contradictory elements in his makeup. One is man's "aggressive or self-assertive" character which causes him to place his demands and desires first and seek "to satisfy them at the expense of others" by overcoming any resistance by any means.[8] The other is man's desire to live in association with his fellow-man.[9] It is unknown whether an original and ideal balance exists between these two drives, or which one is the more fundamental, Pound says, but man's history, dominated as it is by associations and groups, suggests that "social instinct prevails over the instinct of self-assertion".[10]

Social organization requires that the aggressive character of man be controlled, and this is the task of most social institutions. Religion, the family structure, and morality all teach the individual to restrain his destructive and self-assertive instincts and to behave so as to promote social order.[11] Nevertheless, the very existence of man's aggressiveness requires the presence of force that will keep such aggressiveness under control when necessary.[12] Pound observes:

> The task of social control and hence of the highly specialized form of social control which we call law, is to control this individual tendency to aggressive self-assertion to satisfy individual desires.[13]

Social order does not emerge spontaneously nor can it exist without conscious effort. Social control, Pound maintains, is composed of the pressures brought to bear on man by his fellow-man. These pressures are designed to "deter him from anti-social conduct, that is, conduct at variance with the social order."[14]

Although Pound is aware that such control can be achieved by social arrangements that do not involve law,[15] his major concern is to discuss the role of law in meeting man's need for a civilized society by managing and resolving conflicting and overlapping claims.[16] Pound observes that "there are very many of us but there is only one earth." and, therefore, men are bound to conflict with each other, in their attempt to fulfill their demands and expectations.[17]

According to Pound, the law does not create the interests men seek to protect, for these would exist even if there were no legal order;[18] and, therefore, the law must deal with these interests, since these unchecked aggressive instincts would destroy civilization.[19] The law should recognize and classify these interests in a manner that will protect, as far as possible, the overall scheme of interests in society,[20] and, the law must determine the limit to which any of these interests can be secured, for, Pound believes, no interest can ever receive total recognition and protection to the exclusion of all others. The law must develop the means for securing these recognized and delimited interests; prescribe the canons of value to determine which interests to recognize; the limits within which the recognition will operate; the weight the interests should be accorded; and the limits of legal protection to be provided.[21]

In recognizing, delimiting, and securing these interests, four critical factors—justice, force, security and balance—must be considered.[22] The justice of which Pound writes relates in part to "impartial authority".[23] He argues that men are willing to subordinate their claims to principles and rules, which are the components of law, when "it is known that they will be applied uniformly and systematically to all alike."[24] Such impartial authority, when it is equally applied, meets the normal man's expectation of external control which is "compatible with his human dignity".[25]

Pound argues that law without force to compel obedience is a contradiction in terms. Men abide by law in part because of the threat of force. Yet if force is allowed to operate without restraint or limit, "we shall give up what has made law a prime agency of civilization since the days of classical Roman jurists."[26] A civilized order must recognize that, although force is an "instrument of justice," it is "not something which can justify itself," for its real function is to achieve security.[27]

Pound maintains that security reinforces man's cooperative instincts whereas a lack of security encourages his aggressive ones. Security requires that limits be placed on each individual in order to curb his aggressive urges. Historically the security which constituted the law's major concern, has had as its chief purposes order, self-preservation, and the advancement of civilization. Without such security, chaos and disorder ensue.[28]

In Pound's view, then, security provides conditions favorable for an acceptable working balance between man's cooperative character and his individual self-assertiveness.[29] In order to achieve this necessary balance, the law must provide the force needed to insure such order and security. Adjustment of inevitable human conflicts must be made, therefore, in a manner that achieves justice and security.[30]

Because Pound is persuaded that social existence is unthinkable without law, his own definition of law is critical to an understanding of his view of law's other functions which enable it to serve man's needs in a modern society. Pound identifies three separate meanings which are given to the law in the philosophical treatment of it, which he feels are necessary to understand.

First, the term denotes a legal order which, Pound says, is:

> a regime of social control-the regime of adjusting relations and ordering conduct by the systematic and orderly application of the force of politically organized society.[31]

The term legal order, therefore, refers to "a specialized phase of social control",[32] because it is backed by and enforced by the power of the state, and is thus distinguished from other modes of social control which guide, condition, and restrain individual conduct.[33] The concept of legal order, in Pound's writing, does not refer to forms of social order which are randomly applied. In Pound's view, the concept of legal order is tied to the concept of civilization, and he observes:

> law is not only a means to civilization, it is a product of civilization.[34]

The legal order, Pound feels, is processive in its composition and touches on judicial, executive, legislative, and administrative action, which are cumulatively involved in the idea of "social control" by law. The legal order, Pound says, is properly conceived of "a task or as great a series of tasks of social engineering."[35]

In its second usage law is considered to mean:

> the body of authoritative guides to our models or patterns of decision, whether judicial or administrative. ...[36]

Three elements compose this idea of law, which, Pound feels, enables one to predict legal outcomes to a certain extent. This idea of law includes the precepts by which the law is guided, the technique by which it is employed, and the received ideals of society which direct its end or purpose.[37] As Pound notes, the precepts which are central to this definition are not specifically created nor arrived at in a given point in time.[38]

At the outset legal rules emerge. Their value lies in the certainty and predictability they provide, for they relate to "a definite detailed legal consequence for a definite detailed state or situation of fact."[39] Rules in turn are followed by forms in providing remedies for injuries and wrongs.[40] However, experience shows the impossibility of providing rules and forms for each contingency and consequently legal principles arise.[41] As Pound notes:

> Limitless human ingenuity, straining against the restriction of the legal order, the endless variety of circumstances of life, the changes to which all things are subject, continued progress and invention and discovery put it out of the question to have an absolutely complete body of rules [and] if it were not for principles to which these [complex situations] could be referred as they come before the courts, it would not have been possible for the courts to keep pace with them in their rapid development and succession. ...Without that authoritative starting point for reasoning the court could not decide with assurance the multitude of controversies which press upon them. ...[42]

Thus, if order is to survive and function it must be able to handle each new disturbance or claim.[43] Consider says Pound, the principle "that one person is not to be unjustly enriched at the expense of another".[44] Here, as with all principles, there is no detailed set of facts identified, nor a specific legal consequence established. Yet when two parties are involved in a transaction from which one is unjustly enriched by an unjust loss to another, a legal order which seeks to serve the value embodied in this principle must choose an authoritative starting point from which reasoning may proceed. Principles, Pound maintains, provide such starting points. Following the development of rules and principles, law, viewed in the sense being discussed here, developed two other elements which aided in fashioning a certain and equitable process and substance—these are legal conceptions and legal standards.

Of the former Pound says they are:

> generalized categories into which we may put particular situations of fact, whereupon certain rules, principles, and standards become applicable.[45]

Legal conceptions greatly assist the law in refining problems and reasoning to their solution in a coherent and rational fashion.[46] As Pound notes, although no definite state of facts or specified consequences are spelled out for legal conceptions, a decision must be made as to which conception is to apply to a given set of facts. For example, in a transaction involving a chattel, one must decide whether to consider it in terms of a contract sale, a bailment, an abandonment of property, or a gift. The conception selected determines which rules, principles, and standards are applicable.[47] Pound believes that the importance of principles and conceptions lies in the fact that they make "it possible to get along with many fewer rules and to deal with assurance with new cases for which no rules are at hand."[48]

The standards to which Pound refers aid in establishing:

> certain limits of conduct from which one subject to the standard departs at a peril of liability or of the invalidity of what he does. The chief characteristic of a standard is that it is not to be applied absolutely, like a ruling, but is to be applied according to the circumstances of each case.[49]

For example, standards of due care, reasonable service, etc., all operate to give to the law a certain flexibility in its application, which in turn, permits individualization of treatment of problems without abandoning the degree of generality needed for the survival and coherence of the law.[50]

These precepts serve as authoritative guidelines for the understanding and application of law, and constitute an important element of Pound's understanding of law as an authoritative guide to conduct. Of the technique which is central to law's meaning, Pound says, that it is:

> a traditional technique of working out the grounds of deciding particular cases on the basis of received legal ideals; a technique of applying legal precepts, and of working out their limits and developing new ones to meet cases to which existing precepts are not adopted, or for which no precepts are at hand.[51]

Technique encompasses the "lawyer's craft" as Pound calls it, which is no less important or authoritative than the precepts which constitute authoritative grounds for legal decisions.[52] Technique distinguishes the two great legal systems of the western world—Roman and Common Law—and refers to the modes used in looking at and handling the legal precepts. Pound points out that in the Common Law tradition, statutes determine what cases fall under their provisions, and serve as starting points for reasoning in cases analogically related to them. In this latter instance reference is made to the reported cases of the courts.[53] The Roman Law tradition, on the other hand, reasons by analogy from the code itself. Judicial decisions are regarded as establishing only the specific point which is litigated, not as starting points for legal reasoning.[54] Pound further illustrates the distinction between the techniques of Common and Roman Law by pointing to the fact, that, in the former, specific relief is the exception while substitutional relief, in the form of monetary damages, is the rule, while the opposite is true in the Roman Code. As Pound notes, in both traditions, the technique "is not less authoritative than the precepts."[55]

According to Pound's definition of law, both the precepts and the technique of law are governed by the "authoritative ideals" of the society. He describes the significance of the ideal element in law as follows:

> This element comes at bottom to the picture of the social order of the time and place, the legal tradition as to what that social order is and so as to what is the background of interpretation and application of legal precepts and is crucial in new cases in which it is necessary to choose from many equally authoritative starting points for legal reasoning.[56]

For Pound, the "ideal" is as significant as the precepts.[57] It is, Pound notes, necessary to understand the ideals on which law is based in order to understand the purposes of the legal order.[58] Ideals perform a critical role in giving effect and meaning to the authoritative precepts.[59] Pound correctly says that when men embrace certain ideals and base their actions on them, these ideals are given force. Therefore, ideals have been a decisive factor in legal development.[60] The ideals on which laws are based come down to the present from the past, but this is part of their strength and value. Pound cites with approval Justice Holmes' statement that "Continuity with the past is only a necessity and not a duty."[61]

Pound in tracing the enduring ideals on which western law has developed from antiquity until the modern era, feels that perhaps the most valuable part of the tradition is natural law, which he carefully distinguishes into two types—"natural, natural law," and "positive natural law." Of the former, he says, it is:

> ideal law simply as ideal. It is a body of ideal precepts derived independent of the actual positive law by some method which is regarded as guaranteeing universal moral validity and applicability.[62]

On the other hand, positive natural law is merely an idealization of the positive law in which the jurist is trained, and then is transferred by him into an assertion of unchanged and unchallengeable universal precepts of law.[63]

Pound observes that law must provide answers to society's pressing and practical conflicts, which do not clearly involve a solution reflecting the standards of natural law, but he urges that attempts at conformity with such norms be made.[64] The great task of natural law, as Pound sees it, is to provide the basis for critiquing the ideal elements in positive law, but it cannot serve as a test of their validity or as a concrete guide for the development and application of the positive law.[65]

The ideals which guide and control law are not fixed and static; rather, civilization develops from previous conditions of man.[66] The ideals, values, and interests of a civilization should be used to meet human expectations and interests so far as possible with a minimum of friction and waste.[67] If there are no ideals to guide men in ordering their relations and to condition the exercise of force in society, then that exercise tends to arbitrariness.[68] Such a development, Pound feels, substitutes force for law,[69] since a uniform, regular, and predictable system of law is the antithesis of a regime of force.[70] The ideals which should condition the operation of law must allow for the proper balancing of justice (the ideal relation among men), morals (the ideal development of human character), and the overall security needed for society and the individual. None of these may be fully pursued to the exclusion of the others, and the limit of law in giving effect to justice, and morals, and security must be recognized.[71]

The limit of what law can achieve, Pound argues, should be considered in relation to the role of other institutions which deal with social control, but this is not to suggest that law should not attend to morals and justice. Law must be directed toward giving value to certain interests and achieving the ideals of the society.[72]

Even though the law must often lay down guidelines to assure only uniformity and certainty, its application is to be guided by ideals. Pound agrees that argument should continue over what constitutes an absolute measure of values, however, he says, "the received ideals of the purpose of the legal order and of justice as the ideal relation among men" as they exist in a given time and place, must serve in providing law with the guides for its practice.[73]

Thus the ideals upon which Pound wishes to focus are those prevailing in a society at a given time and place which serve to maintain and promote the values of that civilization.[74] These values Pound feels are included in what he calls the five postulates of a civilized order: First, that men must be able to assume that others will commit no intentional aggressions against them; second, that everyone will exercise care not to cast an unreasonable risk of injury upon others; third, that men will act in good faith and adhere to their promises; fourth, that men may control for beneficial purposes, what they have discovered, produced, or acquired;[75] and fifth, that others using things which are harmless in their sphere of use, but harmful in their normal uses elsewhere, will confine such items to where they are safe.[76] These postulates, he points out, are not fixed and permanent, for new conditions may effect their content and scope, but they are the basic ideals which characterize western civilization. Pound feels that these postulates should guide the use of law, in order to allow men to achieve the greatest control over their internal nature, master their environment, and distribute the goods needed for existence as far as possible with a minimum of friction and waste.[77]

Justice, Pound feels, is what we seek to obtain through the legal ordering of society; and even if man cannot lay down unchallengeable, universal formulations of an ideal justice, the existing ideals of a society provide a foundation for a workable ideal, which man can strive to approximate as far as possible.[78]

Each of these postulates bear significantly on Pound's assumptions regarding the degree of stability needed in a legal order set over against change, and judging what is more transient in a legal order set over against what is more permanent. Precepts, rules, conceptions, principles, and standards he believes are by their very nature more transient in comparison with technique and ideals which are less so. The more important point, however, is that law's survival and successful function are tied in large measure to its capacity to change and adapt. Pound feels the history of law has been marked by alterations between periods of legal development in which the stability of the legal order is emphasized and periods of change in which the liberalization and "loosening up" of the prevailing canons and orthodoxies is prevalent.[79]

It is Pound's opinion that much of the interplay between stability and flexibility of the legal order is reflected in the emphasis placed in some periods on the "traditional" element in law in contrast with other periods where emphasis is placed on the "imperative" element of the law. Pound feels it is fortunate that, at least in the context of civilization, equilibrium can be maintained between the centrifugal forces of imperative law and the centripetal influences of traditional law. The reciprocal influence of these two emphases of the law are reflected in alternating periods of growth and stability in the law which Pound sees reflected in the historical periods into which he classifies law,[80] and which he presumes are unavoidably present in any legal order which seeks to survive.[81] In each of the historical periods Pound observes:

> the law for a time had become overrigid and it attained the necessary measure of flexibility though the absorption of ideas developed outside of the law....[82]

The imperative dimension of law, however, arrived late in the development of the legal order. In Pound's chronology of law one does not see imperative law employed in the earlier stages. The notion of imperative law appears in the stage of maturity of law. Tracing imperative law's origin, development and purpose Pound argues that in the earliest stages of law, men did not conceive of "making" law, since it was presumed to derive from some higher authority and social control was exercised by other institutions than the state. The modern era, according to Pound, has witnessed a resurrection of the idea of law as the will of the ruler, which came from Roman thinking about the law. The consequence has been that law is now used as a regularly employed instrument to give effect to the will of the ruler, and Pound observe of this development:

> What, however, marks the stage of legislation in the development of a legal system is the use of legislation not as an instrument of occasional legal revolution, but as the regular, everyday agency of growth and development of law.[83]

Pound points to the longer presence of the traditional element in any recording of legal history, and it is that traditional body of law which gives effect to legal precepts even though it is neither enacted, nor, perhaps, written down.[84] The traditional in the law, however, Pound observes does not refer to popular, customary modes of thought, but to:

> customary modes of professional or juristic handling of controversies developed by writing and teaching.[85]

This traditional element appears in primitive stages of law as religious tradition as it was developed and understood by priests. In turn it appears, he argues, as "popular" tradition embodied in and incorporated into Germanic law.[86] The emergence of traditional law in a truly juristic sense, Pound argues, awaits the emergence and development of relatively complex legal orders.[87] Pound suggests, that the traditional element in legal systems goes through five stages of development. In the first stage a decision is reached based on claim of inspiration, or a divine intervention in a mechanical mode of decision such as trial by ordeal. Second, rules begin to emerge which embody the ethos of a decision as it has become reflected in repeated decisions. Third, there emerged an oligarchical class which possessed the knowledge of method, procedure, and substance to decide a given case. Fourth, the traditional law is committed to writing in the form of codes or monographic literature. Fifth, the traditional materials become directly influenced and controlled by "juristically" trained persons such as lawyers and commentators.[88]

Pound observes that the imperative element derives in large measure from notions which appeared early in the law, *i.e.*, that law is the will of the sovereign enunciated in formal enactment.[89] Such a notion of imperative law is often viewed as a device that can be used to effect changes and alteration in the legal order, even though this was not the original use to which legislation was put in the early stages of law. He writes:

> the first thing that comes to our notice is that [the imperative element] is a relatively new feature of the legal system. Conscious, deliberate, intentional lawmaking is something relatively modern. The beginnings of legislation are not attempts at conscious lawmaking. They are simply attempts at formulating what has been the law already.[90]

As Pound observes, legislation probably began in those circumstances where a choice between competing laws of two or more peoples which had joined in union became necessary. He says this was the case of Alfred the Great in amalgamating the laws of the diverse kingdoms which constituted his realm. The progress from legislation, viewed as setting in the record the law as it exists to conscious law making is incremental and often not even deliberate. It is not, as Pound says:

> until the maturity of law, that we find the lawmaker deliberately making something new and establishing it as something that has been made conscious for the first time.[91]

The changes that law underwent prior to the mature stage of law were those achieved by means of the traditional element of law,[92] which, Pound says:

> truly represent a human experience of the rules which, if I may use such a phrase, have "made good" in the practical administration of justice.[93]

The traditional element as it has developed in the western tradition has served effectively in preventing law from being shaped in conformity with specific class interests; it has also had the advantage of being formed from decisions made in concrete circumstances and not derived from abstract speculation; and, in Pound's opinion, most important, is the fact that the traditional element or law combines certainty and flexibility effectively. As he observes:

> It [traditional law] admits of flexibility because it deals with cases one at a time as they arise. It admits of certainty because it proceeds by a logical technique which enables you, given the premises, to determine the results in cases as they arise with a reasonable certainty.[94]

Thus, according to Pound, these two dimensions of law—imperative and traditional—work in a symbiotic relationship that permits both stability and change. Together they provide the legal order with the capacity to adjust to and to meet the needs of a legal order over extended periods of time. Thus, precepts of law may be traditionally derived or they may be the result of conscious articulation, and precepts therefore, move back and forth between traditional elements of the law and the imperative. As Pound notes, in truth the two act upon and correct each other so that when either, from occupying the field too long, becomes too fixed and rigid, the needed flexibility is restored by law to its rival.[95]

The third, and most recent notion of law, according to Pound, is that employed by "self-styled realists," who, Pound argues, consider law to be the process primarily by which adjudication—whether judicial, legislative, or administrative—is conducted, and, therefore, for this group:

> The term "law" is used in the sense in most neo-realist writings of today, and in such pronouncements as that of Professor Llewellyn that he includes under "law": all that is done officially.[96]

This third definition is inadequate in defining the law because it ignores what in Pound's view is the *sine qua non* of law, *i.e.*, law conceived as a measure and limit of action. Therefore, to assume that all that is done officially is law, Pound argues, would deny to law its very essence of function and purpose which is—the limiting official action. According to Pound:

> law is not what is done officially but the measuring of what ought to be done officially and how it ought to be done.[97]

Pound maintains that the value of these three meanings is enhanced when one synthesizes or combines elements of all three, because individually none of them fully describe the complex meaning of the type of social control achieved by the law. Thus, Pound offers is a more satisfactory definition of the law which he feels encompasses more completely law's protean nature. "Law", he says:

> is a body of authoritative guides to or grounds for determination, developed and applied by an authoritative technique on a background of received ideals of the social and legal order.[98]

This meaning of law, he feels, explains the function of law as the over-arching system or mechanism that provides the framework within which social control,

century. To be taken in by modern realism and the threat theory it favors, he argues, is to lose that great tradition.[138] Law can transmit, further, and protect civilization only by applying values in the process of recognizing and serving interests as they emerge in the legal system.

Pound suggests that much of the law's success at social control depends on its continuing authority.
Historically, men have sought to determine the source of authority of the legal order[139] and to examine this question's various corollaries—what is the immediate practical source of authority, what is the ultimate practical source, and what is the ultimate moral source of authority. Pound notes that the answers to these questions have been provided mainly by social or political philosophy. But for him, the answer is found in a more practical test. He observes that:

> the legal order goes on, whatever may be the basis of whatever rightful authority it has, and I submit it has kept and holds as actual authority because it performs, and performs well, its task of reconciling and harmonizing conflicting and overlapping human demands and so maintains a social order in which we may maintain and further civilization. So long as it does this well there will be the habit of obedience that makes practicable the employment of force upon those who require it.[140]

Although Pound believes the test of the legal order to be a practical one, he feels that a realistic assessment of that standard requires insight into and an understanding of the limitations under which law operates. Through such an understanding, one can also come to understand the extent to which law can handle its task of social control.

Pound notes that there are five major limitations which impinge on the capacity of the law to control society. The first "grows out of the difficulties involved in ascertainment of the facts to which legal precepts are to be applied".[141] Pound notes that, the facts of a specific case may not be a given, but that the efficacy of the application of legal precepts to the case still depends upon the facts being known, but facts can be withheld, distorted, or unobtainable. Thus, the law proceeds on the fragile and frequently mistaken assumption that the facts can be known, while the reality of the legal order is that they may not. Consequently justice may and does miscarry because of this severe, but unavoidable, shortcoming. Second, Pound points to the "intangibleness of many duties which morally are of great moment but defy legal enforcement."[142] Some attempts to hold individuals to high standards of disinterested benevolence, therefore, fail because the very character of the standard one seeks to impose is too intangible to lend itself to legal enforcement. For example, attempts by law to force disinterested benevolence upon corporations or to create laws defining youthful incorrigibility fall short of their ends. Third, Pound cites the limitations that result in infringement on interests that result from the protection of them.[143] Such matters as protecting individuals from damage by "neighborhood gossip" or from intrusions on their privacy do not lend themselves to the controlling actions of the law because of the difficulty in pinpointing the source of the injury.

Fourth, law often is unable and unequipped to deal with many areas of human conduct.[144] In discussing this limitation, Pound notes the incapacity of the law to handle problems of domestic relations, which most properly are controlled by morals and community sentiment, and not the law.[145] Fifth, law is limited by the fact that it must be set in motion by individuals.[146] The individual must have some personal motive in seeking the law's redress, and the abstract content of the rule and its conformity to an ideal justice or an ideal social interest are not sufficient to set the law in motion.[147] Pound observes that there are those who wish to engage the law in order to protest against such wrongs as bias and prejudice. But for that purpose, he notes. "a prophet rather than a lawmaker is the proper mouthpiece."[148]

Pound's observations regarding the limitations of the law in dealing with problems are important. When too much is expected of the law, and when the limitations of the law are ignored, disappointment and disillusionment result, thus preparing the way for the use of force.

In discussing what the law can achieve, Pound finds only four remedies it can use to reconcile conflict: punishment, prevention, specific redress, and substitutional redress. He observes, "The wit of man has discovered no further possibilities of judicial action."[149] The first three of these remedies have serious limitations. Punishment is restricted in the role of enforcing absolute duties and is effective mainly in criminal law. Prevention is not always useful because many injuries are accomplished before the law is called into play. Specific redress applies only to possessory rights and certain acts which are purely economic. Because of these limitations, Pound notes:

> in the great majority of cases redress by way of money damages is the only recourse and this has been the staple remedy of the law at all times.[150]

Substitutional redress, therefore, is the most frequently available and practical remedy, though it, too, has drawbacks. It is employed most satisfactorily, Pound believes, in dealing with conflicts involving items of easily measured value, such as property exchanges and contractual agreements related to property. Conflicts concerning such personal matters as pride, mental comfort, and privacy, however, do not lend themselves easily to financial measurement, and this fact has given rise to the complaint that the law honors property more than the person, In response, Pound maintains that:

> if the law secures property and contract more elaborately and more adequately than it secures personality, it is not because the law rates the latter less highly than the former, but because legal machinery is intrinsically well adapted to securing the one and intrinsically ill adapted to securing the other.[151]

This point is well taken, for although one may bemoan the fact that redress for mental suffering is incalculable in money terms, the law can do little else than award the damages.

Pound observes that, although these mechanisms for resolving conflict are not fully satisfactory, they are the only ones which enable the law to perform its practical task. Morals or ethics alone are inadequate, because often they cannot provide a clear-cut principle on which to base a resolution. Moreover, Pound notes, some conflicts involve equally blameless parties, yet the law must resolve them. In so doing, the law restores stability and predictability, which are values in themselves although the substantive issue being resolved does not admit of a clearly discernable value.[152]

Finally, in addressing what the law can do Pound points to the fact, often ignored in legal theory and practice, that law needs a support of other institutions of social control such as the church and the home, which are better equipped to handle certain areas of social control, and whose support is critical.[153] These other institutions must provide the background against which the law operates, if it is to be effective.[154]

For Pound law is the basic foundation on which civilized society is built. His concern with the abandonment of law motivated many of his later concerns.[155] It was, however, not a losing cause, for he felt reason and experience would work to restore and preserve the legal order. The "give it up philosophy" of modern realists and positivists was of growing concern to him, and to correct the change that these modes of thought had brought about in the legal order required a recognition that the law is a civilizing agency and is to be used to restrain force and power.

In one of his last major publications, Pound argues for the restoration of the proper role of law, *i.e.*, as the protector of civilized society, in which human liberty could flourish, and a rejection of the authoritarian ideas which he considered to be so dominant in legal thinking and practice. He was not willing to concede the victory to those who subscribe to the "cult of force," and did not feel that the task of law in fashioning conditions in which human liberty could flourish was at an end, and feels that use of the past in fashioning a new road to human liberty and civilized society is more than possible. This new path would be fashioned from the law as it had developed in the preceding centuries and be directed toward a preservation and furtherance of civilization.[156] Pound feels his conception of law—its function, purpose and limit—would contribute to the restoration of the legal order.

ENDNOTES

CHAPTER ONE

1. R. Pound, "Making Law and Finding Law," Vol. 13, *Ohio Law Reporter*, August, 1915, pp. 283-300, p. 284. See also: *Vol. 1*, PB 72. (Hereinafter referred to as "Making Law..."). Permission granted by Anderson Publishing Company, Cincinnati, Ohio.

2. See Chapter Four Legal Philosophy: Nineteenth Century.

3. See Chapter Two Pound on Legal History.

4. R. Pound, *The Task of the Law*, Franklin and Marshall College, Pa., 1941, p. 12. *Vol. 2*, PB 2. (Hereinafter referred to as *Task...*). Permission granted by Franklin and Marshall, Lancaster, PA. See also: Roscoe Pound, *The Ideal Element...Tagore*, pp. 177-178.

5. Pound, *Task...*, p. 15. See also: Pound, *The Ideal Element...Tagore*, pp. 177-178.

6. Pound, *The Ideal Element...Tagore, p. 28.* See also: Roscoe Pound, *Social Control Through Law,* New Haven, Connecticut, Yale University Press, 1942, pp. 130-134. Vol. 2 PB 7. (Hereinafter referred to as *Social Control...*). Roscoe Pound, *Jurisprudence (Vol. 3*), 5 vols., St. Paul, Minn., West Publishing Co., 1959, vol. 3, pp. 5-6. Vol. 2 PB 44. (Hereinafter referred to as *Vol. 3*).

7. Pound, "Law and the Christian Code." In: *An Outline of Christianity; The Story of Our Civilization Vol. 5.* New York, Bethlehem Publishers, Inc. 1926. p. 106, Vol. 1, PB 144 (Hereinafter referred to as "Law and Christian..."). See also: Roscoe Pound, *The History and System of the Common Law*, New York, P. F. Collier & Son Publishers, 1939, pp. 1-3. *Vol. 1*, PB 249 (Hereinafter referred to as *History and System...Common....*). Pound, *Vol. 3*, pp. 5-8. Roscoe Pound, *Interpretations of Legal History*, Cambridge, England, Cambridge University Press, 1930, 1923, pp. 141-166. Vol. 1 PB 118. (Hereinafter referred to as *Interpretations of Legal...*).

8. Pound, *Task...*, p. 26. See also: Pound, *The Ideal Element...Tagore*, p. 52. Pound, *Social Control...*, pp. 130-135. Pound, *Vol. 3*, pp. 5-8. Pound, *Interpretations of Legal...*, pp. 141-166.

9. Pound, *Task...*, p. 26. See also: Pound, *The Ideal Element...Tagore*, p. 52. Pound, *Social Control...*,, pp. 130-135. Pound, *Interpretations of Legal...*, pp. 141-166. Pound, *Vol. 3*, pp. 5-8.

10. Pound, *Task...*, p. 24. See also: Pound, *The Ideal Element...Tagore*, p. 224. Pound, *Social Control...*, pp. 130-135. Pound, *Interpretations of Legal...*, pp. 141-166. Pound, *Vol. 3*, pp. 5-8.

11. Pound, *The Ideal Element...Tagore*, pp. 223, 225. See also: Pound, *Task...*, pp. 21, 182. Pound, *Social Control...*, pp. 25-26. Pound, *Interpretations of Legal...*, pp. 141-166. Pound, *Vol. 3*, pp. 5-8.

12. Pound, *Task...*, p. 21. See also: Pound, *The Ideal Element...Tagore*, p. 222. Pound, *Social Control...*, pp. 25-26. Pound, *Interpretations of Legal...*, pp. 141-166. Pound, *Vol. 3*, pp. 5-8.

13. Pound, *Task...*, p. 21. See also: Pound, *The Ideal Element...Tagore*, p. 222. Pound, *Social Control...*, pp. 25-26. Pound, *Interpretations of Legal...*, pp. 141-166. Pound, *Vol. 3*, pp. 5-8.

14. Pound, *Task...*, p. 12. See also: Pound, *Social Control...*, pp. 18-20. Roscoe Pound, *Justice According to Law*, New York, New York Evening Post Job Printing Co., 1914, pp. 30-31. Vol. 1 PB 60. (Hereinafter referred to as *Justice According...*). Pound, *Interpretations of Legal...*, pp. 141-166. Pound, *Vol. 3,* pp. 5-8.

15. Pound, *Justice According...*, pp. 32-33. See also: Roscoe Pound, An *Introduction to the Philosophy of Law,* New Haven, Connecticut, Yale University Press, 1922, Reprinted, 1976, pp. 167-168. Vol. 1 PB 111. (Hereinafter referred to as *Introduction...*). Roscoe Pound, *Jurisprudence (Vol. 2) 5 vols.*, St. Paul, Minn., West Publishing Co., 1959. Vol. 2, pp. 349-351. Vol. 2 PB 44. (Hereinafter referred to as *Vol. 2*).

16. Pound, *Justice According...*, pp. 28-30. See also: Pound, *Social Control...*, pp. 131-132. Pound, *Vol. 3,* pp. 7-8.

17. Pound, *Social Control...*, p. 64. See also: Pound, *The Ideal Element...Tagore*, pp. 223-225. Pound, *Vol. 3*, pp. 327-33.

18. Pound, *The Ideal Element...Tagore*, pp. 86-88. See also: Pound, *Social Control...*, pp. 66-68. Pound, *Vol. 3,* pp. 22-26.

19. Pound, *Task...*, p. 30. See also: Pound, *The Ideal Element...Tagore*, pp. 223-225. Pound, *Vol. 3*, pp. 22-26.

20. Pound, *Social Control...*, p. 109. See also: Pound, *The Ideal Element...Tagore*, pp. 99, 282. Pound, *Vol. 3*, pp. 327-334.

21. Pound, *The Ideal Element...Tagore*. pp. 86-88. See also: Pound, *Social Control...*, p. 68. Pound, *Vol. 3*, pp. 327-334. Pound, Task..., pp. 32-34.

22. Pound, *Task...*, pp. 30, 32-34. See also: Pound, *The Ideal Element...Tagore*, pp. 82-83.

23. Pound, *Task...*, pp. 32-34. See also: Pound, *The Ideal Element...Tagore*, pp. 76-77.

24. Pound, *Task...*, pp. 16-17. See also: Pound, *The Ideal Element...Tagore*, pp. 76-77.

25. Pound, *Task...*, p. 30. See also: Pound, *The Ideal Element...Tagore*, pp. 76-77.

26. Pound, *Social Control...*, p. 97.

27. Pound, *Task...*, p. 31.

28. Pound, *Task...*, p. 32. See also: Pound, *The Ideal Element...Tagore*, pp. 182-184.

29. Pound, *Task...*, p. 33. See also: Pound, *The Ideal Element...Tagore*, pp. 182-184.

30. Pound, *The Ideal Element...Tagore*, pp. 182-183. See also: Pound, *Interpretations of Legal...*, p. 160.

31. Pound, *Justice According...*, p. 48.

32. Pound, *Social Control...*, p. 41. See also: Pound, *The Ideal Element...Tagore*, p. 1.

33. Pound, *Social Control...*, p. 40.

34. Pound, *Interpretations of Legal...*, p. 143. See also: Pound, *The Ideal Element...Tagore*, p. 80.

35. Pound, *Interpretations of Legal...*, p. 156. See also: Pound, *The Ideal Element...Tagore,* p. 178. Pound's view of law's role in "social engineering" is discussed in Chapter Five Sociological Jurisprudence, and Chapter Two Pound on Legal History.

36. Pound, *Justice According...*, p. 48. See also: Pound, *Task...*, p.43. Pound, *The Ideal Element...Tagore*, p. 2.

37. Pound, *The Ideal Element... Tagore*, p. 2. See also: Pound, *Social Control...*, pp. 39-41. Pound, *Vol. 2*, pp. 99-122.

38. Pound, *Task...*, p. 44. See also: Pound, *Social Control...*, p. 45. Roscoe Pound, "The Theory of Judicial Decision," Vol. 36 *Harvard Law Review*, April, 1923, pp. 641-662, 645. Vol. 1 PB 113. (Hereinafter referred to as "The Theory..."). Pound, *Vol. 2*, pp. 99-122.

39. Pound, *Task...*, p. 44. See also: Pound, *Justice According...*, p. 56. Pound, *Social Control...*, p. 45. Pound, *Social Control...*, pp. 45-47. Pound, *The Ideal Element...Tagore*, pp. 3-4. Pound, "The Theory...," pp. 645-648. Pound, *Vol. 2*, pp. 99-122, 124-125.

40. Pound, *Task...*, p.44. See also: Pound, *The Ideal Element...Tagore*, pp. 3-4. Pound, "The Theory...," pp. 645-648. Pound, *Vol. 2*, pp. 99-122.

41. Pound, *Justice According...*, p. 56. See also: Pound, *Social Control...*, pp. 46-47. Pound, *The Ideal Element...Tagore*, pp. 3-4. Pound, *Vol. 2,* pp. 99-122, 125-126. Pound, "The Theory...," pp. 645-648.

42. Pound, *Task...*, pp. 44-45. See also: Pound, *Justice According...*, p. 56. Pound, *Social Control...*, pp. 45-47. Pound, "The Theory...," pp. 645-648. Pound, *Vol. 2*, pp. 99-122.

43. Pound, *Task...*, p. 44. See also: Pound, "The Theory...," pp. 645-648. Pound, *Vol. 2*, pp. 99-122.

44. Pound, *Social Control...*, p. 46. See also: Pound, "The Theory...," pp. 645-648. Pound, *Vol. 2*, pp. 99-122.

45. Pound, *Task...*, p. 46. See also: Pound, *Social Control...*, p. 46-48. Pound, *The Ideal Element...Tagore*, pp. 3-4. Pound, *Vol. 2*, p. 127. Pound, "The Theory...," pp. 645-648.

46. Pound, *Task...*, p. 46. See also: Pound, *Social Control...*, p. 47. Pound, *The Ideal Element...Tagore*, pp. 3-4. Pound, *Vol. 2*, p. 127. Pound, "The Theory...," pp. 645-648.

47. Pound, *Social Control...*, p. 46. See also: Pound, *The Ideal Element...Tagore*, pp. 3-4. Pound, *Vol. 2*, p. 127. Pound, "The Theory...," pp. 645-648.

48. Pound, *Social Control...*, p. 47. See also: Pound, "The Theory...," pp. 645-648. Pound, *Vol. 2*, pp. 99-122.

49. Pound, *Task...*, p. 46. See also: Pound, *Social Control...*, p. 48. Pound, *The Ideal Element...Tagore*, pp. 3-4. Pound, *Vol. 2*, pp. 127-128. Pound, "The Theory...," pp. 645-648.

50. Pound, *Task...*, pp. 46-47. See also: Pound, *Social Control...*, pp. 48-49. Pound, *The Ideal Element...Tagore*, p. 3. Pound, *Vol. 2*, pp. 127-128. Pound, "The Theory...," pp. 645-648.

51. Pound, "The Problems of the Law," Vol. 12 *American Bar Association Journal*, February, 1926, p. 84. Vol. 1, PB 134 (Hereinafter referred to as "The Problems..."). See also: Pound, *Vol. 2*, pp. 111-112. Pound, "The Theory...," pp. 648-651.

52. Pound, *Justice According...*, p. 50. See also: Pound, *Task...*, pp. 43, 48. Pound, *Vol. 2*, pp. 111-112. Pound, "The Theory...," pp. 648-651.

53. Pound, *Justice According...*, p. 51. See also: Pound, *Social Control...*, pp. 41-42. Pound, "The Theory...," pp. 648-651. Pound, *Vol. 2*, pp. 99-122.

54. Pound, Justice According..., p. 51. See also: Pound, *Social Control...*, pp. 41-42. Pound, "The Theory...," pp. 648-651. Pound, *Vol. 2*, pp. 99-122.

55. Pound, *Justice According...*, p. 54. See also: Pound, *Social Control...*, p. 41. Pound, "The Problems...," p. 84. Pound, *Task...*, pp. 67-70. Pound, "The Theory...," pp. 648-651. Pound, *Vol. 2*, pp. 99-122.

56. Pound, *Social Control...*, p. 42. See also: Pound, *The Ideal Element...Tagore,* pp. 5-6, 25. Pound, *Vol. 2*, pp. 99-122. Pound, "The Theory...," pp. 651-662.

57. Pound, *The Ideal Element...Tagore*, p. 25. See also: Pound, "The Theory...," pp. 651-662.

58. Pound, *The Ideal Element...Tagore*, p. 25. See also: Pound, *Social Control...*, pp. 5-6. Pound, "The Theory...," pp. 651-662. Pound, *Vol. 2*, pp. 116-123.

59. Pound, *The Ideal Element...Tagore*, p. 5. See also: Pound, *Social Control...*, pp. 5-6, 12-16. Pound, "The Theory...," pp. 651-662. Pound, *Vol. 2*, pp. 116-123.

60. Pound, *The Ideal Element...Tagore*, pp. 5-6. See also: Pound, *Social Control...*, pp. 5-6, 12-16. Pound, "The Theory...," pp. 651-662. Pound, *Vol. 2*, pp. 116-123.

61. Quoted in: Pound, *The Ideal Element...Tagore*, p. 19.

62. Roscoe Pound, "Natural Natural Law and Positive Natural Law," Vol. 68 *The Law Quarterly Review*, July, 1952, pp. 330-336, at p. 330. Vol. 2 PB 30. (Hereinafter referred to as "Natural Natural..."). See also: Pound, *The Ideal Element...Tagore*, p. 48. Pound, *Social Control...*, pp. 3-4.

63. Roscoe Pound, "Natural Natural...," p. 330. See also: Pound, *Social Control...*, pp. 3-4.Pound, *The Ideal Element...Tagore*, p. 49.

64. Pound, *The Ideal Element...Tagore*, p. 50. See also: Pound, "Natural Natural...," p. 330.

65. Pound, *The Ideal Element...Tagore*, p. 50. See also: Pound, "Natural Natural...," p. 330.

66. Pound, *The Ideal Element...Tagore*, p. 97. See also: Pound, *Vol. 2*, pp. 116-123. Pound, *Social Control...*, pp. 42-44, 121-124.

67. Pound, *The Ideal Element...Tagore*, p. 97. See also: Pound, *Vol. 2*, pp. 116-123. Pound, *Social Control...*, pp. 42-44.

68. Pound, *The Ideal Element...Tagore*, p. 51. See also: Pound, *Social Control...*, pp. 42-44, 122-124.

69. Pound, *The Ideal Element...Tagore*, p. 51. See also: Pound, *Social Control...*, pp. 42-44, 122-124.

70. Pound, *The Ideal Element...Tagore*, p. 77. See also: Pound, *Social Control...*, pp. 42-44, 122-124. Pound, *Task...*, pp. 61-62.

71. Pound, *The Ideal Element...Tagore*, pp. 82-83. See also: Pound, *Task...*, pp. 31-33, pp. 61-62.

72. Pound, *The Ideal Element...Tagore*, pp. 82-83. See also: Pound, *Social Control...*, pp. 108-110. Pound, *Task...*, p. 87.

73. Pound, *The Ideal Element...Tagore*, pp. 106-107. See also: Pound, *Vol. 2*, pp. 116-123. Pound, *Social Control...*, pp. 108-110.

74. Pound, *The Ideal Element...Tagore*, p. 186. See also: Pound, *Vol. 2*, pp. 116-123. Pound, *Social Control...*, pp. 81-83, 112-118.

75. Pound, *The Ideal Element...Tagore*, p. 187. See also: Pound, *Vol. 3*, pp. 8-11. Pound, *Social Control...*, pp. 81-83, 112-118.

76. Pound, *The Ideal Element...Tagore,* p. 191. See also: Pound, *Vol. 3*, pp. 8-11. Pound, *Social Control...*, pp. 81-83, 112-118.

77. Pound, *The Ideal Element...Tagore*, pp. 191-194. See also: Pound, *Social Control...*, pp. 81-83, 112-118. For further analysis of the role of jural postulates see Chapter Seven Theory of Interests.

78. Pound, *The Ideal Element...Tagore*, p. 109. See also: Pound *Justice According...*, pp. 28-29.

79. See Chapter Two Pound on Legal History.

80. See Chapter Two Pound on Legal History.

81. Pound, *The Ideal Element...*, p. 109. See also: Pound, "Making Law...," p. 284. Pound, *Social Control...*, p. 87.

82. Pound, "Making Law...," p. 285. See also: Roscoe Pound, Jurisprudence (Vol. 1) 5 vols., St. Paul, Minn., West Publishing Co., 1959, pp. 361-366. Vol. 2 PB 44. (Hereinafter referred to as *Vol. 1*).

83. Pound, *Vol. 3*, pp. 574-575. See also: Roscoe Pound, *Spirit of the Common Law,* Boston, Mass., Marshall Jones Co., 1921, reprinted 1931, pp. 172-176. Vol. 1 PB 107 (Hereinafter referred to as *Spirit...*).

84. To illustrate this difference Pound points to the distinction of *jus scriptum* and *jus non-scriptum* as they developed in Roman law. Pound, *Vol. 3*, p. 440. See also: Pound, *The Ideal Element...Tagore*, pp. 29-33. Pound, *Justice According...*, pp. 60-61. Pound, *Social Control...*, pp. 2-3. Pound, *Spirit...*, pp. 173-175.

85. Pound, *Vol. 3*, p. 440. See also: Pound, *Justice According...*, pp. 41-43. Pound, *The Ideal Element...Tagore*, pp. 25-26. Pound, *Justice According...*, pp. 60-61.

86. Pound, *Vol. 3*, pp. 440, 445. See also: Pound, *Vol. 1*, p. 143. Pound, *Vol. 2*, pp. 32-34.

87. Pound, *Vol. 3*, pp. 440, 445-446. Pound observes that the tradition of law in German custom, was really a class-type tradition which had different effects on members of one class as opposed to another. See also: Pound, *Vol. 1*, p. 143. Pound, *Vol. 2*, pp. 32-34. Pound, *Social Control...*, pp. 2-3.

88. Pound, *Vol. 3*, pp. 446-447. See also: Roscoe Pound, "The Legal Profession in the Middle Ages," Vols. 19 & 20, *Notre Dame Lawyer*, 1943-1945, pp. 229-244. Vol. 2 PB. (Hereinafter referred to as "The Legal Profession..."). Roscoe Pound, "The Legal Profession in England from the End of the Middle Ages to the Nineteenth Century," Vol. 19 *Notre Dame Lawyer*, June, 1944, pp. 315-333, Vol. 2 PB. (Hereinafter referred to as "The Legal Profession in England...").

89. Pound, "Making Law...," pp. 288-289. See also: Pound, *Vol. 3*, pp. 573-584, 654-672. Pound, *Social Control...*, p. 3.

90. Pound, "Making Law...," p. 296. See also: Pound, *Vol. 3*, pp. 573-584, 654-672. Pound, *Social Control...*, p. 3.

91. Pound, "Making Law...," p. 297. See also: Pound, *Vol. 3*, pp. 573-584, 654-672.

92. Pound, "Making Law...," p. 296. See also: Pound, *Vol. 3*, pp. 437-570. Pound, *Social Control...*, p. 3. Pound, *Justice According...*, pp. 41-43.

93. Pound, "Making Law...," p. 294. See also: Pound, *Vol. 3*, pp. 437-570. Pound, *Social Control...*, p. 3. Pound, *Justice According...*, pp. 41-43.

94. Pound, "Making Law...," pp. 295-296. See also: Pound, *Vol. 3*, pp. 437-570. Pound, *Social Control...*, pp. 2-3. Pound, *Justice According...*, pp. 41-43.

95. Pound, *Spirit...*, pp. 173-174. See also: Pound, *The Ideal Element...Tagore*, pp. 25-26. Pound, *Vol. 1*, p. 14. Pound, *Vol. 3*, pp. 654-672. Pound, *Justice According...*, pp. 40-44.

96. Pound, *Vol. 1*, p. 14. See also: Pound, *Justice According...*, pp. 89-91. Pound, *Social Control...*, pp. 97-99.

97. R. Pound, "The American Idea of Government," Vol. 10, *Vital Speeches*, September, 1944, p. 501. *Vol. 2,* PB 98. (Hereinafter referred to as "The American Idea..."). See also: Pound, Social Control..., pp. 106-109. Pound, *Justice According...*, pp. 90-91.

98. Pound, *Task...*, pp. 43-44. See also: Pound, *The Ideal Element...Tagore*, p. 2. Pound, *Social Control...*, pp. 39-41. Pound, *Vol. 2*, pp. 99-122.

99. Pound, *Social Control...*, pp. 20-26. See also: Pound, *Vol. 1*, p. 15. Pound, *Task...*, pp. 78-79.

100. Pound, *Vol. 1*, pp.15-16. See also: Pound, *Social Control...*, pp. 20-26. Pound, *Task...*, pp. 24-25, 42-44, 66-71. Pound, *Justice According...*, pp. 16-27.

101. Pound, *The Ideal Element...Tagore*, pp. 52-53. See also: Pound, *Social Control...*, pp. 20-26. Pound, *Task...*, pp. 24-25. Pound, *Justice According...*, pp. 16-27.

102. Pound, *The Ideal Element...Tagore*, p. 53. See also: Pound, *Social Control...*, p. 20. Pound, *Task...*, pp. 24-25. Pound, *Justice According...*, pp. 16-27.

103. Pound, *Social Control...*, p. 103. See also: Pound, *Task...*, pp. 48-49. Pound, *Vol. 1*, pp. 539-540.

104. Pound, *Social Control...*, pp. 103-104. See also: Pound, *Vol. 1*, pp. 55-61, 113-119. Pound, *Vol. 1*, pp. 361-547. See Chapter Two Legal History.

105. Pound, *Social Control...*, p. 108. See also: Pound, *Vol. 1*, pp. 540-541. Pound, *Task...*, pp. 61-62.

106. Pound, *Social Control...*, p. 109. See also: Pound, *Task...*, p. 15. Pound, *Vol. 1*, pp. 363-367.

107. Pound, *Social Control...*, p. 109. See also: Pound, *Task...*, p. 15. Pound, *Vol. 1*, pp. 363-367.

108. Pound, *Social Control...*, p. 42. See also: Pound, *Vol. 2*, pp. 369-388. Pound, *Task...*, pp. 58-62.

109. Pound, *Social Control...*, pp. 109-110. See also: Pound, *Vol. 2*, pp. 369-388. Pound, *Task...*, pp. 58-62.

110. Pound, *Social Control...*, pp. 110-111. See also: Pound, *Vol. 2*, pp. 369-388. Pound, *Vol. 3*, p. 513. Roscoe Pound, *Jurisprudence* (*Vol. 5*) *5 vols.*, St. Paul, Minn., West Publishing Co., 1959. Vol. 5 pp. 714-715. Vol. 2 PB 44. (Hereinafter referred to as *Vol. 5*). Pound, *Spirit...*, pp. 182-184. Pound, *Task...*, pp. 61-62.

111. Pound, *Social Control...*, pp. 64-65. See also: Pound, *Vol. 2*, pp. 369-388. Pound, *Vol. 1*, pp. 346-347. Pound, *Vol. 3*, p. 328. Pound, *Spirit...*, pp. 195-196. Pound, *The Ideal Element...Tagore*, pp. 178, 195.

112. Pound, *Social Control...*, p. 69. See also: Pound, *Interpretations of Legal...*, pp. 157, 162-165. Pound, *Vol. 3*, pp. 16, 327-334. Pound, *Introduction...*, pp. 42-43, 107. Pound, *Task...*, pp. 23, 112. See a fuller examination of Pound's Theory of Interests, Chapter Seven Theory of Interests.

113. Pound, *Social Control...*, p. 70. See also: Pound, *Interpretations of Legal...*, pp. 162-165. Pound, *Vol. 3*, pp. 99-324. Pound, *Spirit...*, pp. 197-203. See Chapter Seven Theory of Interests.

114. Pound, *Social Control...*, pp. 70-71. See also: Pound, *The Ideal Element...Tagore*, pp. 84-107. Pound, *Interpretations of Legal...*, pp. 162-165. Pound, *Vol. 3*, pp. 25-233. See Chapter Seven Theory of Interests.

115. Pound, *Social Control...*, p. 65,71-72. See also: Pound, *Vol. 3*, p. 71. Roscoe Pound, "Individual Interests in Domestic Relations," Vol 14, *Michigan Law Review*, January, 1916, pp. 177-196. Vol. 1 PB 78. (Hereinafter referred to as "...Domestic Relations").

116. Pound, *Social Control...*, pp. 64-65. See also: Pound, *Vol. 2*, pp. 369-388. Pound, *Vol. 1*, pp. 346-347. See also: Roscoe Pound, "A Theory of Social Interests," *Papers and Proceedings of the American Sociological Society*, Vol. 15, 1921, pp. 16-45, 1921, Vol. 1 PB 108, (Hereinafter referred to as "Theory of Social...").

117. Pound, *Social Control...*, p. 76. See also: Pound, "Theory of Social...", pp. 16-45. Pound, *Vol. 3*, pp. 291-324.

118. Pound, *The Ideal Element...Tagore*, pp. 184, 194. See also: Pound, *Vol. 3*, pp. 291-324.

119. Pound, *Social Control...*, p. 75. See also: Pound, *Vol. 3*, pp. 235-267.

120. Pound, *Social Control...*, p. 78. See also: Pound, *Vol. 3*, PP. 325-276.

121. Pound, *Social Control...*, p. 80. See also: Pound, *The Ideal Element...Tagore*, pp. 84-107. Roscoe Pound, Jurisprudence (Vol.4) 5 vols., St. Paul, Minn., 1959, pp. 56-90. Vol. 2 PB 44. (Hereinafter referred to as *Vol. 4*).

122. Pound, *Social Control...*, p. 83. See also: Pound, *Interpretations of Legal...*, pp. 158-165. Pound, *Vol. 4*, pp. 56-90.

123. Pound, *Social Control...*, p. 83. See also: Pound, *Interpretations of Legal...*, pp. 158-165. Pound, *Vol. 4*, pp. 56-90.

124. Pound, *Social Control...*, p. 85. See also: Pound, *Interpretations of Legal...*, pp. 158-165. Pound, *Vol. 4*, pp. 56-90.

125. Pound, *Social Control...*, p. 85. See also: Pound, *Interpretations of Legal...*, pp. 158-165. Pound, *Vol. 4*, pp. 56-90.

126. Pound, *Social Control...*, p. 86. See also: Pound, *Interpretations of Legal...*, pp. 158-165. Pound, *Vol. 4*, pp. 56-90.

127. Pound, *Social Control...*, p. 87. See also: Pound, *Interpretations of Legal...*, pp. 158-165. Pound, *Vol. 4*, p. 62.

128. Pound, *Social Control...*, p. 91. See also: Pound, *Interpretations of Legal...*, pp. 158-165. Pound, *Vol. 4*, pp. 56-90.

129. Pound, *Social Control...*, p. 88. See also: Pound, *Interpretations of Legal...*, pp. 158-165. Pound, *Vol. 4*, pp. 56-90.

130. Pound, *Social Control...*, p. 89. See also: Pound, *Interpretations of Legal...*, pp. 158-165. Pound, *Vol. 4*, pp. 56-90.

131. Pound, *Social Control...*, p. 89. See also: Pound, *Interpretations of Legal...*, pp. 158-165. Pound, *Vol. 4*, pp. 56-90.

132. Pound, *Social Control...*, p. 92. See also: Pound, *Interpretations of Legal...*, pp. 158-165.

133. Pound, *Social Control...*, p. 96. See also: Pound, *Vol. 4*, p. 73. Pound, *The Ideal Element...Tagore*, pp. 268-269.

134. Pound, *Social Control...*, p. 97. See also: Roscoe Pound, "The Twilight of Liberty," *Nation's Business*, Vol. 28, August, 1940, p. 47. Vol. 2, PB 50, (Hereinafter referred to as "Twilight..."). Roscoe Pound, The Recrudescence of Absolutism, *Sewanee Review*, Vol. 47, January-March, 1939, pp. 26-27. Vol. 1, PB 236. (Hereinafter referred to as "Recrudescence...").

135. Pound, *Social Control...*, p. 97. See also: Roscoe Pound, *Contemporary Juristic Theory*, Claremont, California, Pomona Scripps College, Claremont Colleges, 1940, pp. 1-28. *Vol. 1*, PB 255. (Hereinafter referred to as *Contemporary...*).

136. Pound, *Social Control...*, p. 99. See also: Pound, *Contemporary...*, pp. 1-28.

137. Pound, *Social Control...*, p. 99. See also: Pound, *Vol. 4*, pp. 41-56.

138. Pound, *Social Control...*, p. 102. See also: Pound, *Justice According...*, p. 91.

139. Pound, *Social Control...*, p. 51. See also: Pound, *Interpretations of legal...*, pp. 25-30.

140. Pound, *Social Control...*, pp. 53-54. See also: Pound, *Interpretations of legal...*, p. 47.

141. Pound, *Social Control...*, p. 55. See also: Pound, *Vol. 1*, pp. 72-79, 98-102. Pound, *Vol. 3*, pp. 354-360. Pound, *The Ideal Element...Tagore*, p. 99-100.

142. Pound, *Social Control...*, p. 55. See also: Pound, *Vol. 3*, pp. 354-360.

143. Pound, *Social Control...*, p. 56. See also: Pound, *Vol. 3*, pp. 354-360. Pound, *The Ideal Element...Tagore*, p. 100.

144. Pound, *Social Control...*, p. 57. See also: Pound, *Vol. 3*, pp. 354-360. Pound, *The Ideal Element...Tagore*, pp. 100-101.

145. Pound, *Social Control..., p. 57.* See also: Pound, *Vol. 3*, pp. 354-360. Pound, *The Ideal Element...Tagore*, p. 101.

146. Pound, *Social Control...*, p. 60. See also: Pound, *Vol. 3*, pp. 354-360. Pound, *The Ideal Element...Tagore*, p. 101.

147. Pound, *Social Control...*, p. 61. See also: Pound, *Vol. 3*, pp. 354-360. Pound, *The Ideal Element...Tagore*, p. 101.

148. Pound, *Social Control...*, p. 62. See also: Pound, *Vol. 3*, pp. 354-360.

149. Pound, *Social Control...*, p. 58. See also: Pound, *The Ideal Element...Tagore*, pp. 71-77.

150. Pound, *Social Control...*, p. 59. See also: Pound, *Task...*, pp. 66-72.

151. Pound, *Social Control...*, p. 60. See also: Pound, *Task...*, pp. 66-72.

152. Pound, *The Ideal Element...Tagore*, pp. 70-82.
See also: Pound, *Task...*, pp. 66-72.

153. Pound, *Justice According...*, p. 29. See also: Pound, *Social Control...*, pp. 18-20, 25-26.

154. Pound, *The Ideal Element...Tagore*, p. 53. See also: Pound, *Social Control...*, pp. 25-26.

155. See Chapter Nine, Administrative Law.

156. Pound, *The Ideal Element...Tagore*, pp. 282-283. See also: Pound, *Social Control...*, pp. 95-98.

CHAPTER TWO

POUND ON LEGAL HISTORY

PRIMITIVE LAW

Roscoe Pound speaks of stages in the development of the growth and function of law. More by implication than by explicit statement, Pound sees a commonness in the problems faced by man, which are dealt with, at least in part, by social institutions—the kin group, the family, the church, and increasingly so by the law. The conflicts that appear among individuals within in any society are inevitable and require some form of resolution, which has historically been done by means of law which flows from the comparable role played by other institutions which previously handled the conflicts.[1]

This search for solutions of human problems in the context of society, according to Pound, does not proceed randomly and incoherently. Security and restraint on arbitrary coercion dominates the growth of law, and while there are endless ramifications and permutations in this development, it is steady enough and certain enough to allow it to be described in general terms and assigned to general periods. He notes:

> Thus we see a quest for conformity of action and certainty of result from the very beginning of public administration of justice. This quest has two bases. One is psychological—humans' distrust of our fellowmen when given power over our conduct or our substance, The other is economic—the need of predictability of judicial reaction in assuring economic activity, long-term enterprises and investments of energy and money therein.[2]

Pound often rejected the pretension involved in writing "universal history," and said such efforts were improper because of the method and focus they employed, *i.e.*, the:

> selection of a few facts, taken to be the significant or important factors, as if there could be an absolute significance or importance, which were then taken to demonstrate the principle with reference to which they had been chosen.[3]

Nonetheless, Pound speaks in quite universal terms in describing the stages on law's development. Indeed, he perceives a pattern and a process in such stages which is reflected in eras of relatively fixed and stringent law, which are in turn followed by periods of "loosening up" of the law in order to give it the flexibility needed to accommodate new interests and changes involved in society.[4]

His observations on the history of law's development have a two-fold character. On the one hand, he defines and describes the periods of law in regard to the ends or purposes served in these eras; and , on the other hand, he deals with the periods of the "philosophy of law." Both need examination and description if one is to understand Pound's thinking about the law, for he presumes his own interpretations, statements, and philosophy of law are a culmination of developments in thought and practice that preceded the law he knew. Thus, he looked to past practice and thought to define and explain his own notion of the end, task, purpose, and composition of law. In discussing the treatment he gives to the historical epochs of law he says:

> Approaching the subject historically, the first inquiry should be, what is the end of law as ideas on this subject have developed in connection with the development of legal precepts and doctrines?
>
> In this inquiry it will be convenient to think of four stages of legal development in systems which have come to maturity: (1) the stage of primitive law, (2) the stage of strict law, (3) the stage of equity and natural law, and (4) the stage of maturity of law.[5]

Pound observes, however, that a new stage of law is developing which he refers to as "the socialization of law" which is as distinctive in its characteristics as are the preceding four periods.[6]

The second discussion of Pound's historical treatment of the law involves his examination of the ideas that influenced and governed the law's development. He writes:

> Having attempted to mark the course which the development of law has actually taken in different periods of legal history, with respect to the end

> for which the legal order and law exist, we turn now to the course which juristic thinking has taken during these same periods as to the direction in which law ought to develop and what should be regarded as the end of law.[7]

This chapter will be devoted to reviewing Pound's analysis of the five historical stages of law, while chapters three, four, and five will examine his view of law's philosophical development.[8] Pound's examination of the law's development in historical stages is built on examining the end to which law was directed, and finally, the symbiotic relationship he sees between these legal eras.

Pound notes that anthropological and archaeological studies describe a condition in human society where law does not serve as a differentiated form of social control, and in which the social system works in an almost organic fashion in regulating human conduct.[9] He observes that there is a point in time where law, as a means of social control, begins to distinguish itself from other mechanisms of social control, such as the kin group and the family.[10] When a society makes this transition from a kin or tribally organized society, to a stage of primitive law it exhibits certain characteristics and seeks certain ends,[11] and at this juncture law becomes a separate technique of social control.[12] In this primitive era, the primary concern of law is two-fold: first, to keep the peace and provide for the general security: and second, "to insure that one will should not be subjected arbitrarily to the will of another by reliance upon chance."[13] Consequently he observes that when:

> law was struggling to establish itself alongside of religion and the internal discipline of the household and the clan as an agency of social control, it was first necessary to consider how far the law could interpose effectively in preventing self-help and keeping the peace.[14]

In this era Pound says there were three methods whereby an injured individual or group could seek and obtain redress for injury—self-help, appeal(s) to god(s) for divine retribution, or use of the mechanism of the state.[15] Recourse to self-help threatens the peace and security of the society and, carried to the extreme, permits extended private war. Thus, the end of law becomes fundamentally to "keep the peace,"[16] and law, at the outset sought to regulate self-help and prevent aggression of one person against another.[17] Thus, it arrived at keeping the peace and eliminating private war.[18] In earlier societies—which were kin or tribally oriented—the presence and frequent recourse to self-help to redress injuries made blood feuds and reprisals endemic, and eventually religious sanctions were used to obtain redress.[19] With the advent of a primitive legal order, redress could also be obtained by seeking the aid of king or his magistrate. Initially, however, the king's aid was sought only to prevent interference with the injured party's attempt to obtain redress for this injury.[20] The political force in primitive society thus began to limit the types of reprisals permitted, and the means that could be used,[21] and resulted in the substitution of organized force for private actions for redress of injuries.[22] The mechanism employed by the legal force in society in this early stage involved quite mechanical modes of trial which ignored disputes over the facts involved.[23] This mechanical mode of trial served the major purposes of the legal order quite well, since a more "rational" process designed to elicit the truth of the facts asserted, would have invited even further dispute. Thus, the mechanical mode of trial involved neither disputes over the facts nor partiality in the adjudication of them. Methods such as trial by ordeal, compurgation, and oath provided for a resolution of the conflict without concern for the sufficiency of evidence or the degree of impartiality of the adjudicating body.[24]

In the primitive era the scope of the law in terms of the disputes it would handle was also limited. The law was composed mainly of detailed regulations regarding the employment of self-help, a specified listing of the circumstances under which one might appeal for the king's aid, and mutually prescribed compositions and tariffs which the king could impose for affronts to the dignity and peace of the crown.[25] Pound notes that the reparations provided were not necessarily tailored to the actual scope of the injury, but included only what was necessary to eliminate the desire for revenge.[26]

Primitive law was able to control and satisfy the desire for revenge, and eliminate, for the most part, private war and provide for general security and peace.[27] The construction of a more peaceable order in which men could use law as a means to other ends became possible, and as Pound observes, these conditions of security made:

> possible a division of labor and so an economic order in which research and investigation and experiment are possible which have led to our mastery over external nature.[28]

Pound feels there are five characteristics of this primitive stage of law.[29]

First, consideration was directed to the matter of determining the degree to which a desire for revenge was provoked by the wrongful act involved, and not a determination of the actual extent of the damage that was done. Thus, in the stage of primitive law remedies were designed to effect composition, *i.e.*, a specific remedy for the specific injury, and not compensation directed at repairing the full scope of the damage inflicted. Second, the entire mechanism of rules and procedures were characterized by extreme formality. Third, completely mechanical forms were employed in the conduct of the trials involved, in order that additional disputes would not arise over the truth of the facts asserted, and thus minimize additional controversy and the consequent threat to peace this would entail. Fourth, law that was employed was based on specific rules that tailored the application of such rules to specific and determinant fact situations. Fifth, the unit to which legal protection was extended was the collective—such as a kin group or family—and not the individual person.[30]

During this primitive stage of law, political force developed and eventually this force enabled the political institutions, within which the law developed, to become the dominant force in the ordering of society and the preservation of security and peace. This developed political force replaced the kin or tribal organization, and religion, as the major forms of social control. Primitive law thus constituted the necessary precondition for the development of the era of strict law. It is Pound's view that once primitive law reached a given stage of development, two causes press the social order to move to a stage of strict law—the fear of the arbitrary exercise of magisterial power by the state, and the survival of ideas of form and literal application from the earlier period.[31]

Strict Law

According to Pound, the transition from the stage of primitive law to the stage of strict law brings about a significant and qualitative change in the role of law and the ends which law serves in society:

> [I]n this stage [strict law], law has definitely prevailed as the regulative agency of society and the state has prevailed as the organ of social control. Self-help and self-redress have been definitely superseded for all but exceptional causes. Normally men appeal to the state to redress of wrongs.[32]

In the era of primitive law remedies and wrongs pertained to groups with which the individual was associated,[33] while in the stage of strict law, the major purpose of the law was to secure to individuals' remedies for injuries done to them.[34] As Pound notes:

> while the logical sequence is interest, right, remedy, the historical sequence is the reverse, remedy, right, interest. When remedies were known, but not rights, the only limits of the remedy were formal.[35]

The era of strict law placed the primary emphasis on remedies and these remedies were characterized by great formality and ornateness,[36] and, unlike the era of strict law where remedies were applied only after injury was done, remedies were used in the stage of strict law preventively—to forestall injury.[37] Consequently remedies constituted the central concern of law in the era of strict law,[38] and as appeals to the state to employ these remedies increased, there was a correlative expansion of the concerns of the law.

Pound observes that the era of strict law was characterized by its "hard and fast rules," and its emphasis on form and procedures that were mechanical in their operation. Pound identifies four major characteristics of the era of strict law—formalism, unalterability of the law, individualism, and an unmoral attitude.[39]

The great formalism which characterized this period was evidenced in procedural forms which were exceedingly demanding, and which automatically controlled the responses of the adjudicating agency.[40] For example, Pound observes that the loss of claim in a petition could occur unless the issue was fully and completely identified in the pleading.[41] Such formalism in adjudication and procedure, Pound feels, constituted a midway point between the totally mechanically process of adjudication which characterized the primitive era and the rational process of discovery and adjudication used in more modern times. The forms and procedures used for determining an issue and adjudicating it in the stage of strict law constituted a method not quite as mechanical as that of the primitive era, but not as flexible and rational as those of more modern eras of law. Pound observes, however, that this elaborate formalism did serve the end of certainty which characterized the era of strict law.[42] This formalism also emphasized minuteness of detail. Consequently there was an unbending application of what was expressed in the legal pleadings and responses. Intention and will were not considered germane to the adjudication of disputes or the reconciliation and adjustment of the expectations which were involved.[43]

Formalism necessitated an emphasis on the forms of action in place of the substantive issues involved, and literalness of interpretation was the dominant concern in the adjudication of disputes.[44] Pound feels that there were several reasons which justified such an emphasis on formalism in the era of strict law.

First, the role of forms was prominent because remedies were known and identifiable, whereas interests and rights were not clearly identified in the law. Therefore, procedural forms which called for remedies assumed a preeminence. Only in later periods of law's development, remedies and the forms needed for obtaining them were considered in reaction to the interests and rights which the remedies were to protect.[45] This rigid formalism made sense in the era of strict law, but became irrelevant to the needs of legal orders in the later stages of law's development.[46] In the era of strict law, however, this formalism aided in eliminating further dispute. As Pound says:

> Men's ideas might differ as to whether there was something novel, called a substantive right, contained in or behind the form, and if so, as to what it was. But the form allowed no scope for such disputes, and in the beginnings of a legal system, as well as in the pre-legal period, a chief end is to avoid dispute. In any age or in any place where men are inclined on slight provocation to take the righting of wrongs into their own hands, the law that hesitates is lost.[47]

One must be aware of the fact that the strict law emerged at a time when record keeping was almost non-existent, and that most matters and events needed to be committed to memory and orally transmitted. He says:

> Ceremonial was a stimulus to memory. Men could remember that a ceremony had taken place before them, especially one which everyone knew was the only way to produce legal results. ... They might or might not remember that an informal transaction had taken place in their presence; they might or might not remember its details. The details of formal transactions follow fixed lines. If one knows the kind of ceremony, the details fill themselves in with certainty.[48]

In addition, form served as a brake on arbitrary official acts:

> at a time when there was no elaborate body of substantial rules and principles to furnish standards of decision.[49]

While Pound acknowledges the importance of relatively fixed forms as a protection against arbitrary power and its exercise,[50] he also feels that form helps in identifying and serving interests in all periods of time.[51]

The second characteristic of law during this structure is the law's rigidity and immutability, which Pound feels has three causes.

First, there was the carryover from the stage of primitive law of the belief that there was a certain sacredness to the law, and consequently it was assumed that the law could be changed only by some form of divine intervention. Though this type of divine sacredness was no longer fully attributed to the law, Pound does note that:

> Immutability of a body of religious-legal precepts may persist after law is no longer accounted sacred;...and such is the case during much of the era of strict law.[52]

Second, much of the law, in the era of strict law, existed in codes and statutes, and there was no acceptable and workable method which could be employed to alter these codes and statutes.[53] Judicial treatment of law during this period was based on the assumption that law was found and not made, and that therefore, there was little or no flexibility in the judicial application and interpretation of the law. Such flexibility would come only later in the development of law.[54] It was further assumed, in the era of strict law, that law was a "declaration of custom," and since only some form of "better ascertainment" of custom could warrant law's alteration, this notion also added to the fixity and immutability of the law.[55] Pound says the immutability of law in this era is fully understandable and that in this period of legal development:

> Conscious change seems to be a war with the very idea of law, since there are as yet no fixed rules or settled principles to dictate its course. The idea of formally superseding law by new law is repugnant in such a period, as implying that law is something that may be adopted or rejected at will. Rigidity is connected with the formal character of the strict law because, as Jhering put it, "forms will break but not bend".[56]

The third characteristic in this era of strict law is the overwhelming emphasis on individualism. In the primitive era remedies and interests were related to some form of group association and did not relate to the individual. The stage of strict law, however, imposed responsibility and duty upon individual men of mature age, and thus, remedies and interests related primarily to the individual. In describing this characteristic Pound says that in the era of strict law:

> every man is expected to stand for himself, to look out for himself, to be primarily his own keeper... The law will do little for man. He must not expect the state to look out for his interests. If he goes into anything, he must do so with his eyes open and must abide the consequence.[57]

Given the focus on the individual and the assumption that he exercised his own will, law could not be adjusted to take into account extenuating circumstances. Law was to be applied literally and unbendingly, since it was assumed that no mature man would subject himself to the harshness of the remedies involved except as a result of his own free choice. Pound observes that this:

> whole point of view is that of primitive society and reading the story in TACITUS of how the Germans played dice. They played, he tells us, as a serious business, even staking their own liberty; and if one lost in such a case, he voluntarily went into slavery and patiently allowed himself to be sold. Something of this spirit, which is the spirit of the strict law, may be recognized today in such doctrines as contributory negligence and assumption of risk and the exaggeration of contentious procedure which treats litigation as a game.[58]

The fourth characteristic of the stage of strict law is reflected in its "unmoral attitude," *i.e.*, "a refusal to take account of the moral aspects of situations or transactions. ..."[59] Pound feels that this characteristic was tied closely to the individualism of the period, for it was considered that each individual man should be able to care for himself and his interests, and that the law should not be employed to mitigate the consequences which resulted from one's own choice of action.[60] Pound is critical of this unmoral attitude and the doctrine of individualism to which it was tied. He observes that:

> the stock argument of the strict law for the many harsh rules it enforces is that the situation was produced by the party's own failing and he must abide it. But the whole point of view is that of primitive society, and, despite the eulogies which have been pronounced upon the features of the strict law as molding of strong and self-reliant character, it may be asserted confidently that they were not devised to any such end, that at best they subserve such an end but little, and that they defeat social interests of general security and general morals and individual interests of personality and substance which the law ought to protect.[61]

The individualism of this era of strict law was narrow in its definition of a legal person—and the rights and interests associated with it. For example, Roman law defined only a free man as legal person.[62] In the earliest stages of strict law a legal person had rights and privileges which stood somewhere between the rights and privileges associated with kin groups of the primitive era, and the attachment of rights and privileges to *all* individual human beings which would occur later in legal development.

Despite certain criticisms Pound levels at the era of strict law, he admires its contributions to a better legal order which emerged. He points out, that the era of strict law advanced as a mechanism designed not only to keep the peace, which was characteristic of primitive law, but also adopted a broader and more encompassing idea of security.[63] Second, he feels that the remedies available in the stage of strict law were far advanced over the primitive law's reliance on compositions etc..[64] Finally, he notes that the strict law contributed ideas of certainty and uniformity to the law which it did not have before, and established additional rules and forms that proved to be effective techniques for achieving security and conformity.[65]

Equity or Natural Law

The formalism and rigidity of strict law, Pound argues, were modified by the flexible and adjustable precepts that emerged in the period of equity or natural law. In contrasting the two eras Pound says:

> The watchword of this stage [equity or natural law] is morals or some phrase of ethical import, such as good conscience, *aequin et bonum*, or natural law. The strict law insists on uniformity. Equity and natural law insists on good morals. The strict law insists on form, equity and natural law on justice in the ethical sense; the strict law insists on remedies, equity and natural law on duties; the strict law insists on rule, equity and natural law on reason.[66]

As Pound notes, the era of strict law conceived that formalism with its rigid and immutable forms was necessary in order to curb personal arbitrariness and caprice in the administration of law. In the era of equity and natural law, by contrast, it was felt that such a limitation could be achieved by a reliance on reason and the limitations that it imposed.[67] This view, he notes, comported with the general temper of the times, and says:

> Equity and natural law relied rather upon reason and an attempt to identify law and morals at a time when philosophical or religious systems of morals were generally accepted and appeared to furnish universal standards.[68]

The stage of equity and natural law allowed for a liberalization of law that would modify the rigid system of strict law. This liberalization, Pound feels, was necessary in order to allow the law to adjust to the needs and demands present at the time.[69] Pound suggests that this period of equity and natural law began on the continent with the advent of the law of nature schools which emerged in the seventeenth and eighteenth centuries, and in England at the time of the rise of the courts of chancery and the development of equity in the sixteenth century.[70]

Pound observes that the era of equity and natural law has three major characteristics.

First, the era of equity and natural law is characterized by a close identification of law with morals.[71] In the era of strict law, emphasis was placed on giving effect to agreements as they were expressed, despite any inequity or irrationality of outcomes.[72] It was in response to such rigidity and immutability of law that the stage of equity and natural law arose. In the strict era there was an unbending application of rules and standards regardless of outcome, while the stage of equity and natural law considered the outcome of a decision to be the test of its appropriateness. In conformity with the general tenor of equity and natural law principles, law was considered as a means to assure "correct" outcomes in adjudication. Such outcomes, it was felt, should be consistent with good morals, even if that required altering the law in order to achieve such outcomes.[73] Pound maintains that this characteristic is reflected in such notions as "natural obligation" and the belief that certain moral obligations devolve upon men as reasonable creatures.[74] This characteristic of reasonableness emerged in response to two beliefs which undergirded the stage of equity and natural law, *i.e.*, a:

> 1. theory of limitations on human activities imposed by reason in view of human nature, [and]
> 2. ...a theory of moral qualities inherent in human beings or natural rights demonstrated by reason as deductions from human nature.[75]

Second, the developments in law which reflected moral consideration, were learned from the idea that there is an appropriate "nature of things" and "nature of man".[76] These externally derived moral standards and obligations were applied to the legal order and allowed for the abandonment of the rigid forms and procedures which governed the operation of law in the era of strict law despite the outcomes they caused.

Third, the era of equity and natural law emphasized the application of reason in the use of the law and diminished the emphasis placed on strict rules and forms.[77] Reason was employed to assure that the outcome of the application of law would be moral. The rigid and unbending application of law, which, although it assured certainty, resulted in inequitable and often irrational results was abandoned.[78]

It is Pound's opinion that the application of standards of morality and reason in the period of equity and natural law provided the flexibility needed for law's survival and development. In addition the emphasis on reason and morals resulted in fairer and more beneficial results. According to Pound, the stage of equity and natural law, contributed four enduring ideas which have influenced law in its subsequent development.

First of all, and in Pound's opinion the most significant, is the notion that the concept of "legal personality" should extend to all persons, and that "the moral unit [individual persons] should be the legal unit."[79] This notion extended rights and the capacity for legal action to all natural persons, and not merely to arbitrarily and narrowly defined legal persons, as was the case in the stage of strict law.[80] There was an insistence:

> on throwing off all incapacities for which a "natural reason," as distinguished from an historical explanation, cannot be given, and on making possession of normal will and capacity for legal transaction coincident.[81]

Second, in the era of equity and natural law, law's substance as well as its form was considered. Emphasis, therefore, needed to be placed on the role of reason in determining the substantive dimensions of the law. Such an emphasis on reason reduced, in turn, the reliance on strict unalterable notions of form which were so characteristic of the era of strict law. Pound observes:

> only the systems which, having achieved strict law, went through the change and came to measure things by reason, instead of solely by rule and formula, have become laws of the world.[82]

Third, Pound points to the fact that the era of equity and natural law emphasized the notion that expectations which have reasonably been induced by another's behavior or words should not be disappointed. Consequently, the certainty of the law was to be assured not merely by the observance of forms and formulae, but also by using the law to protect such reasonably induced expectations, and this, in turn, led to using the law to assure the certainty of human conduct.[83] In assuring this certainty of individual conduct, heavy reliance was made on the use of reason to formulate conclusions of law based on substantive concerns which enhanced the tie of law to morals. This association of law with morals enhanced the idea that duties derived from good faith reliance should be considered as legal duties.[84] Legal transactions and legal relations, therefore, became tied to ideas of what should constitute reasonable conduct and the determination that such obligations should be enforced by the operation of the law.[85] As Pound comments, this development in the era of equity and natural law introduced into the law the idea that good faith reliance should be supported by the law so that:

> we know today what moral conduct will be tomorrow. The unprincipled may or may not keep promises, may or may not pay debts, may or may not be constant in business or political or family relations. The term trustworthy, which we apply to one whose conduct is moral, speaks for itself. We say his word is as good as his bond. We have confidence in the stability of his course of life. In the stage of equity or natural law, there is an endeavor to make moral duties of good faith into legal duties, and it largely succeeds.[86]

The fourth idea which emerged in the stage of equity or natural law, was the notion that one should not be unjustly enriched at the expense of another,[87] *i.e.*, one should not profit "by the form if the substance fails."[88] Natural justice, Pound argues, assures that equivalency must be considered an element in justice; consequently doctrines of restitution, and mutuality of performance, became operative in this stage of law.[89]

Even though Pound attributes considerable and enduring benefits to the stage of equity or natural law he, nonetheless, points to two major difficulties which he associates with making morals a basis for law.[90] First, he believes that associating law and morals too closely, induces unrealistic assumptions about what standards may be legally enforced, and that such standards also are far too often too intangible to be of real value in measuring human conduct for legal purposes. For example, he cites, the futility involved in the past attempts to translate gratitude into a legal duty, or create a legally applicable standard of disinterestedness. Fortunately, he concludes, the law, because it is a practical instrument, tends to back away from contrived attempts to enforce moral duties as legal duties when it is evident that this cannot be done successfully.[91]

The second difficulty Pound feels, is far more serious and much less easily corrected. The stage of equity and natural law encourages a "too wide a scope to judicial discretion."[92] Unlike rules—which have a determinant content and are applicable to a determinant set of facts—moral precepts are far less determinant in terms of content or meaning and any attempt to enforce them necessitates that wide discretion be vested in the agent or agency charged with their enforcement.[93] Since it is imperative, in Pound's view, that a legal order minimize all chances for arbitrariness and caprice, this particular development in the stage of equity and natural law, enhanced the opportunity for judges to rely on individual preferences and their own caprice in fashioning rules of behavior and their enforcement. Although this increased opportunity for judicial discretion was not easily correctable, Pound feels that there were two developments which aided in correcting it. First, what initially was discretionary eventually became embodied in rules of equity proceedings which were relatively fixed and determinant.[94] Second, the far reaching moral principles that emerged in this era of law, gradually became subjected to a more mechanical interpretation and application.[95] Both of these developments served to act as a brake on judicial latitude in the application of equitable principles or natural law doctrines. The tightening up of these doctrines and procedures were a part of the course of developments which led to the emergence of the "maturity of law."[96] To be sure, there were benefits that derived from the "loosening up" of the law during the stage of equity and natural law, but at the cost of enhancing judicial discretion with the dangers that involved. Pound, notes that in order to hedge in these developments of personalized justice, there arose a:

> gradual fixing of rules and consequent stiffening of the legal system. Some moral principles, in their acquired character of legal principles, were carried out to logical consequences beyond what was practicable or expedient, so that a selecting and restricting process became necessary and at length the principles became lost in a mass of somewhat arbitrary rules derived therefrom. Others were developed as mere abstractions, and thus were deprived of their purely moral character. In this way transition took place to the next stage. But note a significant feature of this transition. The tribunal no longer tells us that its law is not other than the law of God. It no longer seeks to add legal sanction the whole body of moral principles simply because they are moral. The legal field has again become a limited one, defined by rules, not an unlimited one capable of indefinite extension to cover all things within the reach of the moral zeal of the magistrate.[97]

In comparing the stage of equity or natural law with the two that preceded it, Pound says:

> we may say that whereas the end in primitive law is public peace and in the period of strict law security, in this stage it is an ethical solution of controversies; that whereas the means employed in primitive law is

> composition and in the strict law legal remedies, in this period it is enforcement of duty; and that to the contribution of primitive law, mainly, the idea of a peaceable ordering of society, and to those of strict law, mainly certainty, and uniformity reached by rule and form, it adds the conceptions of good faith and moral conduct to be attained through reason.[98]

Mature Law

The liberalizing era of equity or natural law was followed in turn by the mature stage of law, wherein the law again became fixed and stable. This new fixed and stable ordering, however, reflected many of the liberalizing influences and changes brought about by the stage of equity or natural law.[99] The stability of mature law established restraints on the opportunities for arbitrariness which emerged in the more fluid situation of equity or natural law. Pound comments:

> The maturity of law turned to the logical development of conceptions derived from supposed ultimate metaphysical data, at a time when men believed in the absolute, or to logical deduction from principles derived from history, under the influence of positivist views derived from the analogy of scientific study of nature.[100]

The major ends sought in the stage of the maturity of law were equality and security.[101] Pound observes that the concept of equality as it was understood in this stage embodied the notion, which emerged in the stage of equity or natural law, that all natural persons must be treated as equals before the law and as possessing equal legal capacities. Remedies in the stage of mature law reaffirmed the prevailing idea of the stage of strict law, *i.e.*, that the same remedy should be applied to the same state of facts. Equality in the stage of mature law was reinforced by the fact that the law emphasized that legal precepts were to be applied to all persons equally, and assured the equality of opportunity to all persons to act on their own behalf.[102]

The idea of security in the stage of the maturity of law also bore some relationship to the type of security which was central to the stage of strict law. The stage of equity or natural law developed the idea that legal affects are to be considered as a result of acts of will and not merely the result of the operation of form and mechanical application of the law. This change was reflected in the notion that one should not be enriched at "the expense of another through forms without will."[103] Pound, therefore, suggests that there are two dimensions to the idea of security as it developed in the stage of mature law:

> (1) The idea that every one is to be secured in his interests against aggression by others, and (2) the idea that others are to be permitted to acquire from him only through his will that they do so, or through his breach of rules devised to secure others in like interests.[104]

Pound says that the idea of equality in the stage of mature law was complemented by an emphasis on certainty. The certainty which was sought and achieved was similar to that in the stage of strict law, but differed in the fact that there was an insistence not only on the equal application of remedies, but also upon the equality of rights. He observes that this notion offered to all the:

> equality of capacities to influence others through the power of the state, and conceives of equality of application of legal remedies as only a means thereto.[105]

The concept of security pervading this era is reflected in this stage's emphasis on contract, property, transactions, and acquisitions—all of which were considered crucial to the security of the social order.[106] The idea of freedom of contract was considered to be a privately owned right or asset and was protected as such. Contract law was designed to protect one's given and natural abilities, to acquire what one could by the use of these abilities.[107]

The security of acquisitions and contract were central to the stage of mature law since both were considered to be property rights. The law was considered as a means to protect exercises of human will and contract was the means to be used for the furthermost extension of individual will in the relations of one man with another. Contracts were the most important mechanisms by which one could give and extract resources, goods, services, etc., and contracts were to be given the same scope of protection as other forms of property.[108] Other personal interests—such as the right of privacy or protection against defamation—were also to be protected by the law of the mature era, and were also considered to be property rights.[109]

Liberty—which received protection and recognition in the stage of mature law- was the liberty of each individual to act in conformity with his own will and in pursuit of his own self-interests. Limitation of such liberty could occur only if the willed acts of one person intruded upon the secured rights of another.[110]

In Pound's view the most significant contribution of the stage of mature law was "the idea of individual legal rights" on which the legal order was based.[111] It is Pound's opinion that there is a uniform progression from the idea of "composition" which prevailed in the stage of primitive law, to the concept of remedy in the stage of strict law. This progression continued in the stage of equity or natural law in which legal remedies were used to enforce legal duties, to the stage of strict law where a right was considered to underlie each duty.[112] He observes:

> until the last quarter of the nineteenth century we taught and expounded the common law from the standpoint of actions and remedies rather than of rights. It is only a generation ago that the law of torts began to be emancipated from the bonds fixed by the actions of trespass and trespass on the case and to be expounded upon the basis of the legal rights secured. As often happens in such connections, we are systematizing the whole law upon the basis of rights just as that conception is beginning to yield its central position in legal science because of the discovery of a more fundamental conception behind it.[113]

But in the stage of mature law legal rights were put behind duty and remedy, and constituted the ultimate end for which the legal order existed, and these legal rights, Pound says, served to preserve the interest in general security.[114]

In summarizing the nature of mature law, legal thought and practice maintained: "that legal results should flow from will rather than from power and that one person should not be enriched unjustly at the expense of another because of power without intention. In consequence, its idea of security includes two elements: everyone is to be secured in his interest against aggression by others and others are to be persuaded to acquire from him or to exact from him only through his will that they do so or through his breach of rule devised to secure others in like interests."[115] In contrasting the stage of mature law with the preceding stages in law's development, Pound writes:

> Comparing the maturity of law with the stages which preceded it, the ends of the stage are equality of opportunity and security of acquisitions, the means employed is maintenance of rights; the contribution to the science of administering justice is through the working out of the idea of individual rights. In this stage individual rights are put at the foundation of the legal system, so that duties are but correlative thereto and remedies but indications thereof. As has been said..., all important legal institutions of this stage are property and contract.[116]

As in all the preceding stages of law, however, the stage of mature law was to be succeeded by another stage in which the function of law and administration of justice is improved. This next stage of law is what Pound calls the socialization of law.

Socialization of Law

In the stage of mature law, according to Pound, the focus and emphasis was on the individual—his abstract liberty, property, contract, and security of transactions. The outcomes of such emphases were considered to be those which logically and necessarily followed from freely willed choices. The role of law was to identify the limits of such actions as they were to be applied to all equally.[117] Such emphases in the law, Pound notes, were reminiscent of strict law, and, he says:

> In consequence, a certain opposition between law and morals develops once more, and just as neglect of the moral aspects of conduct in the stage of strict law required the legal revolution through infusion of lay moral ideas into law which we call the stage of equity and natural law, so the neglect of the moral worth of the concrete individual and of his claim to a complete moral and social life, involved in the insistence upon property and contract in the abstract, which mark the maturity of law, have been requiring a like revolution through the absorption into the law of ideas developed in the social sciences.[118]

In the stage of socialization of law the moral worth of the individual is enhanced by the recognition that individuals are best protected when the interests which are vital to them are recognized and properly attended by the law.[119] In describing these new emphases he writes:

> there is a change from the abstract equality of the nineteenth century to an adjustment of burdens with reference to ability to bear them. Thus, there is a concrete individualization of application wherein the last century there was an abstract equality of abstract individuals.[120]

These emphases resulted from external influences exercised by the newly developing social sciences which pointed to areas of human want and need which were ignored by the law. Pound says:

> One perceives a significant divergence between the idea of the end of law which had developed in actual rules and doctrines and obtained in juristic thought at the end of the nineteenth century, on one hand, and, on the other hand, the idea of justice which had come to obtain in the other social sciences. So marked was this divergence that the promoters of social legislation did not hesitate to contrast what they called legal justice with social justice.[121]

Such a disparity between what the law served and what interests needed the recognition and protection of the law, could not last for long. The era of socialization of law abandoned the support of abstract rights and looked to the interests those rights serve. The major inquiry of law then became:

> What claims, what demands are involved in the existence of society in which these individual demands are put forward; how far may these individual demands be put in terms of those social interests or identified with them, and when so subsumed under social interests, insofar as they may be so treated, what will give the fullest effect to those social interests with the least sacrifice.[122]

Thus, in the era of socialization of law there is a shift from the emphasis on protecting the outcomes of individually willed acts, to an emphasis on balancing competing claims and interests in order to achieve as equitable arrangement of them as is possible. Pound notes that in the socialization of law:

> we may think of the task of the legal order as one of precluding friction and elimination of waste; as one of conserving the goods of existence in order to make them go as far as possible, and of precluding friction and elimination of waste in the human use and enjoyment of them, so that where each may not have all that he claims, he may at least have all that is possible. Put in this way , we are seeking to secure as much of human claims and desires—that is as much of the whole scheme of interests—as possible, with the least sacrifice of such interests.[123]

Pound suggests that significant changes have occurred in the operation of the law in order to permit it to protect the interests involved in society, and to maintain and further civilization. These changes in the practice of law were necessary in order to provide flexibility in the law so that laws could protect and serve those interests which are essential to society, and would also enhance those activities needed to advance civilization. According to Pound, these changes occurred in twelve areas of the law and cumulatively constitute the characteristics of the law in the stage of socialization.[124]

The first of the changes occurred in the law of property. Limitations on property's use which characterize the stage of socialization of law reflect a need to limit, what Pound calls, the "anti-social" uses of property. Precedents for such limitations on property rights, he maintains, occurred in the stage of equity or natural law when, for example, the concept of "unconscientious exercise of rights to property" emerged. The difference between the limitations in these two stages of law, however, is reflected in the fact that in the period of equity or natural law such restraints were derived from "moral considerations," while in the stage of "socialization of the law" they are derived from a felt need to restrain usage of property in order to protect vital social interests.[125]

Pound cites as examples of limitations in the era of socialization the changes in the law regarding "spite fences" and "surface and percolating water." In the stage of socialization of the law, a standard of "reasonable use" takes the place of what Pound calls the "equality of abstract liberty of action," which had been used to measure and determine what was an appropriate exercise of a property right in the preceding era.[126] Such changes in the law, he observes, have occurred in both the judicial and legislative spheres of legal activity.[127] The security of property rights in the stage of socialization reflect:

> the tendency to hold that what the law should secure is satisfaction of those wants or claims of the owner with respect to the property which may be generalized and subsumed under certain social interests, especially those claims which consist with the like claims of his neighbors and so are said to be reasonable.[128]

The second, and perhaps the most dramatic, change has occurred in the realm of liberty of contract, which was so central to mature law.[129] As in the use of property, limitations on right of contract have resulted both from judicial decision and legislative enactment. Pound sees, however, some parallel in these developments to legal notions which emerged in the stage of equity or natural law. In that equitable era courts of equity often protected debtors from creditors, and in the era of socialization of law a similar notion is reflected in the law governing employer-employee relations. In this latter era, the law provides for the protection of:

> a class [employees] which is subjected to severe economic pressures against unfair advantages in dealing with employers.[130]

Such intrusions and limitations into the law of employer-employee relations, he argues, is done:

> to secure the social interest in the moral and social life—one might say the human life—of each individual. We say that we insist on social conduct.[131]

The law has further intruded on the liberty of contract in other areas of the law as well, for example, in the areas of sureties, trusts, and in regulation of insurance and public service companies.[132] Each of these intrusions and limitations is justified, in Pound's view, because the law focuses on protecting the social interests which are essential to society and which are superior in their claim to the justification offered in defense of some abstract theory of right to contract without limitation.[133]

The third change, Pound feels has altered one of the most elemental and central notions in the stage of strict law—the guarantee extended to the individual to dispose of his property as he deemed fit. In the stage of socialization of law, a series of restraints and restrictions on such a right has developed. For example, Pound points to the requirement that the wife join in the disposal of the family home even though title to it is held by the husband, or to the requirement that the wife must agree to the assignment of her husband's wages.[134] Such limitations on the right to dispose of property are applauded by Pound because they reflect the law's attention to the protection of social interests which are crucial to a society's well being, and indicate a proper recognition that social interests, such as those involved in the preservation of the institution of the family, are superior in importance to an abstract and unbending notion of security in property.[135]

Fourth, Pound comments on the importance of limitations placed on the power of creditors and injured parties to exact compensation and satisfaction. Similar types of limitations, he notes, emerged in earlier stages of law as, for example, in the common law's development of homestead exemptions, protection of family incomes, and protection of a professional's or craftsman's implements needed for doing business.[136] Such doctrines were looked upon with disfavor in the stage of mature law, where for example, he cites that creditor rights could be limited, but only by a mutual agreement at the outset of the transaction and involved the concurrence of both the creditor and debtor.[137] The protections and changes which have emerged in the stage of socialization of law, he maintains, reflect the notion that the law should be used to spread and adjust risks among creditors and debtors and not be tied to abstract notions of freely executed contracts.[138]

Fifth, in contrast with the law's operation in preceding periods, the era of socialization of law permits the imposition of liability for injuries resulting from "agencies employed and things maintained without proving those employing them or maintaining them were at fault."[139] For example, primitive law limited its inquiry to determining if an injurious act was done. This level of inquiry of the primitive era was ultimately replaced by an inquiry into the "blameworthiness" of the act. This latter test involved the use of an ethical standard regarding "reasonable conduct," which, according to Pound, is an abstract individual standard, and did not inquire sufficiently into the effect which such injuries had on the overall and general interests of society, and thus liability was seldom imposed without proof of fault.[140] It is Pound's view that the socialization of law properly ignores the assumption that liability must stem from action which is blameworthy.[141] Pound identifies two dimensions to this growth of liability without fault. One dimension reflects the extension, by analogy, of the doctrine of *Rylands* v. *Fletcher* so that a:

> wide responsibility for agencies employed and in placing upon enterprises the burden of repairing injuries, without fault of those who conduct them, which are incident to the undertaking.[142]

The other dimension allows for inquiry into the question of which of the parties involved can best bear the costs of the injury inflicted and impose liability on them even where there has been no fault.[143] This dimension is reflected in both legislation—as, for example, Workmen's Compensation Acts—and in judicial decisions.[144] The basis for these changes in the notion of liability for injury results from a recognition that there are significant social interests which must be considered when determining liability. The test of liability, therefore, is not controlled by a determination of whose willful act caused the injury. Determination of liability requires consideration not only of:

> the social interest in the general security but also and quite as much the social interest in the full social life of the individual, especially in classes less able to bear the burden of injuries incident to their tasks.[145]

Sixth, Pound points to the development of the idea that natural resources need to be protected. This recognition embodies a combination of the older doctrines of *res communes* (a resource belonging to no one in particular but which could be appropriated for private use—such as running water), and *res nullius* (a resource which belonged to no one until one took possession of it—such as wild game). The merger of these two doctrines is reflected in the concept of *res publicae*, according to which, Pound says, certain resources:

> are owned by the state or, better, that they are assets of society which are not capable of private appropriation or ownership except under regulations which protect the social interest in the use and conservation of natural resources.[146]

It is Pound's feeling that the concept of *res publicae* is necessary in the crowded and complex society of modern times. This concept of *res publicae* is to be valued more highly than the individualism of enterprise, which encouraged relatively unrestricted use of resources.[147]

Seventh, Pound observes that in the preceding epochs of law, parents were considered to have "a natural right" to control their children in ways they considered appropriate and necessary. In the age of socialization of law he observes, society's general concern with the condition and well-being of dependent children is reflected in "...the social interest of dependents."[148] Society's interest is considered superior to the right of control vested in the parents. He observes that social interest in this instance, are to be considered superior to individual interests, and that the private interest in dependents, which characterized the maturity of law, must give way to other social interests which are characteristic of modern society.[149]

Eighth, in the past, agencies of government were considered to be immune from liability for injuries done to citizens. In the era of socialization of law the rightness of imposing liability on public agencies or government for injuries done to individuals is recognized. Pound feels that this change in the concept of the liability of government and public officials for injuries they may inflict is consistent with the general notions prevailing in the stage of socialization of law and reflects the idea that:

> We are all of us to bear the losses incident to the operation of agencies maintained for the benefit of all.[150]

Ninth, Pound is of the opinion that in the maturity of law, litigation reflected a purely contentious character, and was rigid and inflexible. Such characteristics hampered the capacity of law to serve its necessary and valuable function of resolving conflict in society and making needed adjustments. In the age of socialization of law litigation is enabled, by procedural reform and different emphases and purposes of the law generally, to adjust competing or conflicting interests.[151] He writes:

> Thus, after a period of rigidity in practice, in which substance has been sacrificed to form and end has been subordinated to means, we are evidently about to enter upon a period of liberality in which the substance shall prevail and the machinery of justice shall be restrained by and made strictly to serve the end for which it exists.[152]

Tenth, in the era of mature law contracts were considered to be a manifestation of will and the law was not concerned with the possible inequitable outcome of such contracts. In the age of socialization of law, however, the law develops doctrines which operate to mitigate such inequitability. These developments, he feels, resemble the use of equitable power in the seventeenth and eighteenth centuries, to reform contracts so that they would conform with certain ethical principles. This supervision of contracts has been carried further in the socialization of law, however, and Pound cites as an example:

> the doctrine of the Supreme Court of the United States that all contracts are made subject to the protective power of the state, as an implied reservation, and so statutes which reasonably exercise the reserved power do not impair the obligation.[153]

Eleventh, in the stage of mature law the focus of the law was on natural, individual persons. Because of changes in society, which make relations with groups increasingly more significant, Pound notes that in the stage of the socialization of law, the law begins to extend equivalent protection and concern to "certain historical associations and business devices" and considers them to be analogically the same as individuals.[154] This change of focus and concern is reflected, for example in statutes related to trade unions and the process of collective bargaining.[155]
Finally, Pound points to the relaxation of rules regulating the law of trespass, which he feels reflect the thrust and nature of the period of the socialization of law, and cites the approvingly following development:

> At first, there was a tendency to require the occupier to exercise due care not to injure a perceived or actually anticipated trespasser. Next the requirement came to be extended to unperceived trespassers who might have been perceived with due care and then by some courts to trespassers whose wrongful presence might have been anticipated by the exercise of due care.[156]

In summarizing what he feels to be the beneficial consequences of the age of socialization of law, Pound says it would satisfy as much of the whole body of human wants with the least sacrifice through a politically organized society.[157] While Pound became a critic of extensions of this socialization of law in ways he felt were inappropriate,[158] he nonetheless feels that the changes which occurred were not only beneficial but also necessary in order that law might fulfill its major task which is

> to give the most effect to the whole scheme of expectations of men in civilized society with a minimum of friction and waste.[159]

ENDNOTES

CHAPTER TWO

1. Pound, "Making Law...," pp. 283-284.

2. R. Pound, The Problem of an Ordered Society, *Tennessee Law Review, Vol. 11*, December, p. 1,2 (1932). *Vol. 1* PB 186. (Hereinafter referred to as "The Problem..."). See also: R. Pound, Juristic Science and Law, *Harvard Law Review*, Vol. 31, Nr. 8, pp. 1058-1059, (1918) *Vol. 1*, PB. 911. (Hereinafter referred to as "Juristic Science..."). Pound, *Task...*, pp. 31-36.

3. Pound, *Interpretations of Legal...*, p. 27.

4. Pound, "Making Law...," p. 285. See also: Pound, *Task...*, pp. 61-62.

5. Pound. *(Vol. 1)*, pp. 365-366. See also: R. Pound, "The End of Law as Developed in Legal Rules and Doctrines", Vol. 27 *Harvard Law Review*, January, 1914, p. 195. *Vol. 1*, PB, 64. (Hereinafter referred to as "End of Law...in Legal Rules..."). Roscoe Pound, "The End of Law as Developed in Juristic Thought II," Vol. 30, *Harvard Law Review*, p. January, 1917. 605. *Vol. 1*, P.B. 66 (Hereinafter referred to as "End of Law...Juristic Thought...II"). Pound, *The Ideal Element...Tagore*, pp. 110-111.

6. Pound, *The Ideal Element... Tagore*, p. 118. See also: R. Pound, "End of Law...in Legal Rules...," p. 225. R. Pound, *Vol. 1*, pp. 429-456. This term was first used in R. Pound, "Social Justice and Legal Justice," *Proceedings of the 30th Annual Meeting of the Missouri Bar Association*, p. 110 (1913). *Vol. 1* PB 51 (Hereinafter referred to as "Social...Legal Justice").

7. Pound, *Vol. 1*, p. 463.

8. Pound, *Vol. 1*, p. 463. See Chapters 3, 4, & 5. Whether there is a sixth state in the historical development of law depends on whether one wishes to include as another epoch Pound's infrequent reference to the law of the world. See also: Pound, *Spirit...*, pp. 139-165. Pound, *The Ideal Element...Tagore*, pp. 108-119. Pound, *Introduction...*, pp. 25-47.

9. Pound, *The Ideal Element...Tagore*, p. 110. See also: Pound, *Vol. 1*, pp. 367-370.

10. Pound, *Vol. 1*, p. 369. See also: Pound, *Interpretations of Legal...*, p. 125. Pound, *The Ideal Element...Tagore*, p. 110.

11. Pound, *Interpretations of Legal...*, p. 30. See also: Pound, *Task...*, p. 43. Pound, "End of Law...in Legal Rules...," pp. 198-201. Pound, *Vol. 1*, pp. 369-370.

12. Pound, *The Ideal Element... Tagore*, p. 110. See also: Pound, *Vol. 1*, p. 369. R. Pound, "The Limits of Effective Legal Action," *American Bar Association Journal*, Vol., 3, January, 1917, 55,58. *Vol. 1*, PB 82 (Hereinafter referred to as "Limits...Legal Action.")

13. Pound, "Juristic Science..." p. 1060.

14. Pound, "Limits...Legal Action," p. 58. See also: Pound, "End of Law...in Legal Rules...," pp. 198-199.

15. Pound, "End of Law...in Legal Rules...," pp. 198-201. See also: Pound, *The Ideal Element...Tagore*, p. 111. Pound, *Vol. 1*, pp. 370-371.

16. Pound, *Spirit...*, p. 85. See also: Pound, *Vol.1*, p. 370. Pound, *Interpretations of Legal...*, p. 30. Pound, *The Ideal Element...Tagore*, p. 111.

17. Pound, "End of Law...in Legal Rules...," p. 199. See also: Pound, *Vol. 1*, p. 372. Pound, *The Ideal Element...Tagore*, pp. 110-111.

18. Pound, *The Ideal Element... Tagore*, pp. 110-111. See also: Pound, "End of Law...in Legal Rules...," pp. 198-199. R. Pound. "A Survey of Social Interests," Vol. 57, October, 1943, *Harvard Law Review*, pp. 1, 10. *Vol. 2*, PB 12 (Hereinafter referred as "Survey..."). Pound, *Vol. 1*, p. 370. Pound, "Limits...Legal Action," p. 58.

19. Pound, *Task...*, p. 42. See also: Pound, *The Ideal Element... Tagore*, p. 111.

20. Pound, *The Ideal Element...Tagore*, p. 111. See also: Pound, *Vol. 1*, p. 373.

21. Pound, *The Ideal Element...Tagore*. p. 111. See also: Pound, *Vol. 1*, p. 373.

22. Pound, *The Ideal Element... Tagore*, p. 111. See also: Pound, *Task...*, p. 43. Pound, *Vol. 1*, pp. 367-372. Pound, *Introduction...*, pp. 33-34.

23. Pound, *The Ideal Element...Tagore*, p. 112. See also: Pound, *Vol. 1*, p. 372. Pound, "End of Law...in Legal Rules...," p. 199.

24. Pound, *The Ideal Element...Tagore*, p. 112. See also: Pound, *Vol. 1*, p. 374. Pound, "End of Law...in Legal Rules...," p. 199. Pound, "Limits...Legal Action," p. 65.

25. Pound, *Vol. 1*, pp. 379-380. See also: Pound, *The Ideal Element...Tagore*, p. 113. Pound, *Task...*, p. 44.

26. Pound, *Vol. 1*, p. 372. See also: Pound, *The Ideal Element... Tagore*, p. 113.

27. Pound, *Vol. 1*, pp. 376-377. See also: Pound, *The Ideal Element...*, p. 112. Pound, "End of Law...in Legal Rules...," p. 200.

28. Pound, *Task...*, p. 33.

29. Pound, "End of Law...in Legal Rules...," p. 202. See also: Pound, *Vol. 1*, pp. 378-382. Pound lists only four characteristics of this stage in *The Ideal Element...Tagore*, pp. 112-113.

30. Pound, "End of Law...in Legal Rules...," pp. 202-203. See also: Pound, *The Ideal Element...Tagore*, pp. 112-113. Pound, *Vol. 1*, pp. 378-382.

31. Pound, *The Ideal Element... Tagore*, p. 114. See also: Pound, "End of Law...in Legal Rules...," p. 204. It is difficult to see how Pound concludes the latter to be a cause pressing for a system of strict law, for really what he seems to be making reference to, is a characteristic of primitive law which is retained in the era of strict law. On the other hand, the former—fear of the arbitrary exercise of power—seems to fit the characterization of it as a causal factor for adopting the system of the legal order he describes as strict law. Pound, *Vol. 1*, pp. 378-382. Pound, *Spirit...*, p. 140.

32. Pound, *Spirit...*, p. 140. See also: Pound, *The Ideal Element...Tagore*, p. 113. Pound, *Vol. 1*, pp. 382-383.

33. Pound, "Survey...," p. 57. See also: Pound, "Limits...Legal Action...," p. 59. Pound, *Vol. 1*, pp. 380-381. Pound, *Spirit...*, pp. 17-19.

34. Pound, *Vol. 1*, p. 403. See also: Pound, *The Ideal Element...Tagore*, p. 114. Pound, *Spirit...*, pp. 17-19.

35. Pound, "End of Law...in Legal Rules...," p. 210.

36. Pound, "End of Law...in Legal Rules...," p. 210. See also: Pound, *The Ideal Element...Tagore*, p 114. Pound, *Vol. 1*, pp. 385-396.

37. Pound, *Vol. 1*, pp. 405-406, 385-396. See also: Pound, "The End of Law...in Legal Rules...," pp. 207-208.

38. Pound, "Juristic Science...," p. 160. See also: Pound, *Spirit...*, p. 140. Pound, "End of Law...in Legal Rules...," p. 204. Pound, *Vol. 1*, pp. 385-396.

39. Pound, *Vol. 1*, pp. 397-401. See also: Pound, "End of Law...in Legal Rules...," pp. 208-210. Pound, *The Ideal Element...Tagore*, p. 114.

40. Pound, *Vol. 1*, pp. 384, 392. See also: R. Pound, *Law Finding Through Experience and Reason*, Athens, Georgia, University of Georgia Press, 1960, p. 9. Vol. 2 PB 46. (Hereinafter referred to as *Law Finding...*). Pound, "End of Law...in Legal Rules...," p. 204.

41. Pound, *Vol. 1*, pp. 385, 392.

42. Pound, *Vol. 1*, pp. 387, 392, 406. See also: Pound, *Spirit...*, p. 140. Pound, "End of Law...in Legal Rules...", p. 205. Pound, *The Ideal Element...Tagore*, p. 114.

43. Pound, *The Ideal Element... Tagore*, p. 114. See also: Pound, *Vol. 1*, pp. 387-388.

44. Pound, *Vol. 1*, p. 390. See also: Pound, *The Ideal Element... Tagore*, p. 114. Pound, "End of Law...in Legal Rules..," pp. 205, 207.

45. Pound, *Vol. 1*, p. 396. See also: Pound, *The Ideal ELement... Tagore*, p. 114.

46. Pound, *Vol. 1*, p. 396.

47. Pound, "End of Law...in Legal Rules...," p. 208. See also: Pound, *Vol. 1*, pp. 392-393.

48. Pound, "End of Law...in Legal Rules...," p. 209. See also: Pound, *Vol. 1*, pp. 393-394.

49. Pound, "End of Law...in Legal Rules...," p. 209. See also: Pound, *Vol. 1*, pp. 394-396.

50. Pound, *Vol. 1*, p. 395. See also: Pound, "End of Law...in Legal Rules...," p. 209.

51. Pound, *Vol. 1*, pp. 394-397. See also: Pound, "End of Law...in Legal Rules...", p. 209.

52. Pound, *Vol. 1*, pp. 397-398. See also: Pound, *The Ideal Element...Tagore*, p. 114. Pound "End of Law...in Legal Rules...," pp. 206-207. Pound, *Interpretations of Legal...*, pp. 54-55.

53. Pound, *Vol. 1*, pp. 397-398. See also: Pound, "End of Law...in Legal Rules...," pp. 211-212.

54. Pound, *Vol. 1*, pp. 397-398. See also: Pound, "End of Law...in Legal Rules...," pp. 210-211.

55. Pound, *Vol. 1*, p. 398. See also: Pound, *The Ideal Element... Tagore*, p. 114. Pound, "End of Law...in Legal Rules...," pp. 206-207.

56. Pound, "End of Law...in Legal Rules...," p. 211. See also: Pound, *Vol. 1*, pp. 398-399. Pound, *The Ideal Element...Tagore*, p. 114.

57. Pound, *Vol. 1*, p. 399. See also: Pound, "End of Law...in Legal Rules...," pp. 211-213. Pound, *Spirit...*, pp. 17, 19. Pound, *Law Finding...*, p. 9.

58. Pound, *Spirit...*, p. 19. See also: Pound, *Vol. 1*, p. 399. Pound, "End of Law...in Legal Rules...," p. 212.

59. Pound, *Vol. 1*, p. 400. See also: Pound, *The Ideal Element...Tagore*, p. 114. Pound, *Spirit...*, p. 141. Pound, *Law Finding...*, p. 9. Pound, "End of Law...in Legal Rules...," pp. 211-212.

60. Pound, *Vol. 1*, p. 401. See also: Pound, "End of Law...in Legal Rules...," pp. 210-212.

61. Pound, "End of Law...in Legal Rules...," pp. 212-213. See also: Pound, *Vol. 1*, p. 405.

62. Pound, *Vol. 1*, p. 403. See also: Pound, *Spirit...*, p. 119. Pound, *The Ideal Element...Tagore*, p. 114. Pound, "End of Law...in Legal Rules...," p. 204.

63. Pound, *Vol. 1*, p. 405. See also: Pound, *Spirit...*, pp. 140-141. Pound, "Law Finding...," pp. 9-10. Pound, "End of Law...in Legal Rules...," p. 213.

64. Pound, *Vol. 1*, p. 406. See also: Pound, "End of Law...in Legal Rules...," p. 213.

65. Pound, *Vol. 1*, p. 406. See also: Pound, *Spirit...*, p. 140. Pound, "End of Law...in Legal Rules...," p. 213.

66. Pound, *Vol. 1*, p. 407. See also: Pound, "End of Law...in Legal Rules...," p. 213. Pound, *Spirit...*, pp. 141-142.

67. Pound, *Vol. 1*, p. 407. See also: Pound, "End of Law...in Legal Rules...," p. 214. Pound, *Spirit...*, pp. 141-142.

68. Pound, "Juristic Science...," p. 1060.

69. Pound, *Spirit...*, p. 141. See also: Pound, *Vol. 1*, p. 407. Pound, "Limits...Legal Action," p. 59. Pound, "End of Law...in Legal Rules...," p. 213.

70. Pound, *Spirit...*, p. 141. Pound discusses a period of equity and natural law in the Roman system, but with the collapse of the Roman Empire the stages of law apparently begin again from that event. Thus, the stage of equity and natural law which he places in the seventeenth and eighteenth centuries is that which is central to his treatment of this stage of law's development.

71. Pound, *Vol. 1*, p. 408. See also: Pound, *Spirit...*, p. 141. Pound, "Limits...Legal Action," p. 60. Pound, *Law Finding...*, pp. 10-11. Pound, "End of Law...in Legal Rules...," p. 213.

72. Pound cites *Beaulieu v. Finglum*, Y.B., Hen. IV, (1400), to illustrate his point. In this case the court's reply to the defendant's counsel's argument that "the application of a harsh rule of liability" to the defendant would damage him irreparably was: "What is that to us? It is better that he be wholly undone than that the law be changed for him." Cited in: Pound, *Vol. 1*, p. 399.

73. Pound, *Vol. 1*, p. 408. See also: Pound, *Spirit...*, p. 141. Pound, "End of Law...in Legal Rules...," pp. 213-214.

74. Pound, *Vol. 1*, p. 409. See also: Pound, "End of Law...in Legal Rules...," p. 215. Pound, *Spirit...*, pp. 141-142.

75. Pound, *Spirit...*, p. 88. See also: Pound, "End of Law...in Legal Rules...," p. 216. Pound, *Vol. 1*, pp. 408-410.

76. Pound, *Interpretations of Legal...*, p. 5.

77. Pound, *Vol. 1*, P. 410. See also: Pound, *Spirit...*, p. 141. Pound, *Law Finding...*, p. 11. Pound, "Limits...Legal Action," p. 60. Pound, "End of Law...in Legal Rules...," pp. 214-215.

78. Pound, *Vol. 1*, p. 410. See also: Pound, *Spirit...*, p. 141. Pound, Law Finding..., p. 11. Pound, "Limits...Legal Action," p. 60. Pound, "End of Law...in Legal Rules...," pp. 214-215.

79. Pound, *Vol. 1*, p. 410. See also: Pound, *Spirit...*, p. 141. Pound, Law Finding..., p. 11. Pound, "Limits...Legal Action," p. 60. Pound, "End of Law...in Legal Rules," pp. 214-215.

80. Pound, *Vol. 1*, p. 411. See also: Pound, "End of Law...in Legal Rules...," pp. 214-215. Pound, *The Ideal Element...Tagore*,d p. 115.

81. Pound, "End of Law...in Legal Rules...," p. 215. See also: Pound, *The Ideal Element...Tagore*, p. 115. Pound, *Vol. 1*, pp. 411-412.

82. Pound, *Vol. 1*, p. 413. See also: Pound, "*Law Finding...*," p. 11. Pound, "End of Law...in Legal Rules...," p. 215.

83. Pound, *Vol. 1*, p. 413. See also: Pound, "Limits...Legal Action," p. 61.

84. Pound, *Vol. 1*, p. 413. See also: Pound, *Law Finding...*, p. 11. Pound, "End of Law...in Legal Rules...," p. 215. Pound, *The Ideal Element...Tagore*, p. 115.

85. Pound, *Vol. 1*, p. 414. See also: Pound, "End of Law...in Legal Rules...," pp. 215-216. Pound, *The Ideal Element...Tagore*, p. 115.

86. Pound, *Vol. 1*, p. 413. See also: Pound, "End of Law...in Legal Rules...," p. 216.

87. Pound, *Vol. 1*, p. 415. See also: Pound, "End of Law...in Legal Rules...," p. 217. Pound, *The Ideal Element...Tagore*, p. 115.

88. Pound, *Vol. 1*, p. 415. See also: Pound, "End of Law...in Legal Rules...," p. 217.

89. Pound, *Vol. 1*, p. 416. See also: Pound, "End of Law...in Legal Rules...," p. 217. Pound, *The Ideal Element...Tagore*, p. 115.

90. Pound, Vol. 1, p. 416. See also: Pound, "End of Law...in Legal Rules...," p. 217. Pound, *The Ideal Element...Tagore*, p. 115.

91. Pound, *Vol. 1*, p. 416. See also: Pound, "End of Law...in Legal Rules...," p. 217. Pound, *The Ideal Element...Tagore*, pp. 115.

92. Pound, *Vol. 1*, p. 417. See also: Pound, "End of Law...in Legal Rules...," p. 218. Pound, *The Ideal Element...Tagore*, pp. 115-116.

93. Pound, *Vol. 1*, p. 417. See also: Pound, "End of Law...in Legal Rules...," p. 218. Pound, *The Ideal Element...Tagore*, pp. 115-116. Pound, *Law Finding...*, p. 11.

94. Pound, *Vol. 1*, p. 417. See also: Pound, "End of Law...in Legal Rules...," p. 218. Pound, *The Ideal Element...Tagore*, p. 116.

95. Pound, *Vol. 1*, p. 418. See also: Pound, "End of Law...in Legal Rules...," p. 218. Pound, *The Ideal Element...Tagore*, p. 116.

96. Pound, Vol. 1, p 421. See also: Pound, *Law Finding...*, p. 11. Pound, "End of Law...in Legal Rules...," p. 218. Pound, *The Ideal Element...Tagore*, pp. 116-117.

97. Pound, "Limits...Legal Action," p. 61. See also: Pound, *Vol. 1*, pp. 417-421. Pound, "End of Law...in Legal Rules...," pp. 219-220. Pound, *The Ideal Element...Tagore*, pp. 116-117.

98. Pound, "End of Law...in Legal Rules...," p. 220. See also: Pound, *The Ideal Element...Tagore*, pp. 116-117. Pound, *Vol. 1*, pp. 420-421.

99. Pound, *Vol. 1*, p. 422. See also: Pound, "End of Law...in Legal Rules...," p. 220. Pound, *Spirit...*, p. 142.

100. Pound, "Juristic Science...," p. 160.

101. Pound, *Vol. 1*, p. 422. See also: Pound, "End of Law...in Legal Rules...," p. 220. Pound, *Spirit...*, p. 142.

102. Pound, *Vol. 1*, p. 422. See also: Pound, "Limits...Legal Action," p. 62. Pound, *Spirit...*, p. 142. Pound, "End of Law...in Legal Rules...," p. 221.

103. Pound, *Vol. 1*, p. 423. See also: Pound, *Spirit...*,, p. 143. Pound, "End of Law...in Legal Rules...," p. 221.

104. Pound, *Vol. 1*, p. 423. See also: Pound, "Limits...Legal Action," P. 62. Pound, "End of Law...in Legal Rules...," p. 221. Pound, *Spirit...*, p. 143.

105. Pound, "Limits...Legal Action," p. 62. See also: Pound, *Law Finding...*, p. 12. Pound, *Vol. 1*, pp. 425-426. Pound, *Spirit...*, 142-143.

106. Pound, *Vol. 1*, p. 424. See also: Pound, *Spirit...*, p. 143. Pound, "End of Law...in Legal Rules...," p. 222.

107. Pound, *Vol. 1*, p. 426. See also: Pound, *Spirit...*, p. 143. Pound, "End of Law...in Legal Rules...," pp. 222-223.

108. Pound, *Vol. 1*, p. 425. See also: Pound, "End of Law...in Legal Rules...," p. 222. Pound, *Spirit...*, p. 143.

109. Pound, *Vol. 1*, p. 426. See also: Pound, "End of Law...in Legal Rules...," p. 222. See also: R. Pound, "Equitable Relief Against Defamation and Injuries to Personality," *Harvard Law Review*, Vol. 29., April, 1916. p. 640. Vol. 1, PB 80 (Hereinafter referred to as "Equitable Relief...").

110. Pound, *Vol. 1*, pp. 424-425. See also: Pound *Spirit...*, p. 143. Pound, "End of Law...in Legal Rules...," p. 222.

111. Pound, *Vol. 1*, p. 427. See also: Pound, "End of Law... in Legal Rules...," pp. 223-224. Pound, *Spirit...*, p. 143.

112. Pound, *Vol. 1*, p. 427. See also: Pound, "End of Law...in Legal Rules...," p. 224.

113. Pound, "End of Law...in Legal Rules...," p. 224.

114. Pound, "Survey...," pp. 11-12.

115. Pound, *Spirit...*, pp. 142-143. See also: Pound, *The Ideal Element...Tagore*, p. 119. Pound, "Limits...Legal Action," p. 63.

116. Pound, "End of Law...in Legal Rules...," p. 224.

117. Pound, *Vol. 1*, pp. 430-433. See also: Pound, *The Ideal Element...Tagore*, p. 171.

118. Pound, *Vol. 1*, p. 431. See also: Pound, "End of Law...in Legal Rules...," p. 225.

119. Pound, "End of Law...in Legal Rules...," p. 225. Pound cites Jhering as illustrative of this point. See also: Pound, *Spirit...*, pp. 204-206.

120. Pound, *Vol. 1*, p. 432.

121. Pound, "End of Law...in Legal Rules...," p. 196.

122. Pound, *Spirit...*, p. 203.

123. Pound, *Spirit...*, p. 196. See also: Pound, *Interpretations of Legal...*, p. 157.

124. Pound, Vol. 1, p. 432. See also: Pound in "End of Law...in Legal Rules...," published in 1914, identifies changes in only seven areas, but in his later work—*Jurisprudence*, published in 1959—he expands the number of areas involved.

125. Pound, *Vol. 1*, pp. 433-434. See also: Pound, "End of Law...in Legal Rules...," pp. 226-228. Pound, *Spirit...*, p. 185.

126. Pound, *Vol. 1*, p. 436.

127. Pound, *Vol. 1*, p. 436. See also: Pound, "End of Law...in Legal Rules...," pp. 227-228.

128. Pound, *Vol. 1*, p. 437. See also: Pound, "End of Law...in Legal Rules...," p. 228. Pound, *Spirit...*, p. 186.

129. Pound, *Vol. 1*, p. 438. See also: Pound, "End of Law...in Legal Rules...," pp. 228-230. Pound, *Spirit...*, p. 186.

130. Pound, *Vol. 1*, p. 438. See also: Pound, "End of Law...in Legal Rules...," p. 229. Pound, *Spirit...*, p. 187.

131. Pound, *Vol. 1*, pp. 439. See also: Pound, "End of Law...in Legal Rules...," p. 229.

132. Pound, *Vol. 1*, pp. 439-440. See also: Pound, "End of Law...in Legal Rules...," p. 228.

133. Pound, *Vol. 1*, p. 440. See also: Pound, "End of Law...in Legal Rules...," p. 229.

134. Pound, *Vol. 1*, pp. 441-442. See also: Pound, "End of Law...in Legal Rules...," p. 230.

135. Pound, *Vol. 1*, p. 442. See also: Pound, "End of Law...in Legal Rules...," p. 230.

136. Pound, *Vol. 1*, p. 444. See also: Pound, "End of Law...in Legal Rules...," p. 232.

137. Pound, *Vol. 1*, pp. 443-444. See also: Pound, "End of Law...in Legal Rules...," p. 231.

138. Pound, *Vol. 1*, p. 445. See also: Pound, *Introduction...*, pp. 167-168.

139. Pound, *Vol. 1*, p. 445. See also: Pound, "End of Law...in Legal Rules...," p. 231.

140. Pound, *Vol. 1*, pp. 445-446. See also: Pound, "End of Law... in Legal Rules...," p. 233. It is Pound's view that the socialization of law properly ignores the assumption that liability must stem from action which is blameworthy.

141. Pound, *Vol. 1*, pp. 445-446. See also: Pound, "End of Law...in Legal Rules...," p. 233.

142. Pound, *Vol. 1*, p. 447.

143. Pound, *Vol. 1*, p. 447. See also: Pound, "End of Law...in Legal Rules...," p. 233.

144. Pound, *Vol. 1*, pp. 447-448.

145. Pound, *Vol. 1*, p. 448. See also: Pound "End of Law...in Legal Rules...," p. 233.

146. Pound, *Vol. 1*, p. 449. See also: Pound, "End of Law...in Legal Rules...," p. 234.

147. Pound, *Vol. 1*, p. 450. See also: Pound, "End of Law...in Legal Rules...," p. 234.

148. Pound, *Vol. 1*, p. 450.

149. Pound, *Vol. 1*, p. 450. See also: Pound, "End of Law...in Legal Rules...," p. 234.

150. Pound, *Vol. 1*, p. 452.

151. Pound, *Vol. 1*, p. 452.

152. R. Pound, " A Practical Program of Procedural Reform," Vol. 22, August, 1910, *Green Bag*, p. 438. *Vol. 1*, PB 36. (Hereinafter referred to as "...Practical Procedural Reform."). See also: R. Pound, "Some Principles of Procedural Reform", Vol. 4, January-February, 1910, *Illinois Law Review*, p. 491. Vol. 1, PB 35 (Hereinafter referred to as "Principles...Procedural Reform."). R. Pound, "The Causes of Popular Dissatisfaction with the Administration of Justice," Vol. 29, 1906, *Report of the 29th Annual Meeting of the American Bar Association*, p. 395. *Vol. 1*, PB 20 (Hereinafter referred to as "Popular Dissatisfaction...").

153. Pound, *Vol. 1*, pp. 453-454.

154. R. Pound. "A Feudal Principle in Modern Law," Vol. 25, October, 1914, *International Journal of Ethics*, p. 1. *Vol. 1*, PB 68 (Hereinafter referred to as "Feudal Principles...,").

155. Pound, *Vol. 1*, p. 454.

156. Pound, *Vol. 1*, 455.

157. Pound, *Introduction...*, p. 47. See also: Pound, *The Ideal Element... Tagore*, p. 225.

158. Chapter Five Sociological Jurisprudence.

159. R. Pound, *Justice According...*, p. 29. See also: Pound, *Introduction...*, p. 47.

Chapter Three

Legal Philosophy
Ancient Greek to Eighteenth Century

Introduction

In discussing the evolution of legal philosophy, Pound points to the fact that law must be anchored to some fixed principles, but simultaneously it must also be adaptable to changing conditions. "Thus," he says:

> the legal order must be flexible as well as stable. It must be overhauled continually to the changes in the actual life which it is to govern. If we seek principles, we must seek principles of change no less than principles of stability. Accordingly, the chief problem to which legal thinkers have addressed themselves has been how to reconcile the idea of a fixed body of law, affording no scope for individual willfulness, with the idea of change and growth and making of new law; how to unify the theory of law with the theory of making law and to unify the system of legal justice with the facts of administration of justice by magistrates.[1]

As we have seen in the preceding chapter, Pound argues that the history of legal order reveals how law has expanded in order to encompass more and more of the affairs of men; provide for the distribution of scarce resources; and the reconciliation of disagreements, while, simultaneously, keeping in check waste and conflict.[2] It is his opinion that law responds to newly emerging interests, which press for recognition, and at the same time retains a high degree of security and stability. In the process of historical development law also responds to and is fashioned, to an extensive degree, by the philosophical ideas which emerge and influence the course of legal development. Commenting on the enormous significance of these philosophical activities, Pound notes:

> Because men tend to do what they think they are doing, professional and judicial ideals of the social and legal order have been and are a decisive factor in legal development.[3]

Pound maintains that ancient legal thought was not clearly differentiated from thought stemming from ethics, religion, and commercial activity.[4] Nonetheless, Pound observes even if modern thinking about law:

> begins with the Romans, philosophy of law begins with the Greeks. What went before them is too remote for the present purpose, what went after them was largely shaped by them. Since the Romans took their philosophical ideas from the Greeks, the Greek idea of the end of law not only governed the Roman world but in consequence in large measure governed the medieval world.[5]

In evaluating Greek contributions to the philosophy of law, Pound says that it is necessary to note that this legal philosophy was not the product of juristic thinking; it was conditioned, in part, by the conflict between the concept of "made" law, as opposed to received custom; and that the consciousness grew that assumed law could be the product of conscious, reasoned thought.[6]

Pound observes that even though the Greek Polis was a politically organized order, it more closely resembled the configuration of a kin ordered society. Persons not of the original kin group, present in the city-state, necessitated some form of accommodation of them in order to proceed with commercial activity, and this compelled the development of laws that could realistically deal with these elements, and this type of law differed qualitatively from kin related laws, largely because it had to be consciously formed and developed.[7] It is Pound's opinion that the conflict of these conflicting ideas—custom vs. consciously developed law—engendered the interest of the philosophers,[8] since this conflict raised for consideration and resolution, the respective merits of enacted as opposed to custom dictated laws. Pound observes that:

> the law purported to be a conscious product of human wisdom. But the philosophers began to inquire as to the relation of laws so constituted to the ideas of right and wrong. Was an act right, they asked, because it conformed to law, or were both the act and the law right if and insofar as they coincided with an absolute and eternal standard above the law? One answer was that what corresponded to the latter standard was natural right, but what corresponded only with the humanly enacted standard was

> conventional right, while others held that the whole matter rested upon enactment. Thus we have two ideas in Greek thinking about law; on the one hand the idea of law as human wisdom, ascertained and promulgated through the state, on the other hand, the idea of law as the manifestation of an eternal and inevitable right and justice.[9]

Most of Greek legal thought wrestled with this basic dichotomy between law as enactment and law as custom. Pound feels that the general philosophic resolution of this conflict is testimony to the astuteness of the Greeks, who concluded law was neither unquestioned obedience to unchanging tradition, nor an act of uncontrolled majority will.[10] Basically, Greek philosophers of law concluded that law's purpose and legitimacy was tied to its adherence to the ideal of a *status quo* in which each person occupied a place in the social order commensurate with his ability and role. Thus, a legal order was:

> an ordering of men to keep each in his appointed place in the politically organized society of an ideal Greek city. Right and law had their basis in a harmony or fitness involved in the nature of things. They were independent of human will and had universal validity.[11]

In summarizing the characteristics of legal philosophy in ancient Greece, Pound maintains that it was this emphasis on law's role in maintaining the *status quo* that united the ideas of both Plato and Aristotle, who concluded that law:

> was in the first instance to take account of relations of inequality in which individuals were treated according to their worth. Then each being in his proper place, the law would keep him there and would preserve among equals a unanimity in which there would be no violation of mutual rights.[12]

This Greek notion that law's role was to preserve the *status quo* stemmed in large measure from two sources. First, the Greek philosophers believed a legal order could and should reflect the regularity they had acknowledged as present in the "natural order."[13] Thus, the Greek idea of law was not tied only to preserving security, but also encompassed the idea that law should maintain the *status quo,* and:

> Justice, accordingly, was regarded as maintenance of the social *status quo*, and philosophers were busied in planning an ideal society in which everyone was put in the right place, to be kept there thenceforth by the law.[14]

Second, Pound maintains the Greek philosophers also drew heavily on their understanding of mathematics, and, therefore, they assumed that legal precepts could be discovered by employing the techniques of mathematical reasoning, and:

> that the deduced precepts [thus discovered] could be systematized in a body of logically interdependent propositions after the pattern of geometry. In this way Greek philosophical speculation about social control gave us the idea of natural law and the idea of a systematic positive law developed logically from natural law which governed in the science of politics and the science of law for centuries and have by no means lost their hold even today.[15]

Pound feels that Greek legal philosophy is important, not only because of its impact on Greek historical developments, but also because it focused attention on central concepts such as—the balance between imperative and traditional law, higher law concepts and their relationship to positive law—which would lie at the core of future legal philosophical inquiry and consider whether laws were such:

> by nature rather than by custom or enactment. The right or the just by nature became law by nature or natural law, and thus begins the identification of the legal with the moral that has been characteristic of natural law thinking ever since.[16]

Roman Law

The Romans changed the Greeks' philosophical speculation about the law into a science of law. The initial step in this development of a science of law, Pound asserts, is clearly evidenced in the theoretical foundations the Romans worked out to explain *jus gentium*.[17] *Jus gentium* arose to handle the conflicts resulting from Roman contact with non-Roman groups and societies. *Jus gentium*, Pound maintains, signalled the disappearance of the residue of "kin related" legal ordering, and developed the idea that law was to be applied on a territorial basis,[18] and, as Pound further observes, "Territorial law is an idea of a politically organized society."[19] Cicero's writings constituted the initial step in creating the theoretical and intellectual bases of *jus gentium* and set forth the idea that *jus gentium's* precepts reflect a universality of law's purposes and nature, among all civilized people, and provide the benchmark for identifying what the law ought to be among all persons.[20] As Pound observes, Cicero, in the formulation of *jus gentium*:

> finds the basis of law and governance not in an act but, in the moral spirit that is intrinsic in nature.[21]

This notion of universality which was derived, in part, from the idea of *jus gentium*, also was to be found in the doctrines embodied in the notion of *jus naturale*, which assumes the reality of a set of ideal principles which should be universally applicable, and which provide a "basis of philosophical development of legal materials and criticism."[22] *Jus gentium*, Pound concludes, described an actual body of law to be applied to concrete cases, while *jus naturale* was composed of a set of abstract principles which could be used to critique the operation and nature of law.

Cicero wrote in a period when the view that law was mainly custom was ending, and a new period of extensive juristic writing was beginning. Cicero's writing reflects both,[23] and, as Pound observes:

> While Cicero's formulas are drawn from or modeled upon Greek definitions of VOYOS it is noteworthy that, as he puts them, they have something of the idea of authoritative declaration and command, appropriate to the period just past, and something of the idea of reason and justice, appropriate of the period just beginning.[24]

Thus, Pound feels that Cicero's writings provided the foundation on which legal science was to build. Cicero felt that law was derived from three basic sources. First, the *jus civile*, which was composed of the Twelve Tables of Roman law, and all that derived from them; second, the rules found in edicts; and third, *jurisconsults*' writings. These three elements provided the framework within which legal science would continue to develop,[25] and set the stage for the emergence of professional legal persons whose writings systematized these three elements, and permitted continuing formulation and development of law from them.[26]

This *denouement* set the stage for the important contributions made in the growth of Roman law by the jurisconsults. Pound observes that although Cicero had spoken derogatorily of *jurisconsults*, they would provide the leadership needed for furthered developing of Roman law.[27] Although this group considered law's major function to be the provision of general security, they also wished to identify law with morality, and further, that since they were charged with explaining the development of law, they began to seek a reconciliation of what is with what ought to be. These endeavors of the jurisconsults, Pound observes:

> gave a scientific foundation for the belief of the *jurisconsults* that when and where they were not bound by positive law they had yet to expound the reason and justice of the thing in order to lay down the law.[28]

During the Republican era the writings of the *jurisconsults* were joined with other collections such as commentaries on praetors' edicts, and legal treatises on various subjects. Pound says, they collectively created

> a body of legal writings quite without parallel until recent times and standing in relation to the law as the literature of Greece has stood in relation to letters.[29]

In the period of the empire the significance of *jurisconsults*' writings was greatly enhanced by Augustus' support of them; and under the Emperor Hadrian these writings became binding on all judges, in reaching their decisions. The writings of the *jurisconsults*, Pound says, became the dominant element in Roman legal thinking up through the third century.[30]

Pound notes that what came to dominate was the desire to find an organizing principle which could unify legal thought. The principle was identified as the maintenance of the natural order as it should exist in society. Evaluating law against this ideal order served as an effective guide, since "justice" and "injustice" could be easily identified and, therefore, serve:

> to measure all situations by an idealized form of the social order of the time and place and are so to shape the law as to make it maintain and further this ideal of the social *status quo*.[31]

This notion in Roman law would form the concern for much of subsequent legal philosophical interest and concern,[32] and would affect the development of subsequent case law as well.[33] The affect that the jurisconsults had is reflected clearly in the *Institutes of Justinian*, according to Pound, which enshrined the concept of the *status quo*, and taught that each person should occupy his proper position in society, and justice would, therefore, consist of each person's having those things proper to his station and role and:

> in rendering them to him and in not interfering with his having and using these within defined limits. This is a legal development of the Greek idea of harmoniously maintaining the social *status quo*.[34]

After the middle of the third century, the growth and development of Roman law was evidenced in legislation and not in the writings of jurisconsults, and there were no systematic treatises on law to systematize and identify the course of legislative content and development. According to Pound, therefore, there was little of significance in legal philosophy developed from Justinian's era until the revival of the study of Roman law in the twelfth century.[35] Pound says:

> In the period from the downfall of the Roman empire in the West to the twelfth century, western Europe was governed by remnants of the Roman law and by Germanic law tempered by Christian theology or theological philosophy, and by political and legal ideas which the church had taken over for the Roman lawyers.[36]

Medieval

Specific, formal sources dominated the development of legal philosophy during the period from the twelfth century to the seventeenth century.[37] Pound says of this period:

> In tracing the growth of the conception of law from the revival of legal studies of Bologna in the twelfth century to the time of Grotius, we must bear in mind that the theories of the time implied the acceptance of three great authorities, which might be interpreted or applied, but were not to be questioned—the authority of the Bible, of Aristotle, and of Justinian.[38]

Pound says that following the collapse of Roman authority and during the period of disorder that followed in the wake of this collapse, the focus of legal thought necessarily was on the issue of restoring certainty and order.[39] In order to succeed in establishing such order, it was necessary that legal philosophy synthesize the various and disparate legal influences that had operated during the period of relative disorder, with the canons of Roman law. This could be done most effectively by proceeding within the parameters of the dominant and accepted sources of authority, which conditioned legal thought, and this necessitated, in turn, a focusing on the concept of *status quo*.[40] However, medieval legal philosophy also had to accommodate itself to Christian religious teaching, which called for the development, or revival of some natural law philosophy. Pound observes:

> But another factor was introduced by the survival of the idea of natural law and the consequent appeal to conscience against the positive law.

> This renewal, induced by the study of the Roman law, was no doubt furthered by the acceptance of Aristotle as an authority in philosophy. And through Alexander of Hales, in whose *Summa* it is first noticeable, and in Thomas Aquinas, who developed it into a detailed theory, natural law has a purely theological basis.[41]

Legal philosophy had to reconcile the secular power of the state with the spiritual power of the church. All of the authorities in that period recognized the presence of these two sources of authority, and, sought to have them work conjunctively as agencies capable "of upholding the social and moral order."[42]

Legal philosophy as it developed in the medieval era recognized not only the authority of Roman law, but also had to consider how to incorporate Germanic elements that had become influential following the collapse of Rome.[43] Germanic law, Pound says, was "archaic and without effective organization or development,"[44] and the tenets of Roman and Canon law were employed to make Germanic law compatible with the ends of law as they were derived from Roman and Christian sources.[45] Thus, according to Pound, reconciliation was needed of:

> (1) The Roman-Byzantine, academic idea of enacted law—the civil law as enactments of the emperor Justinian, and the Canon law as enactments of the popes—and (2) the idea of law as authoritatively declared custom, the idea of the customs of the Germanic peoples, authoritatively ascertained and declared by reduction to writing.[46]

There was a marked contrast between the Germanic idea that the ruler and his subjects were both controlled by the customary law of the tribe, and the Roman idea that the law was the manifested will of the ruler. The issue was resolved, however, by proceeding from the argument of the ruler and his subjects being controlled by the customary law of the tribe, to the idea that the ruler and his subjects were both ruled ultimately by divine and natural law. This reconciliation of the same essential idea from two separate sources of argument, Pound says, set the stage for a:

> return to the idea of reason and justice and of the traditional element of the legal system as resting thereon.[47]

The Italian universities served as the forums within which the study of Roman law occurred and its revision took place. The beginning of this work Pound attributes to the writings of the *glossators* who focused their attention on refining the interpretation to be given to the Roman *Corpus Juris*, and formulated rules and maxims which could be applied from that textual exegesis.[48] The completed and compiled writings of the *glossators*, Pound says, provided a full methodological and analytical interpretation of the basic texts of Roman law.[49] Following in the wake of the compiled work of the *glossators* came a series of *commentators* whose exhaustive and systematic series of treatises on various legal issues expanded and completed the work that preceded theirs.[50] The final development in the exposition of law was completed by the *humanists* who, Pound believes, were the true innovators of law during this entire period, and who took the preceding developed legal theories and applied those precepts and maxims to a series of practical issues which they sought to resolve, both theoretically and practically.[51] The unifying academic and intellectual development in the law during this period, Pound says:

> proceeded upon a fundamental conception of a universal state embracing all Christendom and a universal church.[52]

Three sources of authority were universally recognized in this era—the Bible and its exegesis by the Church fathers, the works of Aristotle, and the *Code of Justinian*. Each of these sources affirmed the concept of universalism,[53] which served well the continued development of the law and legal philosophy.[54] As Pound observes, the entire intellectual legal movement of the Middle Ages:

> formed an all embracing body of legislation, the legislation of God, of the church, and of the empire.[55]

This unifying theme of universality was complemented by the development of the universal authority found in the authoritative texts of Roman law,[56] *i.e.*, the works of the *glossators*, the *commentators*, and the humanists—all of whom enjoyed great respect and were employed in the continuing process of developing legal philosophy during this medieval period.[57]

Pound points out that a major concern of law and legal philosophy was examining and explaining the imperative dimension of the law, in light of the revived interest in the ethical ideas involved in the formulation of natural law, particularly in the thought of St. Thomas Aquinas,[58] whose:

> views had the greatest influence on jurisprudence, conceived of natural law as that part of the eternal law, enacted by the supreme lawgiver of the universe, which man's reason reveals to him. Accordingly, positive law

> did not rest merely upon human enactment; it was a recognition of the *lex naturalis* which was above all law and authority.[59]

In addition to Pound's feeling that St. Thomas had a great influence on the development of natural law doctrine, Pound also credits him with synthesizing the Germanic notion of the supremacy of law with the Greco-Roman idea that the state is a natural constituent element of human life and law is the necessary means for preserving this condition.[60] St. Thomas, Pound argues, using the ideas of natural law and eternal law, explained how man's reason is employed in discovering natural law which is then used to provide prescriptions for how men should live.[61] In addition, Pound says, St. Thomas' contribution:

> prepared the way for the more liberal notions of Humanist school of jurists, and for the return in the seventeenth century to the classical conception of reason as the source of authority in law.[62]

This reliance on and emphasis of the central role of reason in the operation and use of the law developed by St. Thomas, Pound says:

> led to a new conception in philosophy, in theology, in politics, and ultimately in juristic theory, as a result of which the legal order came to be regarded as something devised to secure a maximum of individual self-assertion.[63]

Pound sees three major notions stemming from the writing of legal philosophy in the Medieval Era. First were the ideas of universality of precepts. Second, the idea of law governing relationships. Third, the notion of universality of authority.[64]

Reformation, Counter Reformation, and the Seventeenth Century to Hugo Grotius

The writings of Hugo Grotius constitute a watershed in the development of legal philosophy, according to Pound. Hugo Grotius' was the originator of legal thought that was to influence succeeding generations of legal writers, and this thought is characterized, basically, by two central ideas, concerning human nature, which had such enduring influence. These two central ideas Pound says are:

> On the one hand, there was a theory of limitations upon human activities imposed by reason in view of human nature, on the other hand, there was a theory of moral qualities inherent in human beings, or natural rights, demonstrated by reason as deductions from human nature.[65]

The concept of natural law developed by Hugo Grotius had different intellectual foundations than that developed in the Middle Ages, and consequently, Grotius' concept of natural law became separated from the argument in support of natural law that was grounded in theology.[66]

Prior to Grotius' theories, however, there were significant and far-reaching changes that had occurred in society and in thought, which were the result of the Reformation and Counter-Reformation.

One of the effects of the protestant reformation was the challenge this movement and the ideas undergirding it had to the ideas of universalism that were so characteristic of the Medieval Era. In the place of universalism, the reformation resurrected the idea of law as a phenomenon co-existent with a territorial state.[67] Further, the idea of universalism was challenged by the reformation's rejection of the central and universal role of the church, and replaced it with a variety of arguments related to the idea of individual paths to salvation.[68] This latter idea was inherently threatening to the legal order for it raised the possibility it could be used to argue for and support the idea that there was a justifiable role for individualized disobedience to the law stemming from the individual conscience.[69] In response to this possibility, the reformation writers tended to emphasize the sinful nature of such disobedience. In order to support this position, they placed a heavy emphasis on the relationship between law and morals, and, therefore, argued that disobedience of the secular law, which embodied these moral notions, was tantamount to sinful conduct.[70]

Pound notes that one of the effects of the reformation was that it resulted in separating much of intellectual activity from its theological foundation, which had been so characteristic of the Middle Ages. The very nature of the reformation necessitated a rejection of the universal authority of the church, and fashioned the idea that authority stemmed from territorial state organizations, with the consequence that:

> the most significant feature of their work, for the jurist, is their insistence on a national rather than a universal law, their insistence on replacing the universal empire of Roman law and canon law by the civil law of each state.[71]

The major figures of legal thought during the period of the Reformation—Melanchthon, Oldendorp, Hemugsen, and Winkler—had a significant impact on future legal thought.[72] In their rejection of the ideas of universal natural law, as this had been propounded by St. Thomas, they necessarily rejected the idea that such values were discoverable by reason's participation in the eternal law, and divine revelation. They put in place of this idea the notion that values of right and wrong were developed by the reason of man alone.[73]

Acting in response to the challenges raised by the theorists of the reformation, certain writers of the counter-reformation, particularly the Spanish Jurist Theologians, developed a legal theory, which, while not abandoning the concept of universality, tailored this notion to meet the changing intellectual climate. In defending the concept of universality, these writers relied on different bases than those used by Medieval writers. Because of the damage done to the central position of the Church in defending universality, and the corollary impact this had on the universal validity of Roman law, the writers of the counter-reformation had to construct a theory that would show, first of all, that Roman and Canon law were still applicable and reconcile such a contention with the reality of separate and independent sovereign states, and the arguments of the independence of the individual conscience in determining values.[74] The juristic writers of the counter-reformation succeeded in doing this by arguing that there was a universally valid and applicable natural law, from which all legitimate law is properly derived, and of which Roman and Canon law are the most refined expression.[75] These Spanish jurist-theologians, Pound argues, combined morality, reason, and conscience into a workable concept of law which reconciled both natural and positive law, and viewed law as eternal because it contained the fullest expression of eternal notions of justice.[76] Their view on the universality of law also included a doctrine of equality of individual men and states. Since all men and states were equal, the law was to treat them equally. Pound explains the formulation of the counter-reformation writers regarding this point as follows:

> The restraints upon states, limitations upon their activities which they might not overpass, since they were imposed by eternal principles, might fix the limits of the activities of sovereigns in their relations with each other, giving us international law, or the limits of the activities of sovereigns in their relations with their subjects, giving us political theory. The restraints upon individuals had the same basis in eternal principles of universal law and were of the same nature. They fixed the limits of individual activity in the relations of individuals with each other giving us juristic theory.[77]

The importance of the theory these Spanish Jurist Theologians, Pound maintains, was very significant for the future development of legal philosophy. Their construction of a frame of reference within which to discuss the nature and role of legal orders created a major departure from the preceding ideas dominant in the law, that law's purpose was to preserve or establish an ideal *status quo*.[78] Pound describes this contribution further, by saying:

> The theory which begins with the Spanish jurist-theologian thinks, of a limiting of men's activities in the interest of other men's activities because all men have freedom of will and ability to direct themselves to conscious ends and so are equal. Thus, instead of a device to maintain a social *status quo*, the legal order begins to be thought of as a device to maintain a natural equality.[79]

According to Pound, the juristic writers of the reformation and the counter-reformation aided in developing legal thought made possible the transition between the dominant themes of the Medieval world and those of the seventeenth and eighteenth centuries. Indeed, their work set the stage for the contribution to be made by Hugo Grotius. Pound associates Grotius' work with two great contributions to the development of legal thought in the western world. On one hand, Grotius is the founder of the idea of international law which embodies the idea that states are to respond morally in meeting their duties to other states in the international order. In addition, Grotius developed the theory that men should be guided in their conduct toward their fellow men by moral precepts which were the product of their reason and reflected the morality inherent in their being.[80]

Pound maintains that Grotius' theory has a twofold basis of justification of rights. On the one hand, Grotius argues there are identifiable limits which should be imposed on human actions, and that the content and extent of such limitations are discoverable by reason which can determine what they should be in light of the nature of human beings. On the other hand, Grotius argues that human beings possess certain inherent moral qualities because they are human beings. These qualities Grotius calls "rights"; and their composition can be demonstrated by the use of reason which can deduce them from the nature of man.[81]

The first of these notions Grotius derived in part from those who preceded him in the period of the Reformation—particularly Suarez. Pound observes, however, that there is a critical difference between the two in that Suarez derived his argument of limits on human action from the theory of divine obligation, while Grotius, argues for these limitations on the basis of reason alone.[82]

Interestingly, according to Pound, while Grotius was expounding a theoretical formulation of rights and the limits of power of the sovereign based on this argument, the same idea was being expounded in a practical setting by Lord Coke in his arguments with the Stuart kings, and was essentially the same, *i.e.*, that law's role in restraining conduct reflects the discovery of limits that are, in their extent and application, consonant with the nature of man.[83] Thus, while the Grotian formula was being developed in his theory, the same idea was being translated into practicality by the operation of the law in England.

Even though Grotius attempted to construct his theory without reference to authority, he nonetheless relied heavily on authoritative sources and pronouncements for justifying his theoretical arguments.[84] Such a development, Pound finds most understandable given the time and circumstances in which Grotius was writing. Pound does not feel that this fact distracts in any way from the critical role played in the development of legal thought.

Pound feels that Grotius' contribution to the clarification of the idea of rights in the modern world was both substantial and valuable. Medievalists had justified the concept of rights primarily on the basis of preserving intact the benefits attaching to each man by virtue of his position within a relatively unchanging social order.[85] In Grotius' view, however, the doctrine of rights was derivative from the nature of man himself, and that necessitated the conclusion that each man should be protected and served by the law in preserving to him, as well as others, certain powers to act and in guaranteeing to him those values derived from his very nature as man.[86] This Grotian view not only advanced a notion of equality of rights attaching to man by virtue of his being man, but also provided a moral measurement to determine the validity and value of each law.[87]

It is Pound's opinion that there were both positive and negative values to be found in Grotius' theories. On the positive side Pound says that Grotius' theory contained a measure of value that could be employed to test and measure the desirability and value of all law in terms of how well it gave effect to the values that were discoverable by reason with which men were equally endowed.[88] This notion of Grotius' was a liberalizing force in the development of the law as well as legal theory, for it compelled a conclusion that broader protection must be extended to all individuals by the law, and further compelled the liberalization of the prevailing ideas regarding the ends the law should serve, which resulted in greater and greater emphasis on law's role in protecting and serving individual men.[89]

On the other hand, Pound feels that the Grotian concept of rights had a negative effect on the law in that it confused the concept of rights by suggesting it referred to the actual value or interest protected, with the notion of right as the means or mechanism by which a value or interest is protected. This confusion has troubled jurisprudential writing ever since Grotius, and leads, in Pound's view, to unnecessary misunderstanding and confusion concerning what rights are, and what they must be understood to be, if there is to be any clear legal thought.[90] Pound argues, that interests arise independently of any state or legal action, and that the law's recognition of such interests is often necessary, and that when such recognition is extended to these interests, the means for their realization or protection are what are properly denominated as rights. Thus, misapprehending what the proper referent of the term right is, leads to distortion in the operation and application of the law.[91] Because of Grotius's basic misunderstanding of this necessary distinction, his concept served to feed the ideas inherent in most contractarian theories of law and government. Implicit in these theories, and the ideas they in turn influenced, is an overarching emphasis on the individual,[92] with an insufficient attention to other equally significant interests, *e.g.*, property. These other interests are of equally significant importance to the well-being of the social order, and should be equally recognized in juristic thought. The impact of Grotian thought, however, was to overemphasize the role of personality, and resulted in the widespread valuing of contractarian theories of law and government.[93] Implicit in this set of theories is that the search for reconciling the competing wills of men, which is necessary in establishing and maintaining social order, is accomplished through the instrumentality of the contract.[94] The elements of this contract compelled the further conclusion, that all interests of substance were to be determined by reference to the moral quality of each individual man, and consequently the contract was viewed as the measure of determining that to which man was entitled by terms of the contract.[95] Consequently, even though the contract initially was used to argue in defense of a *status quo*, it necessarily began to be interpreted by reference to its role in managing and adjusting varied and altering conditions and relations among men.[96]

The theory of natural rights necessarily implied in these social contract theories, complemented ideas of individualism and the claims an individual might legitimately make of behalf of these rights. Beyond the protection of these individual rights by the terms of the social contract, it was felt that there was little else which the law needed to secure.[97]

The social contract theory, with its concept of individual rights, served to shape the character of law and legal philosophy in the seventeenth century, and as Pound notes:

> Putting the matter in modern phrase, according to the seventeenth century, law exists to maintain and protect individual interests.[98]

Legal Philosophy—
The Seventeenth and Eighteenth Centuries:
Grotius to Kant

The developments of legal thought in the seventeenth century which was dominated by the thought of Hugo Grotius whose thought is described by Pound as follows: As he [Grotius] expounded the new doctrine, it had two sides. On the one hand there was a theory of limitations upon human activities imposed by reason in view of human nature, on the other hand there was a theory of moral qualities inherent in human beings, or natural rights, demonstrated by reason as deductions from human nature... Grotius makes reason the measure of all obligations and the basis of limitations.[99] It is Pound's opinion that the second of these two notions was dominant. Social contract theories were predicated on the assumption that the contract itself did not create rights, but rather that the contract created the mechanisms and methods by which rights would be protected guaranteed in their exercise.[100] Pound summarizes this view as follows:

> (1) There are natural rights demonstrated by reason. These rights are eternal and absolute. (2) Natural law is a body of rules, ascertainable by reason, which perfectly secures all of these natural rights. (3)The state exists only to secure men in these rights. (4)Positive law is the means by which the state performs this function, and it is obligatory only so far as it conforms to natural law.[101]

What was common to each of these themes was the belief that human reason was the method by which one could measure the appropriateness of the law for the ratification and protection of the rights asserted. Because of the subjectivity involved in such judgement, there were certain anarchical elements involved in such an idea.[102] Almost of necessity, modifying ideas emerged which cushioned and restrained these inherent anarchical ideas. Primary among these ideas was the notion that even though each man's conscience could be properly employed to make such a measurement, there was, nonetheless, a type of standard conscience which would compel all men to reach essentially the same judgements in making such decisions.[103] This idea served, therefore, to hedge in the latent anarchy contained in the belief of the inherent efficacy of individualized conscience. Nonetheless, the belief in the correctness of individual conscience was to have an impact on the judgement exercised by individual jurists in dealing with cases before them, and this was to have, according to Pound, both beneficial and negative effects.[104] The benefit derived from this, lay in the fact that individual discretion provided the groundwork for continuing critique and change in the law. Conversely, the bad effect stemmed from the fact that individualized decisions shared the legitimacy associated with final and determinative statements of what the law should be.[105]

There was an intimate relation between the seventeenth century emphasis on the merit of individualized conscience as the measure of rightness, and the belief that rights were inherent in the human character itself. Grotius, and his successors, therefore, adopted:

> a theory of natural rights; not merely natural law, as before, not merely principles of eternal validity, but certain qualities inherent in persons and demonstrated by reason and recognized by natural law, to which therefore the national law ought to give effect.[106]

This theory of natural rights emphasized the notion that rights inhered in human existence, and were not, therefore, anything derived from the operation of the state. The English conception of natural rights, as developed in the common law, differed from this particular view, in that the derivation of rights was from the operation of the common law, and those thus derived were insulated from further state interference and control. The continental natural rights theory posits and assumes the existence of fundamental rights which are neither created nor controlled by the state. However, the common law argument regarding the derivation of rights complemented the natural rights theory stemming from Grotius. In identifying the similarities of the two, Pound, says:

> it followed that the common law was taken to be a system of giving effect to natural rights.[107]

In the course of the development of the natural rights argument, certain interpretations of it came into existence which detracted from its credibility and value. Most significant in these developments was the inordinate emphasis placed on individualism. Indeed, Pound identifies it as an "abstract individualism" based solely on a conception of rights and that the sole obligation of the state was to protect those rights.[108]

Such a view became untenable, according to Pound, in that it obstructed necessary adjustments that had to be made in the law to accommodate a series of newly emerging interests which could not be accommodated in the philosophy of this abstract individualism. But such a change took time, and the influence of this abstract individualist interpretation carried forward through the nineteenth century.[109]

Pound feels that the influence of the thinking of Grotius and the theory of natural rights determined by reason had a substantial impact on natural law thinking as well. Indeed, there was a shift in the natural law arguments away from the belief that the precepts of natural law were derived from authority, to an emphasis on natural law resulting from human reason applied to the condition of human society. Thus, natural law was not generally considered to be derived from a supra-rational authority.[110] Therefore, natural law theories of the seventeenth century also were founded on reason, and derived their obligatory force from their reasonableness. As Pound observes, the seventeenth century notion of natural law explained the obligation of such law as being:

> an obligation resting upon reason, in that reason shows us the dictate of right and justice.[111]

The consequence of this shift of justifying natural law, not by appeal to superior authority, but as a product of reason, had two consequences, which Pound describes as follows.

> (1) Positive law became the application of reason to the civil relations of men, and (2) the *Corpus Juris* stood as its exponent merely because of its inherent reasonableness.[112]

The impact of these developments was to be found in the effect they had on positive law during this period. Pound argues that it reinforced and impelled the development of legislation, since it was believed that the universal principles that should govern such legislative action could be discovered by human reason. Consequently, he says:

> men conceived that it was not merely their duty to criticize existing rules with reference to these principles. Even more they came to hold, it was a duty to work out completely all the applications of these eternal principles and put them in the form of a code. Accordingly, about the middle of the eighteenth century, a strong movement for codification set in.[113]

This emphasis on legislated or imperative law increased in both tempo and scope up to the era of Kant.[114] The period from Grotius to Kant, Pound says, is marked by the continued development of the idea of law as manifested reason, and the belief in the efficacy of legislated law. Thus, Pound says, during the course of the eighteenth century:

> the traditional element, while still important, was beginning to be disturbed by the development of the imperative element. Hence eighteenth century jurists were not clear as between the two ideas of law and their formulas are the result of two opposing tendencies in the law of the time.[115]

Thus, according to Pound, great changes were wrought in both legal practice and legal thinking in the course of the period following Grotius. The stage was set by these developments for the course of the developments that would follow, and what was to characterize legal thinking henceforward was dynamism and expansion, since the abandonment of identifiable sources of authority from which legal reasoning must proceed would engender continued search and examination.

ENDNOTES

CHAPTER THREE

1. Pound, *Interpretations of Legal...*, p. 1. See also: Pound, *...Introduction...Philosophy...*, p. 2. Pound, *Spirit...*, pp. 181-185. Pound, *The Ideal Element...Tagore*, p. 31.

2. Supra., Chapter One.

3. Pound, *The Ideal Element... Tagore*, p. 6.

4. Pound, *Vol. 1*, p. 27. See also: Pound, *Vol. 2*, p. 19. R. Pound, "Natural Natural Law and Positive Natural Law," Law Quarterly Review, Vol. 68, July, 1952, p. 333. Vol. 2, PB. 30. (Hereinafter referred to as "Natural...Law"). Pound, *Vol. 2*, pp. 27-29.

5. Pound, "End of the Law...Juristic Thought...," p. 605. See also: R. Pound, "Theories of Law," Vol. 22, December, 1912, *Yale Law Journal*, pp. 114-150, pp. 116-117. Vol. 1, PB 52. (Hereinafter referred to as "Theories..."). Pound, *Vol. 1*, pp. 34-35. Pound, *The Ideal Element...Tagore*, pp. 28-32.

6. Pound, *Vol. 2*, p. 20. See also: Pound, "Theories...," pp. 117-119. Pound, *Vol. 1*, pp. 27-30.

7. R. Pound, *Contemporary Juristic Thought*, Claremont, California: Claremont Colleges, 1940, pp. 29-30. Vol. 1, PB 255. (Hereinafter referred to as *Contemporary...*). See also: Pound, "Natural...Law...," pp. 333-334. Pound, "Theories...," pp. 117-118. Pound, *Vol. 1,* pp. 27-29.

8. Pound, *Vol. 1*, p. 28. See also: R. Pound, *Law and Morals: The John Calvin McNair Lectures*, Chapel Hill, N.C., 1924. Reprinted, New York: Augustus M. Kelly, 1969, p. 4. Vol. 1, PB 123 (Hereinafter referred to as *Law...Morals*). "Theories...," pp. 117-118.

9. R. Pound, "Political and Economic Interpretations of Jurisprudence," *Proceedings of The American Political Science Association*, Vol. 9, 1913, pp.

95-96. Vol. 1, PB 63 (Hereinafter referred to as "Political and Economic..."). See also: Pound, "Theories...," pp. 117-118. Pound, *Vol. 2*, pp. 22-25.

10. Pound, *Vol. 1*, p. 28. See also: Pound, *Vol. 2*, pp. 22-23, Pound, *...Introduction...Philosophy...*, pp. 34-35. Pound, "Theories...," p. 118.

11. Pound, *Vol. 1*, p. 29. See also: Pound, *Interpretations of Legal...*, p. 130. Pound, Pound *...Introduction...Philosophy...*, pp. 34-35. Pound, *Law...Morals*, pp. 4-6. Pound, "Natural...Law...," p. 334. Pound, *Contemporary...*, p. 30. Pound, *Spirit...*, pp. 85-86.

12. Pound, *Spirit...*, pp. 85-86. See also: Pound, *...Introduction...Philosophy...*, pp. 34-38. Pound, *Vol. 1*, pp. 28-29. Pound, *The Ideal Element...Tagore*, pp. 120-123.

13. Pound, *Contemporary...*, pp. 31-32. See also: Pound, "Theories...," pp. 115-116. Pound, *Vol. 1*, p. 29. Pound, *Spirit...*, pp. 85-86. Pound, *Vol. 1*, pp. 28-29. Pound, *The Ideal Element...Tagore*, pp. 120-123.

14. Pound, "End of Law...in Legal Rules...," p. 606. See also: Pound, *The Ideal Element...Tagore*, p. 123. Pound, *...Introduction...Philosophy...*, p. 7.

15. Pound, *Contemporary...*, p. 32. See also: Pound, *The Ideal Element...Tagore*, pp. 28-31.

16. Pound, *Law...Morals*, pp. 6-7. See also: Pound, *...Introduction...Philosophy...*, pp. 11-12.

17. Pound, *Vol. 1*, pp. 34-35. See also: Pound, *The Ideal Element...Tagore*, p. 123.

18. Pound, *Vol. 1*, pp. 34-35. See also: Pound, *The Ideal Element...Tagore*, pp. 123-124.

19. Pound, *Vol. 1*, pp. 34-35. See also: Pound, *The Ideal Element...Tagore*, pp. 123-124.

20. Pound, *Vol. 1*, p. 36. See also: Pound, *The Ideal Element...Tagore*, pp. 33-34.

21. Pound, "End of Law...in Legal Rules...," p. 608. See also: Pound, *The Ideal Element...Tagore*, pp. 32-33.

22. Pound, *Vol. 1*, p. 37. See also: Pound, *The Ideal Element...Tagore*, pp. 34-35.

23. Pound, *Vol. 2*, p. 27. See also: Pound, *Task...*, p. 119. Pound, "End of Law...Juristic Thought," p. 609. Pound, *The Ideal Element...Tagore*, pp. 34-35.

24. Pound, *Vol. 2*, p. 28. See also: Pound, "Theories...," p. 119. Pound, *The Ideal Element...Tagore*, p. 34.

25. Pound, ...*Introduction...Philosophy...*, pp. 7-9. See also: Pound, *Vol. 2*, pp. 26-27.

26. Pound, ...*Introduction...Philosophy...*, p. 9. See also: Pound, *Vol. 1*, pp. 29-31.

27. Pound, *Vol. 1*, pp. 38-39. See also: Pound, ...*Introduction...Philosophy...*, p. 16.

28. Pound, ...*Introduction...Philosophy...*, pp. 9-10. See also: Pound, "Theories...," pp. 120-122.

29. Pound, *Vol. 1*, p. 40. See also: Pound, ...*Introduction...Philosophy...*, pp. 9-11.

30. Pound, Vol. 1, p. 40. See also: Pound, *Spirit...*, pp. 176-177. Pound, ...*Introduction...Philosophy...*, pp. 9-11.

31. Pound, ...*Introduction...Philosophy...*, pp. 11-12. See also: Pound, "Social...Legal Justice," p. 457. Pound, *Spirit...*, pp. 86-87.

32. Pound, *Vol. 2*, p. 28. See also: Pound, *Law...Morals*, pp. 6-7. Pound, ...*Introduction...Philosophy...*, pp. 11-12. Pound, *Spirit...*, pp. 87-88.

33. Pound, *Vol. 1*, pp. 41-42. See also: Pound, *Spirit...*, pp. 86-88. Pound, ...*Introduction...Philosophy...*, pp.10-11.

34. Pound, ...*Introduction...Philosophy...*, p. 11-12. See also: Pound, "End of Law...Juristic Thought," p. 609. Pound, *Spirit...*, pp. 87-88.

35. Pound, "Theories...," pp. 120-121. See also: Pound, *Vol. 1*, p. 42. Pound, ...*Introduction...Philosophy...*, pp. 8-9, 36.

36. Pound, *Vol. 2*, p. 34. See also: Pound, *The Ideal Element...Tagore*, pp. 124-125. Pound, ...*Introduction...Philosophy...*, pp. 8-9, 141-142.

37. Pound, "End of Law...Juristic Thought," p. 610. See also: Pound, *The Ideal Element...Tagore*, pp. 34-35. Pound, *Vol. 1*, pp. 42-44. Pound, *Vol. 2*, pp. 31-38.

38. Pound, "Theories...," p. 121. See also: Pound, *The Ideal Element...Tagore*, p. 35. Pound, *Vol. 1*, pp. 42-44. Pound, *Vol. 2*, p. 31-38.

39. Pound, ...*Introduction...Philosophy...*, pp. 12, 36-37. See also: Pound, "End of Law...Juristic Thought," pp. 609-610. Pound, *The Ideal Element...Tagore*, pp. 124-125.

40. Pound, ...*Introduction...Philosophy...*, pp. 36-37. See also: Pound, "End of Law...Juristic Thought," p. 610. Pound, *The Ideal Element...Tagore*, pp. 124-125.

41. Pound, "End of Law...Juristic Thought," p. 610. See also: Pound, *The Ideal Element...Tagore*, pp. 35-36. Pound, *Vol. 1*, pp. 470-471.

42. Pound, *Vol. 2*, p. 32. See also: Pound, *The Ideal Element...Tagore*, pp. 131-132. Pound, "Theories...," pp. 122-123.

43. Pound, *Vol. 2*, p. 32. See also: Pound, "Theories...," pp. 122-123. Pound, *The Ideal Element...Tagore*, pp. 124-126, 131-132.

44. Pound, *Vol. 1*, p. 143. See also: Pound, "Theories...," pp. 122-123. Pound, *The Ideal Element...Tagore*, pp. 124-126, 131-132. Pound, ...*Introduction...Philosophy...*, pp. 12-13.

45. Pound, *Vol. 2*, p. 34. See also: Pound, *The Ideal Element...Tagore*, pp. 125-126.

46. Pound, *Vol. 2*, p. 32. See also: Pound, "Theories...," pp. 122-123. Pound, *The Ideal Element...Tagore*, pp. 125-126.

47. Pound, *Vol. 2*, p. 35. See also: Pound, *The Ideal Element...Tagore*, pp. 131-133. Pound, "Theories...," pp. 122-123.

48. Pound, *Vol. 1*, p. 44. See also: Pound, "Theories...," pp. 121-122. Pound, *Vol. 2*, pp. 36-38.

49. Pound, *Vol. 1*, p. 44. See also: Pound, "Theories...," pp. 121-122. Pound, *Vol. 2*, pp. 36-38.

50. Pound, *Vol. 1*, p. 45. See also: Pound, "Theories...," pp. 121-122. Pound, *Vol. 2*, pp. 36-38.

51. Pound, *Vol. 1*, pp. 46-47. See also: Pound, *Vol. 2*, pp. 36-37.

52. Pound, *Vol. 2*, p. 35. See also: Pound, *The Ideal Element...Tagore*, pp. 16-20.

53. Pound, *Vol. 2*, p. 35. See also: Pound, *The Ideal Element...Tagore*, pp. 16-20.

54. Pound, *Vol. 1*, p. 43. See also: Pound, *The Ideal Element...Tagore*, pp. 16-20.

55. Pound, *Vol. 2*, p. 36. See also: Pound, *The Ideal Element...Tagore*, pp. 16-20.

56. Pound, *Vol. 2*, p. 36. See also: Pound, *The Ideal Element...Tagore*, pp. 16-17.

57. Pound, *Vol. 2*, p. 37. See also: Pound, *The Ideal Element...Tagore*, pp. 16-20.

58. Pound, *Vol. 2*, p. 39. See also: Pound, "End of Law...Juristic Thought," pp. 610-611. Pound, "Theories...," pp. 122-123.

59. Pound, "Political and Economic...," p. 96. See also: Pound, "Theories...," p. 123. Pound, *Vol. 2*, pp. 39-42.

60. Pound, *Vol. 2*, pp. 39-40. See also: Pound, "Theories...," pp. 122-123.

61. Pound, "Theories...," p. 123. See also: Pound, *Vol. 2*, p. 40.

62. Pound, *Vol. 2*, p. 41. See also: Pound, "Theories...," p. 123.

63. Pound, "End of Law...Juristic Thought," p. 610. See also: Pound, *The Ideal Element...Tagore*, p. 36. Pound, *Vol. 2*, p. 41.

64. Pound, *The Ideal Element...Tagore*, p. 16. See also: Roscoe Pound, "A Comparison of Ideals of Law," Vol. 47, *Harvard Law Review,* Nr. 1, November, 1933, pp. 1-17. passim. *Vol. 1* PB 195. (Hereinafter referred to as "Comparison...Ideals...").

65. Pound, *Spirit...*, p. 88. See also: Pound, *...Introduction...Philosophy...*, p. 38.

66. Pound, *Vol. 2*, p. 43. See also: Pound, *The Ideal Element...Tagore*, pp. 137-139. Pound, *Spirit...*, p. 89. Pound, *Law...Morals*, pp. 8-9.

67. Pound, "End of Law...Juristic Thought," p. 611. See also: Pound, *The Ideal Element...Tagore*, p. 127. Pound, *Vol 1*, pp. 474-475.

68. Pound, "End of Law...Juristic Thought," p. 612. See also: Pound, *Vol. 1*, pp. 475-476. Pound, *The Ideal Element...Tagore*, p. 128.

69. Pound, *Vol. 1*, p. 476. See also: Pound, *The Ideal Element...Tagore*, pp. 128-129. Pound, *...Introduction...Philosophy...*, p. 14.

70. Pound, "End of Law...Juristic Thought," p. 612. See also: Pound, *...Introduction...Philosophy...*, pp. 14-17. Pound, *Vol. 1*, pp. 474-478.

71. Pound, "End of Law...Juristic Thought," p. 611. See also: Pound, *Vol. 1*, pp. 475-476. Pound, *Spirit...*, pp. 54-55. Pound, *The Ideal Element...Tagore*, pp. 127-128.

72. Pound, "End of Law...Juristic Thought," pp. 612-613. See also: Pound, *Vol. 1,* pp. 477-479. Pound, *The Ideal Element...Tagore*, pp. 129-130.

73. Pound, "End of Law...Juristic Thought," pp. 612-613. See also: Pound, *Vol. 1*, pp. 477-479. Pound, *Spirit...*, p. 88.

74. Pound, "End of Law...Juristic Thought," p. 612. See also: Pound, *Vol. 1*, p. 479. Pound, *The Ideal Element...Tagore*, pp. 133-136.

75. Pound, "End of Law...Juristic Thought," p. 612. See also: Pound, The Ideal Element...Tagore, pp. 135-136. Pound, *Vol. 1*, pp. 481-483.

76. Pound, *Spirit...*, p. 88. See also: Pound, "End of Law...Juristic Thought," pp. 614-616. Pound, *Vol. 1*, pp. 482-483.

77. Pound, *Spirit...*, p. 88. See also: Pound, "End of Law...Juristic Thought," pp. 614-616. Pound, *The Ideal Element...Tagore*, pp. 135-136. Pound, *Vol. 1*, p. 482.

78. Pound, "End of Law...Juristic Thought," p. 616. See also: Pound, Vol. 1, pp. 479-483. Pound, *Interpretations of Legal...*, p. 32. Pound, *The Ideal Element...Tagore*, p. 136.

79. Pound, "End of Law...Juristic Thought," p. 616. See also: Pound, *The Ideal Element...Tagore*, p. 136.

80. Pound, *The Ideal Element...Tagore*, pp. 40, 137. See also: Pound, "Theories...," pp. 126-127. Pound, *Vol. 1*, pp. 483-484. Pound's major concern is with Grotius' writing in regard to the development of a theory of natural law. For a more detailed examination of Grotius' contribution to international law see: R. Pound, "Grotius in the Science of Law," *American Journal of International Law*, 1925. Vol. 1, PB 126.

81. Pound, "End of Law...Juristic Thought," pp. 616-618. See also: Pound, *Vol. 2*, p. 45. Pound, *The Ideal Element...Tagore*, pp. 136-138. Pound, *Spirit...*, pp. 89-90. Pound, *Vol. 1*, pp. 483-484.

82. Pound, "End of Law...Juristic Thought," p. 617. See also: Pound, *The Ideal Element...Tagore*, p. 136. Pound, *Spirit...*, pp. 88-89.

83. Pound, "End of Law...Juristic Thought," p. 617. See also: Pound, *Vol. 2*, p. 45. Pound, *The Ideal Element...Tagore,* p. 138. Pound, *Spirit...*, pp. 89-90. Pound, *Vol. 1*, pp. 485-487.

84. Pound, "End of Law...Juristic Thought," p. 617. See also: Pound, *Vol. 1*, p. 485.

85. Pound, "End of Law...Juristic Thought," p. 618. See also: Pound, *Spirit...*, pp. 87-88. Pound, *Vol. 1*, pp. 485-487.

86. Pound, *Spirit...*, p. 90. Pound, *Vol. 2*, p. 46. See also: Pound, *The Ideal Element...Tagore*, p. 138.

87. Pound, *The Ideal Element...Tagore*, pp. 139-140. See also: Pound, *Spirit...*, p. 91. Pound, "End of Law...Juristic Thought," p. 618. Pound, *Vol. 1*, pp. 486-487. Pound, "Theories...," p. 126.

88. Pound, "End of Law...Juristic Thought," p. 618. See also: Pound, *The Ideal Element...Tagore*, p. 140. Pound, *Vol. 1*, pp. 486-487. Pound, "Theories...," p. 126. Pound, *Spirit...*, p. 91.

89. Pound, "End of Law...Juristic Thought," p. 618. See also: Pound, *The Ideal Element...Tagore*, p. 140. Pound, *Spirit...*, p. 91. Pound, *Vol. 1*, pp. 487-488.

90. Pound, "End of Law...Juristic Thought," pp. 618-619. See also: Pound, *The Ideal Element...Tagore*, p. 140. Pound, *Spirit...*, p. 91. Pound, *Vol. 1*, pp. 487-488.

91. Pound, "End of Law...Juristic Thought," p. 619. See also: Pound, *The Ideal Element...Tagore*, p. 140. Pound, *Spirit...*, p. 91. Pound, *Vol. 1*, pp. 487-488.

92. Pound, "End of Law...Juristic Thought," p. 619. See also: Pound, *Spirit...*, pp. 92-93. Pound, *Vol. 1*, pp. 487-488.

93. Pound, "End of Law...Juristic Thought," pp. 619-610. See also: Pound, *The Ideal Element...Tagore*, pp. 141-143. Pound, *Vol. 1*, pp. 489-493.

94. Pound, "End of Law...Juristic Thought," p. 620. See also: Pound, *The Ideal Element...Tagore*, pp. 142-143. Pound, *Vol. 1*, pp. 489-493.

95. Pound, "End of Law...Juristic Thought," p. 621. See also: Pound, *The Ideal Element...Tagore*, pp. 142-143. Pound, *Vol. 1*, pp. 489-493.

96. Pound, "End of Law...Juristic Thought," p. 621. See also: Pound, *Vol. 2*, p. 46. Pound, *The Ideal Element...Tagore*, pp. 142-143. Pound, *Vol. 1*, pp. 489-493.

97. Pound, "End of Law...Juristic Thought," p. 621. See also: Pound, *The Ideal Element...Tagore*, p. 143. Pound, *Vol. 1*, pp. 489-493.

98. Pound, "End of Law...Juristic Thought," p. 621. See also: Pound, *Vol. 1*, pp. 491-492. Pound, *The Ideal Element...Tagore*, p. 143. Pound, *Spirit...*, p. 81. Pound, *Vol. 1*, p. 493.

99. Pound, "End of Law...Juristic Thought," pp. 622-623. See also: Pound, *The Ideal Element...Tagore*, p. 144. Pound, *Spirit...*, p. 90.

100. Pound, *Spirit...*, p. 91. See also: Pound, "End of Law...Juristic Thought," pp. 620-621. Pound, *The Ideal Element...Tagore*, p. 144.

101. Pound, "End of Law...Juristic Thought," p. 623. See also: Pound, *The Ideal Element...Tagore*, pp. 144-145. Pound, *Vol. 1*, pp. 486-489.

102. Pound, "End of Law...Juristic Thought," p. 623. See also: Pound, *The Ideal Element...Tagore*, p. 145.

103. Pound, "End of Law...Juristic Thought," p. 624. See also: Pound, *The Ideal Element...Tagore*, p. 145.

104. Pound, "End of Law...Juristic Thought," p. 624. See also: Pound, *The Ideal Element...Tagore*, p. 146. Pound, *Vol. 2*, p. 48.

105. Pound, "End of Law...Juristic Thought," p. 624. See also: Pound, The Ideal Element...Tagore, p. 146. Pound, *Vol. 2*, p. 50. Pound, *Spirit...*, p. 89.

106. Pound, *Spirit...*, p. 89. See also: Pound, *Vol. 1*, pp. 486-487.

107. Pound, "End of Law...Juristic Thought," p. 625. See also: Pound, *The Ideal Element...Tagore*, p. 150. Pound, *Spirit...*, p. 95. Pound, *Vol. 1*, p. 486.

108. Pound, *The Ideal Element...Tagore*, p. 150. See also: Pound, *Vol. 1*, pp. 485-493.

109. Pound, *The Ideal Element...Tagore*, pp. 150-151. pp. 150-151. See also: Pound, *Spirit...*, pp. 100-102. Pound, *Vol. 1*, pp. 492-493.

110. Pound, "Theories...," p. 125. See also: Pound, *Vol. 1*, p. 487. Pound, *Spirit...*, pp. 90-91.

111. Pound, "Theories...," p. 126. See also: Pound, *Spirit...*, p. 88. Pound, *Vol. 1*, p. 484.

112. Pound, *Vol. 2*, p. 45.

113. Pound, "Theories...," p. 127. See also: Pound, *Vol. 2*, p. 46.

114. Pound, "Theories...," pp. 127-128. See also: Pound, *Vol. 2*, pp. 46-48.

115. Pound, *Vol. 2*, pp. 54-55. See also: Pound, "Theories...," p. 132. Pound, *The Ideal Element...Tagore*, pp. 151-152. Pound, "Political and Economic...," p. 98.

Chapter Four

Legal Philosophy—Nineteenth Century

According to Roscoe Pound, the contribution made to legal philosophy by Immanuel Kant was equal to that made by Hugo Grotius.[1] Addressing Kant's significance Pound says that Kant:

> struck a decisive blow at the philosophical jurisprudence which had obtained for the past two centuries.[2]

Kant addressed what was the central issue of legal thought in the nineteenth century, *i.e.*, the reconciliation of government and individual human liberty and, according to Pound, contributed significantly to the resolution of this issue.[3] He successfully resolved the problem of whether a belief in untrammelled individual liberty could be reconciled with the preservation of social order. In describing Kant's constructive contribution to the problem Pound notes:

> Kant's solution thereof lies in this, that legal reasoning is the chief instrument by which compromise between the need of stability and the need of change is effected in everyday administration of justice—by which, that is, new needs are met by means of old rules and institutions and adaptation to changing condition is brought about with a minimum of outward infringement or warping of established precepts.[4]

Kant argued that the source and nature of rights were derived from the conscious ego of the individual. Because the individual can will his acts, Kant felt that one must find the means whereby conflicting wills could be reconciled. This, Kant maintained, could be accomplished by subjecting each individual will to:

> the application of a universal rule to each action which would evoke the free will of the actor to co-exist along with the free will of everyone else. The whole course of nineteenth century juristic theory was determined by this conception.[5]

Jurisprudence had become a separate and autonomous discipline in the nineteenth century, and, according to Pound, this logically flowed from the separation of theology from jurisprudence that occurred in the sixteenth century. Following this, separate approaches to jurisprudence emerged, which resulted in three separate schools of thought—analytical, historical, and philosophical,[6] all of which, however, were touched by Kantian influence.

Nineteenth Century Historical School

Pound concludes that, the dominant nineteenth century school of jurisprudence was the Historical School, whose most significant representative was F.C. von Savigny. This school was closely akin to the philosophical school. Central to the thought of the historical school was the notion that law is to be understood as the result of the historical development of a given society. The law's purpose and the purpose of human activity, *i.e.*, the realization of human liberty, was revealed in a society's history. The historical school sought a determinant pattern and process of history, and like the philosophical school believed that law served a common purpose. Pound describes the similarity in the thought of the two schools as follows:

> On the one hand it had to do with the historical unfolding of the idea of liberty as men discovered the rules by which to realize it. This was historical jurisprudence. On the other hand, it had to do with the logical unfolding of the principles involved in the abstract conception. This was philosophical jurisprudence....Philosopher and historian were agreed that law was found, not made. One formed it by deduction from a metaphysical principle, the other by historical study.[7]

The object of the historical school's examination was to discern in the pattern and process of history, canons of the law which were revealed by this history. In the course of its development the historical school maintained that legal history showed that law:

> was declaratory of principles of progress discovered by human experience of administering justice and of human experience of intercourse in civilized society; and these principles were not principles of natural law revealed by reason, they were realizings of an idea, unfolding in human experience and in the development of institutions—an idea to be demonstrated metaphysically and verified by history.[8]

The historical school rejected the idea of imperative law. The existing institutions of a society, according to this school, embodied the real purpose of life and action of a given people. These institutions were the culmination of a pattern of historical development which could not be altered by imperative law. Any examination of these institutions, the school maintains, would show they were not the result of any individuals' particular willed actions. These institutions, like language, were evolved in the process of historical development which has its own momentum and generative power.[10]

According to Pound there are five different characteristics of this school, which reflect both its concerns and its conclusions.

First, the scope of examination of the historical school was very extensive. It sought to consider the entire issue of social control and not just that portion attributed to politically organized society. According to the historical school all contemporary forms of social control are mere continuations of forms that had existed in the past. Consequently, all existing law was merely declaratory of past experience of the society involved,[11] and, the source of all authority—including law—was to be found in "the conviction of a people as to what was right and just."[12]

Second, the historical school believed that law could not be created by the will of the legislator or sovereign. Law was something to be found in the course of historical examination of the society.[13] Proof of this contention the historical school believed could be found in what it called the "paper waste" of the French Revolution, which reflected the futility of attempts at willed legislative activity.[14]

The historical school believed that the precepts of natural law were to be discovered in the history of a people, and rejected the natural law theories of preceding centuries which had maintained that natural law precepts were derived from sources external to the law. Pound notes:

> No system of natural law was ever more absolute than this natural law upon historical premises. For other systems of natural law gave ideas developed from without. ...Under the dominion of the historical school the sole critique of the law was to be found in the law itself.[15]

The historical school's view of law was also diametrically opposed to that of the analytical school, which viewed law as the product of will. The historical school believed that law could be found only by historical examination, and considered the idea that law is derived from sovereign power a very modern notion, which could not aid in understanding the origin and content of law,[16] since law "exists" and is not created out of whole cloth.[17] Attempts to understand law from a fixed standpoint of time and place could not be productive.[18]

Pound is sympathetic to the ideas of the historical school, for he feels that much that is significant in the content of the law is derived from sources other than the state. He notes, however, that the enunciation of the law is a function of the state, and while this fact may not serve as an ethical justification of the law, it does provide a more concrete basis for recognizing its true nature.[19]

Pound argues that although there is value in the historical school's reference to the past in order to understand the present, their overemphasis on the past detracts from the necessary attention that must be given to the role of law in fashioning and conditioning the future.[20]

Third, the historical school maintained that state imposed sanctions did not determine the efficacy and effectiveness of the law. Obedience to the law, they argued, is a product of past experience and habit, and law's success depends on the support extended to it by the entire social order. Consequently, they argued that attempts to distinguish the legal order from the social order were misguided.[21]

The historical school agreed that law was obeyed and recognized in primitive times and did not require enforcement for its efficacy, since compliance was voluntary. According to the historical school the modern notion that compliance is a result of coercion, is at variance with historical evidence.[22] Thus, the writers of the historical school developed a theory of sanction which was quite different from that of the analytical school.[23] The historical school argued that there were two bases for sanctions—the generalized approval of the members of the society, and the inculcation of obedience by habit.[24] The historical school's view of sanction is inadequate, Pound says, and the theory of sanction developed by the analytical school is more relevant and correct. The analytical school, he maintains, correctly and clearly distinguishes between motives and feelings which induce obedience to the law, and the use of sanction to compel such obedience. The historical school, Pound feels, failed to recognize this critical difference.[25] Pound asserts that it is essential to understand this difference between motive and compulsion if one is to comprehend the operation of modern legal systems. Sanction as a result of compulsion, is one of the most important legal developments of modern society.[26] Pound feels that the fear of popular displeasure accurately describes social norms, but that it cannot explain how and why people obey statutes.[27] The historical school's argument that obedience results from habit is equally flawed, Pound argues, since evidence would suggest that some men are habituated to disobedience. Further, given the frequency of new statutes in modern societies, one cannot realistically describe compliance to them as a result of habit.[28]

Fourth, the historical school maintained that a society's customary modes of decision are based on past decisions, which condition the present application and understanding of the law.[29] The historical jurists believed that all principles and all forms of social action are derived from past historical experience. "Hence," Pound says:

> the historical school denied that law was a product of conscious or determinate human will. They doubted the efficacy of legislation, in that it sought to achieve the impossible and to make what cannot by made. They held that the living organs of law were doctrinal writing and judicial decision, whereby the life of a people, expressed in the first instance in its traditional rules of law made itself felt in a gradual development by molding those rules to the conditions of the present.[30]

Fifth, the historical school—greatly influenced by Hegelian thought—assumed the existence of universal principles which can be perceived in history. According to Pound, this view considers "history as the unfolding in human experience of the principles which one has found."[31] For this reason Pound suggests, much of the writing of the historical school contains elements of the idealistic interpretation, and adopts the view that all human historical development reveals the "unfolding of an idea of freedom."[32]

Pound argues that the historical school was just as committed to describing and analyzing the law as a means of justifying freedom of the individual as were members of the analytical school, and that while the school began: "as a political theory of securing en in a natural (*i.e.* ideal) equality, it became a juristic theory of securing them in their natural rights..., and by a further simplification became a theory of securing the men an abstract freedom of will."[33] Accordingly, the historical school is metaphysical and utilizes much of the eighteenth century's notion of natural law.[34] Historicists, Pound says:

> Having no philosophical method of their own,..., overthrew the premises of the Eighteenth Century Law-of-Nature School, [but] they preserved the method of their predecessors, merely substituting new premises. They had,..., neither the capacity nor the desire to put a new philosophy of law in the place of the buried law of nature. They sought the nature of right

> and of law in historical deductions from the Roman sources, from German legal institutions, and from the juristic development based thereon.[35]

The historical school assumed that law and morals have a common origin, and although they may have different paths of development, they are, nonetheless, related.[36] Pound feels that this view of the historical school is correct, and agrees that there is a continuous inter-relationship between law and morals. In this respect the historical school proved more accurate than the analytical school which maintained that law and morals were totally separate. Pound discusses how important the recognition of this linkage between law and morals is, and observes:

> Whenever a legal precept has to be found in order to meet what used to be called a "gap in the law" it is found by choice of a starting point which is governed by considering how far application of a result reached from one or the other will comport with the received ideal. Thus morals are a matter for judge and jurist as well as for the legislator. Yet it is necessary to sound thinking to perceive that moral principles are not law simply because they are moral principles.[37]

Pound maintains that a major weakness of the historical school results from its *a priori* reasoning. Because of this, its evaluations and judgements must conform to these *a priori* principles, which are not and cannot be based on verified evidence.[38] Pound subscribes to the critique of Savigny made by Bluntschli, who writes:

> The critical examination of the past is necessary in order to cover the grounds upon which we rest, but the consideration of the future is none the less necessary in order to determine whither we are going. All law is truly of the present; the past is no more, except in so far as its force operates in the present; and the future is not yet, except in so far as it is already a condition of the present. The present is, therefore, a union of the past and present. It alone is real. This is something that is often not sufficiently recognized by the Historical School.[39]

In his summary statements about the nineteenth century historical school Pound points to the necessary pessimism of their argument. If all the development of human history and law is a product of historical development that is not and cannot be influenced by conscious willed human action, then attempts at affirmative acts by means of imperative law are futile. The study of law, according to the historical school, reflects a Hegelian abstraction of human freedom. This evolving element would be reflected, of course, in the content and purpose of law as well as the institutions that gave effect to these purposes.[40] All in all, Pound feels that the historical school is very close in spirit and methodology to the metaphysical notions embodied in Hegelian thought.

Nineteenth Century Philosophical School

According to Pound, the influence exercised by the nineteenth century philosophical school was confined to the first half of that century, because this school failed to develop a realistic philosophy of law. He says that by the:

> last third of the nineteenth century the abandonment of philosophy had gone so far that the philosophical jurist either had been swallowed up in the dominant historical school or had disappeared.[41]

The only significance of this school resulted from the influence it exercised on the more important historical school of that century. This influence stemmed from the ethical guidelines provided by the philosophical school, which the historical school could use to evaluate the path of development of the law.[42]

The philosophical school concentrated on means and methods for critiquing law, its exercise, and the institutions it employed. This type of critique, Pound suggests, enjoys much more attention in periods when the law is changing than periods when the law is more stable.[43] He notes:

> The appeal to reason and to the sense of mankind for the time being as to what is just and right, which the philosophical jurist is always making, and his insistence upon what ought to be law as binding law because of its intrinsic reasonableness, have been the strongest liberalizing forces in legal history.[44]

According to Pound the nineteenth century philosophical school has four major themes.

First, this school dealt with determining what the purpose of law should be in light of the facts with which this law must deal. It is evident, Pound notes, that such an emphasis in legal inquiry is directed less to determining what the law is in a contemporary setting, than on propositions advanced for its development in the future.[45]

Second, the philosophical school differed little from the historical school in rejecting the notion that imperative law could serve constructive purposes in a society. The historical school assumed this was the case because of past legal development. The philosophical school argued that law can be found only by discovering its true content and purpose as measured by ethical precepts that are to be discovered. Thus the task of legal philosophy is to discover these guiding precepts.[46]

Third, the philosophical school rejected the notion that sanctions were the proper source of obedience to the law. The ethical bases of legal principles which determined the law, mold its true binding force, and these principles legitimate the law and justify obedience to it.[47]

Fourth, the philosophical school's reaction to codified or statute law was the same as its reaction to all law, including customary. The propriety and desirability of all law is to be determined by the degree to which it reflected proper notions of right and justice.[48]

Numerous schools of philosophy composed what Pound calls "the philosophical school" whose most significant representatives were Krause, Hegel, and Kant,[49] although Pound feels that the unquestioned founder of this entire school of thought was Immanuel Kant. It was Kant, Pound maintains, who developed and refined the notions of authority which had their origins in the sixteenth century. According to the view developed in that period of time, the only binding authority for an individual was that discovered by his own reason and adopted for practice and effect by the exercise of his own will.[50] Kant refined this notion further, and Pound observes, concluded individual free wills were to be reconciled by discerning a universal law that could reconcile these acting wills.[51] Kant's formulation had a lasting effect on the nineteenth century philosophical school, whose writers felt that:

> the whole legal system could be deduced from the conception of right and in this way mount a critique of institutions and doctrines. As a rule they carried out Kant's idea of securing the free will into its practical consequences of liberty; of general freedom of action for individuals. Hence in their view the end of law was to secure the widest possible liberty to each individual.[52]

Pound criticizes this Kantian notion because it focuses only on abstract individual liberty and the significance of social and economic conditions.[53] This narrow view assumed that the sole purpose of law was to protect abstract liberty,[54] and to maximize it.[55]

The philosophical school's thought compelled two conclusions about the law. First, all law is suspect because of its restrictive character. Therefore, they argued, the only appropriate measure of law was a result of determining how essential it was to restrict individual abstract liberty.[56] Second, the philosophical school believed sanctions were necessary and unavoidable, and were needed to insure obedience to the law.[57]

Further, the philosophical school maintained that "true law" was an expression of right, and that any enforcement of law must be based on the fact of its rightness.[58] The philosophical school was not concerned about the origin of legal precepts or how such precepts become authoritative. Rather, the school was concerned only with law's moral dimension and how well the law gave expression to these moral ideas.[59] This idea is reflected in Kohler's theory that laws are "derived from the jural postulates of the civilization of the time and place."[60] According to Kohler, the role of the legislator is not to create law by will, but only to give expression to valid moral precepts.[61] The philosophical school believed that law's nature can be discovered only by examining its content, in order to determine if it is consonant with those ideals that are discovered by rigorous philosophical inquiry.[62] Consequently, the philosophical school focused only on the degree of morality embodied in the law. As Pound observes, the writers of the philosophical school assume:

> that jurisprudence is a branch of ethics and that legal precepts are only declaratory of moral precepts. They assume that a rule of decision in the courts cannot be a legal precept unless it is a moral precept; not merely that it ought not to be a legal precept if it runs counter to a moral precept. They assume also that moral precepts as such are legally obligatory.[63]

The content and direction of the philosophy of the philosophical school, Pound says, reflect the type of thinking about the law that is evident in periods of legal change and flux,[64] and in many ways express ideas and sentiments similar to those legal philosophies which are founded on theological bases.[65] As Pound observes, legal philosophy often focuses on the relationship of morals to law, and this is most evident in those societies that have a relatively cohesive belief system. When such homogeneity of belief is not present, legal philosophy serves mainly as a basis of criticism of the law. Because there is great diversity of views among the writers of the philosophical school, Pound maintains, one must conclude that the theories in this school are only the expressed preferences of the particular writers. One cannot find in this school a broad agreement regarding what would constitute the proper moral content of the law. For example, Pound notes that the natural law theories advanced in the eighteenth century only reflected the personal preferences of the various writers and did not compose a cohesive statement about a widely shared moral consensus within the broader community.[66] Pound points to the similarity of the nineteenth century school of metaphysical jurisprudence in this regard:

> An eighteenth-century jurist laying down natural law and Bentham's man who claims to be one of the elect are in the same position; each is giving his personal views and assuming that those views must be binding on every one else.[67]

Kant's philosophical scheme, Pound observes, was predicated on the belief that there is an internal and external dimension that must be taken into account in examining human and social behavior. In evaluating and judging this idea, Pound says, one must recognize that the internal nature of man is the province of morals, while the external nature is properly the province of the law. The correct relationship between these two dimensions requires that law protect one person from the effects of the freely willed acts of another. Thus, law is devoted to protecting the liberty of all individuals, consonant with the protection of the liberty of all others.[68] Therefore, when the law is used to protect liberty, it is to be guided by the concept of right.[69] The philosophical school, following the lead of Kant, attempted to retain this distinction between law and morals, and argued that law is to be used in protecting the liberty of the individual in his actions, and that the perfection of man's internal character is the province of morality.[70] Thus, law and morals are distinguished in terms of what is capable of being realized in the regulation of outward human conduct by the use of the law, in contrast with that which is internally recognizable by the measure of moral necessity.[71]

The beneficial effects of the philosophical school's theories become more evident when one contrasts them with the analytical and historical schools in this period. According to Pound, both the analytical school and the historical school sought to discover the historical causes for the content of law at a given point in time, without concern for the moral desirability of what existed. Pound feels that good legal philosophy must test the propriety and desirability of what law is against some measure of right and justice, and it is this concern that heightens the value of the philosophical school.[72] Pound notes further, that the efforts of the philosophical school had some impact on jurists who became more aware of the principles and values that influence their decisions.[73]

Criticizing the nineteenth century philosophical school, Pound states that there are three problems they did not handle adequately. First, when the philosophical notions of this school are rigidly and inflexibly applied, they do not produce a helpful critique of the law. Rather, they are merely general pronouncements which cannot assist meaningfully in the refashioning of the law to meet the concrete issues which the law must handle. Second, these broad and encompassing theoretical propositions serve little purpose in particularized and discrete areas of the law. Third, given the fact that the focus of the generalized positions of the philosophical school touch only the problems associated with defining the ends of law, they provide little or no assistance in evaluating or assisting in the improvement of the means by which the law is given effect.[74]

Pound points out, however, that the nineteenth century philosophical school had much to commend it, and notes:

> Even when misdirected and overworked, the rationalizing influence of the philosophical school has been invaluable. In civilized countries, men are compelled to administer justice by formulas. These formulas are designed to express ideas of right and justice and as a means to promote right and justice. But there is always a danger that we forget those ideas and lose sight of those ends and treat formulas as existing for their own sake.[75]

Nineteenth Century Analytical School

Pound says that the nineteenth century analytical school:

> sought to take developed systems of law as they were, to analyze the legal institutions and legal precepts and juristic conceptions that actually existed, and to obtain the materials for a universal science of law in that way.[76]

According to Pound, two basic assumptions controlled this school's thought. First, it ignored "backward" systems of law, and focused its attention only on highly developed systems. Second, it studied only imperative legal systems, focusing only on the expressed sovereign will.[77]

Although Pound's writing on this school is extensive, he focused mainly on three stages of development of the English Analytical School.[78] The most detailed treatment of these examined the English Analytical School, particularly the thought of John Austin.

Pound maintains that the three controlling assumptions of the analytical school are erroneous and misleading.[79] First, the analytical school's assumption that the law is merely an "aggregate of laws," reflecting the sovereign's will ignores the more significant precepts, techniques, and ideals that control judicial conduct.[80] This school, Pound says, ignores the fact that law:

> is more than an aggregate of laws. It is what makes laws living instruments of justice. It is what enables courts to administer justice by means of laws; to restrain them by reason when the lawmaker exceeds his reason, and to develop them to the full scope of the reason where the lawmaker's falls short of it.[81]

This error of the analytical school resulted, in part, from their misunderstanding of the theory of the separation of powers. The assumption of legislative supremacy contained in their analysis of the separation of powers mistakenly viewed the courts as ancillary instruments of legislative will.[82] This mistaken notion prevented analytical jurisprudents from understanding the basic nature of law. The school rejected what could not be accommodated to this narrow theory, and failed to treat and explain all that is necessary for the understanding of the law.[83]

The second faulty assumption of the analytical school held that law is merely a series of rules.[84] Clearly, Pound argues, the concept of rule as the only element in the examination of law is erroneous, because it leaves out of account, the more important elements of precepts, technique, and ideals.[85] This narrow approach based on considering only rules ignores more than it can explain. Pound says that this narrow approach, however true it:

> may be with respect to the manner in which norms are established in matured legal systems, its tendency is to lead lawmakers, legislative and judicial, to overlook the need of squaring the rules upon the statute book, or in reports or doctrinal treatises, as the case may be, with the demands of reason and the exigencies of human conduct in the one case, and with the demands of social progress in the other case.[86]

This treatment of law is incomplete.[87] The incompleteness is demonstrated by the fact that the theory is not designed to explain the reaction of judges and lawyers, which in turn shapes and forms the effect of the law in ways that may be at variance with the legislator's intent and stems from different premises and values.[88]

The analytical jurists aspired to develop a complete philosophy of law, to explain the source of the law, its purpose, and what would determine its success.[89] The fixity of the school's boundaries of examination reveals its most significant weaknesses.[90] The analytical school's attempt was a misadventure, because they created an idealized system of law, which shared all the weaknesses of the nineteenth century's philosophical school.[91] He notes that analytical jurisprudence is trapped by the logical scheme it constructs, and what did not fit into that scheme was excluded in their consideration and understanding of law.[92]

The major elements of Austin's theory are all subject to serious criticism according to Pound.[93] The first element in Austin's definition of law—that it is a command issued by a sovereign to a subject—is of limited value, according to Pound, since its conception is relevant only to a mature system of law. Austin relied on the English experience of his day, and the study of codified Roman law to provide support for his contention.[94] As Pound rightly notes, the attempt of the analytical writers, including Austin, to find general principles and precepts of law in these systems is excessively narrow.[95]

Pound notes that Austin's assumptions regarding the notion of command as an elemental part of the definition of law, unacceptably ignores the relationship of law to morals.[96] Oftentimes, Pound observes, courts are faced with cases which have no identifiable and certain precepts to govern their decisions. Consequently, in such cases, judges are compelled to follow their own sense of what is correct legally and morally in the given context. This fact was ignored by the analytical jurists who failed to consider this reality.[97] Pound notes that the analytical view glossed over the discretion and independence involved in judicial decisions and insisted that judges merely fulfill the will of the sovereign. However, as Pound correctly observes, this explanation attempts to mask reality with a fiction, and ignores the fact that when judges act they are not "obeying" a sovereign will, but rather are employing:

> the received technique [of the law] of developing and applying received ideals as grounds [for their] decision[s].[98]

According to Pound, ideals that affect the operation and application of the law cannot be ignored in any realistic interpretation of the law.[99] The Austinian doctrine of imperative law clearly ignores the more substantive character and nature of law, and, as Pound observes:

> What is law depends not merely upon the fact of the past and of the present but also upon the will of those who prescribe and those who administer rules of conduct by the authority of the state; and the will is determined not a little by their theory of what they do and why they do

> it. The rules are not prescribed and administered for their own sake, but rather for social ends. The problem is not merely how law-making and law-adjusting functions are exercised, but also how they may be exercised so as to achieve their purposes, and what conception of these functions by those who perform them will conduct best thereto.[100]

The analytical theorists' attempt to force facts to fit preconceived conclusions required them to ignore the centuries old tradition of law, and replace it with a faulty conclusion that law is a fully self sufficient source of authority and determination.[101] Indeed, Pound notes, this school constructed an ideal concept of law which was as closed in its explanation as that of the philosophic theories of the same century. Pound argues that Austin and his school attempted to create a purely logical and ideal explanation of a legal order run exclusively by legal rule.[102]

Not only did Pound feel that Austin's assumption about sovereign authority was wrong, but also questioned whether any such determinate source of authority could be located in any system of law, except for those few despotic regimes known in world history.[103] Equally in error is the Austinian assumption, that the sources of political authority can be easily defined and separated from those sources of moral authority in society.[104] This attempted separation of law from morals, Pound argues, ignores the identifiable and observable fact that most of the premises and precepts of the legal order are derived from moral ones and must be considered.[105] As Pound observes:

> nineteenth century jurists were inclined to carry this argument [the distinction between law and morals] too far and to ignore moral considerations merely as such—to ignore those which the law can and should take into account, and to assume that they might do so simply on the ground of the distinction between legal and moral.[106]

The third characteristic of law in Austin's definition which Pound finds erroneous is Austin's belief that law is composed of rules which are general in their effect on the sovereign's subjects.[107] Although Pound feels this notion is valuable since it can be used to argue against the type of political, discretionary judgement that has come to be so prevalent in the modern era,[108] he, nonetheless, feels that, in the context of the analytical school's theory, this particular notion fails to take into account those categories of exception which have long been used in the law; the modern attempts at the individualization of justice; and the politically determined exceptions granted by legislative will.[109]

Four, Austin's definition of the law assumes that law can affect only external acts, but that the internal feelings and motives of individuals must be governed by moral principles, which reinforced Austin's other arguments that a distinction must be made between law and morals.[110] Pound suggests that this notion of differences between external acts and internal feelings has some value since it recognizes the limitations of the law in fashioning an ideal political, social, and legal order.[111] However, Austin's use of this idea attempts to prove more than it can. The insistence on the purity of this argument ignores the role morals play in creating starting points for legal reasoning, and in creating legal remedies.[112]

The fifth element in Austin's definition postulates that sanctions give effect to the law.[113] Pound agrees that sanctions are essential for a successful legal order.[114] However, because of law's limitation and the consequent limitations of sanctions, the latter cannot explain men's adherence to and obedience to the law.[115]

According to Pound, the inherent weakness of the Analytical School's theory is clearly evident in Austin's theory which attempts to explain too much, and which fails to provide support for what is argued.[116] Austin's theory is weakened further by insisting that the only source of law in any society is the sovereign will.[117] The Analytical School viewed law as a purely logical order established by authority that did not need or incorporate ideals.[118] Consequently what Austin and his school achieved had no lasting effect in the history of the development of legal philosophy.

In describing the contribution of the analytical school, Pound writes:

> The English utilitarians did not contribute much of moment to the theory of the end of the legal order. they merely strengthened in the minds of the lawyers the extreme individualism which the latter had inherited with the common-law tradition. Perhaps their most significant achievement was in definitely driving the eighteenth century law of nature out of English books.[119]

Nineteenth Century Conclusion

Pound observes that the nineteenth century analytical school examined only mature legal orders, and on the basis of this examination sought to derive universally applicable principles.[120] It attempted to view all legal orders within this narrow and fixed frame of reference,[121] and to explain the pattern and process of all legal development within its scope of inquiry.[122] The analytical school further assumed that law and morality were totally separate phenomena and that law could be understood without reference to morality.[123]

The historical school engaged in a comparative study of legal systems, and argued that law was a result of given historical development. Examining its development would reveal that which was universal in the law since these principles would be embodied in the legal precepts of the people being studied.[124]

The philosophical school predicated its examination of the law on the notion that the principles of right and justice are the only criteria that should be used in examining legal development, and that proper principles of law would reflect such principles of right and justice.[125]

In evaluating these three schools, Pound concludes that they each had as the center of their philosophy the idea of abstract liberty which the law was to protect.[126] Despite the weaknesses of these nineteenth century schools of legal philosophy, Pound was willing to give them importance, for, he says:

> the juristic thought of that time was not wholly in vain. It may teach us that there are inherent limitations upon the efficacy of effort in conscious lawmaking; that for the greatest part law must always be found through application of reason to causes as they arise and the testing of principles in their actual operation; that laws are not like clothes to be thrown off and replaced at will, but, like language, are so intimately a part of all we do that development of the traditional materials will always be the chief agency of growth. Used to temper the enthusiasm of a new period of liberalization, the philosophy of law of the last century may yet save us from the excesses of the stage of equity and natural law, a reaction wherefrom had so much to do with the rigidity of the law under which we live.[127]

Pound believed that the most productive and important legal philosopher in the nineteenth century was Rudolph Jhering. Jhering, he feels, is the legal philosopher who set the stage for the development of sociological jurisprudence, since his influence is to be found in "...every form of social legislation."[128] Jhering developed the theory of interests, which Pound himself adopted, as the most effective and reasonable method of explaining the operation of law, and prescribing its purpose.[129] Legal theory of the nineteenth century provided the impetus for the abandonment of the maturity of law and acceptance of the socialization of law. This development, in Pound's opinion, was essential so that law might meet its responsibility of maintaining and furthering civilization.

ENDNOTES

CHAPTER FOUR

1. Pound, *Vol. 1*, pp. 502-503. *Vol. 2*, pp. 52-53 See also: Pound, *Spirit...*, p. 148.

2. Pound, *Vol. 1*, p. 502. See also: Pound, *Spirit...*, p. 146. Pound, *The Ideal Element...Tagore*, p. 151. Pound, "Theories...," p. 132. Pound, *Interpretations of Legal...*, pp. 28-29.

3. Pound, *Interpretations of Legal...*, pp. 28-29. See also: Pound , *Spirit...*, p. 147. Pound, *The Ideal Element...Tagore*, p. 155-156. Pound, "Theories...," pp. 132-133. Pound, *Vol. 1*, p. 502. Pound, "The End of Law...Juristic Thought...II," pp. 202-203.

4. Pound, *Interpretations of Legal...*, pp. 29-30. See also: Pound, *Vol. 2*, p. 57. Pound, *Spirit...*, p. 148. Pound, "Theories...," p. 133. Pound, "The End of Law...Juristic Thought," p. 204. Pound, "Political and Economic...," pp. 94-105, p. 99.

5. Pound, *Vol. 1*, pp. 502-503. See also: Pound, *Vol. 2*, pp. 52-53. Pound, *Spirit...*, p. 146-148, 152-153. Pound, *The Ideal Element...Tagore*, p. 152. Pound, "Theories...," pp. 132-133. Pound, "The End of Law...Juristic Thought," p. 204-205.

6. Pound, *Vol. 1*, p. 504. See also: Pound, "Theories...," p. 132. Pound, *Vol. 2*, pp. 56-57. Pound, "The End of Law...Juristic Thought II," p. 201. Roscoe Pound, "The Scope and Purpose of Sociological Jurisprudence, I," Vol. 24, June, 1911, *Harvard Law Review*, pp. 591-619, pp. 591-592. Vol. 1 PB 199. (Hereinafter referred to as "Scope and Purpose...I"). Pound, *Law...Morals*.

7. Pound, *Spirit...*, pp. 153-154. See also: Pound, *The Ideal Element...Tagore*, p. 163. Pound, "Scope and Purpose...I," p. 599. Pound, *Vol. 2*, pp. 56-57. Pound, "Theories...," pp. 133-135. Pound, *Law...Morals*, pp. 1-42. Pound, *interpretations of Legal...*, pp. 34-35. Pound, "The End of Law...Juristic Thought II," p. 221. Roscoe Pound, "Law and the Science of Law in Recent

Theories," Vol. 43, February, 1934, *Yale Law Journal*, pp. 525-536. Vol. 1 PB 199. (Hereinafter referred to as "Law...Science...Recent...").

8. Pound, *Interpretations of Legal...*, pp. 9-10. See also: R. Pound. "Scope and Purpose...I," pp. 591, 599. Pound, *The Ideal Element...Tagore*, pp. 162-163. Pound, "The Political...Interpretations...," p. 99. Pound, *Vol. 2*, pp. 56-57. Pound, *Vol. 1*, pp. 81-82. Pound, "Theories...," pp. 133-135. Pound, *Law...Morals*, pp. 1-42. Pound, "The End of Law...Juristic Thought II," pp. 209-210.

9. Pound, *Vol. 1*, p. 82. See also: Pound, *The Ideal Element...Tagore*, p. 132. Pound, "Law...Science...Recent...," p. 527. Pound, Vol. 2, pp. 63-64. Pound, *Spirit...*, pp. 152-154. Pound, "Scope and Purpose...I," p. 599. Pound, *Law...Morals*, pp. 1-41. Roscoe Pound, "Jurisprudence" *Research in the Social Sciences, Its Fundamental Methods and Objectives*. New York, The Macmillan Co., 1929. p. 186. Vol. 1 PB 168.

10. Pound, *Spirit...*, p. 33. See also: Pound, *Law...Morals*, pp. 1-42.

11. Pound, *Vol. 1*, p. 83. See also: Pound, "Scope and Purpose...I," pp. 599-600. Pound, *Spirit...*, p. 155. Pound, "Law...Science...Recent...," p. 527. Pound, *Law...Morals*, pp. 1-42. Pound, "The End of Law...Juristic Thought II," pp. 208-210.

12. Pound, *Vol. 2*, p. 169. See also: Pound, *Interpretations of Legal...*, p. 18. Pound, *Spirit...*, p. 155. Pound, *The Ideal Element...Tagore*, pp. 284-285. Pound, *Law...Morals*, pp 1-42.

13. Pound, *Vol. 1*, p. 85. See also: Pound, "The Scope and Purpose...I," p. 599. Pound, "The Political...Interpretations...," p. 99. Pound, "Law...Science...Recent...," p. 527. Pound, *Spirit...*, p. 155. Pound, "Theories...," pp. 136-137. Pound, *Law...Morals*. pp. 1-42. Pound, "The End of Law...Juristic Thought II," pp. 208-210.

14. Pound, *Vol. 1*, p. 85. See also: Pound, *Vol. 3*, pp. 728-730. Pound, "Scope and Purpose...I," pp. 599-600. Pound, *Interpretations of Legal...*, p. 14. Pound, "Theories...," pp. 136-137. Pound, *Law...Morals*, pp. 1-42.

15. Pound, *Spirit...*, p. 156. See also: Pound, *Law...Morals*, pp. 1-42. Pound, "The End of Law...Juristic Thought II," pp. 221-222.

16. Pound, *Vol. 2*, p. 113-188. See also: Pound, *Spirit...*, p. 155. Pound, "Law...Science...Recent...," p. 527. Pound, *Interpretations of Legal...*, pp. 8-9. Pound, "Theories...," pp. 140-143. Pound, *Law...Morals*, pp. 1-42.

17. Pound, *Vol. 3*, pp. 390-391. See also: Pound, *Spirit...*, p. 155. Pound, *Vol. 2*, p. 171. Pound, *Vol. 1*, pp. 85-86. Pound, "Theories...," pp. 140-143. Pound, *Law...Morals*, pp. 1-42. Pound, "The End of Law...Juristic Thought II," pp. 220-222.

18. Pound, *Vol. 2*, pp. 172-173. See also: Pound, *Vol. 1*, pp. 85-86. Pound, "Scope and Purpose...I," pp. 598-604. Pound, "Theories...," pp. 140-143. Pound, *Law...Morals*, pp. 1-42.

19. Pound, *Vol. 2*, pp. 142-148, 183. See also: Pound, *Task...*, p. 61. Pound, *Vol. 1*, p. 71. Pound, "Scope and Purpose...I," p. 604. Pound, *Law...Morals*, pp. 1-42.

20. Pound, "Scope and Purpose...I," p. 603. See also: Pound, *Task...*, p. 61. Pound, "Law...Science...Recent...," p. 527. Pound, *Interpretations of Legal...*, p. 68. Pound, *Law...Morals*, pp. 1-42. Pound, "The End of Law...Juristic Thought II," pp. 224-225.

21. Pound, *Vol. 1*, pp. 86-87. See also: Pound, "Scope and Purpose...I," pp. 599-600. Pound, *Task...*, p. 64. Pound, "Law...Science...Recent...," p. 527. Pound, *Law...Morals*, pp. 1-42.

22. Pound, *Vol. 2*, pp. 174-175. See also: Pound, *Vol. 1*, pp. 86-87. Pound, *Law...Morals*, pp. 22-23. Pound, "Theories...," p. 137. Pound, *Interpretations of Legal...*, p. 18. Pound, *Law...Morals*, pp. 1-42.

23. Pound, *Vol. 2*, p. 175. See also: Pound, *Law...Morals*, pp. 22-23. Pound, *Vol. 1*, pp. 86-87. Pound, "Theories..." p. 137. Pound, *Interpretations of Legal...*, p. 18. Pound, *Law...Morals*, pp. 1-42.

24. Pound, *Vol. 2*, p. 176. See also: Pound, "Scope and Purpose...I," pp. 599-600. Pound, *Interpretations of Legal...*, p. 18. Pound, *Law...Morals*, pp. 1-42.

25. Pound, *Vol. 2*, p. 175-183. See also: Pound, *Law...Morals*, pp. 1-42.

26. Pound, *Vol. 2*, pp. 154-163, 177-178. See also: Pound, *Task...*, pp. 63-72. Pound, *Law...Morals*, pp. 1-42.

27. Pound, *Vol. 2*, p. 182. See also: Pound, *The Ideal Element...Tagore*, p. 53. Pound, *Social Control...*, p. 20. Pound, *Law...Morals*, pp. 1-42.

28. Pound, *Vol. 2*, p. 182. See also: Pound, *The Ideal Element...Tagore*, p. 53. Pound, *Social Control...*, p. 20. Pound, *Law...Morals*, pp. 1-42.

29. Pound, *Vol. 1*, pp. 86-87. See also: Pound, "Scope and Purpose...I," pp. 599-600. Pound, *Spirit...*, pp. 155-156. Pound, *Law...Morals*, pp. 1-42.

30. Pound, *Spirit...*, p. 155. See also: Pound, *Interpretations of Legal...*, p. 18. Pound, *Vol. 1*, pp. 518-519. Pound, *Law...Morals*, pp. 1-42.

31. Pound, *Vol. 1*, p. 87. See also: Pound, *Spirit...*, pp. 152-156. Pound, *Interpretations of Legal...*, pp. 17-18. Pound, "Scope and Purpose...I," p. 600. Pound, *Law...Morals*, pp. 1-42. Pound, "The End of Law...Juristic Thought II," pp. 209-210, 221-222.

32. Pound, *Vol. 1*, p. 87. See also: Pound, "Scope and Purpose...I," pp. 599-600. Pound, *Interpretations of Legal...*, pp. 17-18. Pound, *Spirit...*, pp. 152-156. Pound, *Law...Morals*, pp. 1-42. Pound, "The End of Law...Juristic Thought II," pp. 209-210, 221-222.

33. Pound, *Interpretations of Legal...*, p. 31. See also: Pound, *The Ideal Element... Tagore*, pp. 161-162. Pound, *Vol. 1*, p. 518. Pound, "Scope and Purpose...I," pp.600-601. Pound, *Law...Morals*, pp. 1-42.

34. Pound, *Vol. 1*, p. 519. See also: Pound, *Spirit...*, pp. 151-152. Pound, "Theories...," pp. 133-134. Pound, *Law...Morals*, pp. 1-42. Pound, "The End of Law...Juristic Thought II," pp. 221-222.

35. Pound, "Scope and Purpose...I," p. 600. See also: Pound, *Interpretations of Legal...*, pp. 17-18. Pound, *Spirit...*, pp. 55-56. Pound, *Law...Morals*, pp. 1-42.

36. *Supra*, Chapter One On Legal History. See also: Pound, *Law...Morals*, pp. 1-42.

37. Pound, *Vol. 2*, p. 221. See also: Pound, *The Ideal Element...Tagore*, pp. 57-58, 70-71, 74. Pound, *Law...Morals*, pp. 1-42.

38. Pound, *Vol. 1*, pp. 519-520. See also: Pound, *Interpretations of Legal...*, pp. 17-18. Pound, *Law...Morals*, pp. 1-42. Pound, "The End of Law...Juristic Thought II," pp. 221-222.

39. Quoted in Pound "Scope and Purpose...I," p. 603.

40. Pound, *The Ideal Element...Tagore*, p. 163. See also: Pound, *Law...Morals*, pp. 1-41. Pound, "Scope and Purpose...I," pp. 60-601. Pound, *Law...Morals*, pp. 1-42. Pound, "The End of Law...Juristic Thought II," pp. 205-206.

41. Pound, *Interpretations of Legal...*, p. 69. See also: Pound, *Spirit...*, p. 152. Pound, *Law...Morals*, pp. 89-117.

42. Pound, *Interpretations of Legal...*, p. 34. See also: "The Political...Interpretations...," p. 99. Pound, *Spirit...*, p. 156. Pound, *Law...Morals*, pp. 89-117. Pound, "The End of Law...Juristic Thought," pp. 206-207.

43. Pound, *Vol. 1*, p. 88. See also: Pound, *The Ideal Element...Tagore*, pp. 43, 58. Pound, *Law...Morals*, pp. 89-117. Pound, "Scope and Purpose...I," pp 604-605. Pound, "The End of Law...Juristic Thought," pp. 206-207.

44. Pound, "Scope and Purpose...I," p. 608.

45. Pound, *The Ideal Element...Tagore*, p. 43. See also: Pound, *Vol. 1*, p. 89. Pound, *Spirit...*, p. 145. Pound, "Scope and Purpose...I," p. 606. Pound, "Law..Science...Recent...," p. 528. Pound, *Law...Morals*, pp. 89-117.

46. Pound, *Vol. 1*, p. 90. See also: Pound, *The Ideal Element...Tagore*, p. 163. Pound, *Spirit...*, p. 145. Pound, "Scope and Purpose...I," p. 606. Pound, "The Political...Interpretations...," p. 79. Pound, "Law...Science...Recent...," p. 528. Pound, *Law...Morals*, pp. 89-117. Pound, "The End of Law...Juristic Thought II," pp. 221-222.

47. Pound, *Vol. 1*, p. 90. See also: Pound, "Scope and Purpose...I," p. 606. Pound, *Law...Morals*, pp. 89-117.

48. Pound, *Vol. 1*, p. 90. See also: Pound, "Scope and Purpose...I," p. 606. Pound, *Law...Morals*, pp. 89-117.

49. Pound, *Vol. 1*, p. 92. See also: Pound, "Scope and Purpose...I," pp. 606-607. Pound, *Law...Morals*, pp. 89-117.

50. Pound, *Vol. 1*, p. 508. See also: Pound, *The Ideal Element...Tagore*, p. 165. Pound, *Law...Morals*, pp. 89-117. Pound, "The End of Law...Juristic Thought II," pp. 205-206.

51. Pound, *The Ideal Element...Tagore*, p. 155. See also: Pound, *Vol. 1*, p. 508. Pound, *Spirit...*, pp. 145,147,152-153. Pound, *Interpretations of Legal...*, pp. 28-30.

52. Pound, *Spirit...*, p. 152. See also: Pound, *Interpretations of Legal...*, pp. 32-33. Pound, *The Ideal Element...Tagore*, p. 52. Pound, *Law...Morals*, pp. 89-117. Pound, "The End of Law...Juristic Thought II," pp. 202-205.

53. Pound, *Vol. 1*, p. 509. See also: Pound, "Scope and Purpose...I," pp. 609-610. Pound, *Law...Morals*, pp. 89-117. Pound, *The Ideal Element...Tagore*, pp. 155-158. Pound, "The End of Law...Juristic Thought II," pp. 202-205.

54. Pound, *Vol. 1*, p. 509. See also: Pound, "Scope and Purpose...I," p. 610. Pound, *Law...Morals*, pp. 89-117. Pound, *The Ideal Element...Tagore*, pp. 155-158. Pound, "The End of Law...Juristic Thought II," pp. 202-205.

55. Pound, *Vol. 1*, p. 510. See also: Pound, *Law...Morals*, pp. 89-117. Pound, *The Ideal Element...Tagore*, p. 167.

56. Pound, *The Ideal Element...Tagore*, p. 157. See also: Pound, *Vol. 1*, pp. 510-511. Pound, *Law...Morals*, pp. 89-117. Pound, "The End of Law...Juristic Thought II," pp. 202-205.

57. Pound, *The Ideal Element...Tagore*, p. 157. See also: Pound, *Vol. 1*, pp. 510-511. Pound, *Law...Morals*, pp. 89-117.

58. Pound, *Vol. 2*, p. 184. See also: Pound, *Spirit...*, p. 155. Pound, *Law...Morals*, pp. 89-117. Pound, "The End of Law...Juristic Thought II," pp. 202-205.

59. Pound, *Vol. 2*, pp. 184-185. See also: Pound, *The Ideal Element...Tagore*, p. 179. Pound, *Law...Morals*, pp. 89-117.

60. Pound, *Vol. 2*, p. 185. See also: Pound, *The Ideal Element...Tagore*, pp. 45, 186. Pound, *Interpretations of Legal...*, pp. 148-149.

61. Pound, *Vol. 2*, p. 185. See also: Pound, *The Ideal Element...Tagore*, p. 45. Pound, *Interpretations of Legal...*, pp. 148-149.

62. Pound, *Vol. 2*, p. 186. See also: Pound, *Interpretations of Legal...*, pp. 142-145. Pound, *The Ideal Element...Tagore*, p. 45.

63. Pound, *Vol. 2*, pp. 223-224. See also: Pound, "Scope and Purpose...I," pp. 608-609. Pound, *Law...Morals*, pp. 89-117.

64. *Supra*, Chapter One Legal History. See also: Pound, *Vol. 2*, pp. 223-224. Pound, *Law...Morals*, pp. 91-93, 106-108.

65. Pound, *Vol. 2*, pp. 223-224. See also: Pound, *The Ideal Element...Tagore*, p. 58.

66. Pound, *Vol. 2*, p. 225. See also: Pound, *The Ideal Element...Tagore*, p. 58. Pound, *Law...Morals*, pp. 93-96.

67. Pound, *Vol. 2*, p. 225. See also: Pound, *The Ideal Element...Tagore*, p. 58. Pound, *Law...Morals*, pp. 89-92. Pound, "The End of Law...Juristic Thought II," pp. 204-205.

68. Pound, *The Ideal Element...Tagore*, p. 156. See also: Pound, *Vol. 2*, p. 226. Pound, *Law...Morals*, pp. 104-108. Pound, "The End of Law...Juristic Thought II," pp. 202-205.

69. Pound, *Vol. 2*, pp. 226-227. See also: Pound, *The Ideal Element...Tagore*, p. 157. Pound, *Law...Morals*, pp. 103-108.

70. Pound, *Vol. 2*, p. 228. See also: Pound, *The Ideal Element...Tagore*, p. 157. Pound, *Law...Morals*, pp. 106-108.

71. Pound, *Vol. 2*, pp. 228-229. 228-229. See also: Pound, *The Ideal Element...Tagore*, p. 157. Pound, *Law...Morals*, pp. 101-105.

72. Pound, "Scope and Purpose...I," p. 608. See also: Pound, *Vol. 2*, pp. 224-226. Pound, *Law...Morals*, pp. 89-117. Pound, *Vol. 1*, pp. 87-89. Pound, "The End of Law...Juristic Thought II," pp. 221-222.

73. Pound, "Scope and Purpose...I," pp. 608-609. See also: Pound, "The End of Law...Juristic Thought II," pp. 221-222.

74. Pound, "The Scope and Purpose...I," pp. 610-611. See also: Pound, *Vol. 1*, pp. 112-117. Pound, *Law...Morals*, pp. 89-117.

75. Pound, "The Scope and Purpose...I," pp. 607-608. See also: Pound, *Vol. 1*, pp. 107-110.

76. Pound, *Vol. 1*, p. 55. See also: Pound, *The Ideal Element...Tagore*, pp. 14-15. Pound, "Scope and Purpose...I," p. 596. Pound, *Law...Morals*, pp. 43-88.

77. Pound, *Vol. 1*, p. 77. See also: Pound, "Scope and Purpose...I," pp. 591, 596. Pound, "The End of Law...Juristic Thought II," pp. 207-208.

78. Pound, *Vol. 1*, pp. 516-518. See also: Pound, *Vol. 2*, pp. 71-76, 511-518.

79. Pound, *Vol. 2*, pp. 132-133. See also: Pound, *Law...Morals*, pp. 45-50.

80. Pound, *Vol. 2*, pp. 132-133. See also: Pound, *Interpretations of Legal...*, pp. 25-26, 45-46. Pound, *Law...Morals*, pp. 42-45. Pound, "Theories...," pp. 132-133. Pound, "Scope and Purpose...I," pp. 595-597.

81. Pound, *Justice According...*, p. 60. See also: Roscoe Pound, "The Progress of the Law—Analytical Jurisprudence, 1914-1917," Vol. 41, *Harvard Law Review*, December, 1927, p. 181. Vol. 1 PB 154. (Hereinafter referred to as "Analytical Jurisprudence...").

82. Pound, *Law...Morals*, pp. 48-49. See also: Pound, *Vol. 2*, pp. 114, 148-149, 150-151.

83. Pound, *The Ideal Element...Tagore*, pp. 15-16. See also: Pound, "Analytical Jurisprudence...," pp. 181-182. Pound, "Scope and Purpose...I," pp. 595-596.

84. Pound, *Vol. 2*, pp. 135, 149-151. See also: Pound, *Law...Morals*, p. 49-50. Pound, *Vol. 1*, p. 77. Pound, "Scope and Purpose...I," pp. 596-598.

85. Pound, *Task...*, p. 43. See also: Pound, *Vol. 2*, p. 136. Pound, *Law...Morals*, pp. 51-54. Pound, *Vol. 1*, p. 76. Pound, "Scope and Purpose...I," pp. 596-597.

86. Pound, "Scope and Purpose...I," p. 596. See also: Pound, *Vol. 2*, p. 135-136. Pound, "Analytical Jurisprudence...," p. 181. Pound, *Vol. 1*, p. 76. Pound, *Law...Morals*, pp. 43-88.

87. Pound, *Vol. 2*, p. 136. See also: Pound, "The End of Law...Juristic Thought II," pp. 217-220.

88. Pound, *Vol. 2*, p. 136. See also: Pound, *Law...Morals*, pp. 50-62. Pound, *Vol. 1*, pp. 75-76. Pound, *The Ideal Element...Tagore*, pp. 14-15. Pound, "Scope and Purpose...I," pp. 596-597. Chapter Eight Judicial Justice.

89. Pound, *The Ideal Element...Tagore*, pp. 14-15. See also: Pound, *Interpretations of Legal...*, pp. 25-26. Pound, "Analytical Jurisprudence...," pp. 181-182. Pound, "Scope and Purpose...I," pp. 595-596.

90. Pound, *Vol. 2*, p. 137. See also: Pound, "The End of Law...Juristic Thought II," pp. 208-212.

91. Pound, *Interpretations of Legal...*, p. 26. See also: Pound, *Law...Morals*, pp. 43-46. Pound, *Vol. 2*, pp. 136-140.

92. Pound, *The Ideal Element...Tagore*, p. 46. See also: Pound, *Interpretations of Legal...*, pp. 25-26. Pound, *Law...Morals*, p. 45-50.

93. Pound, *Vol. 2,* p. 137.

94. Pound, *Interpretations of Legal...*, p. 26. See also: Pound, *Law...Morals*, pp. 43-46. Pound, *Vol. 2*, pp. 136-140.

95. Pound, *Law...Morals*, p. 45.

96. Pound, *Vol. 2*, pp. 138, 140-141. See also: Pound, *Law...Morals*, p. 46-47, 54-56.

97. Pound, *Law...Morals*, pp. 62-63. See also: Pound, *Vol. 2*, p. 138. Pound, *The Ideal Element...Tagore*, pp. 14-15.

98. Pound, *Vol. 2*, p. 147. See also: Pound, *Law...Morals*, pp. 65-67.

99. Pound, *Vol. 2*, p. 147.

100. Pound, "Scope and Purpose...I," p. 598.

101. Pound, *The Ideal Element...Tagore*, pp. 16-21.

102. Pound, *The Ideal Element...Tagore*, p. 16.

103. Pound, *Vol. 2*, p. 140.

104. Pound, *Vol. 2*, p. 151.

105. Pound, *Vol. 2*, pp. 152-153. See also: Pound, *Law...Morals*, pp. 53-60.

106. Pound, *Law...Morals*, p. 71. See also: Pound, *Interpretations of Legal...*, pp. 45-46.

107. Pound, *Vol. 2*, p. 152.

108. See Chapter Eight: Administrative Law.

109. Pound, *Vol. 2*, pp. 154-156. See also: Pound, *The Ideal Element...Tagore*, pp. 16-17. Pound, *Introduction...*, pp. 54-56, 65-69. Pound, *Law...Morals*, pp. 60-62.

110. Pound, *Vol. 2*, p. 154.

111. Pound, *Law...Morals*, pp. 70-71.

112. Pound, *Law...Morals*, pp. 71-74.

113. Pound, *Vol. 2*, pp. 154-156.

114. Pound, *Social Control...*, pp. 32-33.

115. Pound, *Social Control...*, pp. 54-60.

116. Pound, *Vol. 1*, p. 514.

117. Pound, *Vol. 1*, p. 514.

118. Pound, *The Ideal Element...Tagore*, p. 14.

119. Pound, *Vol. 1*, p. 516.

120. Pound, *The Ideal Element...Tagore*, pp. 14-15. See also: Pound, *Vol. 1*, p. 81. Pound, "Law...Science...Recent...," pp. 527-530. Pound, *Interpretations of Legal...*, pp. 129-130. Pound, *Law...Morals*, pp. 42-88.

121. Pound, *Vol. 1*, p. 81. See also: Pound, *Interpretations of Legal...*, pp. 129-130. Pound, *The Ideal Element...Tagore*, pp. 14-15. Pound, "Law...Science...Recent...," pp. 527-530. Pound, *Law...Morals*, pp. 42-88.

122. Pound, *Interpretations of Legal...*, pp. 129-130. See also: Pound, *Vol. 1*, pp. 80-81. Pound, *The Ideal Element...Tagore*, pp. 14-15. Pound, "Law...Science...Recent...," pp. 527-530. Pound, *Law...Morals*, pp. 42-88.

123. Pound, *Vol. 1*, p. 81. See also: Pound, *Law...Morals*, pp. 42-88. Pound, "Law..Science..Recent..," pp. 527-530. Pound, *Interpretations of Legal...*, pp. 129-130. Pound, *The Ideal Element...Tagore*, pp. 14-15. Pound, *Law...Morals*, pp. 42-88.

124. Pound, *Vol. 1*, pp. 81-82. See also: Pound, "Law...Science...Recent...," pp. 527-530. Pound, *Law...Morals*, pp. 1-42.

125. Pound, *Vol. 1*, p. 82. See also: Pound, *Law...Morals*, pp. 88-117. Pound, "Law...Science...Recent...," pp. 527-530.

126. Pound, *The Ideal Element...Tagore*, pp. 162-163. See also: Pound, *Vol. 1*, p. 519.

127. Pound, *Spirit...*, p. 165.

128. Pound, *Vol. 1*, pp. 429-430. See further treatment of Jhering in Chapter Five: Legal Philosophy in the Twentieth Century.

129. See Chapter Seven: Theory of Interests.

CHAPTER FIVE

LEGAL PHILOSOPHY—TWENTIETH CENTURY

According to Pound, the concept of liberty of human action dominated legal thought from the sixteenth to the nineteenth centuries. The prevailing notion argued that law should interfere only minimally with individual liberty. Ultimately this line of argument, Pound says:

> was used as a stabilizing idea, as in the latter part of the nineteenth century, when men proved that law was an evil, even if a necessary evil, that there should be as little law made as possible, since all law involved restraint upon free exertion of the will, and hence that jurist and legislator should be content to leave things legal as they are and allow the individual "to work out in freedom his own happiness or misery" on that basis.[1]

Pound is convinced that this emphasis on free individual will and action was unsuited to the circumstances prevailing at the end of the nineteenth century, since the former agrarian and rural societies disappeared and were replaced by complex and highly industrial ones. Although Pound is not an economic determinist, he feels that the altered needs of society attending this change, resulted in the emergence of new interests which sought recognition and protection by the law.[2] In light of this situation changes were required in how the law would respond to these new conditions and also, new thinking about the law was needed. These factors required a break with the ideas and practices which had prevailed in the nineteenth century. Therefore, according to Pound, legal thought became concerned with evaluating the law's role in satisfying human wants, in place of its previous concern with the liberation of human wills. Jurists, he says:

> began to think of the end of law, not as a maximum of self-assertion, but as a maximum satisfaction of wants. Hence, for a time they thought of the problem of ethics, of jurisprudence, and of politics as chiefly one of valuing; as a problem of finding criteria of the relative value of interests. In jurisprudence and politics they saw that we must add practical problems

> of the possibility of making interests effective through government action, judicial or administrative.[3]

These new needs and emphases altered the views of law's role, and the nature of the ends which the law should serve.[4] Pound classifies these developments into three broad streams of philosophic development—social-philosophical jurisprudence,[5] realist jurisprudence (including economic determinism),[6] and sociological jurisprudence.[7]

Social Philosophical Schools

Pound divides the social philosophical school into five branches: social utilitarian, neo-Kantian, neo-Hegelian, neo-Idealist, and Natural law revivalists.[8]

Social Utilitarian

Social utilitarian thought departed from most nineteenth century legal thought, in viewing the law's role as dealing with:

> a continually wider and broader recognition and securing of social interests, that is, of the claims and demands involved in the existence of civilized society, not the least of which is the social interest in the individual life.[9]

The contribution of social utilitarian thought served legal philosophy beneficially in three different ways, according to Pound. First, he maintains, social utilitarian inquiry improved the understanding of legal history, by focusing on the phenomena of social interests which the law should protect, and rejected the idea that the purpose of law is to protect some notion of "abstract individual liberty."[10] Second, social utilitarian theory was grounded, in part, on the belief that, in order to understand the operation of law historically, one must evaluate the role it played in securing social interests.[11] Third, Pound says:

> as a result of social utilitarianism the legal reason of today in shaping rules and developing traditional premises of the legal system in order to give effect to social interests, looks at them in terms of the concrete situation, not in terms of the abstract claims of abstract human beings.[12]

Pound argues that social-utilitarian thought advanced legal theory when it rejected the notion that evaluation of the effectiveness of law was to be done within a self-contained framework without reference to the larger social task the law was to perform. In looking to standards external to the law itself, the social utilitarians created effective means by which the efficacy of the law could be evaluated and measured.[13] Although modern social utilitarian thought had its intellectual roots in Benthamite Utilitarianism, Pound applauds this school's rejection of the Benthamite assumption that law is designed to serve abstract human liberty, and its emphasis on the role of the law in recognizing and serving social interests.[14]

Pound considers Rudolph Jhering as being the major figure in the development of social utilitarian thought, and the one who most advanced the notion of the role of the law as the protector of social interests, and who, further, linked this role of the law with ethical considerations.[15]

According to social utilitarians, the evaluation of the effectiveness and efficacy of the law is to be accomplished by determining how well it serves the social needs of the society.[16] According to social utilitarian theory, legal precepts are developed in order to aid in reconciling conflicting claims in the society. Consequently, these precepts are to be understood in light of their historical development, and not predicated on some theory of abstract, theoretical conceptions.[17] According to social utilitarians, therefore, legal precepts and legal conceptions are fashioned in response to given circumstances in order that they might deal effectively with pressing needs within the society, and provide practical standards which can be employed in measuring the relative success of the law in performing its major tasks.[18]

According to Pound, there were five important features in Jhering's thought. First, Jhering's theory required the abandonment of the "jurisprudence of conceptions,"[19] which, Pound says, was dominant in nineteenth century legal thought and required that decisions be made to conform to preconceived standards without regard to outcome. Pound notes:

> The result in the particular case was immaterial. The case was to be fitted to the conception after the Manner of Procrustes—Jhering said that the legal conception of the historical school required a world of their own in which they existed wholly for themselves, far from every connection with life.... They were abstract creations with no relation to the life of the past or to that of the present.[20]

The actual and concrete conditions existing in a given society at a given time constituted the focus of Jhering's inquiry, and he held that law's value could be determined by how well it operated to improve the conditions existing in a given society, and, therefore, jurisprudence must be anchored in reality and the measure of success of:

> legal precepts and doctrines and institutions [must be made] with reference to how they work or fail to work and why.[21]

Pound is impressed with the fact that Jhering's theory focuses on law and legal institutions that are consciously fashioned to serve particular purposes and ends. Jhering believed that explaining law's purpose was essential if legal philosophy was to be of any value, since he believed that law fashioned the prevailing notions of right and wrong in a given society. Therefore, Jhering felt: "Law knows but one source—the practical one of purpose."[22]

Second, Jehring felt that the concern of properly framed law, is the protection of interests in a society, and that rights were to be measured and valued only in terms of how well they served these interests.[23] Jhering's view stood in stark contrast to nineteenth century legal thought which had placed rights at the center of the inquiry. Pound notes:

> Whereas the eighteenth century conceived of law as something which the individual worked against society, the idea of our American Bill of Rights, Jhering taught that it was something created by society, through which individuals found a means of securing his [sic] interests, so far as society recognized them...The conception of law as a securing of interests or a protecting of relations has all but universally superseded the individualist theory.[24]

Third, Pound feels that Jhering's contribution in the field of criminal law was beneficial and realistic. Jhering considered that the role of criminal law was not to ratify some abstract ideal but rather it is properly used to serve determinant social ends. This agreement, Pound argues, provides a refreshing change from the nineteenth century notion of using criminal law for pure retribution without concern for the impact such law would have in reshaping and developing society.[25] Pound notes that Jhering's view of criminal provided a:

> means to social ends; [and argued] that punishment must be governed by its social end and must be fixed with reference to the future rather than to the past.[26]

Fourth, Jehring's theory of law placed much less attention on the role of tradition in the law than had nineteenth century theory. For Jhering the law was an instrument to be used creatively in dealing with issues as they emerged in a society, and not an instrument which had as its only or major function the preservation of tradition.[27]

Fifth, and what Pound feels to be Jehring's major contribution, is his belief that the law must deal with each individual case in order to achieve equitable results. According to Pound, this "administrative element" provided the degree of flexibility the law needed to deal with the new issues and interests that were present in complex, industrial societies.[28] According to Pound the law could not have met such new conditions without providing some method for the law to become flexible in developing solutions to these issues and meeting the expectations of such interests.[29]

For these reasons Pound feels that Jhering is properly designated as the founder of the social-utilitarian school. The general idea of this school is that the law is something to be created in society to deal with emerging interests in an industrial age and provide for their recognition and protection.[30] As Pound observes:

> Jhering called creative juristic science by the suggestive name of juristic chemistry. That is, it is a combining of chosen elements of the law, as it were, to make new compounds. But it often goes further and brings in elements from without and develops them by analogy or combines them with elements at hand in the law to make even more novel compounds. Instead of these compounds resulting from the unfolding of an idea, they are oftenest the result of endeavor to provide for a concrete case, leading to the application of a concrete solution behind which others proceed to put tentative generalizations until finally the more inclusive order is worked out. Thus, when we look back at it we say that an idea was realizing. But the idea served after the event to order and arrange and make it intelligible. It had no part in the creation which was the act of a man seeking to satisfy a demand.[31]

Pound appreciates the contributions Jhering made in legal philosophy, but he is aware of the weaknesses in Jhering's argument. First of all, Pound objects to what he calls the "teleological utilitarianism" of Jhering's thought. This weakness, he feels, too easily joins together the "is" and the "ought" of law in its attempt to identify the advantages which men seek to obtain with the use of the law. As Pound notes:

> These "needs" [identified by Jhering] are not so much what men claim they need or actually need as they are what the philosopher thought they ought to need.[32]

This teleological focus in Jhering's thought, Pound argues, greatly weakens the descriptive and analytical value of his theory because of the personalized influence such views have on evaluating the material being examined.[33]

Second, Pound believes that what men wish to have protected by the law varies and alters in the course of time, while Jhering's approach assumes that that which is pursued is known and determines the end which law should serve. Pound feels that the reality of men's search for improving and refashioning the society in which they live is much less determinate than Jhering assumes, and this fact weakens the analytical value of Jhering's thought.[34]

Third, although Pound believed that nineteenth century thought had focused too much on the role of institutions in the operation of the law, he felt that Jhering had erred too far in the other direction and had ignored almost completely the role institutions play in the construction and operation of the law. Jhering's exclusive focus was on the nature of the interests which sought protection by the law and thus he ignored the vital issue of how institutions served in recognizing and protecting such interests. Ignoring the role of institutions in the operation of the law, Pound feels, also weakened the analytical value of Jhering's thought.[35]

Finally, Pound appreciates Jhering's attention to the importance and value of the individualization of justice which, he feels, enables law to fulfill its necessary task in a modern, industrial age. However, he points out that Jhering's overemphasis on this individualization, ignored the importance of settled, and general principles and precepts which constitute an essential part of a desirable legal order. Consequently, Pound concludes that although Jhering's contributions were considerable, his theory was one which was more a theory of "making" law than it was a theory that explained law's complex and varied reality.[36]

There is no doubt that Pound considers Jhering to be a major figure in the development of legal philosophy. However, Pound argues, that Jhering's thought is properly viewed as a part of the social utilitarian school which is really:

> an element in thought of social-philosophical schools rather than the method of a subsisting school.[37]

The major contribution of Jhering and other social utilitarians is their rejection of the nineteenth century's infatuation with abstract legal ideas—particularly the abstract theory of liberty which was so dominant. Discarding such notions enabled the social utilitarians to view realistically the nature and role of law and develop legal philosophy that could contribute constructively to fashioning and explaining the law. Thus, Pound observes:

> The function of legal history [in Jhering's thought] becomes... one of illustrating how rules and principles have met concrete situations in the past, and of enabling us to judge how we may deal with such situations in the present, rather than one of furnishing self-sufficient premises from which rules are to be obtained by rigid deduction.[38]

Jhering's contribution was not confined to the rejection of abstract legal thought, for his writing also contributed significantly to the development of sociological jurisprudence. Pound observes:

> In the latter part of the nineteenth century and in the present century, the influence of Jhering through his directing attention to the end of law and the rise of social philosophical and sociological jurisprudence led to a functional attitude toward the problems of jurisprudence—jurists began to think of a process or activity directed toward ends or purposes rather than state or condition, maintained by command of a sovereign.[39]

Neo-Kantian

The neo-Kantians' major concern was found in their attempt to fashion a legal philosophy which would explain how multiple individual wills operating in a society could be harmonized while serving to provide an ethical set of justifications for the operation and purpose of the law.[40]

Pound considers R. Stammler as the major spokesman of this school. Stammler, like all neo-Kantians, sought to restore the idea that there are ideals against which the value and efficacy of all law can be measured.[41] The concepts of reason and justice were to provide this focus,[42] and the value and efficacy of legal practices and precepts were to measured against these ideals.[43] This idea of the neo-Kantians differed from the nineteenth century notion of measuring law against the value of the abstract and free individual, since the twentieth century neo-Kantians focused on the nature of the ideals of justice and reason as they existed in a given time and place.[44] Stammler's focus, therefore, was on explaining the nature of a community of men all of whom had free will, and determining how justice could be achieved by harmonizing these free wills in order to achieve some broader, and more inclusive synthesis.[45]

Kant had been vitally concerned with the problem of reconciling individual free wills with social authority and had, according to Pound, resolved this problem by:

> formulating what has come to be known by the significant name of legal justice; by working out the idea of an equal chance to all, exactly as they are, with no artificial or extrinsic handicaps. In other words, he put a new philosophical foundation under the idea of justice as the maximum of individual self-assertion... and so enabled it to reach its final logical development in the law of the nineteenth century.[46]

The neo-Kantians, however, rejected Kant's emphasis on this notion of free will, and emphasized the social nature of individual action. Consequently, their solution posited that one could be concerned with individual wills only when viewed in the context of the interests of the society being examined. Thus, although freely willed actions could be taken they could be curbed. However, any limitations that were to be placed on the exercise of the individual's free will must not be done arbitrarily.[47] In order to preclude such arbitrariness Stammler suggests four fundamental principles should govern all legal action.

First, when individual will required limitation, such limitation should not be undertaken without a careful determination of why such limitation was needed, the purpose it would serve, and the scope of the limitation needed. These considerations were to be employed in order to assure that whatever the limitation, the maximum amount of freedom for all individuals in the society would be preserved consistent with the end the limitation was to serve.[48]

Second, in Stammler's theory, while the individual may be the object of legal demands, every care must be given to assure that such demands do not limit too severely another individual's scope of autonomy, since individual personal liberty is, in itself, valuable. Therefore, no one individual interest could be considered to be superior to the social interest of protecting all of the individuals in the society.[49] Pound feels that this idea of Stammler's is reflected in areas of the law that preserve certain properties and resources to debtor individuals, such as mandating the repayment of indebtedness by installments in place of compelling full repayment in one sum.[50]

Third, in a community of free willing individuals, all are to be guaranteed the opportunity to participate fully in the day to day operations of the society. Therefore, any exclusion from such participation must be done only after there has been:

> ...a reasoned weighing of the ends involved and [a] reasoned attempt to reconcile them.[51]

Pound feels that this notion is reflected in the use of criminal penalties which, although they deny to the convicted criminal choices others in the society may make, are justifiable on the basis that such exclusions are the result of the reasoned balancing of the interests involved.[52]

Fourth, when restrictions and punishments are adopted by a society in order to achieve certain ends, such restrictions and punishments must be humane in character and quality. Thus, in Stammler's theory brutal punishments and unlimited powers of control are excluded.[53]

Nineteenth century legal philosophy emphasized the need for general security in a society, and the law's role in preserving this security. Stammler's scheme of thought, while it embraces the need for general security, encompasses other valuable interests which the law is to protect.[54] Pound believes that the neo-Kantian notion of using values to measure the purposes and practices of the law has merit,[55] but that the weakness of this neo-Kantian theory lies in its overemphasis on logic. This overemphasis is revealed in the dogmatism of the neo-Kantian left whose major spokesman is Hans Kelsen.[56] Though the neo-Kantian left, and the neo-Kantian right—represented by Georgio Del Vecchio—are products of the same school of thought, they are substantially different in their arguments and conclusions. The neo-Kantian right, Pound maintains, considers the individual to be the measure of all things in evaluating the law's role and purpose, while the neo-Kantian left has become totally relativistic.[57]

In Pound's view the Neo-Kantian left, represented by Hans Kelsen, has been far more influential than the neo-Kantian right.[58] The neo-Kantian left has, in large measure, responded to three ideas most clearly formulated in the writings of Hans Kelsen, and these are:

> (1) the idea of jurisprudence as a normative science, that is, one having to do with what ought to be in contrast with the natural sciences which have to do with what is, and hence depend on observation and experiment;

> (2) the idea of a body of laws resting upon some ultimate and legally unchallengeable norms—in most modern states a written constitution, which takes the place, in his theory, of Austin's sovereign; and (3) the idea of the unity of the legal order.[59]

Kelsen maintains that law is an implement employed by a state to order the conduct of its citizens in conformity with some normative rules,[60] which, in turn, are derived from what Kelsen calls the "fundamental norm."[61] State and law are synonymous in Kelsen's view and it is in light of this assumption that Kelsen fashions what he calls a "pure theory of law."[62] This theory allows for examining the necessary and logical interdependence of all of the norms existing in the body of law involved.[63] In Kelsen's legal theory all norms of law are derived from the fundamental law of the society involved, and the role of law is to compel compliance with the norms so established.[64] Consequently, Pound points out:

> Kelsen holds that we need not seek to bring law into accord with life. The norms are not to grow out of life, but life is to be adjusted to the norms.[65]

Kelsen's theory constitutes what Pound calls the "threat theory of law," which maintains that law is an instrument of coercion used to compel compliance with whatever rules are enunciated by the state.[66] Although Kelsen's theory, in this respect, is similar preceding legal philosophers who adopted this "threat theory of law," he does differ in arguing that such norms which are enforced are linked to some neo-Kantian notion of normative rule, *i.e.*, the fundamental norm of the society.[67] This fundamental norm conditions the nature and scope of the additional rules which are adopted and enforced,[68] and, as Pound notes, Kelsen's view is that the rule of law:

> involves a pronouncement with respect to unqualified human behavior, *i.e.*, not characterized as good or bad, but with all moral elements excluded, and second, a pronouncement with respect to constraining action of those who willed the force of the legal orders.[69]

Consequently in Kelsen's theory judgements regarding the law are not derived from a moral basis, but relate only to determining the logical nature of all of the laws in light of what is mandated by the fundamental norm of the society involved.[70] Pound maintains that Kelsen's theory really is a reversion to narrow nineteenth century analytical legal philosophy, because it is primarily a methodological theory.[71] Pound's greatest criticism of Kelsen's theory, however, is directed to the conclusion it compels that whatever the state does is law, since the legal order is inseparable from the order of the state. This notion, Pound argues, totally reverses the proper view of the law which holds that law is an instrument to restrain the use of state power.[72]

Neo-Hegelian

Twentieth century neo-Hegelian thought endorses the notion that human history and society are in the process of evolving. Consequently, this neo-Hegelian theory of law and the interests it seeks to protect differs from other twentieth century social philosophical schools. This school believes that in resolving conflicting interests:

> we may discover and formulate the jural postulates of the civilization of the time and place without assuming that those postulates are a complete and final picture of ultimate law by which it must be measured for all time.[73]

For the neo-Hegelians, law is constantly evolving and the interests that emerge in society which seek protection and recognition are to be viewed as:

> claims in terms of civilization, in terms of the development of human powers to the most of which they are capable-the most complete mastery of nature, both human nature and external nature.[74]

Thus, the neo-Hegelians posit a value guideline by which such interests are to be evaluated and the necessity of their recognition determined. Josef Kohler, Pound maintains, is the most prominent of the neo-Hegelian writers and notes that Kohler views:

> government, law, and morality [as] forces working toward the attainment of an ideal of civilization. [and that] Law and morals express and also further a progressive civilization. Hence jurisprudence and ethics are both subordinated to a universal history of civilization from which we determine the course of development of civilization and to a philosophy of right and of economics from which we determine the jural postulates—the presuppositions as to right conduct—of the civilization of the time and place.[75]

The neo-Hegelians' broad view of the legal order assumes that it is the process through which adjustments are made of conflicting claims and interests, and that such adjustments are guided by precepts derived from multiple sources within the society.[76] These values which guide and condition the development of the law are ones which must aid in serving and maintaining civilization. Pound points out that Kohler's view regarding the role of law in maintaining and furthering civilization does not involve a set of values appropriate for all civilizations at all times. Rather, Pound observes, Kohler sees only one constant and universal relationship involved in his construction of legal theory, and this is the notion of a "universal idea" of civilization which involves the forcible fashioning of human affairs. Thus, Kohler argues that even:

> if there is no natural law, there is still the constant factor or the relation between law and civilization, "a relation which takes on a different content with the infinite variety in the condition of human civilization." But law is not only a means toward civilization, it is a product of civilization we must look at it, therefore, in three ways: as to the past as a product of civilization, as to the present as a means of maintaining civilization, as to the future as a means of furthering civilization.[77]

Kohler's conception of civilization resulted from his belief that man must master his internal nature in order to enable him in turn to master external nature. Mastery of internal nature, therefore, is a precondition to the achievement, maintenance, and furtherance of civilization. According to Kohler man's internal nature, in its untrained condition, is basically aggressive and self assertive. If these elements of man's internal nature are not controlled and conditioned then man will seek to pursue his own desires and interests without consideration for the effect such conduct has on other persons' aspirations and needs. Consequently, these elements of human nature threaten civilization. Kohler believes, however, that man also has, as part of his being, a cooperative and collaborative dimension, which when cultivated enables him to work in association with others for constructive ends. This collaborative nature of man, therefore, must be cultivated in order to maintain and further civilization, and this cultivation is an appropriate function of the law.[78]

As Pound observes, both Kohler's method and philosophy are based on his view that law is both a product of civilization and the most effective means for that civilization's maintenance and furtherance. According to Pound Kohler's theory is both historical and social-philosophical. Pound identifies four major elements in Kohler's philosophy which reflect its neo-Hegelian character.[79]

First, Kohler maintains that since law is derived from a particular civilization it must, necessarily, reflect that civilization's past in its present. This essential fact is reflected in the process of continuing evolution that characterizes the law.[80] Pound sees a similarity between Kohler's and Savigny's legal philosophy, since both view law as reflective of a given civilization; and that they both feel that the challenge for legal development lies in the need to have this development adjust the values and prescriptions of past civilization to the present purposes of the law,[81] while preserving the present civilization.[82] Pound notes that Kohler concurred with Savigny's notion that purposeful law making had limited value, but, was more optimistic than Savigny about the possibilities of success of imperative law.[83] Even though, Pound concludes, Kohler adopted much of the Hegelian view of legal evolution, he did not, as did the Hegelians of the nineteenth century, consider law as reflecting the unfolding of the ideal of liberty. Rather, Kohler saw the development as the working out of particularized problems that emerge within a given civilization.[84]

Second, Pound maintains that most nineteenth century thought was influenced by Hegelian notions that held that both legal and political history reflected the gradual unfolding of the ideal of individual liberty.[85] In contrast to this element of Hegelian thought, Kohler maintained that history was a recordation of the variety of conflicts and interests that appear in the course of historical development and the record of a society's means of accommodating them. The consequence of accommodating these interests was reflected in the growing mastery men were able to achieve over their aggressive internal nature which, in turn, enabled them to master the external nature in which they were situated [86] History, for Kohler, was the record of how men have employed the adjustments involved in order to maintain and further civilization.[87]

Third, Pound, who feels that nineteenth century legal thought was captivated by the notion that law is mechanically applied, was most impressed by the sociological interpretation Kohler had regarding the application of the law.[88] Kohler's theory, Pound notes, endorsed the idea of the equitable application of legal precepts, *i.e.*, the desire to treat individual cases on an individual basis. Pound observes that the danger of this "individualization of justice" carries in it the danger of attempting to seek justice without law. Kohler's theory, however, avoids both the danger of the mechanistic view and the danger of overly individualized, administrative justice.[89] Kohler's sociological approach, Pound observes, rejected the prevailing view that law is a result of the will of the prince;[90] and, that the judiciary's only role was to discover what the prince's will dictated.[91] Kohler maintained that viewing the law as the product of the prince's will is quite in error, since the only true lawmaker is society at large, and that those who draft codes and statutes are really only articulating the will of this more encompassing society. Consequently, Kohler insists codes are to be interpreted in light of what they are—products of the society.[92] Further, since civilization is a product of continuous historical development,[93] codes and statutes can be nothing other than "the ethical custom or rationally developed morality of a people,"[94] and that, therefore, the law reflects the ends desired by a civilization of a given time and place.[95]

Fourth, and, Pound says:

> Perhaps the most important of Kohler's contributions is his method of formulation of the jural postulates of the civilization of the time and place. [These jural postulates provide]... certain principles of right... logically assumed by or expressed by a given civilization.[96]

Pound feels that Kohler's jural postulates enable one to measure the effectiveness and desirability of the legal precepts involved in a legal order.[97] Pound suggests, that even though the idea that law should serve to maintain and further civilization is a valuable idea, it is not specific and certain enough to assist judges and legislators in finding guides to use in measuring their actions and decisions. Thus, Kohler's jural postulates serve to create such a detailed guide for evaluation.[98] Kohler's formulation of these postulates, Pound says:

> seeks to formulate the ideas of right and justice, the presupposed expectations as to human relations and human conduct which that civilization postulates, and then to shape the legal materials which have come down to us so that they will express or give effect to those ideas.[99]

Pound feels that the value of Kohler's thought lies in the fact that it employs values, reason, and experience in evaluating, explaining, and prescribing the course of the development of law. Kohler's theory permits concern to be given to the preservation of stability in the law, and yet permits change to occur within these prescriptive guidelines. Pound observes that Kohler's great contribution to legal philosophy stems from his theory of civilization as a developing process in which the purpose of law is not exclusively the protection of the individual in the unfettered exercise of his liberty, but rather the maintenance and furtherance of civilization in which individuals.[100]

Neo-Idealist

"Neo-Idealism" finds its origin in Kant's thought, but has pursued multiple paths of development. One derivative school of thought rejects the importance of values and concentrates on the method employed in examining law.[101] A second development, although it maintained that law and ethics were intimately related, focused its attention on the critical evaluation of judgements and turned into a type of utilitarianism.[102] A third development argued that the only values relevant for the law are those that are a result of critical, logical inquiry.[103] The final development in this neo-Kantian school, linked intimately with the name of Julius Binder, Pound considers purely Hegelian.[104]

While values dominated the thought of the idealists of the nineteenth century, the neo-Idealism of the twentieth century accepted as significant the cleavage between values and facts. Thus, this school considered facts to be the focus of the law, and that the only values which were significant were those that were derived from those facts. Consequently, even though values were not expunged from the thinking of the neo-Idealists, they assumed far less significance than they had among nineteenth century idealists.[105]

Gustav Radbruch, according to Pound, is the leading figure in this neo-Idealist school. Radbruch argued that morals and law stand in direct opposition to one another, and that law must, therefore, operate independently of morals.[106] Legal inquiry according to Radbruch should focus only on those values which are embodied in law and which further the major objects of the law, *i.e.*, stability and productivity. Such an inquiry has no relationship to moral concerns found in moral philosophy.[107] Radbruch argues that, it is possible to consider multiple values which can have an influence on the course of the law's development and content, however, he believes that the proper focus of the legal philosophical inquiry is only on those values which are actually applied in the fashioning and application of the law. He states:

> Law is a fact related to a value and the philosopher of law studies law with respect to the values to which it is related.[108]

In Pound's view Radbruch rejects the idea that law can be studied in reference to values, since one cannot meaningfully relate abstract values to the real world with which the law deals. Therefore, for Radbruch, all values are relative.[109]

Radbruch believes that law and morals stand in direct contradiction of one another and that, therefore, no complete justice or morality is possible. Radbruch's view of the relationship of law to the notion of justice is described by Pound as follows: [Radbruch] holds that justice is the sense of the ideal relation among men, morals in the sense of the ideal development of individual character, and security in the sense of assuring men freedom from aggression by others and good faith on the part of others in the general intercourse of society, are in irreducible antinomy.[110] Radbruch does not believe that most of the theories which seek to explain obedience to the law—force theory, consent theory, or the notion that law is obeyed because it embodies justice—are credible. To him realistic legal philosophy recognizes the relativity of all theories of obedience. The realistic role of the legal philosopher is to recognize the limited value each of these notions which are advanced to explain obedience. For Radbruch, obedience comes from the recognition that law is critical for the maintenance and security in a given social order.[111] Therefore, he concludes that law is considered authoritative and is obeyed:

> not because it is susceptible of making itself obeyed, but because it is only under this condition that it can guarantee security.[112]

Radbruch maintains it is critical for the legal philosopher to recognize that law is interpreted differently as a result of the perspectives that various individuals bring to bear when they consider law's purpose and function. There are, for example, those whose major concern is justice, and who, therefore, feel that law is a constantly progressive activity moving toward the achievement of justice.[113] On the other hand, there are those who believe that the role of law is to conserve what already exists, since the *status quo* embodies justice in a fixed and determinant sense.[114] Because such wide differences exist between these and other perceptions, Radbruch finds it unlikely that one could "...find a harmonious development of a legal mentality."[115] Radbruch's views reflect the relativism of his approach to legal philosophy.

Radbruch maintains there are three characteristics of enacted law:

> (1) It has to do with the law as it is, not as it ought to be, nor as it tends to be; (2) it has to do with norms and rules, not with the intrinsic reality of the law; (3) it has to do with objective signifyings of that reality because those signifyings are norms and imperatives.[116]

While Radbruch is not averse to the value of legislated law, his views regarding its content and purpose comport with his view of the law generally, *i.e.*, that it is mode of control tied to the immediate context of which it is a part and which, therefore, must be studied and evaluated separately from morality and justice.

Pound feels that Radbruch's theory is properly described as a "civilization science;" and that his methodology and purpose differ radically from other disciplines.

Pound feels that there are weaknesses in Radbruch's approach, however, and that one of the most significant of these weaknesses results from Radbruch's rigidly logical evaluation and assessment of the law, which directs attention only on the issue of what the law "is" and ignores, what for Pound is a far more critical issue, *i.e.*, what the law "should be."[117] In Pound's estimation this narrowness and rigidity distorts legal inquiry from its proper focus for, as he observes:

> One has only to compare what judges and jurists taught and wrote on such subjects as "abusive exercise of rights," or the "right of privacy", or equitable protection of personality, fifty years ago, and what they think and write and the courts decide today, in order to see how impossible it is, in considering the positive law, to leave out wholly "what ought to be" or "what tends to be" in any accurate account of "what is".[118]

Despite this criticism, Pound feels that Radbruch is one of the major legal philosophers of this century, for his writing realistically assesses the nature and operation of the law, and his treatment of justice allows for a better evaluation of its role in the law. As Pound observes:

> To my mind Radbruch, the foremost philosopher of law, as I see it, in the present generation, put this matter best when he defined justice as "the ideal relation among men." We are seeing through social control, and so through that highly specialized form of social control we call law, to bring about and maintain an ideal relation among men, It is "an" ideal relation rather than "the" ideal relation because what is "the" ideal relation, as something ultimate and absolute, is not the settled and no longer debatable question we took it to be in the nineteenth century.[119]

In addition, Pound feels that Radbruch's theory, which points to the variations involved in how men think about the nature and use of the law, provides a helpful contribution to the development of legal philosophy, in that it moves the inquiry away from purely abstract notions and focuses on the reality of law's role in maintaining social order.

According to Pound, Julius Binder, who started his career as a neo-Kantian but who became an Hegelian, is representative of another division in the neo-Idealist school. In Binder's theory, one could identify a transcendent norm against which all law could be measured.[120] Thus, according to Binder, freedom was the foundation for any civilized order.[121] Pound feels that Binder's development of this argument enabled him to reconcile effectively the notion of individual liberty and the necessities of social order, by virtue of his argument that the "values of civilization" enable one to measure the propriety of human actions. Thus, Binder's theory provided a schema by which one could balance individual and collective needs, in order to determine what balance would best assist in the preservation and furtherance of civilization.[122]

Natural Law Revivalists

Pound associates the twentieth century revival of natural law with the work of Francois Geny and Leon Duguit.[123] The writings of these two French theorists reflect a combination of the historical and metaphysical schools of the nineteenth century, with the sociological thought of the twentieth century.[124] The animating forces behind this revival, according to Pound, lies in the fact that it was a culmination of:

> (1) the movement to bring law into accord with real life which began with Jhering, (2) the vigorous development of the social sciences in France; (3) and, a resulting agitation for greater flexibility in the application of legal precepts.[125]

This revived natural law contained, therefore, Kantian, Hegelian, and social utilitarian notions, which were employed to strengthen the twentieth century natural law school of thought.[126]

Francois Geny viewed society as a moral phenomenon, and argued that recognition of this fact must be the beginning point for legal scholarship, in order to allow meaningful discussion and conclusions about what pattern of law should prevail in a society.[127] Geny defines law as:

> The ensemble of the rules to which the external conduct of man in his relation with his fellows is subjected, and which, under the inspiration of

> the natural idea of justice, in a given state of the collective consciousness of humanity, appearing susceptible of a social sanction where coercion is required, are or tend to be provided with such a sanction, and thenceforth take the form of categorical injunctions governing particular wills for the purpose of assuring order in society.[128]

According to Pound, Geny reasoned as a scholastic would, *i.e.*, that he believed in both revealed truth and truth that could be discovered by the use of human reason.[128] Geny feels that reason can and should be employed in the examination and evaluation of society, since society is a given in the existence of man, and should be fashioned in order to guide it to the proper end for which it is suited.[129] Even though one can begin the examination of society by reason, this reason must be joined with revealed truth in guiding and fashioning acts of humans that are suited to the proper end society should serve.[130] As Pound observes, Geny's view emphasized the necessity of recognizing the role of the ideal in a system of justice.[131] Pound describes Geny's thought as a peculiar mixture of positivism and metaphysical thinking, since Geny felt that social interdependence, which he considered to be a fundamental principle of legal thinking, could be determined by observation; however, he also believed that this fundamental principle of social interdependence was a metaphysical fact.[132] Thus, Pound points out, Geny's legal theory utilizes both Stammler's:

> social ideal of the time and place, [and]... Kohler's... jural postulates of time and place.[133]

Consequently, Pound concludes that Geny's description and definition of the law results in identifying positive law as merely a means of giving definite expression to the precepts of natural law.[134]

Pound maintains that Geny's contribution to the development of legal philosophy is a significant one, but one which is not fully appreciated in the English-speaking world, where much of Geny's work is unknown.[135] Pound says:

> Geny has been busied with the fundamental problems of values. But what is more important for us here and now, he has called our attention to the technique element in law (using law in the sense of authoritative materials of judicial and administrative determination) and to the non-mechanical and administrative element in application of legal precepts and in adjudication, and has sought to put it in the order of reason.[136]

In Pound's view Leon Duguit's writing in the area of revived natural law is almost the equal in significance to that of Francois Geny.[137] Pound argues that most continental philosophy in the twentieth century was concerned with the nature of values, and even thought Duguit's position in this regard is closer to the views of the realists, he is not as far removed from Geny's view on values as one might assume he would be.[138] Pound states that these two theorists responsible for the revival of natural law:

> set up a higher law, which recent skeptical realism would recognize no more than items of judicial or administrative behavior.[139]

Duguit, like Geny, believes that one of the fundamental factors in all legal research is the recognition of the fact of "social interdependence," which gives meaning to all legal research.[140] Even though there is a "positivist" element in Duguit's thought regarding how this fact of "social interdependence" can be discovered and determined by conscious research, he nonetheless believed metaphysics must remain as the starting point.[141]

Duguit claims he rejects all previous notions of natural law.[142] Nevertheless, he proceeds to create a natural law theory.[143] Duguit argues that one must always evaluate legislative acts in terms of how and if they further the concept of "social interdependence" which, he argues, is the most significant measure to be employed in evaluating legal theory and practice.[144] Even though Duguit places great emphasis on the value and importance of individuality he, nevertheless, argues that all evaluation or valuing of individuality should be done by considering how such individuality contributes to or furthers social interdependence.[145] Duguit's thought also incorporates a number of ideas that are properly denominated as "corporatist" theory, since he believes that the proper theory of representation is one that bases representation on class or occupation.[146]

In evaluating Duguit's contribution, Pound says:

> Duguit worked on the problem of values, but his significant contribution has been to further the conception of the legal order as a part and phase of social control and the bringing to bear upon legal problems of the whole apparatus of the social sciences.[147]

Philosophical Realist Schools

Economic Realism

In contrast to most legal philosophy of the nineteenth century, which had focused on the issue of human liberty, new concerns began to dominate twentieth century legal philosophy as a result of industrialization. Thus, the emergence of an extended industrial class involved:

> a shifting from the political standpoint to the economic standpoint grew out of new conditions with which the social sciences had to deal and of new phenomena which they were required to explain.[148]

In response to these new issues and problems legal theory focused more on the economic interpretation of legal philosophy, and this "economic realism," which found its origins in the Hegelian philosophy of history, began to surface.[149] This was particularly the case in the thought of Karl Max, who developed Hegelian notions from an economic basis, and created an Hegelian materialism which rejected the notion of history as an unfolding of the idea of freedom in favor of viewing history as a development directed to the satisfaction of human material aspirations.[150]

Pound argues that probably the most significant influence in economic realist thought was the Hegelian-Marxist historicist notion that history reflects a predetermined nature and course, and that:

> the conception of history [of both Hegel and Marx] was the same. It was something moving in a fixed orbit according to a foreordained plan toward an ultimate state of perfection.[151]

A second major influence was the notion of the "dialectic" and the role it plays in the affairs of man. Nineteenth century historicists had viewed the dialectic exclusively in terms of its relation to some abstract concept of freedom.[152] The notion of the dialectic in the thought of the modern economic realists, however, was to be observed in the material conditions of human existence.[153]

Modern economic realists, Pound feels, were divided into three major schools—idealistic, mechanical sociological, and mechanical analytical.[154]

Although the idealistic economic realists adapted their theory to Hegelianism, they rejected the notion that history was the record of the unfolding of the idea of liberty, which they replaced with the idea that this unfolding was reflected in material reality.[155] Thus, their focus was on man's drive to satisfy his material wants,[156] and maintained that all history was a reflection of man's material condition, and would ultimately and inevitably result in a perfectly harmonious social order.[157] This school maintained that the ultimate propelling force in human development was economic, that this development proceeded dialectically, and would ultimately fulfill all of man's material wants.[158] As Pound observes:

> History was interpreted [by the idealistic economic realists] not in terms of man's ethical life as a moral entity, nor in terms of his political life as a political animal, but in terms of his economic life. History was the mark in the world of an idea of economic activity to satisfy man's economic wants. Hence, all legal history was economic. It was a "history of wants and of labour".[159]

The mechanical sociological branch of economic realism held as its basic belief the idea that law is exclusively a reflection of economic influences,[160] and that these economic influences inexorably and inevitably:

> produced all sorts of social, political and legal limitations, as completely apart from human will as the motion of the planets.[161]

Pound considers Brooks Adams as the major figure in this school, and notes that Adams maintained that all law is merely a consequence of securing the interests of the dominant economic class in the society.[162] These ideas of Adams, Pound asserts, are a mixture of both those notions derived from the ideas embodied in the English analytical school.[163] According to Adams, all law can be fully explained by recognizing that it is nothing other than the exercise of power by the dominant economic class in a given society at a given time.[164] Thus, all jurisprudential study is the study of dominant class interests and how these are protected by the instrument of the law.[165] Consequently, Pound notes, in Adams' theory there can be no relationship whatsoever between law and ethics, since law is merely a technique for the protection and enforcement of an economic class' interests.[166]

Pound feels that the mechanical analytical school had a unique argument about economics and its relationship to the development and content of the law. The ideas of this school placed less emphasis on the ideas of economic determinism and focused mainly on:

> the ends of groups or persons who are in power for the time being and [who] exercise the force of a politically organized society for their own economic advantage.[167]

This dominant group is not necessarily class determined, but rather, is composed of various interests deemed paramount at a given point in time. Pound feels that the weakness of this interpretation stems from the narrowness of its focus. Pound maintains that, though economic considerations may be involved in the operation of the law, focusing on them exclusively forces one to ignore other considerations that have at least equal significance. This approach of the mechanical analytical school, uses a single causal factor to explain law and its development, and, as a result, it ignores significant non-economic evidence which should be taken into account in examining the nature and role of law in society.[168]

Pound recognizes the significance of the school of economic realism in the development of legal philosophy. He argues that it would be a mistake to reject this school out of hand because of its narrow focus, since attention to economic factors should be involved in legal philosophy.[169] This school's emphasis on economics had a salutary effect on legal philosophy, and forced legal philosophers, generally, to consider the importance of these economic factors. More significant is the fact, that it compelled legal philosophy to consider the reality of new and emerging interests which were the consequence of industrialization, and, Pound continues:

> In this respect the economic interpretation was a powerful stimulus to the functional legal school of today. Again, the idea of a social or sociological legal history, as contrasted with merely doctrinal or institutional or political legal history of the past, has done more for the science of law...Above all, however, the economic interpretation has been a stimulus to faith of the efficacy of effort, even if its adherents thought juristic effort futile. It has helped to overthrow juristic pessimism by sharing the effective power of human action to satisfy human desires even if it exaggerated the extent to which men had deliberately shaped the law to attain class ends.[170]

Although Pound expresses appreciation for the contribution made by the economic realism to the development of legal philosophy, he, nonetheless, points to what he considers to be the three major weaknesses of its theories.

First, the economic realists focus their attention too exclusively on the imperative nature of law, and this narrowness causes them to ignore the:

> traditional element, the element of influence developed by reason, which has played a far more significant role in the development of law than has the imperative element.[171]

Consequently, the economic realists place too much emphasis on the "temporary legislative will" and ignore important, long term developments, embodied in most case law, which contribute so significantly to the history and development of law.[172] Economic realism also largely ignores legal developments which have been employed in establishing and protecting the general security of the society, and which could, in no way, be attributed exclusively to serving particularized economic interests.[173] Even in those instances in legal history where the law has been directed to handling what are purely economic matters, the economic realists ignore the fact that most of these decisions were made to fit within the general framework of the law as it prevailed in other areas, and could not be considered as particularized responses serving the discrete interests of a significant economic class.[174] Thus, the entire edifice of economic realism is constructed on faulty grounds and legal realism ignores the historical development of those principles and precepts which condition and control the development of legal history. As a result, economic realism is far too narrowly constructed to serve as a meaningful explanatory theory.[175]

Second, Pound maintains that legal history does not support the analyses and conclusions advanced by the economic realists. Therefore, he says, their analysis is too seriously flawed to be considered valuable or even correct.[176] He uses evidence of three areas of law to support his argument. First, the economic realism identifies the common law fellow-servant rule as an example of class determined law, which served only the interests of the dominant economic class. Such a distortion of the historical development of this doctrine, Pound asserts, ignores the evidence and the reasons surrounding its emergence and use.[177] This particular doctrine, according to Pound, was not a result of serving the interests of a dominant economic class, but rather was designed to restor a standard of liability related to fault,[178] and spread the risk and burden of liability onto those who could best afford it.[179] Second, Pound examines the diverse interpretations given to the doctrine enunciated in *Rylands v. Fletcher*. The variety of ways in which this doctrine has been accepted into the law, Pound maintains, negates any possibility that the theories of the economic realists can explain it.[180] The historical record surrounding the adoption and use of this rule, reflects the task courts face when they attempt to incorporate a newly fashioned interpretation of the law into the full corpus of the law. These decisions cannot be explained by the narrow presumptions of economic realism.[181] Pound also notes that there are numerous instances where legal decisions reflect principles contrary to the interests of the "dominant class." For example, he shows, how courts of equity often enforced ideas that were derived from traditional ideals embodied in the law, and not their particular groups' economic interests. Doctrines such as constructive notice, constructive fraud, and disinterested benevolence all reflect ideas inconsistent with notions of law as a product of class interest.[182] Pound also observes that there are a number of instances which indicate that:

> There are many cases in which a juristic tradition, logically developed by lawyers drawn from a dominant economic or social class, has withstood the interest of the class.[183]

There are numerous instances in corporate law, for example, where judges were guided by principles that were inconsistent with a view of law as a reflection of the will of the dominant class.[184] Pound observes:

> Every grievance of the American labourer against American law in the last century can be matched by quite as real a grievance of the American businessman and the capitalist. There could be no better example of the tenacity of a taught tradition. If nineteenth-century courts had been but the mouthpieces through which businessmen of America promulgated formulations of their self-interest, then things would have come to an end long ago.[185]

Thus, it is Pound's opinion that economic realism is not supported by historical evidence which shows that economic realism, as a philosophy of law, is greatly weakened because of its rejection of such factors as reason and experience as significant elements in the development and fashioning of law. All of this diminishes economic realism's value as an explanatory and analytical scheme of legal thought.[186]

Pound's third major criticism of the economic interpretation is that its:

> theory of mechanical causation by the inevitable operation of economic laws wholly eliminates efficacy of effort.[187]

Although Pound recognizes the importance of economics in the law, he condemns the economic realists because they ignore an historical record that disproves most of their case. As he points out, the traditional elements of the law are more enduring than dominant class interests which might be reflected in legislative enactments. What the economic realists ignore, however, is the fact that the law's development involves the fashioning of means to reconcile interests in a society, and not the imposition of one class' interest.[188]

In summarizing his critique of economic realism Pound concludes that two factors have operated to restrain the development of the law purely as a reflection of class interest. "These are," he says:

> first, the insistence upon development of law logically from analogies of existing rules and doctrine, both because it was supposed the jurist or the judge could not make law but could only find it and because the demand for certainty and predictability, resting on the social interest in security, was held to require him to deduce according to a known technique from premises already existing, and, second, conscious endeavor to make law express supposed eternal and unchangeable ideals.[189]

Neo-Realism

The "neo-Realists", Pound says, were influenced by:

> "positivist sociology, neo-Kantian relativism, Freudian psychology, and phenomenology, [and] the economic interpretation."[190]

As Pound notes, these influences have caused "the neo- realists" to give up the discussion:

> of the nature of law, seeking instead a theory of single judicial determinations.[191]

According to Pound there is little new in this school's claim that it had discovered the single basis on which all legal development is constructed. This notion had been claimed by numerous schools of thought preceding it.[192] Indeed, Pound criticizes this school for the exceedingly narrow focus of its view and states that: "...a science of law must be something other than a descriptive inventory."[193] The neo- realists' amassing of large amounts of quantified data, Pound observes, really provides no effective basis for analysis or evaluation of law. What is missing, and what is most critical for any effective legal philosophy, is a criterion or set of criteria which can be used to interpret this data. Since the legal realists reject the value of all preceding modes of evaluation they deprive themselves of the ability to make significant use of the data they have assembled. Consequently, neo-realists, Pound observes, are both self-congratulatory and self serving in their claims, since their claims of significance are nothing other than assertions that have no foundation or substance.[194]

The neo-realists' emphasis ignores what is fundamental to all effective legal research, *i.e.*, concern for and utilization of received ideals, authoritative technique, settled modes of doctrine, legal precepts, etc. When these factors are taken into account in legal research this provides for effectiveness of analysis for:

> the question at bottom is whether a faithful representation of realities shall paint them in the foreground or instead shall fit in the foreground the subjective features in the behavior of particular judges, the elements in judicial action which stand in the way of predictability and uniformity, the deficiencies of the received technique, the undefined edges and overlappings of doctrines and the defects of legal reasoning.[195]

Emphasis on these central factors of legal research is necessary, Pound says, because they provide the proper means for explaining and examining changes in the legal order. The neo-realists' emphasis and concern with the discreet and the idiosyncratic accounts for the inherent weaknesses of their mode of legal thinking.[196] The neo realists, choosing to remove themselves from the significant in the study of law:

> have their own preconceptions of what is significant and so of what juristically must be. Most of them substitute an economic or psychological must for an ethical or political or historical must.[197]

Pound identifies five categories of neo-realism—economic determinists, psychological realists, skeptical realists, logical positivist realists, and phenomenological realists. He notes that while each have different types of emphases they share certain common characteristics.[198]

First they all assume that influences which operate on a judge to influence his decision are all of equal significance in understanding his decision.[199] This indiscriminate conclusion, Pound maintains, causes the proponents of legal realism to mix uncritically the essential of the legal order with the non-essential. Willingness to engage in this type of loose examination necessarily prohibits them from developing any intelligible scheme of analysis or evaluation,[200] because it ignores substantially more important factors such as judicial review which assures that the law does not fall prey to the excesses of the idiosyncratic behavior of judges.[201].

Second, the neo-realists tend to believe that determination of law can only proceed from determinate and fixed premises.[202] The thinking of legal realists, therefore, really is a reversion to the antiquated idea of a "jurisprudence of conceptions," and argues that law is nothing other than the selection of what rule to apply in a particular situation. Such a view ignores the central tenets of all legal behavior—ideals, technique, and precepts—which serve to control and fashion the law.[203] The notion that law is merely a system of "rules," Pound observes, has been discredited for a long time.[204] Pound also notes that the neo-realists' argument that legal decisions are merely the outcomes of a judge's preconceived conclusions, totally ignores the vital influence that age old authoritative guides to decision play in conditioning judicial decisions.[205]

The result of the neo-realists' argument has led to their being properly defined as those who adhere to the:

> cult of single determination, ...[who have created an] insistence on what is held to be the unique single case rather than on the approximation to a uniform course of judicial action.[206]

The neo-realists insistence that there is a single interpretation that can be given for the pattern and process of legal development necessitates that they ignore what is central and critical to the understanding of legal development, *i.e.*, the elements of the law which are central to its history and development, which color all judicial behavior, and which provide the substance for the generalizations which can intelligently be made about the law. Pound also argues that the neo-realists' assumption that law is merely the aggregate of rules is archaic. Such a view is in fashion with those who favor considering the law as the "cult of force," or who favor and admire the absolutism of modern administrative law. Also, the view willfully ignores the complexity and richly textured nature of law, and compels its adherents to aspire to the Marxian vision of a society organized and operated without law.[207]

Neo-Economic Realism

Neo-economic realism, which is the intellectual heir of preceding schools of economic determinism, perpetuates the ideas that: (1) all law is a result of the prevailing interests of the dominant economic class; and (2) that economic determinism is the sole factor needed to explain the course of law's development and use.[208]

Pound examines this school of thought in light of what he calls its "positive" and its "negative" sides.[209]

The positive dimension of this legal theory reflects the Marxian idea that once private property is abolished there will be no further need for law.[210] In turn, adherents of this view believe that, after private property is abolished, there will be no source of friction in society, and that, therefore, no reconciliation of conflicting demands or interests will be needed.[211] In commenting on the naivety of such a notion, Pound observes:

> There is nothing in the experience of human relations in a crowded world to warrant faith in any of these propositions. But a doctrine of administrative absolutism is relied on to take the place of the law for such situations as those involved in interference with personality. The state as an organization of compulsion may go on long after law has disappeared. There is to be no law and but one rule of law, namely, that there are no laws but only administrative orders for the individual case. Expediency is to be the guide for each item of judicial-administrative action. A superman administrative official is postulated, ...[212]

Pound cites the repudiation of the theories of Paschukanis, which were built on these notions, by the Soviet government itself, as an illustration of the theory's lack of realism, even in a socialist regime. The weakness of this view, Pound points out, is evidenced by the fact that any realistic evaluation of human society and conduct shows quite clearly that individuals are members of multiple associations, and that any attempt to define the individual's interests exclusively in terms of his economic interests, distorts legal inquiry and analysis.[214]

In discussing the "negative" dimension of neo-economic realism, Pound points to this school's view that any notion that law is a body of "authoritative precepts developed and applied by an authoritative technique," is a "deception and superstition."[215] The neo-economic realists insist that the law operates in mechanical fashion, woodenly applying specific results to specific facts.[216]

These assumptions, of course, ignore what legal history and legal practice reveal so clearly, *i.e.*, that different standards and different precepts necessarily operate in various areas of the law, and any mechanical view, such as that held by the neo-economic realists, is not equipped to provide intelligent or helpful legal interpretation.[217]

Another element of neo-economic realism which Pound criticizes is its belief that the emphasis in law should be placed on "public law" in preference to "private law." Neo -economic realists argue that public law is to be preferred because it is directed to the benefit of all people, while private law is fashioned for the protection of particularized and discreet special interests within society.[218] Pound criticizes this view, and points to the fact that the notion of public law was unknown to the common law, and, that the notion of public law in Roman law dealt only with those matters directly related to the constitution of the state. Thus, the fashioning of the doctrine of public law is not derived from historical experience. Nonetheless, neo-economic realists have consistently sought to extend the notion of public law to describe and guide the entire legal order.[219] The neo-economic realists also believe that public law should be used as an instrument to bring about a redistribution of the resources of society in conformity with their notions of what values should be enhanced by the operation of the legal order.[220] This doctrine, therefore, assumes that it can identify one set of values that should be treated preferentially by the law, and those values which should be made subordinate to those preferred by those wielding the power of the state.[221] In commenting on the dangerous implications of this mode of thinking Pound states that determination of what is lawful will reflect the preferences and the choices of officials in an unlimited fashion.[222]

The only value Pound sees in this school of neo-economic realism is that it tended to reinforce the value and need of judicial objectivity.[223] In spite of this limited contribution, Pound feels neo-economic realism's thought poses a danger to a rational understanding of the law due to the fact that this school's assumption that law reflects any economic and class interest, and that such a narrow focus undermines the type of objectivity and impartiality that has characterized western law since the Middle Ages.[224]

Psychological Realism

Pound says that psychological realism is merely economic realism which has been influenced by the teachings of Sigmund Freud, and the developments in behavioral science during this century.[225] This school considers previous judgements and teaching about the law irrelevant, and concludes that law cannot limit man's internal nature. Thus, this school argues law cannot restrain the biases and preferences of judges when they act judicially.[226] Psychological realists argue that the judicial process is composed only of judgements that reflect individual, idiosyncratic beliefs of the particular judges and, therefore, cannot be considered a rational process. Indeed, it is, they assert, a non-rational process and cannot establish either certainty or predictability.[227]

In summarizing the beliefs of psychological realism Pound says:

> In its extreme form, psychological realism conceives of each item of the judicial process as shaped wholly and inexorably by the psychological determinants of the behavior of the individual judge. It thinks of the judicial process in terms of "the judge" and is largely taken up with consideration of the abstract psychology of the abstract judge as it is dogmatically assumed to dictate every item of concrete judicial behavior. In a less extreme form it conceives of determination by factors of individual psychology which are largely undiscoverable, and hence of judicial action as unpredictable "in a case of any novelty whatever."[228]

Pound states that psychological realisms' focusing on the personal idiosyncracies of judges really provides nothing new in legal scholarship. Legal scholars and practitioners have always known this to be the case. What previous scholars knew, however, which has been purposefully ignored by the psychological realists, is that the nature of the legal process, and the role of ideals, technique, and precepts, all have combined to neutralize the impact that such idiosyncracies could have. While it remains true that there is a possibility that personal idiosyncratic behavior of judges may have some impact, particularly in those areas where the content of the law or the precepts of the law have not been fully and clearly developed, their impact is minimal. He states:

> Looking only at the formulas announced tentatively in the development of a doctrine by judicial inclusion and exclusion, there may seem to be a high degree of unpredictability as to where lines would ultimately be drawn. But looking at the results in each case, not at the successive attempts to generalize from the particular result in a case in hand to a universal precept, as a rule it is by no means difficult to put the actual results in the order of reason and be as sure as one can be in any human activity how cases of that sort, even if they involve some degree of novelty will be determined.[229]

Pound deplores the excessively narrow focus of the method and content of psychological realism, which willfully ignores the very important role that tradition, technique, received ideals, and professional standards all have had in the fashioning and operation of the legal system.[230]

Pound agrees that psychological realists have had some limited positive impact on legal thinking when, for example, they discredit the Marxian notion that all control is exercised for purely economic reasons. Nonetheless, the exceedingly narrow focus of their inquiry prohibits their writing from having any major constructive value.[231] Their rejection of—the traditions, ideals, technique, precepts, and professional standards—that lie at the core of the legal system, assures the ineffectiveness and inconsequentiality of their theory.[232]

Skeptical Realism

The skeptical realists carry to the farthest extent the idea that law is not a coherent system but rather a system composed of discrete and multiple official actions.[233] Skeptical realists' thought has been influenced by every variant of contemporary thought, and they conclude that: "...law is what officials do and what officials do is law".[234] This school fully rejects the idea that tradition, ideals, precepts, and behaviors condition and influence judicial action. Indeed, they argue that the belief that such factors condition judicial behavior is only a: "...pious wish or superstition."[235] Accordingly, this school insist that there cannot be any objectivity in the judicial process. They maintain that whatever is determined in any case, at any level, is the law. Such a notion, Pound notes, ignores the entire hierarchical structure of the court system, and thereby further minimizes the value of such inquiry.[236]

Pound believes the unique American Federal scheme encouraged this mode of thinking among professors of law in "national law schools" who either did not understand the coherence found in the federal scheme or who chose to ignore it in order to promote their desire to create a nationally unified system of law. This misrepresentation of the legal order of law professors was not shared by practicing attorneys, in the various jurisdictions of the country. A practicing attorney, Pound says:

> knows which of the diverging lines of persuasive authority are likely to be followed in his jurisdiction even if the teacher cannot find one which is likely to prevail universally.[237]

In those cases, Pound observes, where it is not clear which legal standard should be applied judges find it necessary to choose:

> between starting points for legal reasoning which have equal authority, and the question is from which to begin, there being no precept to determine this.[238]

In such instances there may not be the type of specificity and objectivity which the skeptical realists assert should be there. History shows, however, that coherence is and has been established between the new precepts and the older ones in the law. Given the received technique and ideals of the legal order, this is not surprising, since judges are not free to wander about and pick and choose in ways the skeptical realists assume they can. The skeptical realists, Pound says, cannot marshall the evidence that is needed to support their arguments.[239] Pound demonstrates that history and proper analysis of the law clearly reveals that law is stable, even in times of extensive social, economic, and political change. This fact is one that skeptical realists are unwilling to admit, despite the evidence.[240]

Skeptical realists argue further, that if one does not accept the premise that law is nothing other than a series of articulated personal preferences, then one must be urging that there should be no discretion permitted in the legal order. Pound rejects this argument because it is insupportable. Discretion is fully harmonious with the judicial function, and is employed to retain or achieve harmony between the ideals, technique, and precepts of the law.[241]

Nonetheless, skeptical realism has, according to Pound, made some limited contributions to legal philosophy and practice. This school, because of its focus, Pound says, has called attention to instances where the law has deviated from the logic of the legal order, and has suggested criteria by which this judgement can be made. In this way this school has served a limited role in assisting in creating means whereby the legal order can be reformed.[242] As Pound points out:

> if we consider law as a social control then out of the work of the skeptical realists there may come a better basis for this side of the task of the science of law even if we cannot admit that the judicial process is all that we mean by law or that an adequate science of law may be built wholly on theories of that process as purely or even primarily independent of guidance by authoritative legal precepts developed by a received technique.[243]

The errors of skeptical realism, however, are substantial and, as Pound says, ignore the effort and practice developed in the law to curb idiosyncracy and partiality in its application.[244]

Logical Positivist Realism

Pound states that this particular branch of the neo-realist school, infatuated by the respect and success of modern science, tried to create a "science of law" that would have the same type of objectivity its followers assumed existed in the natural and physical sciences.[245] In order to fashion its "science" this particular school of realism argued for the adoption and use of "scientific technique" in the operation of "legal science."[246] In the attempt to construct such a science, this school insists upon the importance of statistical information and terminological purity.[247] Pound decries such emphases and points out that they are not suited to the study of law.[248] Pound correctly notes, that statistical data do not provide any insight in and of themselves. Their only value is when they are used to confirm or reject conclusions determined by means other than statistical research. Pound states that if one is looking for effective data to examine the legal order, then these can be found in the history of the legal process itself. He observes:

> In the reported decisions of the past we have a record of experience in the administration of justice, of how precepts or doctrines or institutions have worked or have failed to work, and of how and why they came to be formulated or shaped as we find them, which is as solid a basis for objectively scientific study as any man of figures can be.[249]

Any inquiry into the legal order, Pound maintains, must be focused not only on how social control operates, but also on how social control should operate. If one assumes that research can be tied exclusively to the examination of statistical data, then one necessarily eliminates any inquiry into the "ought" questions, and as Pound observes:

> the question of ought, turning ultimately on a theory of values, is the hardest one in jurisprudence.[250]

Because this school insists that inquiry should be directed exclusively at statistical data, the logical positivist realists have directed their inquiry away from the hardest questions of jurisprudence, and as Pound notes, have given their inquiry only and "illusion of reality."[251]

In regard to the logical positivist realists' insistence on the "purification of terminology," Pound states that such a focus is as misplaced as that on statistics, since "...none of the fundamental problems of jurisprudence is solved by terminology".[252] Pound notes that, by itself, terminological refinement does not and cannot provide solutions to the problems with which the law is confronted.[253] Certain value can be obtained from examining terminology in order to reveal "specious universals" and "generalities", but such inquiry, most assuredly, cannot be the sum and substance of legal philosophy or its methodology.[254]

In summarizing the "logical positivist realists" Pound notes that even modern sciences do not adopt the type of rigidity evidenced by this school either in regard the object of their inquiry or to their methodology. The shifting of the focus from certainty to contingency in modern physics clearly reveals this, Pound argues.[255] Pound also finds disturbing the logical positivists realists' notion that men are affected by forces which lie beyond their control, and their derivative belief that a legal order is beyond the competence of men to control or direct.[256] Pound deplores the school's inability to comprehend the application of the analogy of engineering or science to the operation of law.[257] The logical positivist realists fail to understand that the application of legal precepts and standards cannot be done with the type of precision that can be used in applying engineering standards or the rules of natural science.[258]

Phenomenology

According to phenomenologists' understanding of all phenomena can be derived only from the phenomena itself, and not from approaching the examination of the phenomena with a series of conceptions on how to examine it or what to examine. Thus, phenomenologists believe knowledge is: "...a mode of existence of actuality."[259] Whatever is to be valued or how it is to be valued is to be derived from the object of the inquiry itself. This school has had an impact on legal philosophy, but not one that is to be valued, for, as Pound notes, according to this school:

> Justice is the totality of jural value intuitively recognized through collective experience. But these values are extremely variable. Hence in their [phenomenological] mode of thought justice has no meaning apart from the facts in which values are realized.[260]

Phenomenology, according to Pound, fortunately has enjoyed only limited success in influencing legal philosophy. What little impact it has had resulted from the complementary function it has to other schools of realism.[261] The role that phenomenology has had in legal philosophy, when considered alone, is insignificant.[262]

The Swedish Realists

Swedish Realism, Pound says is the ultimate *reductio ad absurdam* of realism, *i.e.*, it rejects any and all forms of conceptualization to be used in evaluating legal action or the operation of the legal order. The Swedish Realists maintain that law is nothing other than a host of discrete and unrelated acts designed only to influence the behavior of those against whom they are employed. The imperatives involved in the operation of the law cannot be considered as commands, since the maximum of their effectiveness is determined by the predispositions of those to whom they are directed. Consequently, all that composes the legal order—rights, duties, authority, legal obligations, etc.—are derivative in the sense that they only reflect the prevailing dispositions within a society to give them creditability and effectiveness.[263] In summarizing the tenets of this school of legal philosophy, Pound observes that its major significance is related to its role in fostering and supporting the "threat theory" of law. He states:

> The reality [of law] is force applied by officials and the psychological basis of obedience which makes actual application of force largely unnecessary. This is in line with the mean tendency toward a threat-theory of law.[264]

Pound's Assessment of Philosophical Realism

Pound ascribes considerable value to the schools of "realism." Pointing to their contributions, Pound says:

> Thus far the achievement of realism in all its forms has been to rouse jurists and lawyers from what Kant called dogmatic slumber. In this it has carried on the work begun by Jhering.[265]

Nonetheless, his critique of this school points to its misapplication of effort, weakness of technique, and limited constructive contribution to legal inquiry. First of all, he maintains, the choice of the term "realism" compels this school to select as the focus of its inquiry "what is" and not "what ought to be" or "what might be." Consequently, it devotes great effort to cataloging specific facts. As Pound notes, however, once facts are assembled, there is a far more important need to use some standard to examine and evaluate this data.[266]

Second, the modern realists reject the idea that any preconceived system of valuing can be productive. They allege that all preceding schools of legal philosophy are based on illusions. This attitude of the realists, however, is not unique to them, for, as Pound notes:

> there is nothing new in the assumption of those who are starting out new paths of juristic thought in believing that those who have gone before then have been dealing with illusions while they alone and for the first time are dealing with realities.[267]

Previous schools of legal philosophy also assumed that their predecessors had begun their inquiry bound in by "preconceptions." The realists' focus on one basis to guide their inquiry, as Pound observes, is unlikely to be any freer of illusions and preconceptions than those which influenced earlier schools of legal philosophy.[268] Pound notes that most modern philosophy assumes that there is no absolute reality. If this is the case, he asks, then what test can the modern realist make of reality other than significance? As Pound points out, significance too is relative. Therefore, he asks, is significance, considered in relation to the valuing and defining of ends of the legal order, not as valid as looking to the data to test its significance in reference to the alogical and unrational elements in the legal order?[269] Pound sees the problem posed by these questions to be a matter of emphasis. Certainly the traditional elements of the legal order—received ideals, authoritative grounds for decision, authoritative techniques—are all realities of the legal order. The question, then, is whether they will be emphasized more strongly, equally, or less strongly than other realities of the legal order, such as its deficiencies, or examples of its alogical use? Pound recognizes that the new realists focus their attention almost exclusively on these deficiencies and alogical elements. In this respect, he feels some service has been done for legal philosophy since such information provides the grounds for criticism and correction. The problem, however, is not that realists do this, but that they then insist on ignoring the traditional and common features of the legal order which, as Pound notes, are as real as the alogical elements or the deficiencies.[270] As a result the new realists are guided by as strong a set of preconceptions as their predecessors regarding what is significant, and in this respect their inquiry is badly flawed.[271] Pound observes:

> Faithful portrayal of what courts and lawmakers and jurists do is not the whole task of a science of the law. One of the conspicuous actualities of the legal order is the impossibility of divorcing what they do from the question what they ought to do or what they feel they ought to do. For by and large, they are trying to do what they ought to do. Their picture

> of what they ought to do is often decisive in determining what they do. Such pictures are actualities quite as much as the materials of legal precepts or of the ideal element in law, valuing of traditional ideas with respect to the actualities of the social and legal order, and the results to which they lead in the social and legal order of today, are as much in touch with reality (*i.e.*, have to do with things of at least as much significance for the legal order) as psychological theories of the behavior of particular judges in particular cases.[272]

Pound feels "it is much more important to understand than to criticize."[273] For this reason he suggests the guidelines which realists should adopt, since such guidelines would improve the value of their study. He suggests five points that should guide a "realist jurisprudence."[274]

First, Pound agrees that there is some value in studying the elements in the legal order which are alogical or without reason. Those elements which are a result of the purely subjective elements influencing the law, can thus be identified and corrected.[275]

Second, Pound feels that legal inquiry, in the modern era, must focus attention on the relationship between administrative and judicial processes, in order that the judiciary can exercise proper checks on the administrative order.[276]

Third, continued examination of the role and of the "individualization of justice" is desirable, but must be balanced with a continuing concern with those generalizations which are crucial for the functioning and survival of a legal order.[277]

Fourth, legal inquiry should continue to concern itself with the plurality of elements which are involved in adequate description and analysis of the legal order. It would be most helpful, Pound says, to employ Jhering's model of precepts, standards, and doctrines, to guide such an inquiry. This mode of inquiry allows consideration to be given to the issue of how to improve the legal order in a reasonable way.[278]

Fifth, legal realism must abandon its desire to find a single causal explanation for the entire legal order, and recognize the multiplicity of influences that are involved. Legal realism's inquiry should be guided by what such an inquiry can do in enabling legislators and judges to maintain, further and transmit civilization.[279]

In a passage which clearly reflects his judgement of realism and its weaknesses, Pounds says:

> We have always known that the judicial process does not at all times and in all places conform absolutely and in all respects to our ideal of it. Despite all the checks with which we surround it, it does not come out in every case entirely as we could wish. But the striving, I repeat, goes far to realize the ideal. It is the approximation to our ideal of it which is significant, not the falling short, which we seek continually to control and to reduce to a minimum. If a theory of social control through the force of politically organized society is made from the falling short rather than from the achievements, we shall undo what has made increasingly for civilization since the beginnings of modern law in the later Middle Ages.[280]

Endnotes

Chapter Five

1. Pound, *Introduction...Philosophy*, pp. 40-41.

2. See Chapter Seven: The Theory of Interests.

3. Pound, *Introduction...Philosophy*, pp. 42-43. See also: *The Ideal Element...Tagore*, p. 167.

4. Pound, *Vol. 1*, p. 121.

5. Pound, *Vol. 1*, pp. 119-192. See also: Pound, *The Ideal Element...Tagore*, pp. 44-56. R. Pound, "Fifty Years of Jurisprudence, III," Vol. 51, January, 1938, *Harvard Law Review*, pp. 444-472, 446-447. Vol. 1 PB 224. (Hereinafter referred to as "Fifty...III,").

6. Pound, *The Ideal Element...Tagore*, pp. 196-215. See also: Pound, *Vol. 1*, pp. 195-287. Pound, "Fifty...III," pp. 446-447.

7. Pound, *The Ideal Element...Tagore*, pp. 268-272. See also: Pound, *Vol. 1*, pp. 122-124. Pound, "Fifty...III," pp. 446-447.

8. Pound, *Vol. 1*, pp.119-192. See also: Pound, "Fifty...III," pp. 447-473.

9. Pound, *Interpretations of Legal...*, p. 163. See also: Pound, "Scope and Purpose...II," pp. 140-147.

10. Pound, *Spirit...*, pp. 205-206. See also: Pound, "Comparison...Ideals...," p.15. Pound, "Scope and Purpose...II," pp. 140-147.

11. Pound, *Spirit...*, pp. 206-209. See also: Pound, "Comparison...Ideals...," p.15.

12. Pound, *Spirit...*, p. 209. See also: Pound, "Scope and Purpose...II," pp. 140-147.

13. Pound, *Spirit...*, pp. 211-213. See also: Pound, "Scope and Purpose...II," pp. 140-147.

14. Pound, *The Ideal Element...Tagore*, pp. 159-161. See also: Pound, *Vol. 1*, pp. 129-133. Pound, "Scope and Purpose...II," pp. 140-147.

15. Pound, *The Ideal Element...Tagore*, p. 60.

16. Pound, *Vol. 1*, pp. 130-131. See also: Pound, "Scope and Purpose...II," pp. 140-147.

17. Pound, *Vol. 1*, p. 131. See also: Pound, "Scope and Purpose...II," pp. 140-147.

18. Pound, *Vol. 1*, p. 131. See also: Pound, "Scope and Purpose...II," pp. 140-147.

19. Pound, *Vol. 1*, pp. 132-133. See also: Pound, "Scope and Purpose...II," pp. 140-147. Pound, "Law...Science...Recent," pp. 525-536, 530-537.

20. Pound, *Interpretations of Legal...*, pp. 119-120. See also: Pound, "Law...Science...Recent...," pp. 530-533.

21. Pound, *Vol. l*, p. 268. See also: Pound, *Vol. 3*, p.11. Pound, "Law...Science...Recent...," pp. 530-533.

22. Pound, "Scope and Purpose...II," p. 140, 141, 168. See also: Pound, "Law...Science...Recent...," pp. 530-531.

23. Pound, *Vol. 1*, p. 133. See also: Pound, "Scope and Purpose...II," pp. 140-147.

24. Pound, *Spirit...*, pp. 204-205. See also: Roscoe Pound, *Jurisprudence (Vol 3) 5 Vols.*, St. Paul, Minn., West Publishing Co., 1959, Vol. 3, p. 15. Vol. 2 PB 44. (Hereinafter referred to as Vol. 3) Pound, *Vol. 4*, p.62. Pound, "The Scope and Purpose...II," p. 143. Pound, "Law...Science...Recent...," pp. 530-531.

25. Pound, *Spirit...*, pp. 204-205. See also: Pound, *Vol 3*, p. 15. Pound, *Vol. 4*, p. 62. Pound, "Scope and Purpose...II," p. 143. Pound, "Law...Science... Recent...," pp. 530-531.

26. Pound, "Scope and Purpose...II," p. 144. See also: Pound, "Law...Science...Recent...," pp. 530-531.

27. Pound, *Vol. 1*, pp. 134-36. See also: *Spirit...*, p.157. Pound, "Scope and Purpose...II," p. 144. Pound, "Law...Science...Recent...," pp. 530-531.

28. Pound, *Vol. 4*, p. 17. See also: Pound, *Vol. 1*, p. 136. Pound, "Scope and Purpose...," pp. 140-147. Pound, "Law...Science...Recent...," pp. 530-531.

29. Pound, *The Ideal Element...Tagore*, pp. 72-73. See also: Pound, "Principles...Procedural Reform," p. 388. Pound, "Law...Science...Recent...," pp. 530-531. As noted elsewhere in this study, however, Pound's concern with 'too much of a good thing' caused him to see peril in too much 'individualization of justice' and the growth of executive justice as a substitute for judicial justice. See Chapter Eight: Judicial Justice. Chapter Nine: Administrative Law.

30. Pound, *Vol. 1*, pp. 131-132. See also: Pound, "Scope and Purpose...II," pp. 140-147.

31. Pound, *Interpretation of Legal...*, p. 136. See also: Pound, *Vol. 3*, p. 482.

32. Pound, *Vol. 1*, p. 139. See also: Pound, "Scope and Purpose...," pp. 140-147.

33. Pound, *Introduction...Philosophy...*, pp.44. See also: Pound, "Scope and Purpose...II," pp. 140-147.

34. Pound, *Vol. 1*, p. 139. See also: Pound, *Introduction...Philosophy...*, p. 46. Pound, "Scope and Purpose...II," pp. 140-147.

35. Pound, *Vol. 1*, p. 139. See also: Pound, *Introduction...Philosophy...*, p. 46. Pound, "Scope and Purpose...II," pp. 140-147.

36. Pound, *Vol. 1*, pp. 140-141. See also: Pound, *Introduction...Philosophy...*, pp. 44-45. Pound, "The Scope and Purpose...II," p. 146.

37. Pound, *Vol. 1*, p. 140.

38. Pound, *Vol. 1*, p. 142. See also: Pound, "The Scope and Purpose...II," p. 146.

39. Pound, *Vol. 2*, p. 105. See also: Pound, "The Scope and Purpose...II," p. 146.

40. Pound, *Vol. 1*, p. 536. See also: Pound, "Scope and Purpose...II," pp. 147-154. Pound, "Law...Science...Recent...," p. 531.

41. Pound, *Vol. 1*, p. 147. See also: Pound, "Scope and Purpose...II," pp. 147-154. Pound, "Law...Science...Recent...," p. 531.

42. Pound, "The Scope and Purpose...II," p. 148. See also: Pound, "Law...Science...Recent...," p. 532.

43. Pound, "Scope and Purpose...II," p. 148. See also: Pound, "Law...Science...Recent...," p. 532.

44. Pound, *Vol. 1*, p. 148. See also: Pound, *Vol. 2*, p. 232. Pound, "Law...Science...Recent...," p. 532.

45. Pound, *Vol. 1*, pp. 144, 149. See also: Pound, "The Scope and Purpose...II," p. 151. Pound, "Law...Science...Recent...," p. 532.

46. Pound, *Spirit...*, pp. 147-148. See also: Pound, *Vol. 1*, p. 150.

47. Pound, *Spirit...*, pp. 147-148. See also: Pound, "Scope and Purpose...II," pp. 147-154.

48. Pound, *Vol. 1*, pp. 150-151. See also: Pound, *Vol. 2*, p. 382. Pound, *Vol. 4*, p. 525. Pound, "Scope and Purpose...II," p. 151. Pound, "Law...Science...Recent...," p. 532.

49. Pound, *Vol. 1*, pp. 150-152. See also: Pound, "Scope and Purpose...II," p. 152. Pound, "Law...Science...Recent...," p. 532.

50. Pound, *Vol. 1*, p. 151. See also: Pound, "Scope and Purpose...II," pp. 147-154. Pound, "Law...Science...Recent...," p. 532.

51. Pound, *Vol. 1*, p. 152. See also: Pound, "Scope and Purpose...II," p. 152. Pound, "Law...Science...Recent...," p. 532.

52. Pound, *Vol. 1*, p. 152. See also: Pound, "Scope and Purpose...II," pp. 147-154.

53. Pound, *Vol. 1*, p. 153. See also: Pound, "Scope and Purpose...II," p. 152.

54. Pound, *Vol. 1*, p. 153. See also: Pound, "Scope and Purpose...II," pp. 147-154.

55. Pound, *Vol. 1*, p. 155. See also: Pound, "Scope and Purpose...II," pp. 147-154.

56. Pound, *Vol. 1*, pp. 152-156. See also: R. Pound, "The Scope and Purpose of Sociological Jurisprudence, III," Vol. 24, April, 1912, *Harvard Law Review*, Reprint, pp. 489-516, pp. 449-452. Vol. 1 PB 43. (Hereinafter referred to as "Scope and Purpose...III,").

57. Pound, *Vol. 1*, pp. 152-156. See also: Pound, "Scope and Purpose...III," pp. 449-452.

58. Pound, "Law...Science...Recent...," p. 531. See also: Pound, "Scope and Purpose...III," pp. 449-450.

59. Pound, "Law...Science...Recent...," p. 531.

60. Pound, *Vol. 2*, pp. 342-343. See also: Pound, "Scope and Purpose...III," p. 449. Pound, "Law...Science...Recent...," p. 532.

61. Pound, *Vol. 2*, p. 81. See also: Pound, "Scope and Purpose...III," pp. 449-452. Pound, "Law...Science...Recent...," p. 532.

62. Pound, *Vol. 2*, p. 80. See also: Pound, *Vol. 1*, p. 332. Pound, "Scope and Purpose...III," pp. 451-452.

63. Pound, *Vol. 1*, p. 332. See also: Pound, "Law...Science...Recent...," p. 532.

64. Pound, *Vol. 2*, p. 81. See also: Pound, "Scope and Purpose...III," pp. 451-452.

65. Pound, "Law...Science...Recent...," p. 533.

66. Pound, *Vol. 2*, pp. 81, 297. See also: Pound, "Law...Science...Recent...," pp. 532-533.

67. Pound, *Vol. 2*, p. 78. See also: Pound, "Scope and Purpose...III," pp. 449-452. Pound, "Law...Science...Recent...," pp. 532-533.

68. Pound, *Vol. 2*, pp. 163-164. See also: Pound, "Law...Science...Recent...," pp. 532-533.

69. Pound, *Vol. 2, p. 167.*

70. Pound, *The Ideal Element...Tagore*, p. 79. See also: Pound, "Law...Science...Recent...," pp. 532-533.

71. Pound, *Vol. 1*, pp. 332-333. See also: Pound, "Scope and Purpose...III," pp. 449-452. Pound, "Law...Science...Recent...," pp. 532-533.

72. *Supra*. Ch. 6. Pound on the Law.

73. Pound, *Introduction...Philosophy...*, pp. 44-45. See also: Pound, "Scope and Purpose...II," pp. 140, 154.

74. Pound, *Introduction...Philosophy...*, p. 47. See also: Pound, "Scope and Purpose...II," pp. 140, 154.

75. Pound, *Vol. 2*, pp. 232-233.

76. Pound, *Vol. 2*, p. 82.

77. Pound, *Interpretations of Legal...*, p. 143. See also: Pound, *Vol. 3*, p. 6. Pound, *The Ideal Element...Tagore*, p. 180.

78. Pound, *Vol. 3*, pp. 18-19. See also: Pound, *Interpretations of Legal...*, pp. 143-144. Pound, *The Ideal Element...Tagore*, p. 180.

79. Pound, *Vol. 1*, pp. 159-161.

80. Pound, *Vol. 1*, pp. 161-162. See also: Pound, *The Ideal Element...Tagore*, p. 180.

81. Pound, *Vol. 1*, pp. 161-162.

82. Pound, *Vol. 1*, p. 163. See also: Pound, *The Ideal Element...Tagore*, p. 180.

83. Pound, *Vol. 1*, p. 163.

84. Pound, *Vol. 1*, p. 162.

85. Pound, *Vol. 1*, pp. 163-164. See also: Pound, *The Ideal Element...Tagore*, p. 180.

86. Pound, *Vol. 1*, pp. 163-164.

87. Pound, *Vol. 1*, p. 164. See also: Pound, *The Ideal Element...Tagore*, pp. 180-181.

88. Pound, *Vol. 1*, p. 164. See also: Pound, *The Ideal Element...Tagore*, p. 180.

89. Pound, *Vol. 1*, pp. 165-166.

90. Pound, *Vol. 1*, p. 165.

91. Pound, *Vol. 1*, p. 166.

92. Pound, *Vol. 1*, p. 167. See also: Pound, *The Ideal Element...Tagore*, pp. 45, 179-180.

93. Pound, *Vol. 3*, p. 393. See also: Pound, *The Ideal Element...Tagore*, pp. 45, 179-180.

94. Pound, *Vol. 2*, p. 167. See also: Pound, *The Ideal Element...Tagore*, pp. 45, 179-180.

95. Pound, *Vol. 1*, p. 168. See also: Pound, *Vol. 3*, p. 185.

96. Pound, *Vol. 1*, p. 168. See also: Pound, *Vol. 2*, p. 185. Pound, *The Ideal Element...Tagore*, p. 180.

97. Pound, *Vol. 1*, p. 168. See also: Pound, *The Ideal Element...Tagore*, pp. 180, 186.

98. Pound, *Vol. 1*, p. 169. See also: Pound, *The Ideal Element...Tagore*, pp. 180, 186.

99. Pound, Vol. 1, p. 169. See also: Pound, *The Ideal Element...Tagore*, pp. 180, 186.

100. Pound, *The Ideal Element...Tagore*, p. 95. See also: Pound, *Interpretation of Legal...*, p. 144. "Scope and Purpose...II," pp. 155-158.

101. Pound, *Vol. 1*, p. 170. See also: Pound, "Scope and Purpose...III," pp. 454-463. He identifies Rickert, Ssawalski, Haensel, and Lesser as leaders in this development.

102. Pound, *Vol. 1*, p. 170. See also: Pound, "Scope and Purpose...III," pp. 454-463. Radbruch, Euchuena, and Lash are considered by Pound as representatives of this development.

103. Pound, *Vol. 1*, p. 171. See also: Pound, "Scope and Purpose...III," pp. 454-463. Kaufman, Merke, and Verdrass are named by Pound as leaders of this particular school.

104. Pound, *Vol. 1*, p. 171. See also: Pound, "Scope and Purpose...III," pp. 454-463. Pound identifies Bender as the leading figure in this variant of this school.

105. Pound, *Vol. 1*, p. 171.

106. Pound, *The Ideal Element...Tagore*, pp. 61, 184. See also: Pound, "Scope and Purpose...III," pp. 454-463.

107. Pound, *Vol. 1*, pp. 171-173. See also: Pound, "Scope and Purpose...III," pp. 455-456.

108. Pound, *Vol. 1*, pp. 171-173. See also: Pound, "Scope and Purpose...III," pp. 454-463.

109. Pound, *Vol. 1*, p. 172. See also: Pound, "Scope and Purpose...III," pp. 454-463.

110. Pound, *Justice....*, p.21. See also: Pound, *The Ideal Element...Tagore*, p. 78. Pound, *Vol. 2*, pp. 231, 278. Pound, "Scope and Purpose...III," pp. 454-463.

111. Pound, *Vol. 1*, p. 174. See also: Pound, "Scope and Purpose...III," pp. 454-463.

112. Pound, *Vol. 1*, p. 174. See also: Pound, "Scope and Purpose...III," p. 457.

113. Pound, *Vol. 1*, pp. 174-175. See also: Pound, "Scope and Purpose...III," pp. 454-463.

114. Pound, *Vol. 1*, p. 175. See also: Pound, "Scope and Purpose...III," pp. 454-463.

115. Pound, *Vol. 1*, p. 175. See also: Pound, "Scope and Purpose...III," pp. 454-463.

116. Pound, *Vol. 1*, p. 176. See also: Pound, "Scope and Purpose...III," pp. 454-463.

117. Pound, *Vol. 1*, p. 176. See also: Pound, "Scope and Purpose...III," p. 459.

118. Pound, *Vol. 1*, p. 176.

119. Pound, *Justice According...*, p. 19.

120. Pound, *Vol. 1*, p. 177. See also: Pound, "Scope and Purpose...III," pp. 461-463.

121. Pound, *Vol. 1*, p. 177. See also: Pound, "Scope and Purpose...III," pp. 461-463.

122. Pound, *Vol. 1*, p. 178. See also: Pound, "Scope and Purpose...III," pp. 461-463.

123. Pound, *The Ideal Element...Tagore*, p. 46. See also: Pound, "Scope and Purpose...III," p. 463.

124. Pound, *Vol. 1*, p. 179. See also: Pound, "Scope and Purpose...," p. 463.

125. Pound, *Vol. 1*, pp. 179-180.

126. Pound, *Vol. 1*, p. 180. See also: Pound, "Scope and Purpose...III," p. 463.

127. Pound, *Vol. 2*, p. 233. See also: Pound, *The Ideal Element...Tagore*, p. 46. Pound, "Scope and Purpose...," p. 464. Pound, "Law...Science...Recent...," p. 531.

128. Pound, *Vol. 2*, p. 83. See also: Pound, *Vol. 1*, p. 198.

129. Pound, *The Ideal Element...Tagore*, p. 46. See also: Pound, *Vol. 1*, p. 182. Pound, "Scope and Purpose...III," pp. 464-465.

130. Pound, *The Ideal Element...Tagore*, p. 47. See also: Pound, "Scope and Purpose...III," pp. 464-465.

131. Pound, *The Ideal Element...Tagore*, p. 47. See also: Pound, *Vol. 1*, p. 183. Pound, "Scope and Purpose...III," pp. 465-466.

132. Pound, *The Ideal Element...Tagore*, p. 47. See also: Pound, "Scope and Purpose...III," pp. 465-466.

133. Pound, *Vol. 1*, p. 182. See also: Pound, "Scope and Purpose...III," pp. 464-466.

134. Pound, *Vol. 1*, p. 183.

135. Pound, *Vol. 1*, p. 184. See also: Pound, *Contemporary...*, pp. 8-9. Pound, "Scope and Purpose...III," p. 466.

136. Pound, "Law...Science...Recent...," p. 531. See also: Pound, *Vol. 1*, p. 184.

137. Pound, *Vol. 1*, p. 184. See also: Pound, "Scope and Purpose...," pp. 466-468.

138. Pound, *Vol. 1*, pp. 184-185. See also: Pound, "Scope and Purpose...III," pp. 466-468. Pound, "Law...Science...Recent...," pp. 531-532.

139. Pound, *Vol. 1*, p. 186. See also: Pound, "Scope and Purpose...III," pp. 468-469.

140. Pound, *Vol. 1*, p. 187. See also: Pound, *The Ideal Element...Tagore*, p. 48. Pound, "Scope and Purpose...III," p. 469.

141. Pound, *The Ideal Element...Tagore*. p. 47. See also: Pound, *Vol. 1*, p. 187. Pound, "Scope and Purpose...III," pp. 469-470.

142. Pound, *Vol. 1*, p. 187. See also: Pound, "Scope and Purpose...III," pp. 468-471.

143. Pound, *The Ideal Element...Tagore*, p. 48. See also: Pound, "Scope and Purpose...III," pp. 469-471.

144. Pound, *The Ideal Element...Tagore*, p. 48. See also: Pound, "Scope and Purpose...," pp. 469-470.

145. Pound, *Vol. 1*, p. 188. See also: Pound, "Scope and Purpose...III," pp. 469-472.

146. Pound, *The Ideal Element...Tagore*, p. 48. See also: Pound, "Scope and Purpose...III," pp. 466-471.

147. Pound, "Law...Science...Recent...," p. 531. See also: Pound, *Social Control...*, p. 8.

148. Pound, *Interpretations of Legal...*, p. 92.

149. Pound, *Vol. 1*, p. 197. See also: Pound, *The Ideal Element...Tagore*, p. 200.

150. Pound, *Vol. 1*, p. 199.

151. Pound, *Interpretations of Legal...*, p. 93.

152. Ibid.

153. Ibid.

154. Pound, *Interpretations of Legal...*, p. 94. See also: Pound, *Vol. 1*, p. 227.

155. Pound, *Vol. 1*, pp. 227-228. See also: Pound, *Interpretations of Legal...*, p. 95.

156. Pound, *Interpretations of Legal...*, p. 95.

157. Pound, *Vol. 1*, p. 228.

158. Ibid.

159. Pound, *Interpretations of Legal...*, p. 95.

160. Ibid. p. 96.

161. Pound, *Vol. 1*, pp. 228-229.

162. Pound, *Vol. 1*, p. 229. See also: Pound, *The Ideal Element...Tagore*, pp. 200-201. Pound, *Interpretations of Legal...*, p. 97.

163. Pound, *Interpretations of Legal...*, p. 97. See also: Pound, *Vol. 1*, p. 229.

164. Pound, *Interpretations of Legal...*, p. 97. See also: Pound, *The Ideal Element...Tagore,* pp. 200-201.

165. Pound, *Interpretations of Legal...*, p. 98. See also: Pound, *The Ideal Element...Tagore,* pp. 200-201.

166. Pound, *Interpretations of Legal...*, pp. 98-99.

167. Pound, *Vol. 1*, p. 230. See also: Pound, *Interpretations of Legal...*, p. 94.

168. Pound, *Interpretations of Legal...*, p. 109, 113.

169. Ibid. p. 113.

170. Pound, *Interpretations of Legal...*, pp. 114-115. See also: Pound, *The Ideal Element...Tagore*, p. 218.

171. Pound, *Vol. 1*, p. 231. See also: Pound, *The Ideal Element...Tagore*, pp. 201-213.

172. Pound, *Interpretations of Legal...*, pp. 102-103. See also: Pound, *Vol. 1*, p. 231. Pound, *The Ideal Element...Tagore*, pp. 201-213.

173. Pound, *Vol. 1*, p. 231. See also: Pound, *Interpretations of Legal...*, pp. 102-103. Pound, *The Ideal Element...Tagore*, pp. 201-213.

174. Pound, *Vol. 1*, p. 234. See also: Pound, *Interpretations of Legal...*, p. 103. Pound, *The Ideal Element...Tagore*, pp. 201-213.

175. Pound, *Interpretations of Legal...*, pp. 103-104. See also: Pound, *Vol. 1*, p. 235. Pound, *The Ideal Element...Tagore*, pp. 201-213.

176. Pound, *Interpretations of Legal...*, pp. 102-103. See also: Pound, *Vol. 1*, p. 235. Pound, *The Ideal Element...Tagore*, pp. 201-213.

177. Pound, *Interpretations of Legal...*, pp. 109-110. See also: Pound, *Vol. 1*, p. 235. Pound, *The Ideal Element...Tagore*, pp. 201-213.

178. Pound, *Vol. 1*, pp. 234-238. See also: Pound, *Interpretations of Legal...*, pp. 110-111. Pound, *The Ideal Element...Tagore*, pp. 201-213.

179. Pound, *Vol. 1*, p. 239. See also: Pound, *Interpretations of Legal...*, pp. 109-111. Pound, *The Ideal Element...Tagore*, pp. 201-213. R. Pound, "The Economic Interpretation and the Law of Torts," Vol. 53, January, 1940, *Harvard Law Review*, p. 368. Vol 1 PB 252. (Hereinafter referred to as "The Economic...").

180. Pound, *Interpretations of Legal...*, pp. 107-110. See also: Pound, *Vol. 1*, pp. 241-242, citing: 3 Hurlst & C. 774 (1865), L. R. Ex. 265 (1866), L. R. 3 H. L. 330 (1868).

181. Pound, *Interpretations of Legal...*, pp. 107-110. See also: Pound, *Vol. 1*, p. 241. Pound, *The Ideal Element...Tagore*, pp. 201-.213.

182. Pound, *Interpretations of Legal...*, pp. 107-110. See also: Pound, *Vol. 1*, p. 242. Pound, *The Ideal Element...Tagore*, pp. 201-213.

183. Pound, *Vol. 1*, p. 242. See also: Pound, *The Ideal Element...Tagore*, pp. 201-213. Pound, *Interpretations of Legal...*, pp. 102-104.

184. Pound, *Vol. 1*, pp. 242-243. See also: Pound, *Interpretations of Legal...*, pp. 110-111. Pound, *The Ideal Element...Tagore*, pp. 201-213.

185. Pound, *Vol. 1*, p. 244. See also: Pound, *Interpretations of Legal...*, p. 111. See also: R. Pound, "Fifty Years of Jurisprudence, III," Vol 51, March, 1938, *Harvard Law Review*, pp. 777-812. Vol. 1 PB 224. (Hereinafter referred to as "Fifty Years...III").

186. Pound, *Vol. l*, pp. 244-245. See also: Pound, *Interpretations of Legal...*, pp. 114-115. Pound, *The Ideal Element...Tagore*, pp. 211-213.

187. Pound, "Political and Economic...," p.103. See also: Pound, *The Ideal Element...Tagore*, pp. 211-213.

188. Pound, *Vol. 1*, p. 246. See also: Pound, *The Ideal Element...Tagore*, pp. 201-204. Pound, *Interpretations of Legal...*, pp. 109-111.

189. Pound, *Spirit...*, p. 11. See also: Pound, *The Ideal Element...Tagore*, pp. 201-204.

190. Pound, *Vol. 1*, p. 247. See also: Pound, *The Ideal Element...Tagore*, pp. 201-204.

191. Pound, *Vol. 2*, p. 169. See also: Pound, *The Ideal Element...Tagore*, pp. 201-204.

192. Pound, *Vol. 1*, pp. 247-248. See also: Pound, *The Ideal Element...Tagore*, pp. 201-204.

193. Pound, *Vol. 1*, p. 248. See also: Pound, *The Ideal Element...Tagore*, pp. 196, 201-204. Pound, *Justice According...*, pp. 36-37.

194. Pound, *Vol. 1*, p. 249. See also: Pound, *The Ideal Element...Tagore*, pp. 197, 201-204. Pound, *Justice According...*, pp. 35-37.

195. Pound, *Vol. 1*, p. 249. See also: Pound, *The Ideal Element...Tagore*, pp. 201-204.

196. Pound, *Vol. 1*, p. 249. See also: Pound, *The Ideal Element...Tagore*, pp. 201-204. Pound, *Justice According...*, pp. 35-37.

197. Pound, *Vol. 1*, p. 250. See also: Pound, *The Ideal Element...Tagore*, pp. 198, 201-204. Pound, *Justice According...*, pp. 35-37.

198. Pound, *Vol. 1*, p. 250. See also: Pound, *The Ideal Element...Tagore*, pp. 201-204.

199. Pound, *Vol. 1*, p. 250. See also: Pound, *The Ideal Element...Tagore*, pp. 201-213. Pound, *Social Control...*, pp. 98-99.

200. Pound, *Vol. 1*, p. 250. See also: Pound, *The Ideal Element...Tagore*, pp. 198-199.

201. Pound, *Vol. 1*, pp. 250-251. See also: Pound, *The Ideal Element...Tagore*, pp. 198-199.

202. Pound, *The Ideal Element...Tagore*, pp. 198, 204-205. See also: Pound, *Vol. 1*, p. 251.

203. Pound, *The Ideal Element...Tagore*, pp. 198, 204-205.

204. Pound, *Vol. 1*, p. 251. See also: Pound, *The Ideal Element...Tagore*, pp. 198, 204-205.

205. Pound, *Vol. 1*, pp. 251-252. See also: Pound, *The Ideal Element...Tagore*, pp. 198-199, 201-213.

206. Pound, *Vol. 1*, p. 252. See also: Pound, *The Ideal Element...Tagore*. pp. 199, 201-213.

207. Pound, *Vol. 1*, pp. 253-254. See also: Pound, *The Ideal Element...Tagore*, pp. 199-200, 201-213.

208. Pound, *Vol. 1*, pp. 254-255. See also: Pound, *The Ideal Element...Tagore*, p. 200. Pound, "Fifty Years...III," p. 780.

209. Pound, *Vol. 1*, p. 255. See also: Pound, "Fifty Years...III," p. 780. Pound, *The Ideal Element...Tagore*, p. 214.

210. Pound, *Vol. 1*, p. 255. See also: Pound, "Fifty Years...III," p. 780. Pound, *The Ideal Element...Tagore*, p. 214.

211. Pound, *Vol. 1*, p. 256. See also: Pound, "Fifty Years...III," pp. 780-781. Pound, *The Ideal Element...Tagore*, p. 214.

212. Pound, *Vol. 1*, pp. 256-257. See also: Pound, "Fifty Years...III," p. 781.

213. Pound, *Vol. 1*, p. 255. See also: Pound, "Fifty Years...III," pp. 782-783. Pound, *Introduction...Philosophy...*, p. 160.

214. Pound, *Vol. 1*, pp. 258-259. See also: Pound, "Fifty Years...III," pp. 782-783. Pound, *The Ideal Element...Tagore*, pp. 214-215.

215. Pound, *Vol. 1*, p. 259. See also: Pound, "Fifty Years...III," pp. 783-784. Pound, *The Ideal Element...Tagore*, pp. 215-216.

216. Pound, *The Ideal Element...Tagore*, p. 216. See also: Pound, *Vol. 1*, p. 259. Pound, "Fifty Years...III," p. 784.

217. Pound, *The Ideal Element...Tagore*, p. 216. See also: Pound, *Vol. 1*, p. 260. Pound, "Fifty Years...III," p. 784.

218. Pound, *The Ideal Element...Tagore*, pp. 216-217. See also: Pound, *Vol. 1*, pp. 260-261.

219. Pound, *The Ideal Element...Tagore*, pp. 216-217. See also: Pound, *Vol. 1*, p. 261.

220. Pound, *The Ideal Element...Tagore*, pp. 216-217. See also: Pound, *Vol.1*, pp. 261-262.

221. Pound, *The Ideal Element...Tagore*, p. 217. See also: Pound, *Vol. 1*, p. 262.

222. Pound, *The Ideal Element...Tagore*, p. 217. See also: Pound, *Vol. 1*, p. 262.

223. Pound, *The Ideal Element...Tagore*, p. 223. See also: Pound, *Vol. 1*, p. 263. Pound, "Fifty Years...III," p. 785.

224. Pound, *The Ideal Element...Tagore*, p. 218. See also: Pound, *Vol. 1*, p. 264. Pound, "Fifty Years...III," p. 785.

225. Pound, *Vol. 1*, p. 264. See also: Pound, *The Ideal Element...Tagore*, pp. 219-222. Pound, "Fifty Years...III," pp. 785-786.

226. Pound, *Vol. 1*, p. 264. See also: Pound, *The Ideal Element...Tagore*, pp. 223-225. Pound, "Fifty Years...III," p. 786.

227. Pound, *Vol. 1*. p. 265. See also: Pound, *The Ideal Element...Tagore*, pp. 220-222.

228. Pound, *Vol. 1*, pp. 266-267. See also: Pound, *The Ideal Element...Tagore*, p. 221. Pound, "Fifty Years...III," pp. 788-790.

229. Pound, *Vol. 1*, p. 267. See also: Pound, *The Ideal Element...Tagore*, p. 221. Pound, "Fifty Years...III," pp. 788-790.

230. Pound, *Vol. 1*. p. 267. See also: Pound, *The Ideal Element...Tagore*, p. 227. Pound, "Fifty Years...III," pp. 788-790. R. Pound, "The Call for a Realist Jurisprudence," *Harvard Law Review*, Vol. 44, March, 1931, p. 705. Vol. 1 PB 178 (Hereinafter referred to as "The Call for...").

231. Pound, *Vol. 1*, p. 268. See also: Pound, *The Ideal Element...Tagore*, pp. 220-227. Pound, "Fifty Years...III," pp. 788-790.

232. Pound, *Vol. 1*, pp. 268-269. See also: Pound, *The Ideal Element...Tagore*, pp. 220-227. Pound, "Fifty Years...III," pp. 788-790.

233. Pound, *Vol. 1*, pp. 269-270. See also: Pound, *The Ideal Element...Tagore*, pp. 220-227. Pound, "Fifty Years...III," pp. 790-797.

234. Pound, *Vol. 1*, p. 270. See also: Pound, *The Ideal Element...Tagore*, pp. 227-228. Pound, "Fifty Years...III," pp. 790-797.

235. Pound, *Vol. 1*, pp. 270-271. See also: Pound, *The Ideal Element...Tagore*, p. 228. Pound, "Fifty Years...III," pp. 790-797.

236. Pound, *Vol. 1*, p. 271. See also: Pound, *The Ideal Element...Tagore*, p. 228. Pound, "Fifty Years...III," pp. 790-797.

237. Pound, *Vol. 1*, p. 272. See also: Pound, *The Ideal Element...Tagore*, p. 231. Pound, "Fifty Years...III," 790-797.

238. Pound, *Vol. 1*, p. 273. See also: Pound, *The Ideal Element...Tagore*, p. 231. Pound, "Fifty Years...III," 790-797.

239. Pound, *Vol. 1*, p. 274. See also: Pound, *The Ideal Element...Tagore*, p. 231. Pound, "Fifty Years...III," 790-797.

240. Pound, *Vol. 1*, p. 274. See also: Pound, *The Ideal Element...Tagore*, pp. 231-233. Pound, "Fifty Years...III," pp. 790-797.

241. Pound, *Vol. 1*, p. 275. See also: Pound, *The Ideal Element...Tagore*, pp. 231-232. Pound, "Fifty Years...III," pp. 790-797.

242. Pound, *Vol. 1*, p. 275. See also: Pound, *The Ideal Element...Tagore*, pp. 231, 237-238. Pound, "Fifty Years...III," pp. 790-797.

243. Pound, *Vol. 1*, p. 276. See also: Pound, *The Ideal Element...Tagore*, pp. 237-238. Pound, "Fifty Years...III," 790-797.

244. Pound, *The Ideal Element...Tagore*, p. 232. See also: Pound, "Fifty Years...III," pp. 790-797.

245. Pound, *Vol. 1*, p. 276. See also: Pound, *The Ideal Element...Tagore*, pp. 238-239. Pound, "Fifty Years...III," pp. 797-799.

246. Pound, *Vol. 1*, pp. 276-277. See also: Pound, *The Ideal Element...Tagore*, pp. 238-239. Pound, "Fifty Years...III," pp. 797-799.

247. Pound, *Vol. 1*, p. 277. See also: Pound, *The Ideal Element...*, p. 239. Pound, "Fifty Years...III," pp. 797-799.

248. Pound, *Vol. 1*, p. 277. See also: Pound, *The Ideal Element...Tagore*, pp. 237-240. Pound, "The Call for...," pp. 700-701. Pound, "Fifty Years...III," 797-799. R. Pound, "What Use Can Be Made of Judicial Statistics," *Oregon Law Review*, Vol 12, February, 1933, Vol. 1 PB 191. (Hereinafter referred to as "What Use...").

249. Pound, *Vol. 1*, p. 278. See also: Pound, *The Ideal Element...Tagore*, p. 239. Pound, "Fifty Years...III," 797-799.

250. Pound, *Vol. 1*, pp. 278-279. See also: Pound, "Fifty Years...III," pp. 797-799.

251. Pound, *Vol. 1*, p. 279. See also: Pound, "The Call for...," pp. 701-702. Pound, "Fifty Years...III," pp. 797-799.

252. Pound, *Vol. 1*, p. 281. See also: Pound, "Fifty Years...III," pp. 797-799. Pound, *The Ideal Element...Tagore*, pp. 240-241.

253. Pound, Vol. 1, p. 281. See also: Pound, *The Ideal Element...Tagore*, pp. 240-241. Pound, "Fifty Years...III," pp. 797-799.

254. Pound, *Vol. 1*, p. 281. See also: Pound, "Fifty Years...III," pp. 797-799. Pound, "The Call for...," pp. 702-703.

255. Pound, *Vol. 1*, p. 279. See also: Pound, "Fifty Years...III," pp. 797-799. Pound, "The Call for...," p. 703.

256. Pound, *Vol. 1*, p. 279. See also: Pound, *The Ideal Element...Tagore*, pp. 238-240. Pound, "Fifty Years...III," pp. 797-799.

257. Pound, *The Ideal Element...Tagore*, pp. 238-240. See Chapter Five, Sociological Jurisprudence; Chapter Seven, Theory of Interests.

258. Pound, *Vol. 1*, p. 280. See also: Pound, "The Call for...," p. 703. Pound, "Fifty Years...III," pp. 797-799. Pound, *The Ideal Element...Tagore*, pp. 238-241.

259. Pound, *Vol. 1*. p. 282. See also: Pound, *The Ideal Element...Tagore*, p. 241

260. Pound, *Vol. 1*, p. 282. See also: Pound, *The Ideal Element...Tagore*, p. 241.

261. Pound, *Vol. 1*. p. 283. See also: Pound, *The Ideal Element...Tagore*, p. 242.

262. Pound, *Vol. 1*, p. 283. See also: Pound, *The Ideal Element...Tagore*, pp. 241-242.

263. Pound, *Vol. 1*. p. 283. See also: Pound, *The Ideal Element...Tagore*, p. 243.

264. Pound, *Vol. 1*, p. 283. See also: Pound, *The Ideal Element...Tagore*, p. 242.

265. Pound, *Vol. 1*, p. 284. See also: Pound, *The Ideal Element...Tagore, pp. 198-200.*

266. Pound, "The Call for...," pp. 697-698. See also: Pound, *The Ideal Element...Tagore*, pp. 198-200.

267. Pound, "The Call for...," p. 698. See also: Pound, *The Ideal Element...Tagore*, pp. 198-200.

268. Pound, "The Call for...," p. 699. See also: Pound, *The Ideal Element...Tagore*, pp. 198-200.

269. Pound, "The Call for...," p. 699. See also: Pound, *The Ideal Element...Tagore*, pp. 198-200.

270. Pound, "The Call for...," p. 699. See also: Pound, *The Ideal Element...Tagore*, pp. 198-200.

271. Pound, "The Call for...," p. 700. See also: Pound, *The Ideal Element...Tagore*, pp. 198-200.

272. Pound, "The Call for...," p. 700. See also: Pound, *The Ideal Element...Tagore*, pp. 198-200.

273. Pound, "The Call for...," p. 709.

274. Pound, *Vol. 1*, pp. 285-287. In his article "Call for Realist Jurisprudence" Pound suggests a seven point program. The three not covered in his later statement, being used here, are: (1) a functional examination of how institutions operate, without excessive focus on atypical and individualized instances of this operation. Numbers five and six seem to be subsumed under number five in the later study, for they urge a focusing on values and ends of the legal order. The second item in the listing from *Jurisprudence* and *The Ideal Element in the Law*, was not in Pound's original list, and reflects, it seems, his growing concern with executive justice and administrative law.

275. Pound, *Vol. 1*, p. 285. Pound, "The Call for...," p. 710. See also: Pound, *The Ideal Element...Tagore*, p. 243.

276. Pound, *Vol. 1*, p. 285. See also: Pound, "The Call for...," p. 710. Pound, *The Ideal Element...Tagore*, p. 243.

277. Pound, *Vol. 1*. pp. 285-286. See also: Pound, "The Call for...," p. 710. Pound, *The Ideal Element...Tagore*, p. 243.

278. Pound, *Vol. 1*, p. 286. See also: Pound, "The Call for...," pp. 706-710. Pound, *The Ideal Element...Tagore*, p. 243.

279. Pound, *Vol. 1*, pp. 286-287. See also: Pound, "The Call for...," pp. 710-711. Pound, *The Ideal Element...Tagore*, p. 244.

280. Pound, *Justice According...*, p. 91.

Chapter Six

Sociological Jurisprudence

Pound believed that the "socialization of law," with its balancing and reconciling of interests, which press for recognition in the legal order, is parallelled by a new philosophical theory of law, *i.e.*, the "sociology of law", or "sociological jurisprudence". According to Pound, Oliver Wendell Holmes was the forerunner of this theory, and believed that law required a balancing of legal facts with legal theory, in order to assume a constructive conclusion in any given situation. Pound concludes that Holmes had:

> faith in the efficacy of effort to make the law more effective for its ends; in a functional point of view in contrast with the purely anatomical or morphological standpoint of the last century; in giving up the idea of jurisprudence as a self-sufficient science in each of these respects he foreshadowed, if he did not develop, the characteristic methods and ideas of a sociological science of law.[1]

Sociological jurisprudence, Pound believes, constitutes a great advance in legal thinking. Among its advantages is that it abandons the rigidity and narrowness of the historical and analytical schools of the nineteenth century, and accounts for the "realities" that must be considered in order that law can manage effectively a changing, industrial society.

Pound describes graphically the scope of the change he perceives to have occurred and says:

> The situation created by the economic order is analogous to that presented by the social order in the Middle Ages when the individual land-owner, unequal to protecting himself, entered into a relation of service and protection with a lord. For the days when the individual business man was self-sufficient are also in the past. More and more he has proved insufficient for any but the smallest businesses. He has had to commend

> himself by transferring his business to a corporation and taking shares in its stead.[2]

Law was compelled to deal with these new conditions. Legal thinking which was tied to the abstract formalism of most of the nineteenth century schools of legal philosophy could not do this. Ideas, however, that were sensitive to the realities of the practical world, and took into account the effects of industrialization, urbanization, and technological advancement could, if they utilized data from other disciplines that were relevant to the law, be equal to the task. This new legal philosophy could preserve and transmit civilization in the face of the altered circumstances of the modern era. Commenting further on the need for this new legal philosophy, Pound observes:

> Looked at functionally, the law is an attempt to satisfy, to reconcile, to harmonize, to adjust their [interests'] overlapping and often conflicting elements and demands, either through securing them directly and immediately, or through securing certain individual interests, so as to give effect to the greatest total of interests or to the interest that weighs most in our civilization, with the least sacrifice of the scheme of interests as a whole.[3]

Because of the altered circumstances in modern society, a more realistic jurisprudence was required that would not be tailored to serve the abstract notions of freedom and individualism. Such abstractions were hostile to the idea that legislative and administrative reforms which could and should be used to adjust the law to a changed reality. Pound observes, further, that in effecting this change in legal philosophy:

> the technicalities of the nineteenth century lawyer and the anti-social obstruction of the nineteenth-century judge who was content to follow patiently a circuitous and uneven road, so it led ultimately to justice—these things, too, it may be, shall be forgotten as the twentieth-century lawyer learns to lay out for us a straight and level, and smooth and secure highway, which also shall lead to justice.[4]

Turning the law from the narrowness of formal, nineteenth century jurisprudence was the major task faced by sociological jurisprudence. Pound notes that the difference between sociological jurists and those who preceded them lies in the fact that the sociological jurisprudential writers:

> 1. ...[L]ook more to the working of the law than to its abstract content.

> 2. They regard law as a social institution which may be improved by intelligent human effort, and hold it their duty to discover the best means of furthering and directing such effort.
> 3. They lay stress upon the social purposes which law subserves rather than sanction.
> 4. They urge that legal precepts are to be regarded more as guides to results which are socially just and less inflexible modes.
> 5. Their philosophical views are very diverse. Beginning as positivists, recently they have adhered to some one of the groups of the social philosophical school, from which, indeed, the sociological school, on many essential points, is not easily distinguishable.[5]

Many of the principles and precepts of the common law, which developed prior to the stage of industrialization, urbanization, and technological change, hampered the law's ability to face the challenges created by these altered circumstances.[6] Information from other disciplines, such as sociology and economics, must be taken into account by legal philosophers and practitioners, according to Pound, since this data would be most helpful in fashioning sociological jurisprudence.[7] Altered circumstances which the law must acknowledge and the use of data from other academic disciplines would both contribute to the fashioning sociological jurisprudence. Pound says:

> It is their [law leaders] task to create in this country a true sociological jurisprudence, to develop a thorough understanding between the people and the law, to ensure that the common law remain, what its exponents have always insisted it is— the custom of the people, the expression of these habits of thought and action as to the relation of men with each other.[8]

Sociological jurisprudence had moved through several stages of development before it had become the coherent legal philosophy which Pound admired. According to Pound these prior stages of development were: (1) the mechanical, (2) the biological, and (3) the psychological.[9]

Mechanical

The mechanical stage of sociological jurisprudence was greatly influenced by the theories of August Comte and Pierre Laplace,[10] both of whom had suggested that society was produced by laws which were equivalent to the laws of mathematics and mechanics.[11] Their arguments were based on those similar to the historical school, Comte and Laplace argued that law was the product of evolutionary processes which were determined by mechanical laws.[12] Notions of economic determinism that are reflected in the ideas of Karl Marx and Brooks Adams were evident in this mechanical view,[13] which maintained that legislative and juristic activity was of no avail. As Pound observes, this view holds that:

> Law is an inevitable resultant; in making or finding it, legislator or judge is merely bringing about "conformity to the *de facto* wishes of the dominant forces in the community."[14]

This mechanical view assumed, therefore, that neither legislative nor judicial action can alter or improve the legal order. Despite the terrible flaws Pound sees in this school, Pound, nonetheless, feels that it made two contributions that improved jurisprudential thought. He describes these contributions as follows:

> (1) ...[the] displacing [of] the individualist starting-point and the atomistic standpoint of nineteenth-century jurisprudence by insisting upon the importance of the group, or the class, of "the compact plurality," and (2) in compelling us to relate the law more critically to other social phenomena.[15]

It is Pound's opinion that the emphasis of the mechanical jurisprudents on this pattern and process of development made further inquiry about the law and its foundation necessary.[16]

Biological

The second stage in the development of sociological jurisprudence is the biological one, which derived mainly from Charles Darwin's theory of evolution.[17] This school had three subdivisions to it—mechanical, ethnological, and philosophical.[18] The mechanical-sociological stressed the evolutionary notions found in early sociological jurisprudence, but placed a heavy emphasis on the idea of "natural selection."[19] Pound observes that this mechanical-biological-sociological school:

> brought us by another path to the same position to which the historical school and the mechanical sociologists had led us before them. The position was the same. But they state it otherwise. As they put it, the end of law is to give play in an ordinary manner to the elimination of the

> unfit; it is to further natural selection by a well-ordered struggle for existence.[20]

Favoring the "survival of the fittest," in terms of groups and individuals, led in turn to an emphasis on collective interests and goals, in contrast to the emphasis on abstract individualism associated with the philosophy of law prevailing in the nineteenth century.[21]

The ethnological emphasis in early sociological jurisprudence, at one stage, focused on *primitive* peoples, and assume that the:

> study of the social institutions of the most primitive peoples [would]...reveal the fundamental laws of legal development.[22]

The proponents of this approach argued that it provided an explanation for social and legal development in general.[23] This ethnological view emphasized the racial idea of legal development, i. e., it argued that the legal developments of a particular race reflects the unfolding of an idea which bears the impress of "the development of the legal institutions of this or that people."[24] Thus, law and legal institutions are expressions of the:

> character, mentality, or temperament of the race in whose social institutions it has developed.[25]

Although this theory argued that such development might be influenced by external forces,[26] it maintained that legal development is, nonetheless:

> a product of race character and temperament, arising from a conflict of interests and the need of *harmonizing* them in action if the race is to endure.[27]

The second variant of the ethnological-sociological, at another stage emphasizes a demographic method which Pound says proceeds:

> on an idea that the jurist had, first, to gather as materials the legal institutions...of all primitive peoples and describe them, and then, second to generalize from them.[28]

The only contribution of this demographic method was to call attention to the fact that preceding historical and philosophical schools of jurisprudence did not examine legal origins sufficiently, since primitive societies were generally excluded from their inquiry.[29] Outside of this limited utility, however, the demographic method did not make any major contribution to the development of legal philosophy.

The final variant in the "philosophical" school reflects nineteenth century metaphysical jurisprudence, which considered all legal phenomena from the standpoint of an abstract philosophical precept—liberty. This metaphysical view focused attention on this single concept and ignored all other evidence and material. The biological-sociological writers corrected this to some extent. Pound feels that the influence of the philosophical approach was both short-lived and minor, and writes:

> Here we have a precursor of the threat theory of law and the theory of rights as influences from the threats. But it is a philosophical theory of law as the outcome of a struggle between the social and anti-social. This type of sociological jurisprudence is quite as barren as the metaphysical jurisprudence which it imitates.[30]

Another variant of this philosophical school, which had a little more to recommend it, is reflected in those studies which viewed law as the outcome of class conflict.[31] This view emphasized the belief that all of law is a reflection of dominant class interests. Consequently the content of law and its purpose is relative to the time and condition of a particular dominant class.[32] This view is quite incomplete and inadequate, and this interpretation, Pound feels, cannot explain most of the legal precepts which give vitality and meaning to law generally. For example, precepts derive their meaning and their content from the nature of law's purpose in civilizing human conduct and cannot be read as results of only class conflict. Despite this serious weakness, however, Pound does feel that there is one important result coming from this variant of the philosophical school. He writes:

> [I]t drew attention to the unequal operation of doctrines derived by the nineteenth-century method of abstraction upon the basis of assumed natural equality when applied in a society in which industrial progress had resulted in well-defined classes.[33]

Psychological

The third stage in the development of sociological jurisprudence was tied to psychology, and had more to commend it. According to Pound, this stage was divided into three major types of examination, which Pound describes as follows:

> (1) study of group personality and group will [which was associated with the work of Gierke] leading to a psychological movement in legal and political philosophy, (2) the complete change in method in the social sciences which resulted from Ward's theories that "psychic forces are as real and natural physical forces—and that they are the true causes of all social phenomena," and, (3) Tarde's demonstration of the extent to which imitation is a factor in the development of legal institutions and his working out of the psychological or sociological laws of imitation.[34]

According to Pound, Gierke is the legal philosopher who most successfully separated legal philosophy from its attachment to the idea that the core of analysis of legal thought is the individual will.[35] Gierke's theory emphasized the notion that man must be considered as a creature of his social development,[36] and believed recognition must be given to the fact that the group's will is qualitatively different from individual will. Consequently, Gierke maintains that law must be viewed in its role as the means of effecting to the collective will.[37] This shift of attention and emphasis from individual to group will contributed to the recognition that law must be viewed as an evolving and growing mode of social control. This view of Gierke's resulted also in focusing attention on the fact that social-psychological theories of sanction must be considered in legal theory and philosophy.[38] Jellinek, who had emphasized this contribution of Gierke's theory is praised by Pound, who says:

> His [Jellinek's] conception of the social psychological *guarantee*, whereby rules are made effective and so are made laws, is one of the most important contributions of the psychological movement.[39]

Concurrently with the developments in the field of legal philosophy which focused on psychological concerns, there were other developments outside of jurisprudence, which had a profound effect on the course of legal philosophical development.[40] Pound feels that the most significant of these external developments was the result of the work of Lester F. Ward, who had argued in opposition to the mechanical sociological theories which were so popular, and endorsed ideas of psychic forces that operated on laws in the course of legal development.[41] Pound says that in Ward's theory:

> sociology rests upon psychology, and not directly upon *biology*, that we must know not only how nonsentient nature works, but "how mind combines it with the non-sentient factors of human conditions," and that this part of nature may be harnessed to man's use as so much of physical nature has been so harnessed.[42]

Ward's work, according to Pound, gave encouragement and respectability to the idea that legal reform could and would be efficacious. His ideas dealt a mortal blow to the prevailing nineteenth century notions that had rejected the idea of law as a means to be used in fashioning society purposefully.[43]

Pound also feels that much credit must be given to the contribution made by Gabriel Tarde, whose emphasis on the importance and significance of "imitation" in human behavior contributed to a reemphasis on the importance of taught tradition in the maintenance and operation of the law. As Pound observes:

> Tarde knew the importance of taught tradition, of doctrinal writing and of judicial decision. He knew the significance of the traditional element in a legal system and of the modes of juristic theory that gave continuity to legal systems. These modes of thinking and mental habits as to the development and application of legal precepts are the most enduring elements in the law.[44]

Pound firmly believes in the value and importance of the taught tradition in the law. The common law is built on such a tradition, and Pound's own endorsement and praise for the role of judicial justice, clearly reveals his attachment to the significance of the taught tradition of law.[45]

Pound considered these early developments in the growth of sociological jurisprudence to be of varied importance and significance. The psychological influences had assisted significantly in reconciling the apparent dichotomy between imperative and traditional law, and thus contributed to the eventual emergence of sociological jurisprudence. As Pound notes:

> Not only does social psychology occupy a chief place in recent sociological jurisprudence but modes of juristic thought, the world-view of judges and doctrinal writers and the psychology of juridical methods are coming to be the subject of special study.[46]

The unification of sociological jurisprudence followed in the wake of the previously cited developments. The unification resulted, in part, from sociologists' recognition that the multitude of approaches and methods they had employed were all necessary to the further development of their study, but that no one method or approach was sufficient.[47] The unification was a result not only of the coherency established among the variants of sociological theory, but also when it was recognized that sociology must be placed:

> into relation with other social sciences; that it was needful to unify the social sciences by recognizing that after all, in a large view, they are departments or phases of a science of human society or, what that comes to, civilization.[48]

Developments in the social sciences had a beneficial effect on the future course of jurisprudential thought which, according to Pound, had been far too insular and removed from the realities with which law must deal. The division of juristic practice and jurisprudential thought from the data needed accounted for the discontent with the law that had been so characteristic of the early twentieth century.[49] The recognition that social science and law had a common task, and that these areas of study and interest were interrelated, served in giving impetus to the implication of sociological jurisprudence.[50] Sociological jurisprudence, Pound argues, enables one to see law as a means of social control which works in conjunction with and not in isolation from other forms of social control.[51]

The emergence of sociological jurisprudence paralleled the development of the socialization of law.[52] As Pound observes these two concepts are "closely related." "The one [sociological jurisprudence] is a theoretical, the other [sociology of law] an applied science."[53] Sociological jurisprudence, which focuses on the social control exercised by law, acknowledges the close relationship of the three meanings which are fittingly ascribed to the law, *i.e.*:

> the regime of adjusting relations and ordering conduct through the force of a politically organized society, the body of authoritative guides to decision and patterns of conduct by which that regime is maintained, and the judicial processes by which those guides to determination are found and applied.[54]

The means needed for the successful ordering of society, Pound feels, cannot be fashioned without expanding the scope of legal inquiry so that it incorporates data drawn from other sciences directed to the understanding of social order.[55] Pound notes:

> In the modern world, law has become the paramount agency of social control. Our main reliance in the society of today is upon the force of politically organized society. We seek to adjust relations and order conflict through the orderly and systematic application of that force. At the moment this side of the law, its dependence upon force, is the one most insisted upon.[56]

The role of law in the context of these broader social issues and concerns, according to Pound, is to adjust relations, interests, and conflicts in society, and achieve justice compatible with a legal order. The legal order, at a minimum, should make it possible for men to achieve as many satisfactions as they can within that social order consistent with the other needs of that order, *e.g.*, peace and security. It is in this sense that justice can be achieved. As he notes, we may consider the task of the legal order:

> as one of precluding friction and eliminating waste; as one of conserving the goods of existence in order to make them go as far as possible, and of precluding friction and eliminating waste in the human use and enjoyment of them, so that where each may not have all that he claims, he may at least have all that is possible. Put in this way, we are seeking to secure as much of human claims and desires—that is as much of the whole scheme of interests—as possible, with the least sacrifice of such interests.[57]

For Pound, the merit of sociological jurisprudence is found in the fact that it provides practical solutions to real problems. Law and jurisprudence cannot ignore values and ethics. Thus, its primary task is the preservation and transmission of civilization, which can be done only if there is a realistic management of conflicts which arise from the competing interests arising in a social order. The task of law is to balance justice, morals, and security.[58] As Pound observes, morality cannot be the only measure of the law or its effectiveness since the purpose of law is more expansive than that. It must provide security and this fact cannot be ignored in any resolution that law makes of conflicting claims and interests. Further, other agencies of the society, he notes, are better equipped to maintain moral relationships among men. Nonetheless, the law must not ignore the question of morals completely, and although one should not attempt to use the law to perfect morality, one still should not eliminate moral concerns from the law.[59]

Social control provides the means for maintaining and furthering civilization, and is achieved through the use of the law.[60] The technique to be employed in the operation of the law is to be found in the balancing and reconciling of competing interests; while ethics and ideals are to be used to condition the choice of the solutions selected.[61] Critical to the success of Pound's formulation is his use of social engineering, which Pound describes as follows:

> It [social engineering] is formed in an idea of giving the most complete security and effect to the whole scheme of human demands or expectations, which have pressed or are pressing for recognition and securing, with the least sacrifice of the scheme as a whole, the least friction, and the least waste.[62]

For Pound, the concept of social engineering, although it is analogically related to the methodology of the industrial engineer,[63] differs in substantial ways from the latter.[64] The concept of social engineering employed by Pound does not refer to a technique that is employed to create or achieve a preformed conception of society. Rather, it is a descriptive term which describes the technique already in operation in the law, which serves to reconcile and adjust competing interests in the society. According to Pound, the sociological school enables lawmakers and jurists:

> to take [a] more complete and intelligent account of the social facts upon which law must proceed and to which it is to be applied.[65]

Pound maintains that sociological writers emphasize five major points which enable them to understand the relationship of fact and value.

First, Pound says, sociological jurisprudence compels the "study of the actual social effect of legal institutions, of legal precepts, and of legal doctrines."[66] The cost of the absence of such information, he says, is suggested by Hermann Kantorowicz, who writes:

> I advise one who does not believe this to read a section of the German Civil Code in the following way: Let him ask himself with respect to each statute...what harms would social life undergo if instead of this statement the opposite were intended. And then let him turn to all textbooks, commentaries, monographs, and reports of decisions and see how many questions of this sort he will find answered and how many he will even find put. Paradoxically, also, statistics upon civil law are almost wholly wanting, so that we can be sure of almost nothing as to the social function of civil law, particularly as to the measure of its realization.[67]

The use of data and information, drawn from the social sciences, including jurisprudence, assists in enabling law to perform its task of social engineering. This focus on reality eliminates the use of abstract formulae and concepts in reconciling and adjusting competing interests. As Pound observes:

> Let us put the new point of view in terms of engineering;... Let us think of the problem of the end of law in terms of a great task or great series of tasks of social engineering.... Thus we may think of the task of the legal order as one of precluding friction and elementary waste; as one of conserving the goods of existence in order to make them go as far as possible, and of precluding friction and eliminating waste in the human use and enjoyment of them, so that where each may not have all that he claims, he may at least have all that is possible. Put in this way, we are seeking to secure as much of human claims and desires—that is as much of the whole scheme of interest—as possible, with the least sacrifice of interests.[68]

Second, sociological jurisprudence links sociological study, broadly defined, with the operation of law in order to "...study their [legislated laws'] social operation and the effect which they produce, if any, when put into action."[69] Such a blending of disciplines, Pound feels, is necessary to developing the concept of "social engineering", which requires that the abstraction of law be tempered by determining its "real" effect, when applied to conflict and discord. As he states:

> Looked at functionally, the law is an attempt to satisfy, to reconcile, to harmonize, to adjust these overlapping and often conflicting claims and demands...so as to give effect to the greatest total of interests or to the interest that weighs most heavily in our civilization, with the least sacrifice by the scheme of interests as a whole.[70]

Third, sociological jurisprudence is concerned with how law is made effective through its enforcement.[71] Previous approaches to the study of law focused mainly on its origins or its creation, and gave little attention to the fact and necessity of effective enforcement. As Pound observes:

> ...the life of the law is in its enforcement. [Thus]...serious scientific study of how to make our huge annual output of legislative and judicial interpretation effective is imperative.[72]

A legal order that does not reflect the moral sentiments and real needs of the society for which it is designed fails to achieve a proper ordering of the affairs of the people within that society. Thus, Pound says:

> Legal science must exhibit some practical results. It must show that it has something to offer before it may hope for public recognition.[73]

Criticizing American law in the early part of the twentieth century, Pound says that it reflected a sterility of form, and that the "reasons" offered in justification of existing rules and interpretation did not conform in any realistic manner to the needs and interests which had emerged in the society which remained unprotected and unrecognized.[74] Sociological jurisprudence, however, takes into account economics, politics, and sociology in examining the content, application, and enforcement of law.[75] The socialization of law enables it to shift the emphasis away from the abstract individualism which characterized the era of maturity of law,[76] and focuses on the collective needs, and duties, which are a fundamental reality in the industrial age.[77] The theory of law which provides the understanding and grasp of these developments is sociological jurisprudence. As Pound writes:

> In all cases of divergence between the standard of the common law and the standard of the public, it goes without saying that the latter will prevail in the end. Sooner or later what public opinion demands will be recognized and enforced by the courts. A Bench and Bar trained in individualist theories and firm in the persuasion that the so-called legal justice is an absolute and a necessary standard, from which there may be no departure without the destruction of the legal order, may retard but cannot prevent progress to the newer standard recognized by the sociologist. In this progress lawyers should be conscious factors, not unconscious followers of popular thought, not conscious obstructions of the course of legal development. To this end it is the duty of teachers of law, while they teach scrupulously the law that the courts administer, to teach it in the spirit and from the standpoint of the political, economic, and sociological learning of today. It is their task to create in this country a true sociological jurisprudence, to develop a thorough understanding between the people and the law, to insure that the common law remains, what its exponents have always insisted it is—the custom of the people, the expression of their habit of thought and action as to the relation of men with each other.[78]

Fourth, Pound believes sociological jurisprudence must develop a sociological history of law which would:

> study not merely of how doctrines have evolved and developed, considered solely as jural materials, but of what social effects the doctrines of the law have produced in the past and how they have produced them.[79]

The sociology of law, therefore, requires a history of law:

> which shall show us: (1) How or how far the law of the past grew out of social, economic, and psychological conditions; (2) how it accommodated itself to them; (3) how far we can proceed today on the basis of the law of the past or in disregard of it with well-grounded expectations of producing the results desired.[80]

To be sure Pound's own scheme of interpreting legal history—the stages through which it passes, the values that are enshrined, and the purposes that are served—was an attempt to formulate the type of legal history which he felt was needed to illuminate the pattern and process of legal development.[81]

Fifth, Pound feels that an important task of sociological jurisprudence involves the development of theory and practice which would assure "reasonable and just solutions of individual causes," which he argues, often is not achieved by law since there has always been an incentive to secure law by ignoring the injustice its application might create in individual cases.[82] Pound argues that where the narrow application of legal precepts and rules had served the law's role in assuring security and stability, such applications often led to "unfair" and "inequitable" consequences for the individual litigants.[83] Sociological jurisprudence explains the nature of developments in the era of the socialization of law which have modified the rigid application of abstract formulas. Sociological jurisprudence has departed from the abstractions so common to nineteenth century thinking about the law, and has focused on the socialization of the law, which requires realistic and balanced adjustments of competing interests. This is reflected in the changed attitude about taxation which moved to a concept of graduated tax and away from:

> the abstract equality of the nineteenth century to an adjustment of burdens with reference to ability to bear them. Thus there is a concrete individualization of application where in the last century there was an abstract equality of abstract individuals.[84]

While Pound feels that the individualization of justice is a development to be applauded, and that sociological jurisprudence must take such developments into account and seek to guide them in their further development,[85] he was alarmed by the degree to which the individualization of justice and the demands for it threatened the role of law as a force for harmony and order.[86]

In summarizing the development and content of the sociological school Pound says:

> Sociological jurists seek to enable and to compel lawmaking, whether legislative or judicial or administrative, and also the development, interpretation, and application of legal precepts, to take more complete and intelligent account of the local facts upon which law must proceed and to which it is to be applied.[87]

Pound was a major spokesman of the sociological school of jurisprudence and an advocate of the socialization law. Later in his life he condemned the direction both had taken and the forms they had assumed. What concerned him most was the capturing of this term by those who translated its meaning into some form of socialist theory, and used it to further the extension of the service state. The creation of an expanded state threatened the life of the law as it had developed in the preceding centuries. In contrast to this development, Pound's own conception of socialization of law abjured the desirability and necessity of socialism and the inflated view of the "service state." For Pound, law should never be viewed as anything other than a brake on the power of the state; and, consequently, never as an instrument of that power.[88]

ENDNOTES

CHAPTER SIX

1. Pound, *Vol. 1*, p. 338.

2. Pound, "The Problem...," p. 6. See also: Pound, *Spirit...* pp. 27-29. Pound, *Interpretations of Legal...*, pp. 57-63.

3. Pound, "Survey...," p. 39. See also: Pound, "Law and Christian...," p. 106. Pound, *Justice According...*, p. 48. Pound, *Spirit...*, p. 196. Pound, *Interpretations of Legal...*, p. 157. Pound, Social Control..., pp. 63-65. See further discussion in Chapter Seven Theory of Interests.

4. Pound, "The Renewal of Personal Government," Proceedings of the Nebraska State Bar Association, Vol. 9, 1916, p. 124. Vol. 1 PB 89 (Hereinafter referred to as "...Renewal of Personal...").

5. Pound, "The Scope and Purpose...III," pp. 515-516. See also: Pound, *Spirit...*, pp. 212-215. Pound, *Vol. 1*, pp. 291-298.

6. Pound, "The Need of a Sociological Jurisprudence," Green Bag, Vol. 19, October, 1907, pp. 607-609. Vol. 1 PB 24 (Hereinafter referred to as "The Need of..."). See also: Pound, *Spirit...*, pp. 35-37. Pound, *The Ideal Element...Tagore*, pp. 182-184. Pound, *Interpretations of Legal...*, pp. 146-147.

7. Pound, "The Need of...," p. 609. See also: Pound, *Vol. 1*, pp. 325-350.

8. Pound, "The Need of...," p. 615. See also: Roscoe Pound, "The Socialization of the Common Law," Green Bay, Vol;. 26, April, 1914, pp. 166-170, Vol. 1 PB 65. (Hereinafter referred to as "Socialization...Common Law").

9. Pound, *Vol. 1*, p. 298. See also: Pound, "The Scope and Purpose...III," pp. 491-509. Pound, *Interpretations of Legal...*, pp. 69-91.

10. Pound, *Vol. 1*, p. 299. See also: Pound, "The Scope and Purpose...III," p. 491. Pound, *Interpretations of Legal...*, pp. 70-72.

11. Pound, "The Scope and Purpose...III," p. 491. See also: Pound, *Vol. 1*, pp. 299-300. Pound, *Interpretations of Legal...*, pp. 70-72.

12. Pound, "The Scope and Purpose...III," p. pp. 491-492. See also: Pound, *Vol. 1*, pp. 299-300. Pound, *Interpretations of Legal...*, pp. 70-71.

13. Pound, *Vol. 1*, p. 301. See also: Pound, "The Scope and Purpose...III," pp. 492-493. Pound, *Interpretations of Legal...*, pp. 92-115.

14. Pound, "The Scope and Purpose...III," p. 494. See also: Pound, *Interpretations of Legal...*, pp. 70-72. Pound, *Vol. 1*, pp. 299-303.

15. Pound, "The Scope and Purpose...III," p. 494. See also: Pound, *Vol. 1*, p.p. 302-303. Pound, *Interpretations of Legal...*, p. 72.

16. Pound, "The Scope and Purpose...III," p. 495. See also: Pound, *Vol. 1*, pp. 302-303.

17. Pound, *Vol. 1*, pp. 305-309. See also: Pound, "The Scope and Purpose...III," pp. 495-496. Pound, *Interpretations of Legal...*, pp. 72-91.

18. Pound, *Vol. 1*, p. 304. See also: Pound, *Interpretations of Legal...*, pp. 72-91. Pound, "The Scope and Purpose...III," pp. 495-496. (Pound mentions four types of biological-sociological jurisprudence in the earlier article—"Scope and Purpose...III," p. 496, but drops consideration of the "organismic" type in *Vol. 1*, p. 304.)

19. Pound, *Vol. 1*, pp. 304-305. See also: Pound, "The Scope and Purpose...III," pp. 498-499. Pound, *Interpretations of Legal...*, pp.85-91.

20. Pound, *Vol. 1*, p. 305. See also: Pound, *Interpretations of Legal...*, pp. 87-90.

21. Pound, *Vol. 1*, p. 305. See also: Pound, *Interpretations of Legal...*, p. 91. Pound, "The Scope and Purpose...III," p. 501.

22. Pound, *Vol. l*, p. 305. See also: Pound, "The Scope and Purpose...III," pp. 496-497.

23. Pound, *Vol. 1*, p. 305. See also: Pound, "The Scope and Purpose...," p. 497.

24. Pound, *Vol. 1*, p. 223. See also: Pound, "The Scope and Purpose...III," p. 497. Pound, *Interpretations of Legal...*, pp. 78-83.

25. Pound, *Vol. 1*, p. 224. See also: Pound, "The Scope and Purpose...III," p. 497. Pound, *Interpretations of Legal...*, pp. 78-83.

26. Pound, *Vol. 1*, p. 224. See also: Pound, "The Scope and Purpose...III," p. 497. Pound, *Interpretations of Legal...*, pp. 78-83.

27. Pound, *Vol. 1*, p. 224. See also: Pound, "The Scope and Purpose...III," p. 497. Pound, *Interpretations of Legal...*, pp. 78-83.

28. Pound, "The Scope and Purpose...III," p. 497. See also: Pound, *Vol. 1*, p. 306.

29. Pound, "The Scope and Purpose...III," p. 497. See also: Pound, *Vol. 1*, p. 306.

30. Pound, *Vol. 1*, p. 308.

31. Pound, *Vol. 1*, p. 309. See also: Pound, "The Scope and Purpose...III," p. 500. Pound, *Interpretations of Legal...*, pp. 94-97.

32. Pound, *Vol. 1*, p. 309. See also: Pound, "The Scope and Purpose...III," p. 500. Pound, *Interpretations of Legal...*, pp. 92-115.

33. Pound, *Vol. 1*, p. 310. See also: Pound, "The Scope and Purpose...III," p. 501. Pound, *Interpretations of Legal...*, pp. 73-75.

34. Pound, "The Scope and Purpose...III," p. 504. See also: Pound, *Vol. 1*, pp. 312-313. Pound, *Interpretations of Legal...*, pp. 73-75.

35. Pound, "The Scope and Purpose...III," p. 504. See also: Pound, *Vol. 1*, p. 314. Pound, *Interpretations of Legal...*, pp. 73-75.

36. Pound, *Vol. 1*, p. 314. See also: Pound, "The Scope and Purpose...III," pp. 504-505.

37. Pound, *Vol. 1,* pp. 314-315. See also: Pound, "Scope and Purpose...III," p. 505. Pound, *Interpretations of Legal...*, pp. 73-75.

38. Pound, *Vol. 1*, pp. 316-317. See also: Pound, "Scope and Purpose...III," p. 505. Pound, *Interpretations of Legal...*, pp. 73-75.

39. Pound, "The Scope and Purpose...III," p. 506. See also: Pound, *Vol. 1*, pp. 318-320.

40. Pound, "The Scope and Purpose...III," p. 506. See also: Pound, *Vol. 1*, p. 320.

41. Pound, *Vol. 1*, p. 313. See also: Pound, "The Scope and Purpose...III," pp. 506-507. Pound, *Interpretations of Legal...*, pp. 73-74.

42. Pound, "The Scope and Purpose...III," p. 507. See also: Pound, *Vol. 1*, pp. 321-322.

43. Pound, "The Scope and Purpose...III," p. 507. See also: Pound, *Vol. 1*, pp. 320-321. Pound, *Interpretations of Legal...*, pp. 73-74.

44. Pound, *Vol. 1*, p. 323. See also: Pound, "The Scope and Purpose...III," p. 508. Pound, *Interpretations of Legal...*, p. 73.

45. See Chapter Eight: Judicial Justice.

46. Pound, "The Scope and Purpose...III," pp. 508-509. See also: Pound, *Vol. 1*, PP. 320-323.

47. Pound, *Vol. 1*, pp. 325-326. See also: Pound, "The Scope and Purpose...III," pp. 507-508.

48. Pound, *Vol. 1*, p. 326. See also: Pound, "The Scope and Purpose...III," p. 510.

49. Pound, *Vol. 1*, p. 327. See also: Pound, "The Scope and Purpose...III," pp. 510-511. Pound, *Interpretations of Legal...*, p. 91. Pound, "Popular Dissatisfaction...," *passim*.

50. Pound, *Vol. 1*, p. 328. See also: Pound, "Scope and Purpose...III," pp. 510-511. Pound, *Interpretations of Legal...*, p. 91.

51. Pound, *Vol. 1*, p. 328. See also: Pound, "The Scope and Purpose...III," p. 511. Pound, *The Ideal Element...Tagore*, pp. 52-53. See also, Pound, *Social Control....*

52. See Chapter Two.

53. Pound, *Vol. 1*, p. 344. See also: Pound, "Sociology of Law...," *passim.* Pound, *Spirit...*, pp. 194-195. Pound, "The End of Law...in Legal Rules...," pp. 225-234.

54. Pound, *Vol. 1*, p. 345. See also: Pound, *Social Control...*, pp. 40-41. Pound, *Spirit...*, pp. 195-196.

55. Pound, *Vol. 1*, p. 346. See also: Pound, *Social Control...*, passim. Pound, "The Need of...," p. 609.

56. Pound, *Social Control...*, p. 20. See also: Pound, *The Ideal Element...Tagore*, pp. 223-225. Pound, *Interpretations of legal...*, pp. 160-165.

57. Pound, *Spirit...*, pp. 195. See also: Pound, *Social Control...*, pp. 64-65. Pound, *History and System...Common...*, pp. 2-3. Pound, *Interpretations of Legal...*, pp. 158-159.

58. Pound, *Vol. 1*, p. 346. See also: Pound, *Interpretations of Legal...*, pp. 147-150. Pound, *The Ideal Element...Tagore*, pp.86-88. Pound, *Social Control...*, p.68. Pound *Vol. 3*, pp. 327-334. Pound, *Task...*, pp. 32-34.

59. Pound, *The Ideal Element...Tagore*, pp. 82-83. See also: Pound, *Vol. 2*, pp. 278-279.

60. Pound, *The Ideal Element...Tagore*, p. 28. See also: Pound, *Spirit...*, pp. 193-216. Pound, *Interpretations of Legal...*, pp. 143-150. Pound, *Social Control...*, pp. 127-131. Pound, *Task...*, pp. 35-36. Pound, *Vol. 3*, pp. 5-24.

61. See Chapter Seven: Theory of Interests.

62. Pound, *Vol. 1*, p. 279, pp. 346-347. See also: Pound, *The Ideal Element...Tagore*, pp. 178-179. Pound, *Social Control...*, pp. 64-65. Pound, *Vol. 2,* pp. 369-388. Pound, *Spirit...*, pp. 195-196. Pound, "Theory of Social...," pp. 16-45.

63. Pound, *Interpretations of Legal...*, pp. 152-165. See also: Pound, *The Ideal Element...Tagore*, pp. 178-179.

64. See Chapter Seven: Theory of Social Interests.

65. Pound, *Vol. 1*, pp. 291-294, 350. See also: Pound, *Social Control...*, p. 7. Pound, "The Scope and Purpose...III," pp. 509-515.

66. Pound, *Vol. 1*, p. 351. See also: Pound, "Scope and Purpose...III," p. 513.

67. Quoted in Pound, "Scope and Purpose....III," p. 513, and in Pound, *Vol. 1*, p. 351.

68. Pound, *Spirit...*, pp. 195-196. See also: Pound, *The Ideal Element...Tagore*, pp. 179, 222. Pound, *Vol. 1*, p. 545. *History and System...Common...*, pp. 1-3. Pound, *Task...*, p. 21. Pound, *Social Control...*, pp. 25-26.

69. Pound, "The Scope and Purpose...III," p. 514. See also: Pound, *Vol. 1*, p. 352. Pound, *Spirit...*, pp. 91-93.

70. See: Pound, "Survey...," in which he cites, as an example, the role of the Legislative Reference Bureau of the day. See also Chapter Seven: Theory of Social Interests.

71. Pound, "The Scope and Purpose...III," p. 515. See also: Pound, *Vol. 1*, p. 352.

72. Pound, "The Scope and Purpose...III," p. 514. See also: Pound, *Vol. 1*, p. 353.

73. Pound, "The Need of...," p. 608.

74. Pound, "The Need of...," p. 610.

75. Pound, "The Need of...," p. 610.

76. See Chapter Two: Socialization of Law.

77. Pound, "Justice According...," p. 78. See also: Pound, "The Need of...," *passim*. Roscoe Pound, "Preventive Justice and Social Work," *Proceedings of*

the National Conference of Social Work, May, 1923, pp. 151-163. Vol. 1 PB 115. (Hereinafter referred to as "Preventive...").

78. Pound, "The Need of...," p. 615. This passage clearly points to a tension which Pound recognized existing in explaining and evaluating legal systems, *i.e.*, on the one hand the need of law to impose values on facts and thus to condition the behavior of men to values embodied in the law. (See particularly Pound, *The Ideal Element...Tagore*), and, on the other hand, Pound recognizes that law is to reflect popular custom and the need to adjust the value embodied in the law to comport with the customs and practices prevailing in a society. (See Chapter Seven: Theory of Social Interests). See also: Pound, "Scope and Purpose...III," p. 514.

79. Pound, "The Scope and Purpose...III," p. 514. See also: Pound, *Vol. 1*, p. 354. (In *Vol. 1*, this point is listed as fifth in his categories.)

80. Pound, *Vol. 1*, p. 355. See also: Pound, "The Scope and Purpose...III," p. 514.

81. See Chapter One: Legal History and Chapter Two: Legal Philosophy: Ancient Greek to the Eighteenth Century.

82. Pound, "Scope and Purpose...III," p. 515. See also: Pound, *Vol. 1*, p. 355. (In *Vol. 1*, this is listed as number six in his categories.)

83. Pound, "The Scope and Purpose...III," p. 515. See also: Pound, *Vol. 1*, p. 350. See also: Pound, "Preventive Justice and Work," *Proceedings of the National Conference of Social Work, (50th Anniversary Session)*, May, 1923, pp. 160-161. Vol. 1 PB 115 (Hereinafter referred to as, "Preventive..."). Pound, "Enforcement of Law," *Green Bag*, Vol. 2, August, 1908, p. 401. Vol. 1 PB 28 (Hereinafter referred to as,"Enforcement...").

84. Pound, *Vol. 1*, p. 432. See also: Pound, "End of Law...in Legal Rules...," p. 196.

85. Pound, "Scope and Purpose...III," p. 515. See also: Pound, *Vol. 1*, pp. 350-354.

86. See Chapter Nine: Administrative Law.

87. Pound, *Vol. 1*, p. 350. See also: Pound, "Scope and Purpose...III," pp. 512-515.

88. Pound, *The Ideal Element...Tagore*, p. 268.

CHAPTER SEVEN

THEORY OF INTERESTS

An examination of Pound's theory of interests, which is so central to his jurisprudential writing, requires one to recognize that this theory was not a neutral one, in that Pound's utilization of it was intended only to provide an objective and analytical scheme for understanding the nature and operation of the law. Indeed, he decried this narrowness in legal thought. He writes:

> The conception of every branch of organized knowledge as science, where it had been thought of as a philosophy, so that natural philosophy became the science of physics, mental philosophy the science of politics, moral philosophy the science of ethics, and philosophy of law the science of jurisprudence, the urge to make everything that was called a science conform in its method to experimental physical science, did nothing less than eliminate from the social sciences their fundamental problems. For if the physical sciences have for their function to discover what is, the social sciences have for theirs to discover what ought to be and how to bring it about. If newly observed phenomena do not accord with the physicist's hypothesis, he must reject it and frame a new one. If particular facts of human conduct do not accord with some formula of justice or politics, or law, the trouble may be with those facts, not with the formula, and conduct may have to be shaped to what-ought-to-be, not formulas of what-ought-to-be shaped with facts of conduct which controvert the jural postulates of civilization. What-ought-to-be has no place in physical science. It has first place in the social sciences.[1]

As we have seen, Pound was devoted to the historical examination of the law.[2] In identifying the relationship of legal history to his theory of interests, he said he was:

> content to see in legal history the record of a continually wider recognizing and satisfying of human wants or claims or desires through social control; a more embracing and more effective securing of social

> interests; a continually more complete and effective elimination of waste and precluding of friction in human enjoyment of the goods of existence—in short, a continually more efficacious social engineering.[3]

One author says the following regarding the role and use of this theory of interests as an explanatory scheme of legal development and history:

> In fact the theory of social interests can be applied to all sets of situations and to all complexes of circumstances... I know of nothing at once so subtle, so comprehensive and so safe as the theory of social interests.[4]

Only brief further mention needs to be made of Pound's use of this theory for purposes of historical method. Pound constructed an entire scheme of historical analysis predicated on the use of the theory of interests that explained the major thrusts of law during given historical epochs, or, as he preferred to call them, stages of legal history.[5] It seems apparent that this scheme of historical interpretation has considerable merit and is capable of being utilized to describe and evaluate how law progresses in terms of emphases and concerns. The theory of interests developed by Pound, however, was intended to do more than merely describe past conduct—it was designed to be a tool to guide future legal action and development. It is in this respect that his theory will be examined.

Frequently Pound's theory of interests is thought to be an objective type of examination of the nature of law in terms of the data with which it deals and the method it uses to provide solutions to the problems that these data create. Pound would frequently assert that the theory of interests focused on *de facto* claims.[6] He intended to show that this theory could classify a set of reliable data that needed to be understood. He assumed also, however, that these data could be balanced against one another in order to provide the most effective and viable solution for the conflicts involved. Pound reveals the objectivity to which he aspired in saying that his conception of jurisprudence was that:

> It is an organized body of knowledge with respect to the means of satisfying human demands, securing interests, giving effect to claims or desires, with the least friction and the least waste, so far as these things can be brought about by the legal order, whereby the means of satisfaction may be made to go so far as possible.[7]

Pound feels that the major task of jurisprudence is to discover how control in a legal order can best be achieved.[8] What is interesting in Pound's thought is the emphasis he places on the body of knowledge which he felt was germane to this inquiry. In this respect he partly emulated the focus of the social sciences in terms of the data he felt were to be considered and the method to be used for its evaluation. While Pound would often speak of the science of law he was careful to stipulate that his use of that term was not identical to its use in relation to natural or physical science. He indicated that his use of the term referred to a disciplined body of knowledge about society.[9] Therefore, he continued:

> by the term "science of law" we mean an organized and critically controlled body of knowledge both of legal institutions and legal precepts and of the legal order, that is, of the legal ordering of society.[10]

If one assumes that Pound conceived his role to be only description or analysis, certainly the value of his jurisprudence would be severely limited. In reading Pound, however, one must conclude that he intended to develop a scheme of jurisprudential thought that would, in addition to its descriptive and analytical function, provide a means of molding the legal order, and more important, prescribe for a society a set of values which it should forward and protect. Roscoe Pound's theory of interests is best understood as a part of his general theory of jurisprudence which is designed to achieve certain results, and obtain fairly definite aims. Therefore, his theory of interests is subsidiary to these purposes.

Pound's theory of jurisprudence may be schematically described as follows:

- I. The End of Law is Understood to be
  - A. The achievement of justice
  - B. The Retention and Furtherance of Civilization defined by:
    - 1. The Jural Postulates
    - 2. The ability of man to be fully developed.
- II. The Factors or Conditions to be taken into account in Achieving the End of Law are the Interests that Operate in The Society.
  - A. Individual
  - B. Public
  - C. Social
- III. Social Interests are the most important in Achieving the Ends of Law.
- IV. In Reconciling the Conflict of these Interests Law engages in Social Engineering which operates through
  - A. Legislative Reconciliation of Conflict

B. Administrative Reconciliation of Conflict
C. Judicial Reconciliation of Conflict

Pound understood that law is neither all realism, nor all idealism. Rather, jurisprudence has value when it recognizes the inevitable tension between the ideal and the real. A paraphrased statement of Bluntschli about politics is appropriately descriptive of Pound's conception of jurisprudence.

> [Law] should be realistic; [Law] should be idealistic: Two principles which are true when they complement one another, wrong when they are kept apart.[11]

In discussing the ideal element in law, Pound says:

> When we seek to exclude them [ideals] from our formal conception of law we do not only attempt to exclude phenomena of the highest significance for understanding the actual functioning of judicial justice, but, as things are, we do the courts much wrong by laying them open to a charge of deciding lawlessly when they do what they must do, and what courts always have been compelled to do when they administer justice according to law.[12]

Pound believes that the law, in addition to maintaining and furthering civilization should achieve justice. In Pound's thought the end of law involved:

> the task of making the goods of existence, the means of satisfying the demands and desires of men living together in a politically organized society, if they cannot satisfy all the claims that men make upon them, at least go around as far as possible. This is what we mean when we say that the end of law is justice. We do not mean justice as an individual virtue. We do not mean justice as the ideal relation among men. We mean a regime. We mean such as adjustment of relations and ordering of conduct as will make the goods of existence, the means of satisfying human claims to have things and do things, go round as far as possible with the least friction and waste.[13]

It seems that Pound, in his discussion of justice, seeks to view its composition in a fairly neutral sense, *i.e.*, that it does not presume a fixed ideal, or perfect individual virtue. However, a careful reading of the above definition indicates quite clearly that this stipulative definition does in fact refer to a relation among men which, even if it is not ideal, is nonetheless directed toward the achievement of an ideal. His concept of regime must be understood in its qualitative signification, *i.e.*, for example, his concept of justice does not encompass a caste ordering of society, in which men are tied to positions of inferiority, and receive the goods of existence solely on the basis of positions assigned to them by birth. Further, Pound's definition cannot be understood to mean an order of society, which is predicated on insurmountable and arbitrary caste divisions which are legally sanctioned and legally enforced.[14] His understanding of the meaning of justice is revealed in his conclusion that justice is not served in balancing conflicts of class interests, when it means either a minority dominating the majority or the majority dominating the minority. If either were allowed to dominate, this would violate Pound's conception of justice, even though the majority's domination of the minority might be achieved with less friction.[15] One must conclude that Pound's conception of justice is a qualitative and prescriptive one which dictates that law should operate to achieve a certain quality of justice.

Like his definition of civilization Pound's conception of justice is closely linked to the jural postulates which will be discussed below.

As we have seen, central to Pound's identification of the end of law, is his belief that the function of law is to maintain and further civilization.[16] Pound's conception of this role of law is clearly indicated by the following statement:

> I am content to think of law as a social institution to satisfy social wants—the claims and demands and expectations involved in the existence of civilized society...[17]

In another connection Pound was to say that the function of law is to maintain, and transmit civilization.[18], and he cites with approval Kohler's view that judgment of the operation of the law must occur on the following bases:

> As to the past as a product of civilization, as to the present as a means of maintaining civilization, as to the future as a means of furthering civilization.[19]

Pound cannot be understood to be using the term civilization in a neutral sense, *i.e.*, referring to any configuration of a society. Rather, he was discussing civilized society in direct contrast to an uncivilized society. This dichotomy one can safely say refers to a qualitative distinction between societies in terms of how they function and the relationships that exist among men. Pound's "jural postulates" provide a clear understanding of what he had in mind when he spoke of the law's role in maintaining and furthering civilization. Because these postulates are so central to Pound's jurisprudential scheme it is desirable to set them out with the specificity that Pound did. In Pound's theory one must understand that these postulates mean, at least, that their converse would characterize an uncivilized order, and that law's role is to give effect to these postulates and thus maintain and further a civilized society.

> JURAL POSTULATE I. In civilized society men must be able to assume that others will commit no intentional aggressions upon them.[20]
>
> JURAL POSTULATE II. In civilized society men must be able to assume that they may control for beneficial purposes what they have discovered and appropriated to their own use, what they have created by their own labor, and what they have acquired under the existing social and economic order.[21]
>
> JURAL POSTULATE III. In civilized society men must be able to assume that those with whom they deal in the general intercourse of society will act in good faith and hence
>
> (a) will make good reasonable expectations which their promises or other conduct reasonably create;
>
> (b) will carry out their undertakings according to the expectations which the moral sentiment of the community attaches thereto;
>
> (c) will restore specifically or by equivalent what comes to them by mistake, or failure of the presuppositions of a transaction, or other unanticipated situation whereby they receive at another's expense what they could not reasonably have expected to receive under the actual circumstances.[22]
>
> JURAL POSTULATE IV. In civilized society men must be able to assume that those who engage in some course of conduct will act with due care not to cast an unreasonable risk of injury upon others.[23]
>
> JURAL POSTULATE V. In civilized society men must be able to assume that others who maintain things or enjoy or employ agencies, harmless in the sphere of their use but harmful in their normal action elsewhere, and having a natural tendency to cross the boundaries of their proper uses, will restrain them or keep them within their proper bounds.[24]

The jural postulates which Pound uses to define his conception of civilization, have a direct bearing on his concept of the operation of a legal order. They condition, indeed determine, what the legal order is to achieve and how it is to operate. Pound rejects the notion that these jural postulates are absolutes. He says:

> It is said that an absolute element creeps into the method of jural postulates. But it must be said also that a relative element has in the past stood out as controlling in the absolute measure. No doubt one will think with relation to some end or purpose. But it need not inexorably be a universal end with fixed definitions and details.[25]

What is interesting about his attempt to reject the notion that these jural postulates are absolutes is the fact that Pound does not categorically deny that these postulates are to be viewed as absolute. Nor does he categorically deny that these postulates do suggest, and indeed, may require that they be viewed as involving a necessary relationship of means to ends.

The fact that Pound asserts that there is a difference between civilized and uncivilized society further indicates that he embraced a much more absolute than a relative standard. In attempting to reject these postulates as absolutes, Pound points to the fact that over the years he has engaged in some modification of these postulates, and even suggested new ones,[26] but has not removed any of the former ones. His discovery of the new postulates that contribute to the furtherance of civilization is similar in tone, if not in content, to the Thomist conception that natural law precepts do not remain unchangeable, *i.e.*, they can be added to, but not reduced as man's participation in Divine Reason expands. Similarly Pound's argument is that the jural postulates are reflective of a time and place, but he allows for their increase in scope and purpose but not their reduction. This would suggest, it seems, his implicit acceptance of the idea that there is above any given civilization of time and place a more perfect concept of civilization, and that law is ultimately directed to achieving that ideal.

Another element in Pound's definition of civilization is reflected in Pound's belief that:

> one of the major functions of civilization is the raising of human powers to their highest possible unfolding, of the maximum of human control over external nature and over internal nature.[27]

The success of law in maintaining and furthering civilization according to Pound has enabled mankind to dominate the earth and continually improve his control over the natural world.[28]

In order to aid humans in restraining their individual aggressiveness, this element must be brought under the control of their fellow men.[29] Thus, law is to be used to control individual conduct so that men's relationships with their fellow men will serve to further the cooperative values of a civilized order. Pound recognizes that in the modern world social control is primarily the function of the state and is exercised through law, which is used to restrain certain behaviors and relationships in order to achieve the positive goods of civilization.[30] However, Pound points out:

> If one will is to be subjected to the will of another through the force of politically organized society, it is not to be done arbitrarily, but is to be done upon some rational basis, which the person coerced, if reasonable, could appreciate.[31]

Pound sees the role of law involved in the application of the armed force of the state on recalcitrant individuals to alter their conduct in order to achieve justice and to realize the jural postulates which he feels define civilization. However, the coercion that is to be used is to be rational and consistent with the nature of a civilized order, and is to be used only to restrain that behavior which is inimical to civilized society.

We have seen that Pound recognizes that the law's ultimate effectiveness depends on the utilization of the force available to the state, but he correctly notes that because it does rely on force, it has all the weaknesses inhering in that dependence.[32] For this reason, an effective legal order cannot rely exclusively on force to resolve conflicts in society. According to Pound, law succeeds because it performs, and performs well, its task of:

> reconciling and harmonizing conflicting and overlapping human demands and so maintains a social order in which we may maintain and further civilization. So long as it does this well there will be the habit of obedience that makes practicable the employment of force upon those who require it.[33]

According to Pound, therefore, a legal order should be devoted to the achievement of justice, the maintenance and furtherance of civilization, and the fullest development of human capabilities. To do so it must subject men to control through the operation of the state, and yet it cannot succeed if it relies on force alone. If it is to obtain the allegiance of men and obtain their obedience on a basis other than force, it must reconcile conflicts intelligently and effectively. Pound believes that the theory of interests provides the best means for formulating the resolutions of such conflicts in society.

In order to evaluate these interests in the most acceptable and intelligent way requires a full recognition of what these interests are, how they are to be classified, and a determination made of their composition.

According to Pound, interests are those demands, claims, desires or expectations which humans seek to satisfy "through the force of politically organized society..."[34]

Pound's classification of these interests is illustrated in the following table.

Individual Interests	Public Interests	Social Interests
1. Personality 2. Domestic Relations 3. Individual Interests a. Property b. Freedom of Contract c. Promised advantages d. Advantageous relations with others e. Freedom of association f. Continuity of Employment	1. Interest of the State as a juristic person 2. Interest of the State as guardian	1. The General Security 2. Security of Social Institutions 3. Conservation of Social Resources 4. General Progress 5. Individual Life

Man's desire to satisfy his wants, which are reflected in these interests, cause the conflicts which society must reconcile in order to achieve justice and further civilization. Reason, unaided by force, however, is not equipped to reconcile these conflicts. As Pound says:

> Reason—rational adjustment of individual expectations and demands to the expectations and demands of others on recognized knowledge that all the

> expectations and demands of all men cannot be satisfied from the goods of existence to their full extent—has proved to require the force of a politically organized society behind it in order to be effective.[35]

For this reason force will be brought to bear in order to resolve these conflicts, but such force can be intelligently employed by reference to the interests which will benefit or suffer as the case may be. Therefore an understanding of these interests and some measure of their relative importance is necessary, in order to determine when the force of politically organized society should be brought to bear in deciding which interest should be advanced. Pound identifies the composition and scope of these interests.

Individual Interests

Pound rejects the notion that individual interests can be deduced from an abstract concept of man.[36] Such an assumption, he argues, is historically false, since the first interests recognized in legal orders are those of the group.[37] It is only in the process of economic development that "individual interests gradually arise and come to be recognized..." and that the concern of "individual rights as distinguished from group rights..." was evolved over time. Individual rights, which have pressed for recognition and which have come to be recognized, he maintains, are divisible into three subcategories or types. "...interests of personality...domestic interests...and interests of substance..."[38]

Pound agrees that such divisions seem arbitrary since one interest can easily shade into another, but he maintains such a division is helpful for analytical purposes and that the divisions are defensible both logically and historically.[39]

The "interest of personality" involves the individual's physical security; the guarantee that the individual can act freely and autonomously; protection of his reputation; and the guarantee of his right to free speech and publication.[40] One cannot properly evaluate the scope of these elements of interest of personality without doing so in reference to the social interests that are involved. For example, Pound observes:

> The individual interest in free belief and opinion must be considered along with the social interest in the general security and the social interest in the security of social institutions, political, religious, domestic, and economic.[41]

Pound argues that when individual interests are in competition with each other and a reconciliation of the conflict is required, these individual interests should not be balanced against one another as though such a conflict was dependent and unrelated to the social and political interests involved. Rather, in evaluating them for purposes of reconciliation they must be viewed in light of the social interests which they involve, for:

> In weighing individual interests in view of the social interest...we must also take account of the social interest in the human life of such individual.[42]

It would seem that Pound's explanation of the individual interests leads to the conclusion that they are best viewed as subcategories of social interests which are balanced against each other by using the technique of social engineering to achieve justice, and further civilization.

What Pound identifies as individual interests in domestic relations involve the status relationships characterizing family relationships, *e.g.*, husband and wife.[43] The protection and definition of such relationships involves not only determining the relationship between the persons involved, but also their rights set over against all others.[44] Again Pound argues that this must be done in the context of the social interests involved.[45] Thus, for example, the social interest in the security of social institutions (the family), and the social interest in the general morals of the community, need to be considered in resolving conflicts related to the status relationships within a family.

Individual interests of substance, Pound points out, refer to those individual "claims asserted in title of economic life interests of substance."[46] These interests of substance include claims to:

> (1) corporeal things,...
> (2) freedom of industry and contract,...
> (3) claims to promised advantages,...and
> (4) claims to be secured against interference by outsiders with economically advantageous relations with others.[47]

This area of interest is very important in Pound's theory of interests, for, as he says:

> The law of property in the widest sense, including incorporeal property and the growing doctrines as to protection of economically advantageous

> relations, give effect to the social want or demand...that is formulated in the jural postulate that in...civilized society men must be able to assume that they may control for purposes beneficial to themselves what they have discovered and appropriated to their own use, what they have acquired by their own labor, and what they have acquired under the existing social and economic order.[48]

Securing the interest of property by law is, for Pound, reflective of "a wise bit of social engineering in the world as we know it,"[49] since it has secured the most to all with the least cost to others.[50] Despite Pound's praise of the treatment of property in western society, he feels compelled to add as a cautionary statement that, even though private property is to be valued, one may:

> believe this without holding that private property is eternally and absolutely necessary and that human society may not expect in some civilization which we cannot forecast, to achieve something different and something better.[51]

Proper measure of individual interests can be done, however, only if they are evaluated in reference to social interests to which they are related. For example, in his discussion of individual interests in freedom of industry and contract, Pound points out that decisions touching these types of individual interests of substance must be made with reference to the social interests that would be affected. He argues that during the nineteenth century, liberty of contract and industry were carried to extremes and threatened serious damage to vital social interests, and he concludes:

> It was seen that the social interest in the general security was to be maintained by supervision of the professions and callings which have special social importance and that other aspects of the social interest in the individual life are to be secured by limitations upon the contracts which the individual may make.[52]

Pound is arguing that individual interests of substance should be left untouched unless, or until, they impinge on or adversely affect significant social interests, which should be paramount in such situations.

Pound points out that the major task of the legal order, *i.e.*, the balancing of interests is complex and difficult. It is his opinion that the fate of the trade union movement illustrates the point well. Pound recognizes the individual interest in free association as very important. However, in determining how far this interest should be secured and within what limits, he feels, the historical record of the trade union movement has:

> compelled attention to the practical difficulty of so limiting legally the individual interest in free association that exercising of the right securing it shall neither infringe the interest of other individuals to free self-assertion nor shake the supreme legal authority of the state, that is, in the end, impair the social control on which civilization rests.... No small part of the difficulty must be attributed to the number of overlapping interests which must be taken into account: the social interest in the general security, the social interest in the individual life, *and the different individual interest which must be referred ultimately to the last named.*[53]

In this passage Pound touches on the central concern of his analytical scheme, *i.e.*, the evaluation of conflict in the context of the social interests involved. Before turning to the description of social interests, however, some attention must be given to what Pound calls public interests.

Public Interests

Pound maintains that what he calls public interests are only a subcategory of social interests, and are:

> claims asserted in title of a politically organized society; as one might say for convenience; the claims of the state, the political organization of society—as Blunthschli puts its, *the politische organisierte Volksperson. Ultimately these come down to a social interest in the security of social institutions, of which political institutions in the world of today have taken the first place.*[54]

In Pound's scheme of interests there are only two public interests: the interest "of the state as a juristic person," and the interest "of the state as guardian of social interests."[55] The interest of the state as a juristic person requires protecting the political order.[56]

Pound maintains that individual interests cannot be weighed against public interests since any reconciliation of such matters would be predetermined in favor of the state. In such instances he suggests the conflict must be viewed in the context of the social interests involved. To illustrate his argument he provides a discussion of the scope the individual's interest in free association, and how it should be evaluated. He writes:

> If delimitation of the liberty of free association with others is looked at solely as involving an individual interest, on the one hand, and a public on the other, in the very way of putting the matter overweighting of the latter is assured. The ultimate conflict is between the social interest in the individual life and the social interest in the security of social institutions. When looked at in this way, the infringement of the latter involved in a very wide liberty of association may seem very small under the circumstances of today.[57]

The interest of the state as a juristic person, Pound says, resulted from a variety of historical factors, but in light of modern conditions, the identification of the "dignity" of the state with the concept of general security is largely outmoded.[58]

In discussing the interests of the state as the guardian of social interests Pound says that, strictly speaking:

> these are not public interests since these are social interests in relation to which the state merely acts as guardian.[59]

According to Pound, the modern state's major function is to protect and enhance the various social interests in the society. In this respect, he notes, the state has assumed an active role in that it actively forwards and enhances particular social interests. Pound notes that in the modern era the state is obliged to perform:

> ... [a] great variety of services [which] suggests a wider conception of the state as a *parens patriae*—as not merely guardian but as guardian and promoter of the general welfare.[60]

Social Interests

Social interests constitute the central core of Pound's theory of interests, and their treatment is most significant in understanding Pound's theory of law.

Pound says that past attempts at discovering the nature of social interests have been badly marred by the presuppositions that have been employed and the deductive method that has been used and notes:

(4) *Conservation of Social Resources*—This interest encompasses the demands that characterize life in a civilized society that:

> the goods of existence shall not be wasted; that where all human claims or wants or desires may not be satisfied, in view of infinite individual desires and limited natural means of satisfying them, the latter may be made to go as far as possible; and, to that end, that acts or courses of conduct which tend needlessly to destroy or impair these goods shall be restrained.[75]

Pound believes that this interest pressed for recognition early in history. It has grown in importance in the face of the developments of modern society, since increased demand and development have placed even greater pressure on the physical resources of society. Consequently greater demands for government protection of social resources have emerged, and the protection which the state provides involves greater restrictions and controls of owners' use of property.[76]

This interest has now been extended to a concern for the physically and mentally handicapped according to Pound,[77] and Pound also feels that the emergence of juvenile agencies and social security schemes are designed to deal with this social interest.[78] These more recent developments dealing with newer dimensions of this interest, Pound notes, initially were received with hostility, since the use of the state for such purposes was felt to be contrary to the requirements stemming from the nineteenth century's concept of abstract individual liberty and responsibility.[79] With the emergence of the notion of "socialization of the law," however, such developments are considered consonant with the "social interest in the individual life."[80]

(5) *General Progress*—According to Pound this interest relates to:

> the claim or want or demand involved in social life in civilized society, that the development of human powers and of human control over nature for the satisfaction of human wants go forward; the demand that social engineering be increasingly and continuously improved; as it were, the self assertion of the social group toward higher and more complete development of human powers.[81]

The general areas of concern of this interest relate to economics, politics, and general cultural concerns.[82] Pound argues that all actions which served to liberate economic activity and restrict monopolization reveal concern with this social interest. These developments, he maintains, were not designed to serve particularized and selfish interests, but, rather, were designed to assure economic progress.[83]

Service to the needs of political progress, Pound feels, are reflected in the increase of free speech doctrines and free economic activity.[84] Pound does not explain, however, why developments such as these would not more properly be considered under the social interest in the individual life.

The interest in cultural progress is also poorly explained by Pound. Free scientific inquiry and freedom to publish, he says, are more limited because of the potential conflict they threaten to the security of religious and political institutions.[85] It is Pound's opinion that actions to promote education and further developments in the arts have tended to fare better, because of constitutional protections accorded to them.[86] He does not comment on why constitutional protections apply more to existing arts and letters generally, than to the encouragement of arts and letters. He also leaves unexplained the distinction he has made between a policy of free arts and letters and a policy of their encouragement.[87] Additionally, Pound maintains that there has been growing appreciation for aesthetic concerns of society,[88] and that such appreciation is evidenced, for example, in zoning codes.[89]

(6) *The Social Interests in the Individual Life*—Probably no more normative interest is involved in Pound's scheme than his identification of the social interest in the life of the individual. This interest, he says:

> is the social interest in the individual life—the claim or demand asserted in title of social life in civilized society that each individual be secure in his freedom, have secured to him the opportunities, political, social and economic, and be able to live at least a reasonably minimum human life in society.[90]

Although he admits that translating this formulation into action is complicated, Pound, nonetheless, assumes that when decisions are made in reference to it, they will not be arbitrary and will reflect a reasonableness of conclusion and purpose.[91] The consideration of how the social interest in the individual life may be more effectively and fully developed in modern industrial society must include concern, for example, of the opportunity for economic security.[92] Additional changes reflected in the scope and content of law, which reflect the attention given to this crucial social interest are to be seen in the acceptability of providing for additional amenities of life by the use of the state;[93] increased attention to employment security and industrial safety;[94] and attention to the "quality" and "equitability" of the conditions touching most human existence.[95]

One might criticize Pound for the failure to be more specific in explaining the intended meaning he gives to such qualitative concepts as "reasonable," "equitable," and "fair," for example, but when one considers his endorsement of the evolutionary nature of law, and how its content and scope are tied to the jural postulates he advances, which, are the characteristics of a civilized society, one may logically conclude that a certain specificity attaches to the meaning of such terms in light of the value context in which they are advanced.

Pound feels that the conflict of interests, such as those described above, are characteristic of all societies. Legal orders, Pound observes, can be understood properly if looked at from the point "from which we must start," that is:

> the claim or want or demand of the individual human being to have something or do something, or, it may be not to be coerced into doing what he does not want to do.[96]

These claims, wants, demands, and expectations which emerge spontaneously in society, according to Pound, are the interests to which the legal system must respond by recognition, delimitation, protection, and reconciliation.[97]

According to Pound, no society has ever existed or could exist in which there had been or could be sufficient resources and materials to recognize the claims and demands of all fully, or even adequately. Consequently, Pound says:

> Conflicts or competition between interests arise because of the competition of individuals with each other, and the competition of groups or associations in their endeavor to satisfy human claims and wants and desires.[98]

The success of law in reconciling conflict and maintaining order in society, while allowing for development and change, is a fragile undertaking. Pound says that what enables a legal order to succeed "is its ability to perform well and satisfactorily the resolution of conflicts that result from competing interests."[99] In order to resolve these two apparently contradictory objectives law "must be stable and yet it cannot stand still."[100] For Pound the success of the legal order in balancing stability with needed change is accomplished by what he refers to as the "great task of social engineering."[101]

In jurisprudence as well as in other social science, Pound says:

> We must consider how men do act, (or, if one prefers, behave) in their relations and contacts with others, how they ought to act in those relations and contacts in order to maintain, further, and transmit civilization, political, and legal institutions, or by ethical precepts, a correspondence of what takes place with what ought to be.[102]

Pound's notion of social engineering does not refer to expedient and discrete adjustments of controversies at a given point in time, but rather refers to a reasonable and intelligent ordering of such conflicts in conformity with what is required for the maintenance and furtherance of civilization and the achievement of justice. Delimitation of how, when, and why to act will be determined by both reason and experience; the consciousness of the limitations which affect law; and the significant roles other institutions of social control play in determining the necessity and desirability of a legal remedy. If the data of society are to be ordered intelligently, in order to transmit and further civilization, then the process by which decisions are made must be able to take those data and subject them to a balancing and ordering that will comport with the ends the law is designed to serve. In relating his theory of interests to the concept of social engineering Pound indicates that, in order for social engineering to be effective, it must be prescriptive, that is, social engineering must conform to certain values in the development of law. Pound is careful to point to the problems in using the analogy of engineering. To be sure, there are significant similarities between law and engineering since both draw heavily on the lessons of experience and reason.[103] There are, however, important differences which must be acknowledged, not the least of which is the fact that legal formulas are pressed to the limit by those who wish to determine the limit of their applicability, while the formulas of the engineer are never tested so extremely.[104] Engineering formulas and prescriptions suggest outer boundaries which should be avoided in making calculations and decisions,[105] thus such boundaries are designed to specify the limits of action.[106] Legal formulas, on the other hand, are viewed as only relatively determinative of the scope of action which can be taken, and individuals will act, very often, in ways to test whether the boundary can be removed, or at least extended.[107] Confronted with the multitude of interests emerging in society,[108] and the need to reconcile those with interests already recognized and protected by the law, Pound says, that the task of the law may be viewed as:

> [the] adjusting and ordering of conduct which will give the most effect to the whole scheme of interests with the least friction and waste.[109]

Intelligent and effective reconciliation requires that, in most instances, attention be given to the social interests that are involved.[110] Conceivably and logically, some conflicts might be considered purely from the standpoint of the individual interests involved,[111] however, it is far more productive and profitable to consider them in light of the social interests under which they might be properly classified, since:

> in contrast with the nineteenth century it appears...emphasis...[should be placed] upon social interests; upon the demands or claims or desires involved in social life rather than upon the qualities of the abstract man *in vacuo* or upon the freedom of will of the isolated individual.[112]

The method employed by the law in recognizing, delimiting, and securing these interests vary from criminal law to law that encourages cooperative action and behavior.[113] The method employed, of course, is subsidiary to the object of its employment, *i.e.*, the maintenance and transmission of civilization, while protecting as many interests as are consistent with this objective.

Because the law, viewed as social engineering, is so flexible, adaptable, and rational, Pound felt that it could simultaneously reconcile conflicts of interests, and serve as a brake on absolutism, and a check on the dominance of force and will in society.[114]

Further, it seems abundantly clear, after a careful reading of Pound, that he felt his theory of interests would constitute a system of jurisprudential thought that would bridge the gap between the ideal and real in the operation of a legal system. He sought to develop a theory or law that would aid it in achieving justice and maintaining and furthering civilization. It is necessary to emphasize that his use of these terms is not relative, for throughout his writing whenever he analyzes the operation of law he judges it on the basis of the degree to which law achieves a Western liberal definition of justice and civilization.

Although on occasion Pound speaks of civilization in a relative sense, he was a man who was appreciative of the values represented by Western culture, and his definition of civilization, his attachment to the jural postulates, and his view of the function of civilization to provide for the fullest development of the individual human being, clearly reflect the meaning he attached to this concept. It is not intended to fault his writing by this observation; it is rather to emphasize that to understand Pound one must recognize these somewhat unspoken assumptions and unexpressed values which dominate his thought, and which control the development of his theory of law and its function.

The scheme of jurisprudence which he created is strengthened by the value foundation on which it is built. Indeed, the value of Pound's theory is enhanced by his desire to give form and purpose to the law in its development and application, in order to achieve justice and maintain and further civilization as these terms are understood in the Western liberal tradition.

ENDNOTES

CHAPTER SEVEN

1. Pound, *Contemporary...*, p. 36.

2. See Chapter Two: Pound on Legal History.

3. Pound, *...Introduction...Philosophy*, p. 47.

4. J.C. Wu. "The Juristic Philosophy of Roscoe Pound", Vol. 18 *Illinois Law Review*, January, 1924, p. 300. Vol. 1, PBS A3. (Hereinafter referred to as "The Juristic Philosophy...").

5. See Chapter Two: Pound on Legal History.

6. Pound, *Vol. 3*, p. 15. See also: Pound, *The Ideal Element...Tagore*, pp. 88-89. Pound, "A Theory of Social Interests," Vol. 15 *Papers and Proceedings of the American Sociological Society*, 1921, pp. 32-33. Vol. 1, PB 108. (Hereinafter referred to as "Theory...").

7. Pound, *Vol. 1*, p. 545. See also: Pound, *Task...*, pp. 22-23. Pound, *Social Control...*, pp. 23-24.

8. Pound, *Vol. 1*, p. 545. See also: Pound, *Social Control...*, pp. 63-102.

9. Pound, *Vol. 1*, p. 10. See also: Pound, *Social Control...*, pp. 41-43. Pound, *Task...*, pp. 37-62.

10. Pound, *Vol. 1*, p. 16. See also: Pound, *Introduction...*, pp. 48-49. Pound, *The Ideal Element...Tagore*, p. 85.

11. J.K. Bluntschli, *Politik Als Wissenschaft, Lehre vom Modernen Stat.*, Vol. 3, Stuttgart, J.G. Cotta. 1893, p.4. Quoted in Pound: *Vol. 2*, p. 278.

12. Pound, *Vol. 2*, p. 123. See also: Pound, *The Ideal Element...Tagore*, Ch. 1, *passim*. Pound, *Social Control...*, pp. 42-44. Pound, *Task...*, p. 43. Pound, *Justice According...*, pp. 54-56.

13. Pound, *Social Control...*, p. 65. See also: Pound, *The Ideal Element...Tagore*, pp. 194, 225-226, 246. Pound, *Introduction...*, p. 47. See also: Pound, *Spirit...*, pp. 110-111, 196-197.

14. Pound, *Vol. 4*, p. 372. See also: Pound, *Introduction...*, pp. 39-40. Pound, *Spirit...*, pp. 196-205.

15. Pound, *Vol. 2*, p. 386. See also: Pound, *Spirit...*, pp. 107-108. Pound, *The Ideal Element...Tagore*, p. 90. Pound, *Social Control...*, p. 108.

16. See Chapter One: Pound on the Law.

17. Pound, *...Introduction...Philosophy...*, p.47. See also: Pound, *Social Control...*, p.54. Pound, *Vol.1*, p. 278. Pound, *Spirit...*, p. 196. Pound, *The Ideal Element...Tagore*, pp. 180-184. Pound, *Justice According...*, pp. 30-31.

18. Pound, "A Comparison of Ideals of Law," *Harvard Law Review*, Vol. 47, November, 1933, p. 17 *Vol. 1*, PB 195 (Hereinafter referred to as "A Comparison..."). See also: Pound, *Introduction...*, pp. 46-47. Pound, *The Ideal Element...Tagore*, pp. 180-181.

19. Pound, *Vol. 3*, p. 5. See also: Pound, *The Ideal Element...Tagore*, p. 181. Pound, *Introduction...*, p. 47. Pound, *Social Control...*, pp. 131-133. Pound, *Task...*, pp. 35-36. For a clear statement of Pound's distinction between civilized and non-civilized social orders see particularly: Roscoe Pound, "Justice According to Law I," Vol. 13 *Columbia Law Review* December, 1913, pp. 696-713, (Hereinafter referred to as "Justice...I"); Pound, *Vol. 2, pp. 355-357.*

20. Pound, *Vol. 3*, pp. 5,8. See also: Pound, "Theory...," pp. 33-35. Pound, *Social Control...*, pp. 113-118. Pound, *The Ideal Element...Tagore*, p. 187. Pound, *Introduction...*, pp. 85-86.

21. Pound, *Vol. 3*, p. 9. See also: Pound, "Theory...," pp. 35-36. Pound, *Social Control...*, pp. 113-118. Pound, *The Ideal Element...Tagore*, p. 188.

22. Pound, *Vol. 3*, p. 10. See also: Pound, "Theory...," pp. 36-37. Pound, *Social Control...*, pp. 113-118. Pound, *The Ideal Element...Tagore*, p. 187. Pound, *Introduction...*, pp. 107-109.

23. Pound, *Vol. 3*, p. 10. See also: Pound, "Theory...," pp. 38-39. Pound, *Social Control...*, pp. 113-118. Pound, *The Ideal Element...Tagore*, p. 187. Pound, *Introduction...*, pp. 86-89.

24. Pound, *Vol. 3*, p. 10. See also: Pound, "Theory...," pp. 39-40. Pound, *Social Control...*, pp. 113-118. Pound, *The Ideal Element...Tagore*, p. 191. Pound, *Introduction...*, pp. 89-96.

25. Pound, *Vol. 3*, p. 13. See also: Pound, *Social Control...*, pp. 113-118. Pound, *The Ideal Element...Tagore*, pp. 186-187.

26. Pound, *Vol. 3*, p. 13. See also: Pound, *Social Control...*, pp. 115, 118. Pound, *The Ideal Element...Tagore*, pp. 186, 192.

27. Pound, *Social Control...*, p. 132. See also: Pound, *The Ideal Element...Tagore*, pp. 28, 181-183. Pound, *Introduction...*, pp. 46-47. Pound, *Task...*, pp. 24-28, 35-36. Pound, "Law and Christian...," p. 106. Pound, *History and System...Common...*, pp. 1-3.

28. Pound, *Social Control...*, p. 132. See also: Pound, *The Ideal Element...Tagore*, pp. 28-181. Pound, *Task...*, pp. 12, 23-25. Pound, *Vol. 3*, pp. 5-7.

29. Pound, *Social Control...*, p. 18. See also: Pound, *The Ideal Element...Tagore*, pp. 176, 224. Pound, *Vol. 3*, pp. 5-7. Pound, *Task...*, pp. 12, 23-25.

30. Pound, *Social Control...*, p. 25. See also: Pound, *The Ideal Element...Tagore*, p. 52. Pound, *Vol. 3*, pp. 5-7. Pound, *Task...*, p. 12.

31. Pound, "Theory...," p. 42. See also: Pound, *Vol. 3*, p. 318. Pound, *Task...*, pp. 86-87. Pound, *The Ideal Element...Tagore*, pp. 194-195. Pound, *Spirit...*, pp. 182-183. Pound, *Social Control...*, pp. 101-103.

32. Pound. *Social Control...*, p. 20, 32-35. See also: Pound, *The Ideal Element...Tagore*, p. 53. Pound, *Task...*, pp. 88-89.

33. Pound, *Social Control...*, p. 20. See also: Pound, "Theory...," p. 44. Pound, *Task...*, pp. 72-74. Pound, "Making Law...," pp. 296-297. Pound, *Interpretations of Legal...*, p. 21.

34. Pound, *Vol. 3*, p. 16. See also: Pound, *Task...*, pp. 23, 112. Pound, *Interpretations of legal...*, p. 157. Pound, *Introduction...*, pp. 42-43, 107. Pound, *Spirit...*, pp. 91-93. Pound, *Social Control...*, pp. 66-67. Pound, *The Ideal Element...Tagore*, pp. 84-88.

35. Pound, *Vol. 3*, p. 19. See also: Pound, *Task...*, pp. 56, 109-110. Pound, *Social Control...*, pp. 109-112. Pound, *Spirit...*, pp. 91-93. Pound, *Interpretations of Legal..*, pp. 151-158. Pound, *Introduction...*, p. 47. Pound, *Social Control...*, p. 106.

36. Pound, *Vol. 3*, p. 25. See also: Pound, *The Ideal Element...Tagore*, pp. 86-88. Pound, *Introduction...*, p. 42. Pound, *Task...*, pp. 22-23.

37. Pound, *Vol. 3*, p. 27. See also: Pound, *Task...*, pp. 23-24. Pound, "End of Law...in Legal Rules...," pp. 202-203. Pound, *Vol. 1*, pp. 378-382. Pound, *The Ideal Element...Tagore*, pp. 112-113.

38. Pound, *Vol. 3*, p. 28. See also: Pound, *Vol. 1*, pp. 382-384. Pound, *Social Control...*, p. 69. Roscoe Pound, "A Survey of Social Interests," Vol. 57, October, 1943, *Harvard Law Review*, pp. 1-39, pp. 1-2. *Vol. 2*, PB 12. (Hereinafter referred to as "Survey...").

39. Pound, *Vol. 3*, p. 29. See also: Pound, *Social Control...*, p. 69. Pound, "Survey...," pp. 2-3. Pound, *Spirit...*, pp. 91-93. Pound, *Interpretations of Legal...*, pp. 158-164. Pound, *The Ideal Element...Tagore*, pp. 86-88.

40. Pound, *Vol. 3*, p. 33. See also: Pound, "End of Law...in Legal Rules...," pp. 226-229. Pound, *Social Control...*, pp. 70-71. Roscoe Pound, "Interests of Personality," Vol. 28, *Harvard Law Review*, February, March, 1915, pp. 343-365, pp. 445-456. *Vol. 1*, PB Nr. 71. (Hereinafter referred to as "...Personality").

41. Pound, *Vol. 3*, p. 65, see also Pound's comments regarding such balancing of interests in regard to the physical person, p. 43; honor and reputation, pp. 46-52; and privacy, p. 59. Pound, *Social Control...*, pp. 70-71.

42. Pound, *Vol. 3*, p. 321. See also: Pound, "Survey...," pp. 2-3. Pound, *Task...*, pp. 25-26. Pound, *Introduction...*, pp. 45-47.

43. Pound, *Vol. 3*, p. 74. See also: Pound, *Social Control...*, pp. 71-72. Pound, "...Domestic Relations," pp. 177-196.

44. Pound, *Vol. 3*, p. 71. See also: Pound, Social Control..., pp. 71-72. Pound, "...Domestic Relations," pp. 177-196.

45. Pound, *Vol. 3*, p. 76. See also: Pound, "Theory...," pp. 32-33. Pound, *Introduction...*, pp. 45-47. Pound, *Task...*, pp. 25-26.

46. Pound, *Vol. 3*, p. 101. See also: Pound, *Social Control...*, pp. 73-74.

47. Pound, *Vol. 3*, p. 103. See also: Pound, *Social Control...*, pp. 71-74.

48. Pound, *Vol. 3*, p. 103-104. See also: Pound, *The Ideal Element...Tagore*, pp. 188-189. Pound, *Spirit...*, pp. 144, 209. Pound, *Social Control...*, p. 73.

49. Pound, *Vol. 3*, p. 140.

50. Pound, *Vol. 3*, p. 140. See also: Pound, *The Ideal Element...Tagore*, pp. 193-195. Pound, *Justice According...*, p. 30.

51. Pound, *Vol. 3*, p. 140. See also: Pound, *The Ideal Element...Tagore*, p. 225.

52. Pound, *Vol. 3*, p. 158, 328-330. See also: Pound, "Theory...," pp. 32-33.

53. Pound, *Vol. 3*, pp. 231-232. (Emphasis added) 328-330. See also: Pound, "End of Law...in Legal Rules...," pp. 226-227.

54. Pound, *Vol. 3*, p. 236. (Emphasis added). See also: Pound, *Social Control...*, p. 75. Pound, *The Ideal Element...Tagore*, pp. 87-88.

55. Pound, *Vol. 3*, p. 236. See also: Pound, *The Ideal Element...Tagore*, pp. 87-88. Pound, *Social Control...*, pp. 75-76.

56. Pound, *Vol. 3*, p. 236. See also: Pound, "Theory...," pp. 42-43. Pound, *Social Control...*, p. 75.

57. Pound, *Vol. 3*, p. 247. See also: Pound, "Theory...," pp. 42-43. Pound, *Social Control...*, p. 75. Pound, "Survey...," pp. 1-2.

58. Pound, *Vol. 3*, p. 262. See also: Pound, "Theory...," pp. 31-32. Pound, *Social Control...*, p. 75.

59. Pound, *Vol. 3*, p. 263. See also: Pound, *Social Control...*, pp. 75-76.

60. Pound, *Vol. 3*, p. 267. See also: Pound, *The Ideal Element...Tagore*, pp. 217, 224.

61. Pound, *Vol. 3*, pp. 287-288. See also: Pound, "Theory...," pp. 22-25. Pound, *Spirit...*, pp. 203-207. Pound specifically mentions the theory of interests, since in his early formulations of the concept of social interests he relied heavily on the theory of interests as a causal factor. See: Pound, "Theory...," *passim*. Pound, "Survey...," pp. 1-39.

62. Pound, *Vol. 3*, p. 291. See also: Pound, "Theory...," pp. 29-31. Pound, *Spirit...*, pp. 91-93. Pound, *The Ideal Element...Tagore*, pp. 86-89. Pound, "Survey...," pp. 1-39.

63. Pound, *Vol. 3*, p. 291. See also: Pound, *Social Control...*, pp. 76, 117. Pound, "Theory...," pp. 33-35. Pound, "Survey...," pp. 8-10, 17. Pound, *The Ideal Element...Tagore*, pp. 246-253. Pound, *Spirit...*, pp. 197-203, 206-210.

64. Pound, *Vol. 3*, p. 292. See also: Pound, *Social Control...*, p. 76. Pound, "Theory...," pp. 33-35. Pound, "Survey...," pp. 10, 17. Pound, *The Ideal Element...Tagore*, pp. 246-253. Pound, *Spirit...*, pp. 197-203, 206-210.

65. Pound, *Vol. 3*, p. 292. See also: Pound, *Social Control...*, p. 76. Pound, "Theory...," pp. 33-35. Pound, *The Ideal Element...Tagore*, pp. 246-253. Pound, *Spirit...*, pp. 197-203, 206-210. Pound, "Survey...," pp. 1-39.

66. Pound, *Vol. 3*, p. 292. See also: Pound, *Social Control...*, p. 76. Pound, *Spirit...*, pp. 197-203, 206-210. Pound, "Theory...," pp. 32-35. Pound, *The Ideal Element...Tagore*, pp. 246-253. Pound, "Survey...," pp. 1-39.

67. Pound, *Vol. 3*, pp. 295-296. See also: Pound, Social Control..., p. 76. Pound, *Spirit...*, pp. 197-203, 206-210. Pound, "Theory...," pp. 34-35. Pound, *The Ideal Element...Tagore*, pp. 246-253. Pound, "Survey...," pp. 1-39.

68. Pound, *Vol. 3*, pp. 295-296. See also: Pound, "Theory...," pp. 35-36. Pound, *Spirit...*, pp. 197-203, 206-210. Pound, *Social Control...*, pp. 76-77. Pound, *The Ideal Element...Tagore*, pp. 246-253. Pound, "Theory...," pp. 34-35. Pound, "Survey...," pp. 1-39.

69. Pound, *Vol. 3*, p. 294. See also: Pound, *Social Control...*, pp. 76-77. Pound, *Spirit...*, pp. 197-203, 206-210. Pound, *The Ideal Element...Tagore*, pp. 246-253. Pound, "Survey...," p. 1-39. Pound, "Theory...," pp. 34-35.

70. Pound, *Vol. 3*, p. 296. See also: Pound, "Theory...," pp. 35-37. Pound, "Survey...," pp. 1-39. Pound, *Spirit...*, pp. 197-203, 206-210. Pound, *Social Control...*, p. 77. Pound, *Interpretations of Legal...*, pp. 158-164. Pound, *Introduction...*, pp. 47, 164-168.

71. Pound, *Vol. 3*, p. 301. See also: Pound, "Theory...," pp. 35-37. Pound, "Survey...," pp. 1-39. Pound, *Spirit...*, pp. 197-203, 206-210. Pound, *Social Control...*, p. 77. Pound, *Interpretations of Legal...*, pp. 158-164. Pound, *Introduction...*, pp. 47, 164-168.

72. Pound, *Vol. 3*, p. 302. See also: Pound, "Survey...," pp. 1-39. Pound, "Theory...," pp. 35-37. Pound, *Spirit...*, pp. 197-203, 206-210. Pound, *Social Control...*, p. 77. Pound, *Interpretations of Legal...*, pp. 158-164. Pound, *Introduction...*, pp. 47, 164-168.

73. Pound, *Vol. 3*, p. 304. See also: Pound, "Theory...," pp. 37-38. Pound, "Survey...," pp. 1-39. Pound, *Spirit...*, pp. 197-203, 206-210. Pound, *Social Control...*, pp. 77-78. Pound, *Interpretations of Legal...*, pp. 158-164. Pound, *Introduction...*, pp. 47, 164-168.

74. Pound, *Vol. 3*, p. 304. See also: Pound, "Theory...," pp. 37-38. Pound, "Survey...," pp. 1-39. Pound, Spirit..., pp. 197-203, 206-210. Pound, *Social Control...*, pp. 77-78. Pound, *Interpretations of Legal...*, pp. 158-164. Pound, *Introduction...*, pp. 47, 164-168.

75. Pound, *Vol. 3*, p. 305. See also: Pound, "Theory...," pp. 38-39. Pound, "Survey...," pp. 1-39. Pound, *Spirit...*, pp. 197-203, 206-210. Pound, *Social Control...*, pp. 77-78. Pound, *Interpretations of Legal...*, pp. 158-164. Pound, *Introduction...*, pp. 47, 164-168.

76. Pound, *Vol. 3*, p. 306. See also: Pound, "Theory...," pp. 38-39. Pound, "Survey...," pp. 1-39. Pound, *Spirit...*, pp. 197-203, 206-210. Pound, *Social Control...*, pp. 77-78. Pound, *Interpretations of Legal...*, pp. 158-164. Pound, *Introduction...*, pp. 47, 164-168.

77. Pound, *Vol. 3*, p. 307. See also: Pound, "Theory...," pp. 38-39. Pound, "Survey...," pp. 1-39. Pound, *Spirit...*, pp. 197-203, 206-210. Pound, *Social*

Control..., pp. 77-78. Pound, *Interpretations of Legal...*, pp. 158-164. Pound, *Introduction...*, pp. 47, 164-168.

78. Pound, *Vol. 3*, p. 309. See also: Pound, "Theory...," pp. 38-39. Pound, "Survey...," pp. 1-39. Pound, *Spirit...*, pp. 197-203, 206-210. Pound, *Social Control...*, pp. 77-78. Pound, *Interpretations of Legal...*, pp. 158-164. Pound, *Introduction...*, pp. 47, 164-168.

79. Pound, *Vol. 3*, p. 310. See also: Pound, "Theory...," pp. 38-39. Pound, "Survey...," pp. 1-39. Pound, *Spirit...*, pp. 197-203, 206-210. Pound, *Social Control...*, pp. 77-78. Pound, *Interpretations of Legal...*, pp. 158-164. Pound, *Introduction...*, pp. 47, 164-168.

80. Pound, *Vol. 3*, p. 311. See also: Pound, "Theory...," pp. 38-39. Pound, "Survey...," pp. 1-39. Pound, *Spirit...*, pp. 197-203, 206-210. Pound, *Social Control...*, pp. 77-78. Pound, *Interpretations of Legal...*, pp. 158-164. Pound, *Introduction...*, pp. 47, 164-168.

81. Pound, *Vol. 3*, P. 311. See also: Pound, "Theory...," pp. 39-41. Pound, "Survey...," pp. 1-39. Pound, *Spirit...*, pp. 197-203, 206-210. Pound, *Social Control...*, pp. 77-78. Pound, *Interpretations of Legal...*, pp. 158-164. Pound, *Introduction...*, pp. 47, 164-168.

82. Pound, *Vol. 3*, p. 311. See also: Pound, "Theory...," pp. 39-41. Pound, "Survey...," pp. 1-39. Pound, *Spirit...*, pp. 197-203, 206-210. Pound, *Social Control...*, pp. 77-78. Pound, *Interpretations of Legal...*, pp. 158-164. Pound, *Introduction...*, pp. 47, 164-168.

83. Pound, *Vol. 3*, p. 312. See also: Pound, "Theory...," pp. 39-41. Pound, "Survey...," pp. 1-39. Pound, *Spirit...*, pp. 197-203, 206-210. Pound, *Social Control...*, pp. 77-78. Pound, *Interpretations of Legal...*, pp. 158-164. Pound, *Introduction...*, pp. 47, 164-168.

84. Pound, *Vol. 3*, p. 313. See also: Pound, "Theory...," pp. 39-41. Pound, "Survey...," pp. 1-39. Pound, *Spirit...*, pp. 197-203, 206-210. Pound, *Social Control...*, pp. 77-78. Pound, *Interpretations of Legal...*, pp. 158-164. Pound, *Introduction...*, pp. 47, 164-168.

85. Pound, *Vol. 3*, p. 314. See also: Pound, "Theory...," pp. 39-41. Pound, "Survey...," pp. 1-39. Pound, *Spirit...*, pp. 197-203, 206-210. Pound, *Social*

Control..., pp. 77-78. Pound, *Interpretations of Legal...*, pp. 158-164. Pound, *Introduction...*, pp. 47, 164-168.

86. Pound, *Vol. 3*, p. 314. See also: Pound, "Theory...," pp. 39-41. Pound, "Survey...," pp. 1-39. Pound, *Spirit...*, pp. 197-203, 206-210. Pound, *Social Control...*, pp. 77-78. Pound, *Interpretations of Legal...*, pp. 158-164. Pound, *Introduction...*, pp. 47, 164-168.

87. Pound, *Vol. 3*, p. 314. See also: Pound, "Theory...," pp. 39-41. Pound, "Survey...," pp. 1-39. Pound, *Spirit...*, pp. 197-203, 206-210. Pound, *Social Control...*, pp. 77-78. Pound, *Interpretations of Legal...*, pp. 158-164. Pound, *Introduction...*, pp. 47, 164-168.

88. Pound, *Vol. 3*, p. 315. See also: Pound, "Theory...," pp. 39-41. Pound, "Survey...," pp. 1-39. Pound, *Spirit...*, pp. 197-203, 206-210. Pound, *Social Control...*, pp. 77-78. Pound, *Interpretations of Legal...*, pp. 158-164. Pound, *Introduction...*, pp. 47, 164-168,

89. Pound, *Vol. 3*, p. 315. See also: Pound, "Theory...," pp. 39-41. Pound, "Survey...," pp. 1-39. Pound, *Spirit...*, pp. 197-203, 206-210. Pound, *Social Control...*, pp. 77-78. Pound, *Interpretations of Legal...*, pp. 158-164. Pound, *Introduction...*, pp. 47, 164-168.

90. Pound, *Social Control...*, p. 78. See also: Pound, *Vol. 3*, p. 316. Pound, "Theory...," pp. 41-44. Pound, "Survey...," pp. 1-39. Pound, *Task...*, pp. 76-77.

91. Pound, *Vol. 3*, p. 318. See also: Pound, "Theory...," pp. 41-44. Pound, "Survey...," pp. 1-39. Pound, *Social Control...*, pp. 77-78. Pound, *Task...*, pp. 76-77.

92. Pound, *Vol. 3*, p. 320. See also: Pound, "Theory...," pp. 41-44. Pound, "Survey...," p. 36. Pound, *Social Control...*, pp. 77-78. Pound, *Task...*, pp. 76-77.

93. Pound, *Vol. 3*, p. 320. See also: Pound, "Theory...," pp. 41-44. Pound, "Survey...," p. 36. Pound, *Social Control...*, pp. 77-78. Pound, *Task...*, pp. 76-77.

94. Pound, *Vol. 3*, p. 321. See also: Pound, "Theory...," pp. 41-44. Pound, "Survey...," pp. 37-38. Pound, *Social Control...*, pp. 77-78. Pound, *Task...*, pp. 76-77.

95. Pound, *Vol. 3*, p. 323. See also: Pound, "Theory...," pp. 41-44. Pound, "Survey...," pp. 37-38. Pound, *Social Control...*, pp. 77-78. Pound, *Task...*, pp. 76-77.

96. Pound, *Social Control...*, p. 65. See also: Pound, *Task...*, pp. 12-13. Pound, *Justice...*, pp. 16-27. Pound, *The Ideal Element...Tagore*, pp. 86-87.

97. Pound, *Social Control...*, p. 68. See also: Pound, *Task...*, p. 87. Pound, *The Ideal Element...Tagore*, p. 86-87. Roscoe Pound, "Justice According to Law II," Vol. 13 *Columbia Law Review*, January, 1914, pp. 16-27. Vol. 1 PB 60. (Hereinafter referred to as "Justice...II,").

98. Pound, *Social Control...*, p. 66. See also: Pound, "Survey...," *passim*. Pound, *The Ideal Element...Tagore*, pp. 86, 95-107. Pound, *Spirit...*, p. 196. Pound, *Task...*, pp. 12-16, 44-48.

99. Pound, *Social Control...*, p. 54. See also: Pound, *Task...*, pp. 49-62. Pound, *The Ideal Element...Tagore*, pp. 95-107.

100. Pound, *Interpretations of Legal...*, p. 1. See also: Pound, *Social Control...*, pp. 133-134. One must note that this theme permeates all of Pound's writing.

101. Pound, *Social Control...*, p. 64. See also: Pound, *Justice According...*, p. 30. Pound, "The Call for a Realist Jurisprudence," *Harvard Law Review*, Vol. 44, March, 1931, pp. 697-711, Vol. 1, PB 178. (Hereinafter referred to as "Call for..."). Pound, *Spirit...*, pp. 195-196. Pound, *The Ideal Element...Tagore*, pp. 176-195. See also Chapter Two, "Legal History."

102. Pound, *Vol. 1*, p. 278. See also: Pound, *The Ideal Element...Tagore*, pp. 176, 195. Pound, *...Introduction...Philosophy...*, p. 47.

103. Pound, *Vol. 1*, p. 279. See also: Pound, *Social Control...*, pp. 64-65. Pound, "Call for...," p. 704. Pound, *Spirit...*, p. 183. Pound, *Task...*, pp. 62-63, 83.

104. Pound, *Vol. 1*, p. 279. See also: Pound, "Theory...," pp. 44-45. Pound, "Call for...," p. 704.

105. Pound, *Vol. 1*, p. 279. See also: Pound, "Call for...," p. 704. Pound, "Theory...," pp. 44-45.

106. Pound, *Vol. 1*, p. 279. See also: Pound, "Call for...," p. 704. Pound, "Theory...," pp. 44-45.

107. Pound, *Vol. 1*, p. 279. See also: Pound, "Call for...," p. 704. Pound, "Theory...," pp. 44-45.

108. Pound, *Vol. 3*, pp. 21-22.

109. Pound, *Vol. 3*, p. 324. See also: Pound, *Social Control...*, pp. 63-64. Pound, *Spirit...*, p. 196. Pound, *...Introduction...Philosophy...*, p. 47. Pound, *The Ideal Element...Tagore*, pp. 87-88.

110. Pound, *Vol. 3*, p. 328. See also: Pound, *Spirit...*, pp. 195-196. Pound, *The Ideal Element...Tagore*, pp. 178, 195. Pound, *Social Control...*, pp. 68-69, 78-79. Pound, "Call for...," pp. 703-706.

111. Pound, *Vol. 3*, p. 328. See also: Pound, "Theory...," pp. 32-33. Pound, "End of Law...in Legal Rules...," pp. 226-229.

112. Pound, *Social Control...*, pp. 126-132. See also: Pound, *Spirit...*, p. 195. Pound, *Vol. 3*, p. 330. Pound, "Theory...," pp. 52-53.

113. Pound, *Social Control...*, pp. 109-134. See also: Pound, *Vol. 3*, pp. 335-344. Pound, *Vol. 4*, pp. 90, 101, 110, 118-126, 192, 278. Pound, "Theory...," pp. 32-33.

114. Pound, *Social Control...*, pp. 103-134. See also: Pound, *The Ideal Element...Tagore*, pp. 177-195.

CHAPTER EIGHT

ADMINISTRATIVE LAW

Pound believes that the modern era is one wherein the "cult of force" flourishes. In speaking of this in respect to America, he says:

> There has come to be a cult of force throughout the world. In place of the political and legal theory on which our government was founded and under which America has grown to be a land to which people have been eager to come from every part of the world in order to live the lives of free men and enjoy life, liberty, and property in security, new theories are being advanced. Instead of our fundamental doctrine that government is to be carried on according to law we are told that what the government does is law. Instead of a law which thinks of citizens and officials as equally subject to law, we are told of a public law which subordinates the citizen to the official and enables the latter to put the claims of one citizen over those of another, not according to some general rule of law but according to his personal ideas for the time being.[1]

This triumph of force, according to Pound, has occurred in all lands including western democracies where the tradition of liberal governance had emerged and where the tradition of law used as a control of governmental power and force originated. Pound correctly notes:

> One phase of the current cult of force is an idea that if there is to be a democracy it must be an absolute democracy—which certainly was not the idea of our constitutions, national or state. We are told that from its very nature a democracy must be an absolute subjection of a politically organized society to the unlimited and unrestrained rule of the majority or even of a plurality for the time being, just as an autocracy is an absolute subjection of such a society to the unlimited rule of a personal ruler.[2]

The attraction of the notion of unrestrained democracy is evident everywhere, and in Pound's view, is a consequence of the rejection of law, new currents of legal philosophy, and the growth of administrative absolutism, all of which have created perilous conditions for man, the concept of limited governance, civilization, and the law.

As we have seen Pound recognizes that in all times men have pursued the phantom notion of an ideal and just society existing without law.[3] Such "utopian" thinking, however, ignores the need men have for governance and restraint, which, according to Pound, results from man's dual character and the necessity of controlling and limiting his actions. Man's "aggressive or self-assertive" character induces him to act in any fashion he will toward his fellowman.[4] Man's sociable self, however, requires that his aggressive character be controlled by the elaborate social institutions which characterize human order.[5] Almost paradoxically, however, even though these social institutions control man's inherent and potential aggressiveness, social organization itself creates a threatening condition for man. As Pound notes:

> The very features of human nature that make government and law necessary, yet [sic] make government and its legal agencies dangerous to the freedom they are set up to maintain and further.[6]

In Pound's view, the great achievement of civilization is that it has handled this dilemma in a constructive manner. He writes:

> At least half of civilization, and the half without which the other could not have been achieved, is the conquest of internal nature to the exigencies of social life. If, in the course of the conquest, men have developed or set up political power and agencies of exercising it, they have also developed or set up legal institutions for making the exercise of that power uniform and systematic and predictable.[7]

As we have seen,[8] civilization for Pound was the end toward which both social order and law should be directed, for, as Pound notes, civilization involves the:

> control over external or physical nature and control over internal or human nature. These are independent. On the one hand, the control over external nature which has been carried so far through the advancement of science has enabled mankind to inherit the earth, making it possible for the enormous increase in population to maintain itself in security and relative plenty. On the other hand, control over internal or human nature has made possible the investigation, experimentation and research by which the advancement of science has been brought about. Assured

> conditions of peace, freedom from attack or molestation are indispensable to the study and research which are kindred to miracles wrought by science.[9]

A civilized social order strives to resolve justly those conflicts which occur, and:

> make the goods of existence, the means of satisfying human claims to have things and do things, go round as far as possible with the least friction and waste.[10]

The means of achieving this has been one of the great accomplishments of law, and, in Pound's view, it is the consciousness of human action directed to the task of preserving law that will assure the continuation of both law and civilization.[11]

The threat to law from administrative absolutism, however, is great enough to imperil this task of preserving a legal order, for as Pound observes:

> In the cycle of events the world has been swinging round again to absolutism; to the autocratic ideas of the latter Roman empire, of the old regime in France, and of the seventeenth and eighteenth-century governments on that model. Are we also to be caught up in the general movement? Are we to give up our quest for justice through law, our plan of government measured by reason rather than government of unlimited force, our faith in judicial justice, attained after full and fair hearing of all, grounded on findings established by evidence, and directed by principles derived from experience and tested by reason?[12]

The great tradition of liberty and security under the law, which characterizes western civilization is, in Pound's view, the product of the common law, which taught that:

> no one was above the supreme law of the land; that whatever was done was to be done reasonably and in accordance with the settled principles of law, whether done by a private individual, or by the chief executive, or by any agency of government whatever.[13]

The cult of force and the attendant notion of absolutism in government, can only be controlled by law, which employs both reason and experience in resolving conflicts and ordering society.[14]

In Pound's opinion, probably the most pernicious result of administrative law is that it tends to substitute laws for law. As Pound notes:

> Any sort of form of government, an autocracy, a limited monarchy, a republican democracy, or a simple democracy..., can operate according to law, or without law but through laws, or without either law or laws through administrative orders. For we must not yield to those who assert that law is a mere aggregate of laws. Law is something that gives vitality to rules of law and makes it possible to use them as instruments of justice. It develops laws to meet situations which the lawmaker forgot or never knew or did not appreciate. It limits laws to their reason and spirit when the lawmaker fails to pursue his end with exactness. It supplies gaps in the lawmaker's scheme when he fails to pursue his end with completeness. Law has continuity while rules of law are set up, decay, and are abrogated. It has a vitality and a tenacity that survives repeal of laws, One may know every rule of law which obtains in the time and place and yet not know what to do with them unless he knows law. Laws are relatively simple things. Law is complex. It involves a regime of adjusting human relations and ordering human conduct. It involves a body of precepts including more than rules of law; with principles, conceptions, and standards which are at least no less important, and along with them a received authoritative technique and received ideals. It involves finally a judicial and an administrative process, which are a significant part but by no means the whole....[15]

The triumph of the rule of law and the subjection of administrative action to judicial scrutiny was presumed to have been settled by the Revolution in 1688, and by the adoption of the American Constitution. Pound maintains, however, that the "contest between courts and administrative bureaus is [still] going on all over the English-speaking world,"[16] where:

> democracy is taken to be an end, not a form of government, and the people are identified with a majority which then becomes something like an object of worship in political and juristic thought. Where power is in a totalitarian state, the state is worshipped as an end in itself, where it is in a majority, the sanctity of demos deifies the majority.[17]

The growth of the cult of force and the notion of unlimited democracy have created peril to rights, liberty, property, and law, all of which, Pound observes:

> are losing with the rise of new absolutism: The omni-competent state, an institution in which only groups, associations and relations are regarded and the individual is no longer the unit: the totalitarian state under the unchecked rule of a superman leader to whose wisdom all individual interests must give way: the bureaucratic democracy ruled by absolute bureaus and boards and administrative agencies, by discretion instead of by law, freed from hampering constitutional checks, and free to impose their views of expediency in what they take to be the public interest or general welfare.[18]

Because of his concern with the dangers of administrative absolutism Pound identifies the threat that such an absolutism poses to the concepts of limited constitutional government, law, and the liberty of man. Indeed, he views the emergence of administrative absolutism as revolutionary. Commenting on this development in the United States, he says:

> Today, exception from judicial scrutiny of its action seems to be the ambition of every federal administrative agency, and is urged by a group of writers and teachers with increasing insistence. As a result, with the multiplication of these agencies in the Federal Government, the increasing subjection of every form of activity to administrative regulation, and hostility of administrative agencies to all attempts to impose effective legal checks upon them, we have been coming in practice to a condition of what may well be called administrative absolutism. This is nothing short of revolutionary in an American polity.[19]

Administrative law, Pound feels, leads to the erosion of guarantees to rights, liberty and property which should be secured by constitutional, limited government. What he believes we are witnessing, is the destruction of security of man and his property through increasing encroachments by the state through administrative action. The notions of absolutism which undergird the development rest on premises of absolute rule under the guise of law, which is, in Pound's view, the negation of law.[20]

Pound believes that Justice Frankfurter accurately pointed to the danger in saying:

> The accretion of dangerous power does not come in a day. It does come, however, slowly, from the generative force of unchecked disregard of the restrictions that fence in even the most disinterested assertion of authority.[21]

Pound emphasizes the dangers inherent in administrative rule, and proposes the means to be used to control such administrative absolutism.

Liberty and security have been preserved, Pound says, by developing a working relationship between them. He writes:

> Liberty as a political and legal idea presupposes a balance. It presupposes a balance between the general security which makes possible the liberty of all and the individual life, which is what is to be free and is realized in the liberty of each. Concretely, this involves a balance between society and the individual, between the local government, between administration and the judiciary. Balance is by no means an obsolete idea of the eighteenth century, It is only by achieving and maintaining those balances that a single political organization can rule a whole continent otherwise than as an autocracy. Great areas have never been ruled otherwise than by an autocracy or by a federal government built on the idea of balance. But balance in political organization presupposes law. It is a balance maintained by law.[22]

The balancing of these potentially contradictory elements permits stable, orderly and free societies to develop in which men are able to pursue productive and creative activities.[23] This working balance, however, is due to the acceptance of the idea of society under law, wherein both the rulers and the ruled are controlled by the law which protects this balance. As Pound notes, such limited and effective government is not assured, for

> a government in form and theory democratic may rule by bureaus and boards and administrative officials who act absolutely, whose every action is taken for law, or may rule by administrative agencies which act under and according to law.[24]

In Pound's view, unlimited administrative rule is contrary to western liberal governance, for he notes:

> To us law is not what is done officially but the measuring of what ought to be done officially and how it ought to be done.[25]

Current developments in the philosophy of law have weakened the tradition to which Pound refers, and have encouraged the development of uncontrolled and unrestricted administrative action. Pound maintains this development can attributed, in large part, to the belief in unlimited democracy. In his critique of

Kelsen and others, he illustrates why this is so. These theorists have argued that the notion of a society contracting to limit the force and power of government is a contradiction. The idea that popular will should be limited by a higher law which limits how, when, and why such will can be exercised is an erroneous belief. Thus, such theory inevitably embraced the idea of absolute majoritarian rule, which is no different in quality from absolutist theories in support of an absolute ruler which were present in Europe through the sixteenth and seventeenth centuries.[26]

Pound, in effect, sees these intellectual developments as the major causal factors in the growth of administrative absolutism, for all of these intellectual developments reject the notion of law as a limit on power and government. Such currents of thought, he observes, reflect the age-old optimism that so long as administration of justice is needed:

> justice would be better administered if there were no authoritative body of legal precepts and no adherence to the course of decision in the past, but each case were determined by the common sense and sense of justice of a strong and upright judge unhampered by rules or technical principles or technical conceptions. Today the idea takes the form of belief in boards and commissions and administrative officials, adjusting human relations and directing individual conduct on a conception of each case as unique, to be disposed of without reference to any other, with a strong hand on such considerations of fair play or sympathy for the oppressed or weaker party or of distribution of the economic surplus as appeal to them for the time being. The ideal is taken to be a society of just men who require no law and just judges who are equal to administering justice without law.[27]

Such aspirations for justice without law are present in the major intellectual currents that have created modern legal relativism and realism which are:

> modes of thinking which lend aid and comfort to that rise of absolutism in legal and political thought, and are being urged in the assaults upon our legal and constitutional polity, which go on all about us.[28]

The first of such currents stems from Karl Marx's thought. Marx rejected previous ethical, religious, or political interpretations of history and replaced them with a materialist view—in which all phenomena are considered from an economic perspective. This, in Pound's view, has resulted in a doctrine of economic determinism according to which all institutions, law, etc., are considered to be mere reflections of the interests of the dominant class. According to this view, all attempts at judicial impartiality and objectivity are myths and one need look only for the economic interest which is represented and protected.[29]

The second current flows from Freudian psychology and results in what Pound calls "psychological determinism," which maintains, that it is psychologically impossible for a judge, administrator, or legislator to act impartially or objectively. According to this notion, judicial and legal actions are determined by deep-seated subconscious wishes which "...conjure up a principle of reason behind what they have done."[30]

The third major current is what Pound labels "skeptical relativism." Einsteinian relativism, he argues, joined with neo-Kantian relativism, complements both Marxian and Freudian notions and rejects the view of impartial and objective law. To the skeptical relativists:

> Laws are only threats, and the making and enforcing of these threats are relative to the personalities of those who wield the power of a politically organized society for the time being.[31]

According to the "skeptical relativists" there are no core values or purposes to the law, because class interests, subconscious motivations, and relative values are what are involved and law is law only because it is declared to be so and nothing else justifies or commands it.

Finally, there is phenomenalism. According to Pound, this notion teaches that there is nothing behind or beyond a phenomenon other than the phenomenon itself. Thus all phenomena "...are equally significant and equally insignificant," and therefore, nothing is inherently good or bad.[32] Thus, according to the phenomenalists, whatever is done officially, is as lawful as anything else that might have been done.[33]

These sources help cultivate the cult of force and contribute to the growth of absolutism, which Pound sees as characteristic of the modern era. Further, they each support the conclusion that law should reflect what is the immediate, and dominant power, interest, or passion which exists at a given point in time. Such "relativistic realism", Pound notes, argues that since we must accept the phenomena of physical nature as a given, then we should accept the "realities" of man's condition at a given point in time and tailor our laws accordingly, since there are no criteria to determine what ought to be.[34] Pound rejects this line of argument, and says it assumes:

> that we cannot do a great many other things that experience of civilized mankind has shown that we can. It is true that a man cannot by taking thought add one cubit to his stature; but he can, by taking thought add many cubits to his moral stature, and that is something that the relativist and phenomenalist does not take into account.[35]

Another dimension in the growth of absolutism in the modern era, Pound says, is the acceptance of the idea of "subordinating law" in place of the idea of "coordinating law", or, alternatively phrased, public law over private law. In the common law tradition, Pound notes, the concept of law is "not what is done officially but the measure of what ought to be done officially and how it ought to be done." In that tradition public law was tied intimately and inseparably to private law.[36] The distinction between "coordinating" and "subordinating" law Pound says is that "coordinating law:"

> secures interests by separation and the like, treating all individuals as equals, [while]...'the subordinating law,'...prefers some of the interests of some to others, according to its measures of values.[37]

The advocates of public or subordinating law argue that it is replacing private law. Pound notes, however, that in the earlier tradition of the common law "public law" was considered:

> a mere branch of the private law of persons, the branch that presents that part of the private law that has to do with the rules governing public persons.[38]

Thus, according to coordinating law all men were considered equal before the law.[39] With the advent of the conception of public law, however, a dramatic shift in the focus and the purpose of law was achieved. Pound says:

> Public law is a "law of subordination," subordinating individual to public interests, and identifying some individual interests but not the interests of other individuals with those of public interests. Moreover..., all "coordinating law," that is, law coordinating individual interests by treating individuals as equal, gets its force from the "law of subordination," which identifies with public interests the interests coordinated, and hence public law has primacy over private law,

> subordination of individual interests over coordination of them. the primacy of public law is a primacy of state established law. Public or subordinating law proceeds from the state and private law depends upon it.[40]

The notion of public law assumes that superior public interests are served by public law. This notion assumes that private interests which are contrary to public ones should be made subordinate to the claim recognized and protected by public law.[41] The decision regarding superiority is given support and enforcement by politically organized society. The result, as Pound properly notes, is that:

> You start with subordinating the individual's claim to the powers of the public official, but presently you come to the remarkable result,... that the administrative official must judge which is the superior interest, and, having determined for himself between two persons which one is of the highest value, he can ignore the other.[42]

Pound concludes that the cult of force is induced and supported by these intellectual currents, and comes to fruition in the growth of administrative absolutism.

Pound believes that modern industrial society requires the use of administrative law. Early in his career he wrote:

> We are now in a position to understand the growth of administrative justice, which has gone forward so rapidly in the last twenty-five years. Administration had little or no place in the pioneer, rural, and agricultural society of the last century. It belongs to a busy age and crowded, urban, industrial society, with a complex economic organization and minute division of labor. In such society economic adjustments are so delicate and all things are so specialized, that men cannot wait for long, drawn-out investigations after the event in order to know their rights and duties and liabilities. The economic order demands that, so far as possible, what they may do and what they may not do be prescribed authoritatively in advance in an accessible and intelligent form. It demands that they be guided or advised or directed in many things, so that they may do well other things which are their immediate task.[43]

Pound maintains that such administrative law is required in order to meet the needs of the industrial age, and states:

> Administrative agencies for promoting the general welfare have come to be a necessity and have come to stay.[44]

Despite his recognition of the necessity for, and in many instances the desirability of, administrative law, he was concerned about its conflict with the notion of rule under law and notes:

> In the present century, the hegemony of the executive, the rise and multiplication of administrative agencies, and consequent increased and increasing control of all activities by the government have become outstanding features of our polity. These things, indeed, seem to go along with the rise of absolute political ideas throughout the world.[45]

Though granting that administrative law is necessary, Pound feels that the mere expansion of government poses a threat to the working balance between security and individual liberty which, he feels, has been the great achievement of western civilization, and which must be preserved. The threat to the elements of western liberal development stems from the dangers of "administrative or executive justice". He writes:

> Let me be understood. I am not preaching against administration, much less against an administrative law which is a true law, and not a calling of everything law that is done by a commission or board or bureau because it does it. I recognize the need of administration, and a great deal of it, in the urban industrial society of today. It is needed as an administrative element in the judicial process. It is needed as a supplement to the judicial process. It is needed as a directing process in a society so organized economically and so unified economically that they must be done more speedily, with more adjustment to unique situations, with more coordination of special skills and technical requirements than the judicial process, looking at controversies after the event, can afford. But to admit that development of the administrative process is necessary does not involve admitting that it should be free of checks such as a due balance between the general security and the individual life has led us to impose on both the legislative and judicial process.[46]

Pound feels it is imperative to establish a means of controlling administration, because of tendencies inherent in administrative or executive justice which cause this threat to western liberal development.[47] Advocates of administrative justice argue that its efficiency and effectiveness, in dealing with the problems of the industrial era, require its use. In Pound's view, however, the very nature of administrative activity threatens the balance achieved in a civilized society under law.[48] His preference, of course, was to place the efficiency and effectiveness of administrative action under the guarantees and values of the rule of law. In his earlier writing, Pound assumes that this could and would be achieved. If this were achieved then some injuries could be repaired after they occurred by the use of the traditional judicial process, and, other injuries could be prevented by the application of administrative standards, because administrative law was uniquely equipped to handle the problems of the modern era.[49] In light of the developments in the twentieth century, Pound's attention, however, focused on the threat that administrative action posed to western liberal society. He observes:

> Administration, of course, is with us, but the question is: Is administration to be a law unto itself or is administration to be conducted as the common law has always believed everything should be conducted—under God and the law?[50]

Pound became particularly alarmed at the arbitrariness of administrative action, and observes that:

> for absolutisms of any kind there are no individual rights. Indeed, for recent modes of thought there are no such things as rights anywhere. For administrative absolutism there is no such thing as law. There are only administrative orders made for each case treated as a unique case, independent of all others. If there is a law, it is only a threat of administrative action in a particular case. If there is law, it is the sum of whatever is done officially.[51]

Pound feels that a virtual revolution is occurring in the western world as a result of this growth of unchecked administrative power, and states that administrative justice is typified by:

> increasing assumption of unlimited powers, increasing assumption of unchecked discretion, a group tendency to enforce policies of their own making with no basis in, or even contrary to legislation, and characteristic disregard of individual rights.[52]

Such developments, he feels, are the unavoidable consequence of certain characteristics inherent in administrative justice.

First, and in Pound's view the most damaging of the tendencies in administrative justice, is the failure "...to hear both sides fully and with scrupulous fairness."[53] Pound feels that administrators ignore the crucial need to provide a full hearing for all sides which, he argues, is one of the most fundamental axioms of the tradition of justice under law.[54] This lack of a fair and full hearing is manifested in several ways. First, there is a tendency to decide or make rules even without hearings. He says:

> Administrative rule-making is, in striking contrast [to judicial, and legislative rule-making] in its want of checks, in its failure to give those to be affected opportunity to be heard, in its ignoring of interests which have constitutional title to be kept in mind. Too often it seems to make rules for the convenience of the agency at the expense of the citizen... At times it seems to make rules for the sake of making them, reminding us of the mother who said, 'Nurse, run upstairs and see what Tommy is doing and tell him not to do it.' Such things are inevitable where there are no effective checks. Rules made without affording an opportunity of hearing to those who are to be bound have the essential vice of taxation without representation and of absentee government. They are certain to be arbitrary.[55]

This particular tendency reflects the belief that justice can be administered without law, and rationalizes administrators ignoring proper hearings as these are understood in the common law tradition. As Pound notes, such decisions

> however much guided in a general way by custom or current morality or consideration of humanity, have the characteristic features of summary, impulsive action, without hearing both sides, without calling for evidence of rational probative force, and without consideration beyond the case in hand, which mark what we may fairly call justice without law.[56]

The absence of a fair and full hearing, in which the interested parties can present their evidence and arguments in an orderly and full fashion, Pound observes, reflects a "...want of appreciation of the need of hearing the other side if a just determination is to be arrived at. ..."[57] Pound contrasts the elaborate requirements that control legislative and judicial rule-making with the absence of fair hearings which characterize administrative rule-making. He states:

> Often administrative rules and regulations having the force of laws affect interests of as much or even more significance to individuals as those affected by statutes or rules of court. But there are no such checks upon

> administrative rule-making power. Usually the first knowledge that those affected have of a rule is after it has gone into effect. The first opportunity they have to object to it or to its details is after it is sought to be enforced against them and they may be afforded an opportunity to attack it in the courts. But by this time, serious and irreparable injury may have been done to an individual and his business. Moreover, the scope given to administrative rule-making today is so wide that challenging of details in the courts is not easy and often is not effectively available.[58]

The possibility of a fair hearing is minimized further by the administrator's tendency to engage in private consultation, to participate in *ex parte* proceedings, and to use private reports not disclosed to the affected party.[59] Pound argues that these practices call into question the propriety of administrative decisions, since such decisions are made without providing the opportunity for an affected party to present evidence related to the matter at hand.[60] Administrators, he argues, who use such practices and make decisions which touch significant interests of individuals and businesses act in ways which would never be permitted in the operation of judicial justice.[61]

A second characteristic which Pound feels makes administrative justice threatening to a society under law is excessive zeal:

> one might say often crusading zeal—on the part of officials and particularly on the part of subordinates, which lead them to see their relatively narrow task out of proportion.[62]

The threat from such zeal, Pound notes, leads administrators:

> to look at their special task out of proportion and to consider individual rights, constitutional guarantees, and the law of the land as negligible.[63]

In turn, such zeal encourages administrators to set up and effect policies:

> beyond or even at variance with the statute or the general law governing the action of the administrative agency.[64]

As Pound notes, such action in excess of statutory authority is relatively easily justified by administrators who maintain that the public interest being served by the administrative agency demands such excess.[65] Such excesses, he notes, reflect the "inherent and deep-seated characteristic of lay administration of justice..."[66]

Because of the administrator's zeal and commitment to the perceived goals or ends his agency is to serve, he tends to prejudge the case before him, [67] and, as Pound notes, this attitude manifests itself in the administrative assumption:

> that businesses and enterprises are characteristically wrongdoers and that their rights are inimical to policies which the administrative agencies claim the power to identify with the public interest.[68]

The third tendency of administrative justice which concerns Pound is the fact of administrative agencies judging their own case. He observes:

> One of the most serious features of administrative adjudication is that administrative agencies act as judges in cases in which they are also prosecutors and so in effect act as judges in their own cases. Many of these agencies entertain complaints, institute investigations upon them, begin what are in effect, prosecutions before themselves, allow their own subordinates to act as advocates for the prosecution, and often make the adjudications in conference with those same subordinates. All this runs counter to the most elementary and universally recognized principle of justice. So thoroughly grounded were the common-law judges in this principle that in no less than four cases between Coke and Holt the courts laid down that even an Act of Parliament could not make one a judge in his own case.[69]

These practices, as Pound observes, are at direct variance with:

> "the fundamental maxim of justice that no one is to be judged in his own case, no one is to be both accuser and judge."[70]

Pound feels that this mixing of functions within administrative agencies, prohibits the chance for a complaint or problem to receive an objective, impartial, and fair treatment.[71] Even when the functions are separated within the administrative agency, this can provide no corrective to this problem, for Pound argues, agency loyalty and the *esprit de corps* eliminate the effect of such separation.[72] Investigative, legislative, prosecutorial and judicial functions, being vested in one agency, Pound points out, enable the administrators to decide on a policy prior to a hearing, and "promulgate it in an order after the form of a hearing."[73] In addition, Pound feels, that this combination of functions within an agency forces the adjudicative and rule-making officials within an agency to rely excessively on their subordinates to make decisions.[74] As Pound properly notes, most individuals whose lives or livelihood are touched by such decisions:

> cannot afford the expense of formal hearings and judicial review. Their only reliance is on the fairness of a multitude of subordinates. There is need of emphasizing that these subordinates have a responsibility beyond that of carrying out in every way the general aims of the organization. They ought to feel that they are under a responsibility of dealing fairly with all parties whose interests are involved.[75]

Thus, the powers vested in the subordinates of an administrative agency, and the zeal which characterizes administrative action cause administrators to view their activities as being "...of such paramount importance as to justify the means by the end"[76] Pound notes further:

> This attitude on the part of high officials of government may well aggravate the features of exercise of administrative authority which have been growing up. Under such conditions an idea of using these powers not merely to advance the policy of the statute but of using them to change the whole social and economic order and reach visionary ultimate social objectives beyond or against the policy of the statute easily takes possession of subordinates entrusted with large authority.[77]

The argument that this mixture of functions in administrative agencies is necessary so they can achieve their purposes is in error. Pound, in excusing this argument, says:

> But I submit that their investigating functions can be carried on by methods which will give full hearing to both sides and full opportunity to those under investigation to meet, refute or explain everything that is to be used against them, and that if after investigation the agency desires to prosecute it should be required to do so in the courts and not before itself. The Bill of Rights in Massachusetts lays down: 'It is the right of every citizen to be tried by judges as free, impartial, and independent as the lot of humanity will admit.' Is this to be a guarantee as to the courts only or does it apply even more to administrative tribunals where the ethics of adjudication, born of long experience, do not obtain and the checks which surround judicial action in the courts are absent?[78]

Thus, the very nature of the administrative agency and its *raison d'etre* work against the capacity for fairness and objectivity.

Fourth, Pound maintains, administrative agencies seldom have the expertness they need to perform their tasks adequately and effectively. First of all, administrators lack the basic abilities needed for their "deciding function." Pound says:

> They, administrators, are very likely to have the layman's idea that decision is an easy task involving no acquired expertness through training and experience and to be conscientiously unconscious of what the lawyer soon learns, namely, that there are two sides to every case. Without training in grounding their action upon certain known standards, they are prone to act in deciding, as very likely they properly may in directing, as if every case were unique.[79]

Administrators do not compose a common profession, and therefore, their action does not permit of criticism by similarly trained persons. Further, administrators do not feel that laymen have grounds on which to base their criticisms, and consider such criticisms as valueless.[80] Pound argues that it is not proper to identify administrators as experts since they are, in reality, "ex-officio" experts, *i.e.*, an administrator "...is not appointed because he is an expert; he is an expert because he is appointed."[81]

Another argument advanced in favor of administrative agencies engaging in extensive governance is that their "simplicity of procedure and want of mechanical method" provide advantages to all parties.[82] Pound rejects this argument, and views it rather as another weakness of administrative justice, for, as he observes:

> in the hands of agencies and subordinates of agencies not disposed to be scrupulously fair, these simple, non-technical methods may easily serve as traps for the citizen who is seeking to obey the law.[83]

Finally, Pound argues that the combination of functions in administrative agencies is made more dangerous because of "administrative *esprit de corps*," with its built-in practice:

> of delegating decisions to subordinates, where the law requires decisions to be made by the head, makes decisions by the responsible authority, a perfunctory matter. Such delegation was forbidden in judicial justice in antiquity. It was forbidden in Roman law and in the canon law; and no such thing is know to the common law as delegation of the judge's duty of decision to a subordinate.[84]

The most important consequence flowing from these tendencies which inhere in administrative practices, however, is the peril it presents to government under law, for as Pound observes:

> There is little idea of fairness as between the government and the citizen. The interests of private persons are held negligible in the zeal of the administrative agency to get results. The tendency is to weight procedure heavily in favor of the government or the bureau.[85]

Pound believes that these elements of administrative justice pose grave threats to western liberal society and the notion of rule under law, and discusses the correctives, he feels, are needed.[86] As Pound properly notes, one can argue against the notion of checks on administrative action only if one argues the case for administrative absolutism. Pound accepts the necessity and desirability of allowing administrative procedures to develop out of and in response to experience, and concludes:

> Lawyers are not seeking to tie administrative agencies down by a mass of detail,...What they seek is to secure the basic requirements of just determination of facts and sound application of law.[87]

Pound poses four measures which he feels must be adopted in order to provide the checks necessary to combat administrative absolutism and assure that administrative agencies operate under law. These proposals are:

> (1) That both sides and all persons injuriously affected be heard fully before orders and determinations are made against them.
>
> (2) That nothing which is to be used as the basis of an administrative determination adverse to a party's interest be withheld from his scrutiny so as to deprive him of full opportunity to explain or refute it, and nothing used in arriving at the determination be withheld from the record for review.
>
> (3) That whenever determinations are made injuriously affecting individual interests, findings of fact and a record, showing fully and clearly on what they are based be required so as to make review possible and effective to insure that the findings have a basis in evidence of rational probative force.

> (4) That a simple procedure be provided by which order and determination may be reviewed to determine whether there has been a full hearing of all sides, whether the findings have support in evidence of rational probative force, whether the order or determination is in accord with the statute governing it, rightly interpreted and applied according to the law's standard committed to it by statute or has applied a different one (perhaps of its own making) or has acted upon no standard.[88]

Pound feels that these proposals provide the corrective needed, and would assure that checks would be placed on administrative absolutism. Commenting on the situation in America, Pound observes that:

> the question is not whether administration shall be constrained to due process of law. According to the constitution it is so constrained. The question is whether that constraint shall be made available to all who need to invoke it or shall remain generally inaccessible except to the litigant of exceptional means.[89]

Pound feels it is necessary to give the judiciary the task of controlling administrative action. He writes:

> There are certain general characteristics of administrative determination of controversies which have developed in the country in the present generation which call for effective judicial review if our American legal and constitutional polity is to be preserved. Back of them are want of checks upon administrative determination and want of any ethos of determination in any way comparable to the ethos of adjudication which has been developed and maintained in the court.[90]

For example, Pound is greatly concerned over administrative discretion. The dangers inherent in administrative discretion are not correctable by review of administrative action within the agency, for as Pound observes, there are two very different types of discretion. One type of discretion

> commonly bears in the law, it is a power of determination of questions to which no rule of law is applicable, which is left to the personal judgment of the tribunal, to be exercised according to settled principles. This is judicial discretion and is always reviewable to the extent of ascertaining that a real judgment has been exercised according to the governing principles and not arbitrary will or caprice. In another sense it [discretion] means a power of determination left wholly to the judge or

> official with no principle to guide its exercise and no review unless for fraud. The law has always sought to restrain this sort of discretion by subjecting it to judicial review to prevent abuse. When any agency for adjusting human relations or regulating human conduct seeks to be given a discretion freed from judicial scrutiny, we may well suspect it seeks a discretion of the second type.[91]

The tendencies inherent in administrative action—excessive zeal, acting in excess of or in opposition to statutory authority, failure to provide fair hearings, lack of expertness, and internal agency *esprit de corps*—make judicial review of administrative action absolutely essential. According to Pound, judicial justice is the most effective institution for declaring law and making decisions, because:

> it combines the possibilities of certainty and flexibility better than any other form of administrative justice. It provides for certainty through the training of judges in logical development and systematic exposition of authoritative material for decisions. It provides for growth by permitting a testing of received premises with reference to concrete causes and correction of rules by extension or restriction through experience of their application and a gradual process of inclusion and exclusion upon rational principle.[92]

Currently, much administrative activity is directed toward preventive action, and this causes such agencies to treat each case as being unique. Further, most administrative action seeks to serve immediate ends without careful regard to means, with the result that such action tends to be arbitrary and capricious.[93] Administrative activity, therefore, is prone to impinge on guaranteed rights, the standards of the legal order, and:

> to override what judicial experience has taught us are fundamental principles of securing full and fair hearing to all interested parties and objective decisions. It has no well defined ideals. Each administrative agency is likely to think of its immediate practical purpose as paramount and so as something to which all individual interests must give way.[94]

For these reasons, Pound argues that judicial review is imperative in order:

> to make the court effective in securing to individuals the rights guaranteed by our constitution and the fundamentals of full and fair hearings by an impartial tribunal and determination according to the law of the land.[95]

The judiciary is best equipped to secure individual rights and lawful procedure because of its characteristics. As we have seen, Pound argues the judiciary, better than any other agency of government, is able to achieve certainty and flexibility in the administration of law.[96] Judges are guided by the standards and guides to action inherent in the judicial administration of justice, and in the evaluation of problems and evidence.[97] Judges are also bound to utilize legally determined premises, authoritative technique, and the received ideals of the legal order.[98]

Second, the decision of courts are subject to the criticisms and evaluation of fellow members of a common profession, the foundation, purposes, and ideals of which are understood by all of its members.[99] Judges cannot easily ignore the law's determination of which controversies are appropriate to adjudicate, the relationship of all the facts elicited to the law governing the case, and the remedies that can lawfully be provided.[100] In addition, courts of law operate on the basis of a full record of proceedings,[101] and this full record provides the basis on which individual court proceedings are reviewed by superior courts, and which are also available for review by all members of the profession.[102] None of these characteristics are present in administrative activity.

Third, as Pound observes, the judiciary has shown itself in history to be better able than other branches of government to be guided by the law and resist the passions and pressures of the moment.[103] This enables the judiciary to:

> uphold ultimate and more significant interests against those who urge the nearer and in the end less significant claims which are on the surface.[104]

Because of the court's reliance on past judicial decisions, they rely on "authoritative grounds of decision and authoritative technique in applying them...,"[105] and, therefore, in contrast to administrative agencies, the courts have restraints placed on them which keep them from succumbing to temporary advantage and desire.[106] The courts, Pound says, are frequently criticized for being too rigid and unbending in the face of new demands[107] but, he observes, the judiciary takes care to preserve long term interests, for judicially determined law

> moves with the main body, not with the advanced guard, and much in the reconnoitering of the latter often turns out not to be in the line of final progress.[108]

Roscoe Pound often expressed his belief that law must respond to the changing pressures and demands that follow in the wake of industrialization. As we have see, he did not reject the need for administrative law, but, on the contrary, valued the role it could and would play in responding to the pressures and demands which inhere in industrial society.[109] In addition, one must note that Pound's acceptance of the need for law to change was predicated on the belief that such change should not entail abandoning law.[110]

In Pound's earlier writings in administrative law he endorsed the growth of administrative law and conceived it to be a positive response to the new demands that industrial society placed on the legal order,[111] because administrative law could cope preventively with the problems resulting from industrial society such as: industrial safety, child welfare, and public health. In his opinion, the preventive measures of administrative law would greatly facilitate the ongoing needs of society, and would bypass the more difficult and time consuming processes of court remedies which, as a rule, were generally available only after the injury was done. He writes:

> The modern state more and more forestalls controversy by prescribing rules through legislation, or deals with the conditions that produce controversy by subjecting conduct, and especially the conduct of enterprises, to the guidance of administrative regulation.[112]

Consequently, Pound applauds many of the early developments in administrative law which were regulatory and ameliorative, and feels they are in no way inconsistent with a legal order since they were grounded on and conditioned by the established precepts and purposes of the law. He writes:

> We are in a busy, crowded world, and when we do anything today we must specialize. Our activities today must be chiefly our specialties. We cannot waste our time and substance on the mere incidents of our life; and so for those incidents the law is coming more and more today to do what we do with our traffic on the streets. These lines drawn upon the sidewalks and in the streets are examples of what we try to do by legislation. We try to tell men in advance what they may do and what they may not, as far as it is possible; and our administrative commissions are nothing but traffic officers, as it were, with signals to tell us when to cross and when not to cross, and where to cross. In the old days there was no such thing as a jaywalker. You could cross the street wherever you pleased, subject to your liability for negligence. Today we cannot permit a freedom of that kind. It impedes traffic, it imperils life, it creates an impossible tangle in our highways; so we station a man at the crossing to tell people what to do.[113]

The advent of the "New Deal" in American politics around 1936, however, triggered Pound's critique of administrative law. Pound's concern about administrative law is a consequence of his previously expressed concerns about law generally, *i.e.*, that law was to preserve civilized society; that law in its substance and development should be the result of reason and not will or power; and that law is to facilitate the operation of a great society and not to control it. Pound perceives developments in administrative law which are antithetical to the nature of western civilized society.

The changes which Pound observed in the nature of law from his earlier career to his later career caused him unending concern about the fate of a liberal civilized order. It was his judgment that western legal orders were falling wholesale into authoritarian molds, and that preservation of rights of property and liberty were under serious assault and stood in real peril of being destroyed.

The fact, however, that the western legal order had survived other historical epochs in which authoritarian notions and practices had sought to submerge the legal order caused Pound to feel that there were reasons to be optimistic about the survival of a liberal society. Critical to this survival was the need of western society to reconsider the development of administrative law which had transpired since the turn of the century. Critical to this task were the reinstatement of controlling notions of established law, the restoration of the right to a fair hearing, the requirement of decisions based on known law, and the delimitation of administrative discretion.

The preservation of the legal order in Pound's opinion, necessitates judicial review of administrative action. Pound was convinced that judicial justice is best equipped to preserve the legal rights of individuals, and he felt that the major corrective to the real and threatened abuse of administrative action would be provided by judicial review, which should be made easily available to all parties. Pound does not advocate stripping administrative bodies of functions properly committed to them by the legislature, but urges that judicial review be used to assure that administrative agencies comply with the law, that administrative decisions be made on the basis of rational evidence of probative value, and that constitutionally preserved rights and due process be adequately protected from overzealous administrative agencies. He says:

> [W]e do have to have, of course, certain applications of particular experience, particular expert skill to handle unique situations, and we must be careful in judicial review of administrative action not to take what has been committed by the legislature to an administrative body away from

> that body and commit it to a judge, and it seems to me the only way we can do that is by providing a modern, speedy, reasonable, inexpensive mode of review, compelling these administrative agencies to have a record that can be reviewed and providing an easy, simple, inexpensive way of transmitting that record to a court and having a court pass upon it to see that the proceedings conform to the law of the land.[114]

Such judicial review is compelled by the need to assure that due process is available to all individuals. As Pound notes:

> Due process of law involves a treatment of individuals as equals, having constitutionally secured rights. But that is the coordinating law of the courts. The administrative tribunals are dispensing subordinating law which enables them to put a higher value on one side than on the other and so authorizes them to ignore the other or give it a merely formal hearing.[115]

In Pound's writing, one finds growing alarm over the advance of "administrative absolutism" which involves practices and beliefs that are antithetical to western liberal society. Unfettered power, unchecked discretion, violation of due process, and ignoring of individual rights and liberties—all are products of unchecked administrative power. As Pound notes, the intellectual currents of legal realism induce and enforce these tendencies, and, in his view, action must be taken immediately to reverse this trend. As Pound notes:

> A give-it-up philosophy of law and government is being widely taught. We are told that law is to disappear in the society of the future. We are told of a society in which omnicompetent and benevolent government will provide for the satisfaction of the material wants of everyone and there will be no need of adjusting relations or ordering conduct by law since everyone will be satisfied. Thus there will be no rights. There will only be a general duty of passive obedience. We need to be vigilant that where we are combating regimes of this sort, as they have developed in dictatorships and totalitarian governments, we do not allow a regime of autocratic bureaus to become so entrenched at home as to lead us in the same direction.[116]

ENDNOTES

CHAPTER EIGHT

1. Roscoe Pound, "Administrative Agencies and the Law," *New York, Public Affairs Pamphlets, National Industrial Conference Board, Inc.*, p. 26, 1946. *Vol. 2*, PB 22 (Hereinafter referred to as "Administrative Agencies..."). See also: Roscoe Pound, "Administrative Law and the Courts", *Vol.24 Boston University Law Review*, November, 1944, p. 223. *Vol. 2*, PB 101, (Hereinafter referred to as "Administrative Law...Courts").

2. Roscoe Pound, "The American Idea of Government," *Vol. 30 American Bar Association Journal*, September, 1944, p. 497. *Vol. 2, PB 98* (Hereinafter referred to as "The American Idea...").

3. Pound, *Task...*, p. 12. See also: Pound, *The Ideal Element...Tagore*, pp. 177-178.

4. Pound, *Task...*, p. 23. See also: Pound, *The Ideal Element...Tagore*, p. 52.

5. Pound, *The Ideal Element...Tagore*, pp. 52, 223, 225. See also: Pound, *Task...*, pp. 25, 182.

6. Roscoe Pound, *Administrative Law*, Pittsburgh, Pennsylvania, University of Pittsburgh Press, 1942 p. 50, *Vol. 2*, PB 4 (Hereinafter referred to as *Administrative...*). See also: Pound, "Recrudescence...," pp. 26-27.

7. Pound, "Twilight...," p. 47.

8. Chapter One: Pound on the Law.

9. Pound, *Vol. 3*, p. 6. See also: Pound, *Task...*, p. 26. Pound, *Social Control...*, pp. 130-135. Pound, *The Ideal Element...Tagore*, p. 52. Pound, *Interpretations of Legal...*, pp. 141-166.

10. Pound, *Social Control...*, p. 65. See also: Pound, *The Ideal Element...Tagore*, pp. 194, 225-226, 246. Pound, *Introduction...*, p. 47. Pound, *Spirit...*, pp. 110-111, 196-197.

11. Roscoe Pound, *The Development of Constitutional Guarantees of Liberty*, New Haven, Conn., Yale University Press, 1957. *Vol. 2*, PB 39. (Hereinafter referred to as *Development...Constitutional*).

12. Pound, *Administrative...*, p. 85.

13. Roscoe Pound, "Disappearance of the Law", Vol. 2 *Alabama Lawyer*, October, 1941, p. 365. *Vol.* 2, PB 62 (Hereinafter referred to as "Disappearance...").

14. Roscoe Pound, *Justice According...*, p. 91. See also: Pound, *Spirit...*, pp. 64-64. Pound, *Social Control...*, p. 108. Pound, *Task...*, pp. 55-60. Pound, *The Ideal Element...Tagore*, pp. 268-269.

15. Roscoe Pound, "Place of the Judiciary in a Democratic Polity," Vol. 26 *American Bar Association Journal*, March, 1941, p. 135. *Vol.* 2 PB 58. (Hereinafter referred to as "Place of the Judiciary...").

16. Pound, "Recrudescence...," p. 25.

17. Pound, "Twilight...," p. 42.

18. Pound, "Twilight...," p. 15.

19. Roscoe Pound, "What is Happening to the Law," *American Affairs*, April, 1946, p. 119. (Not in Pound Bibliography). (Hereinafter referred to as "What is...").

20. Pound, *The Ideal Element...Tagore*, p. 273.

21. Quoted in Pound, *The Ideal Element...Tagore*, p. 279.

22. Pound, "Recrudescence...," p. 20.

23. Pound, *Task...*, pp. 30-32. See also: Pound, *Social Control...*, pp. 47-68. Pound, *The Ideal Element...Tagore*, pp. 82-83.

24. Pound, "Recrudescence...," pp. 36-37.

25. Pound, "The American Idea...," p. 501. See also: Pound, "Twilight...," p. 46.

26. Pound, *The Ideal Element...Tagore*, p. 237.

27. Roscoe Pound, "Law and Laws in the Twentieth Century," *Dedicatory Exercises of the Law Quadrangle of the University of Michigan*, June 13, 1934, pp. 30-31. *Vol. 1* PB 215. (Hereinafter referred to as "Law...Twentieth Century").

28. Pound, "Disappearance...," p. 368.

29. Pound, "Disappearance...," p. 369. See also: Pound, "Recrudescence...," pp. 22-23. Pound, "The American Idea...," p. 502. Roscoe Pound, "Modern Administrative Law," *Virginia State Bar Association Reports*, 1939, p. 383. *Vol. 1* PB 251, (Hereinafter referred to as "Modern Administrative Law") See Chapter Four Legal Philosophy: Twentieth Century.

30. Pound, "Disappearance...," pp. 369-370. See Chapter Five: Legal Philosophy: Twentieth Century.

31. Pound, *Administrative...*, p. 22. See also: Pound, "Disappearance...," pp. 370-371. Pound, "The American Idea...," p. 502. Pound, "Modern Administrative Law," p. 25. See Chapter Four Legal Philosophy: Twentieth Century.

32. Pound, *Administrative...*, p. 25.

33. Pound, *Administrative...*, pp. 25-26. See also: Pound, "Recrudescence...," pp. 22-23. Pound, "The American Idea...," p. 502. Pound, "Modern Administrative Law," p. 384. See Chapter Four: Legal Philosophy: Twentieth Century.

34. Pound, "Disappearance...," pp. 378-379. See also: Roscoe Pound, "Administrative Law: Its Growth Procedure and Significance," Vol. 7 *University of Pittsburgh Law Review*, June, 1941, pp. 280-281. *Vol. 2*, PB 4 (Hereinafter referred to as "Administrative Law: Its Growth...").

35. Pound, "Disappearance...," pp. 378-379.

36. Pound, "The American Idea...," p. 501.

37. Pound, "Administrative Law: Its Growth...," pp. 274, 281. See also: Pound, *The Ideal Element...Tagore*, p. 217.

38. Pound, "Disappearance...," p. 375.

39. Pound, "Disappearance...," p. 375.

40. Pound, "Administrative Law: Its Growth...," pp. 272-273. See also: Pound, *The Ideal Element...Tagore*, pp. 217-218. Pound, "Place of the Judiciary...," p. 137.

41. Pound, "The American Idea...," p. 501.

42. Pound, "Disappearance...," p. 376. See also: Pound, "Administrative Law...Courts," p. 223. Pound, "Modern Administrative Law," p. 378.

43. Pound, "Preventive...," p. 78. See also: Pound, *Justice According...*, p. 78.

44. Pound, "Justice According...," p. 79.

45. Pound, *Task...*, p. 52. See also: Roscoe Pound, "Proposed Legislation as to Federal Administrative Procedure," Vol. 20 *Indiana Law Journal*, October, 1944, p. 31. *Vol. 2* PB 100 (Hereinafter referred to as "Proposed Legislation...").

46. Pound, *Administrative...*, p. 26. See also: Pound, "Modern Administrative Law," p. 373. Pound, "Place of Judiciary...," p. 135.

47. Pound, *Spirit...*, p. 7.

48. Pound, "Recrudescence...," pp. 26-27.

49. Pound, "Preventative...," p. 78. See also: Pound, *Justice According...*, p. 78.

50. Pound, "Modern Administrative Law," p. 373.

51. Pound, "Recrudescence...," p. 26.

52. Roscoe Pound, "The Challenge of the Administrative Process," Vol. 30 *American Bar Association Journal*, March, 1944, p. 121. *Vol. 2* PB 96 (Hereinafter referred to as "The Challenge...").

53. Roscoe Pound, "For the 'Minority Report'," Vol. 27 *American Bar Association Journal*, November, 1941, p. 665. *Vol. 2* PB 63 (Hereinafter referred to as "'Minority Report'..."). See also: Pound, *Administrative...*, pp. 66-67. Pound, "The Challenge...," pp. 122-123.

54. Pound, "Recrudescence...," p. 25.

55. Pound, "The Challenge...," pp. 124-125. See also: Pound, *Administrative...*, p. 66. Pound, "Proposed Legislation...," p. 32.

56. Pound, *Administrative...*, p. 86. See also: Pound, "Proposed Legislation...," p. 32.

57. Pound, "Administrative Agencies...," p. 17.

58. Pound, "Proposed Legislation...," p. 32.

59. Pound, "Proposed Legislation...," p. 43.

60. Pound, "'Minority Report'...," p. 666. See also: Pound, *Administrative...*, pp. 70-72.

61. Pound, "'Minority Report'...," p. 666. See also: Pound, "Administrative Agencies...," p. 17. Pound, "Proposed Legislation...," p. 32.

62. Pound, "Administrative Agencies...," p. 62. See also: Pound, "The Challenge...," p. 126. Pound, "Proposed Legislation...," pp. 37, 49. Pound, *Administrative...*, p. 67.

63. Pound, "Proposed Legislation...," p. 37.

64. Pound, "'Minority Report'...," p. 667. See also: Pound, "Proposed Legislation...," p. 40. Pound, *Administrative...*, p. 73. Pound, "What is...," p. 120.

65. Pound, "Proposed Legislation...," p. 40.

66. Pound, *Administrative...*, p. 73.

67. Pound, "Administrative Agencies...," pp. 20-21. See also: Pound, "'Minority Report'...," pp. 667-669.

68. Pound, "Administrative Law...Courts," p. 218. See also: Roscoe Pound, "Judicial Trial or Administrative Investigation?," Vol. 24 *NACCA Law Journal*, November, 1959, pp. 139-145, *Vol. 2* PB 256. (Hereinafter referred to as "Judicial Trial...").

69. Pound, "Administrative Law...Courts," p. 214. See also: Pound, "What is...," p. 120. Pound, "Disappearance...," p. 378.

70. Pound, "Proposed Legislation...," p. 45.

71. Pound, "Proposed Legislation...," p. 46.

72. Pound, "Proposed Legislation...," p. 47.

73. Pound, "Proposed Legislation...," p. 47.

74. Pound, "Proposed Legislation...," p. 47.

75. Pound, "Proposed Legislation...," p. 48.

76. Pound, "Proposed Legislation...," p. 49.

77. Pound, "Proposed Legislation...," p. 50.

78. Pound, "Administrative Agencies...," p. 15.

79. Pound, "Administrative Law...Courts," p. 206.

80. Pound, "Administrative Law...Courts," p. 206.

81. Pound, "Modern Administrative Law," p. 387.

82. Pound, "Administrative Agencies...," p. 15.

83. Pound, "Administrative Law...Courts," p. 206.

84. Pound, "What is...," p. 122.

85. Pound, "Administrative Law...Courts," p. 207.

86. Pound, *Administrative...*, p. 67.

87. Pound, *Administrative...*, pp. 75-76.

88. Pound, *Administrative...*, pp. 83-84. See also: Roscoe Pound, "Executive Justice," *Selected Essays on Constitutional Law*, Chicago, Foundation Press, Inc., 1938, pp. 63-75. Vol. 1, PB 22 (Hereinafter referred to as "Executive Justice").

89. Pound, "Place of the Judiciary...," p. 134.

90. Pound, "Administrative Law...Courts," pp. 204-205.

91. Pound, "Twilight...," p. 42.

92. Pound, *Administrative...*, p. 101.

93. Pound, *Administrative...*, pp. 5-7.

94. Pound, *Administrative...*, pp. 6.

95. Pound, "Administrative Agencies...," p. 6.

96. Pound, *Administrative...*, p. 101.

97. Pound, "Administrative Law...Courts," p. 205. See also: Pound, "Making Law...," pp. 11-12.

98. Pound, *Vol. 2*, p. 456.

99. Pound, "Administrative Agencies...," pp. 11-12. See also: Pound, "Administrative Law...Courts," p. 205.

100. Pound, *Task...*, p. 32.

101. Pound, *Justice According...*, p. 88.

102. Pound, *Vol. 2*, p. 457.

103. Pound, *Vol. 2*, p. 459.

104. Pound, *Administrative...*, p. 101.

105. Pound, *Administrative...*, p. 89.

106. Pound, *Administrative...*, p. 89.

107. Pound, *Administrative...*, p. 95.

108. Pound, *Administrative...*, p. 89.

109. Pound, *Administrative...*, p. 26. See also: Pound, "Modern Administrative Law," p. 373. Pound, "Place of the Judiciary...," p. 135.

110. Pound, *Task...*, pp. 34-35. See also Chapter One: *Pound On The Law.*

111. Pound, *Administrative...*, p. 26. See also: Pound, "Modern Administrative Law," p. 373. Pound, "Place of Judiciary...," p. 135.

112. Pound, "Preventive...," p. 150.

113. Roscoe Pound, "The Growth of Administrative Justice," Vol. 2 *Wisconsin Law Review*, January, 1924, pp. 321, 335. Vol. 2, PB 117 (Hereinafter referred to as "Growth Administrative...").

114. Pound, "Modern Administrative Law," p. 388. See also: Pound, *Administrative...*, p. 67. Pound, "Place of the Judiciary...," pp. 135-136. Pound, "What is...," p. 124.

115. Pound, "Place of the Judiciary...," p. 138.

116. Pound, "Administrative Agencies...," p. 26.

CHAPTER NINE

JUDICIAL JUSTICE

As we have seen, Pound views the maintenance and furtherance of civilization as the central role of law, and that the subjection of the coercive force of the state to the limitations of the law constitutes a central feature in this view.[1] As Pound observes:

> The real foe of absolutism is law. It presupposes a life measured by reason, a legal order measured by reason, and a judicial process carried on by applying a reasoned technique to experience developed by reason and reason tested by experience.[2]

Thus, Roscoe Pound evidenced continuing concern over the question of how western liberal civilization could best be maintained and furthered. Western liberal civilization, he feels, needs to be preserved and continued since it offers the best means for resolving human conflict, and creates the best conditions for human existence. It becomes essential, therefore, to determine which institution of government—legislative, executive, judicial—is best designed and equipped to protect and further this civilization. Pound maintains that judicial justice is diminishing in the twentieth century, and provides a substantial argument for why it should be preserved and why other governmental institutions cannot perform the task of preserving or furthering western civilization.[3]

Pound believes that humans are possessed of two contradictory tendencies—one selfish and aggressive behavior, and the other sociable.[4] It is apparent to Pound that man's success in developing society results from cultivating his social nature.[5] According to Pound, therefore, society must develop the means of social control which channel and direct human behavior toward ends conducive to the maintenance and furtherance of civilization.[6] This social control enables man to control his inner nature, *i.e.*, his aggressive, anti-social conduct, and enables him collectively to gain greater control over external nature, and, thus, improve the conditions of life for all. Without effective social control, general progress is impossible and civilization cannot be achieved or maintained.[7]

Pound is aware that human affairs can be ordered by force alone. Indeed, Pound feels that this alternative means of arranging human affairs and managing conflicts has great attraction in the modern world. He attributes this attraction to human dissatisfaction with the orderly and slow processes which characterize the law. Man in the twentieth century has been and still is attracted to the notion that progress is the result of the desires of a superior person or an unrestrained popular majority. In either case there is a willingness to use the force of the state to effect their will. In Pound's view, this reliance on force is antithetical to the operation of a lawful, civilized social order for, according to Pound, the critical role of law in a civilized order is to restrain and limit the operation of the force of the state.[8]

There exists a significant relationship between the maintenance and furtherance of civilization and the civilization's foundation of a system of justice based on law. The legal order is necessary to resolve human conflict which is inevitable because the resources available to man are finite, and their scarcity engenders conflict among men for their use and control.[9] Men must fashion the means whereby such conflict will be controlled and managed in a manner consistent with a civilized order, *i.e.*, a system of justice based on law. A civilized society, respects the interdependence of individuals, but it is also devoted to preserving individual independence.[10] Thus, even though individual action needs to be restrained, such restraint must be must be achieved in a reasonable manner consistent with human liberty.[11] Reasoned control of individual life can be achieved only by the operation of the law, which is designed to maintain and further civilization.[12] The five jural postulates which characterize a civilized society are the starting points for structuring and applying the law in the management of human conflict, and assure that justice will be done.[13] According to Pound, justice is not an utopian dream that postulates a society in which men live in perfect harmony with one another, or where every individual is perfectly virtuous.[14] These abstract ideals should not be rejected out of hand, but, Pound argues, they are unable to serve as a substitute for the type of ideals which must guide the law. Consequently, Pound believes that a realistic and practical resolution of conflict by law is possible when the jural postulates guide the resolution of such conflict in society.[15] Law is a practical enterprise which must deal with men as they are and adjust and resolve their conflicts as they arise in the context of society of a given time and place. Abstract ideals that aim to achieve the ultimate good, although they provide a basis for critique, cannot serve to do what law must do. For example, Pound points to the fact that the law must often deal with conflict in which there is no clear-cut, morally-correct answer, and yet such conflict must be resolved if society is to function.[16] Given the fact that law must deal with practical problems, the justice which it can achieve is defined by Pound as the adjusting:

> of relations and ordering of conduct...[that]...will make the goods of existence, the means of satisfying human claims to have things and do things, go round as far as possible with the least friction and waste.[17]

This is the prescription for the resolution of conflict which is consistent with a civilized order and, according to Pound, outlines the major tasks of the law.

Law and civilization are mainly the products of human fashioning and are not assured of preservation without the conscious human activity being to assure that preservation.[18] The precepts of law developed in the western world, are designed to limit regimes of force and provide the bases on which reasoning about conflict can be developed.[19] These precepts reflect the wisdom and experience of the past and are flexible enough to meet the demands of the present.[20] The technique of the law determines the way in which conflicts may be resolved in order to reduce arbitrariness and lack of predictability, and is fashioned by past experience which is judged by reason.[21] The authoritative ideals on which both the precepts and techniques are based are those of a civilized society and have as their foundation the jural postulates.[22]

The administration of justice according to law has often been subject to criticism, because it is alleged that it does not reflect the people's will, and that courts of law are flawed because they do not reflect that will.[23] Such an argument, Pound observes, is as:

> out of place in a developed social and economic order as the corresponding sixteenth and seventeenth century doctrines that in every case the courts ought to administer the will of the king for the time being....[24]

In Pound's view, the law is not to be confused with popular majoritarian ideas, or the principles of the superhuman leader, or an utopian ideology. As he points out, law enables man to predict the course which the administration of justice will take, and the predictability of this course is critical if a civilized society is to be maintained and furthered.[25]

Pound points out that modern societies are not different from other societies, in their need for peace and order. However, modern societies must manage conflict if men are to be encouraged to commit their time and resources to productive activity, and be assured that such investments and commitments will be secure. The fulfillment of these expectations depends, in turn, on property and transactions affecting it, being secure from the whim of those who hold power. Unless such security is provided, then the chance for commercial and economic development is minimal. As Pound notes:

> No one devotes his life to a specialized bit of labor, becoming a minute cog in an industrial machine, or engages in complex commercial undertakings, or makes large investments trusting to uniform exercises of unchecked discretion or free judicial search for the right.[26]

Pound does not feel the law is a set of complete and exhaustive rules which are automatic and self-executing. Rather, he considers law to be the mixture of precepts, techniques, and ideals, which provides a framework within which decisions can be made which maintain and further civilization. Law viewed in this manner provides security from errors of individual judgment and improper motives on the part of those who administer justice.[27] Judges who are not limited in their discretion by rules and precepts, Pound argues, have proven to be arbitrary and corrupt. It is true, he notes, that such limitations may prohibit a wise judge from making as fair a determination of an issue as is possible, but it does not prohibit him from being fair. More important, however, is the fact that such limits prevent a weaker, less able, or corrupt judge from making an imminently unfair judgement.[28] According to Pound, the control and limitation of the force and will of those who wield power is one of the greatest achievements of the western legal order, for:

> a civilization involves subjection of force to reason, and the agency of this subjection is law.[29]

Further, Pound argues that law provides to the magistrate, standards which reflect the ethical ideas of the community and enables him to act with the benefit of the experience of his predecessors.[30] Law, therefore, reflects both the authoritative ideals of a given society and the ethical notions of the community, and not the particular biases or prejudices of the judge.[31] In addition, the law embodies the experience and wisdom of the past which no individual can acquire on his own.[32] Pound cites the situation of the engineer who could not possibly rediscover all the information involved in creating the formulas which he uses in his work. The efforts, knowledge, and experience of the past, however, enable him to conduct his work efficiently and expeditiously. So it is with the judges, he argues, who deal with massive amounts of litigation, but who can utilize the experience and reason embodied in the law, and do not have to rely on their limited individual reason and experience to resolve conflicts.[33]

Finally, Pound maintains, law:

> prevents the sacrifice of ultimate interests, social and individual, to the more obvious and immediately pressing but less weighty immediate interests.[34]

The nature and purpose of law, Pound maintains, are not well served if it creates judgments on an *ad hoc* basis to deal with problems after they have occurred. However, when the law utilizes past experience—with its precepts, standards, ideals, and technique—to approach issues as they arise it is better equipped to effect a just and reasonable resolution. These means enable the law to approach issues at "an arms length," and, it is not swayed by the passions and powerful interests of the time. Reliance on techniques which are not fashioned in the heat of the moment, allow the law to avoid, for the most part, whim and caprice in the resolution of conflict and, at the same time, reaffirm the principles that will be employed for the resolution of future conflicts. All of these factors, Pound says, serve best to maintain and further civilization.[35]

Since the benefits of justice and civilization are served by a regime of law better than they are by a regime of force it is necessary, according to Pound, to determine which institution of government—legislature, executive, judiciary—is best equipped to provide such an administration of justice. According to Pound, the legislature is least equipped to perform this task. There is, he maintains, an abundance of historical evidence to demonstrate this. There is a desire in modern society, he argues, to revive the idea that the legislature should be charged with handling the development of justice.[36] Pound deplores this for, he says, history shows legislative justice to be "unequal, uncertain, and capricious."[37] Self-serving interests and corruption, he points out, have marked past efforts at legislative justice. Legislative assemblies are too susceptible to passion and prejudice to provide the balanced, and even-handed justice which is necessary to a civilized order.[38] Legislatures also will reflect partisan and political motives in all of their acts.[39] Pound notes, that those who favor legislative justice, argue that it will reflect the popular will.[40] Neither popular will nor majority will are compatible with the administration of justice by law, Pound says, indeed, they are often contrary to it.[41] Legislative justice, he concludes, exhibits all the bad features of justice without law.[42]

While historical evidence clearly reveals the undesirability of legislative justice, Pound maintains, this is not the case for executive or administrative justice. Indeed, the modern concept of the welfare state has led to a demand for an increase in the function and scope of the administration of justice by the executive branch.[43] The resurrection of the archaic demand for executive justice began at the end of the nineteenth century.[44]

This growth of executive justice, and the parallel decline of judicial supervision of that justice, results from three developments, according to Pound. First, economic growth and development have brought in their wake greater complexity and interrelatedness which have created a demand for more expeditious and efficient adjudication and resolution of conflict than would, perhaps, be offered by the courts. Second, the expansion of executive supremacy, has been matched by the growth of administrative boards and tribunals through which the executive operates. Third, throughout history the notion that justice can be achieved without law enjoys credibility, particularly when people believe that law does not resolve conflicts and protect interests as fully and as rapidly as it should.[45]

According to Pound the revival of executive justice is not a result of an inherent inability of the judiciary to adjust conflict in the context of modern society. He maintains, history has shown the ability of the judiciary to modify its practices to meet new and altered conditions.[46] Though this is the case, the advocates of executive justice argue that it provides benefits which the judiciary cannot provide. The proponents of executive justice argue that it has:

> directness, expedition, conformity to the popular will for the time being, freedom from the bounds of traditional rules, freedom from technical rules of evidence, and power to act upon the everyday intuition of ordinary man. In addition, it is claimed that the administrative agency may be composed of or may have a staff of experts with special competency to decide particular cases.[47]

Pound feels such arguments are dangerous to a civilized society. He maintains that traditional rules embodied in the law reflect the degree of deliberation and reason that should be employed in reconciling all legal issues.[48] Executive justice, however, is predicated on the basis of power and passion, and if left unchecked will replace a system of law with a system of force.[49]

In summarizing his critique of legislative and executive justice, Pound comments:

> Legislative and executive justice fail in two respects. In that part of the administration of justice in which rule is the best means toward the end of the legal order they are not governed by rule nor do they apply rule uniformly and consistently, and intelligently. In that part where discretion is best adopted to the ends of the legal order, trained reason and disciplined judgment are required, and the mental habit of those whose primary function is to deal with political rather than legal questions, or to investigate and guide rather than to judge, is often such as to make wide discretion and adjudication intolerable in their hands.[50]

It is Pound's firm conviction that justice according to law and the advancement and maintenance of civilization are best achieved by the judiciary. He writes:

> The advantages of justice are best secured by judicial justice administered by professional lawyers or by specialists. This is true of that most important advantage of justice according to law that it insures that the more valuable ultimate interests, social and individual, will not be sacrificed to immediate interests which are more obvious and pressing but of less real weight.[51]

This reasoning constitutes the crux of Pound's major argument regarding the desirability, indeed the necessity, of judicial justice as the most effective means for the maintenance and furtherance of civilization.[52]

Civilization, he maintains, is the product of past experience tested by reason which is brought to bear on present conflicts in order to resolve them, and protect stability and order. When this is done, a social order can be maintained in which individual initiative will function and which will also provide the degree of human cooperation needed to further a civilized order.[53]

Judicial justice has distinct advantages over legislative and executive justice, that serve to maintain and further civilization.

First of all, the judiciary embodies the flexibility needed to adapt the law to changing circumstances, but it is able, simultaneously, to retain the fixity and certainty required in law.[54] The law is administered by a trained professional group, whose common learning and training provide a cohesive and rational process. Consequently, judges operate within fixed canons of interpretation and application of the law, because of the common background and training they have. They are equipped, therefore, to guard the stability and protection provided by the law.[55] As he notes, judges unlike legislators who will make law on the basis of any ground they choose, make:

> the actual law by a process of trying principles and rules and standards in concrete cases, observing their practical operation and gradually discovering by experience of many causes how to apply them so as to administer justice by means of them.[56]

In performing the task of testing reason by experience and experience by reason, the courts maintain the certainty needed by a civilized order. As Pound argues:

> Certainty is insured within reasonable limits in that the court proceeds by analogy of rules and doctrines in the traditional system and develops a principle for the cause before it according to a known technique.[57]

The conserving function of judicial justice, Pound observes, reflects the very nature of law. Critics of the judiciary argue that their procedures are too rigid and unequipped to meet the challenges of new circumstances and situations. He says of this criticism:

> Fixity of premises is not wholly a defect. If tradition sometimes holds too fast, yet it holds fast and so makes judicial justice reasonably uniform and predictable. Stability is at least no less important than power of growth.[58]

Judicial justice, Pound observes, has never remained unchanged or static. If it had, it would not have been able to survive and flourish as it has. The judiciary, because of its training and professionalism, is able to apply the:

> received premises with reference to concrete causes and...to correct...rules by extension or restriction through experience of their applications and a gradual process of inclusion and exclusion upon rational principles.[59]

In doing so, the judiciary assures the growth needed by law:

> in that the limits of the principle are not fixed authoritatively once for all but are discovered gradually...as cases arise which brings out its practical workings and prove how far it may be made to do justice in its actual operation.[60]

The legislature and the executive are prone to be moved and motivated by expedient considerations and popular approval. Consequently reason which is the core of law is overlooked. This reason, however, is always reflected in the judiciary, and:

> is as Coke put it, 'the artificial reason and judgment of the law,' not every man's natural reason.[61]

Unlike legislators, executives, or administrators, judges are not free to do what they wish, when they wish, and how they wish.[62] As Pound observes, the judge's respect for the law requires that he reach his decisions by using the received precepts, techniques, and ideals developed by the judiciary in the past. The judge may not, as the legislator may, predicate his decisions on any basis he wishes.[63] Judicial justice is conditioned by the fact that judges operate under limitations and controls that do not pertain to either legislators or executives. Consequently judges must tailor their actions and decisions to standards that are not a product of their own will.[64] In addition, their background, their training, and their intimate and inseparable relationship with a similarly trained professional group limit the degree of discretion and choice available to them.[65] Juristic thought, Pound observes, teaches the lawyer and the judge that:

> there are inherent limitations on what may be achieved through law and inherent limitation upon the efficacy of effort in conscious lawmaking; that for the greatest part, law must always be found through application of reason to causes as they arise and the testing of principles in their actual operation; that laws are not like clothes to be thrown off and replaced at will, but, like language are so ultimately a part of all we do that development of the traditional materials will always be the chief agency of growth.[66]

Each decision of a judge is always subject to the examination and critique of a professional group which has experienced the same training and development as the judge who makes a decision. All members of this profession judge the decision not on the basis of a particularized preference or value, but on the basis of the received precepts, ideals, and technique in which they have been trained.[67] The importance of Pound's point here is emphasized by his explanation of the role of the legal profession in the administration of justice, and by the nature of the profession itself. Resolution of controversies which occur in a civilized society require trained professionals to present an orderly, intelligible, and relevant statement of the facts. This is needed if any sound and just decision is to be the result. As Pound notes:

> From antiquity experience has shown that adjustment of relations among men and ordering of their conduct requires law and that law requires lawyers.[68]

Pound is aware that regimes of force can operate with some degree of success, but, he argues, they will do so at an unacceptable cost to all civilized values. Civilization, justice, and law are inextricably linked. The judiciary is trained to work out disputes by law and the ideals on which it is built. Judges cannot ignore the law at will in determining which issues to adjudicate, what decisions to make, based on the facts and the law, and what remedies can be given.[69]

It is the judiciary which provides the proper blending of justice, force, security and balance which must be accomplished in achieving justice.[70] Such an approach in resolving conflicts is part of the lawyers' common training and reflects the reasoning on which the profession is based. A profession, Pound notes, is:

> A group of men pursuing a learned art as a common calling in the spirit of public service which is no less a public service because incidentally it may be a means of livelihood.[71]

Pound emphasizes the fact that the legal profession is charged with serving the law.[72] The profession's dedication to service to the society and the law affect the judge's behavior. The standards by which a judge is critiqued by his fellow lawyers are known and accepted by all the members of that profession. The profession's review and control of judges operates both formally and informally. A series of appeals courts may formally review any decision, and if such courts find error or wrong in light of the accepted precepts, technique or ideals, they may overturn a lower court's decision.[73] In addition, the whole profession reviews and critiques the performance of the judiciary informally, and this fact operates to assure the adherence of the judiciary to the precepts, techniques, and ideals known and accepted by the profession.[74] Pound argues therefore, that a judge must, because of his training, background, and the environment within which he works, adhere to these limitations in giving effect to the law.

Judicial justice is better able to maintain and further civilization, because of its ability to stand for the law against "excitement and clamor and local resistance."[75] Pound cites the numerous instances in the history of the West where the judiciary stood as the only defender of civilization based on law. The demand for the administration of justice in conformity with popular will or passion has been resisted by the courts.[76] For example, he cites the courts in the early American Republic which stood steadfastly for the protection of the loyalists' legal rights and contrasts this record with the many legislative lynchings which occurred, and which were devoid of any semblance of lawful procedure and protection.[77] The capacity and desire of the judiciary to protect law is, in Pound's view, attributable to three qualities of the judiciary, which are:

> their training in the law and in the tradition of the lawyer and judges, their habit-of seeking and applying principles whenever called upon to act, and their consciousness that their decisions will be preserved in permanent form and will be subject to expert criticism in the present.[78]

The judiciary is better able than the other institutions of politically organized society to assure the enforcement of rules which will be applied uniformly and systematically to all.[79] This uniformity constitutes one of the most important qualities of justice in a civilized order, and it is the function of law to preserve this uniformity. The legislature and the executive respond to popular pressures and use the argument of majority will as justification for governmental actions that violate uniform and general law. In light of these facts the judiciary's role becomes even more important, for it is the duty of the judiciary to resist those modern tendencies which seek to abandon law in favor of majority will. As Pound observes, individual autocratic rulers must be attentive to the possibility of revolution by those that they rule. An absolute democratic majority need not fear this eventuality.[80] The practices of the judiciary reflect its belief that the law:

> is not to be made arbitrarily by a fiat of the sovereign will, but is to be discovered by judicial and juristic experience of the rules and principles which in the past have accomplished or failed to accomplish justice.[81]

It is the courts, Pound feels, which can balance reason and experience on the basis of the received values of a civilized society and permit the orderly growth of law to meet new circumstances without abandoning those values which are necessary for a civilized order, but which may, for the moment, be under assault by a powerful majority or plurality.

Pound perceives the growing pressure for expansion of governmental power into every facet of society. He feared that this expansion would be carried out either through legislative or executive action, and he desired to control such expansion through the protection of the law. He felt this would be achieved by the operation of the courts. He maintained that the limitations required by law would dissolve in the face of unlimited democratic governance, which would mean unlimited governmental power for the immediate majority or plurality. Were law to be considered as subordinate to the power of majorities or pluralities, it could no longer serve as an instrument of limiting power, but rather became an instrument of power in the hands of the largest or most popular cause. Civilization could not survive.

ENDNOTES

CHAPTER NINE

1. See Chapter One: *Pound On The Law.* See also Chapter Eight: Administrative Law.

2. Pound, *Justice According...*, p.91. See also: Pound, *Spirit...*, pp. 64-65, 73-74, 182-185. Pound, *Social Control...*, p. 108. Pound, *Task...*, pp. 56-60. Pound, *The Ideal Element...Tagore*, pp. 268-269.

3. See Chapter 9, Administrative Law.

4. Chapter One: Pound on the Law. See also: Pound, *The Ideal Element...Tagore*, pp. 224-225. Pound, *Social Control...*, pp. 131-133. Pound, *Task...*, pp. 22-25. Pound, *Vol. 3* pp. 5-7. Pound, *Interpretations of Legal...*, pp. 148-150.

5. Pound, *Task...*, pp. 20-24. See also: Pound, *The Ideal Element...Tagore*, pp. 224-225. Pound, *Social Control...*, pp. 131-133. Pound, *Task...*, pp. 22-25. Pound, *Vol. 3*, pp. 5-8. Pound, *Interpretations of Legal...*, pp. 148-150.

6. Pound, *Social Control...*, p. 8. See also: Pound, *The Ideal Element...Tagore*, pp. 224-225. Pound, *Task...*, pp. 22-25. Pound, *Vol. 3*, pp. 5-8. Pound, *Interpretations of Legal...*, pp. 148-150.

7. Pound, *Vol. 3*, p. 13. See also: Pound, *Social Control...*, pp. 16-19. Pound, *The Ideal Element...Tagore*, pp. 224-225. Pound, *Task...*, pp. 22-15. Pound, *Interpretations of Legal...*, pp. 148-150.

8. Pound, *The Ideal Element...Tagore*, pp. 234-237. See also: Pound, *Social Control...*, pp. 15-16, 32-33. Pound, *Task...*, pp. 14, 22, 31, 59. Pound, *Justice...*, pp. 45-47.

9. Pound, *Social Control...*, p. 64, 106. See also: Pound, *Vol. 3*, p. 25. Pound, *Task...*, pp. 56, 109-110. Pound, *Spirit...*, pp. 91-93. Pound, *Interpretations of Legal...*, pp. 151-158. Pound, *Introduction...*, p. 47.

10. Pound, *The Ideal Element...Tagore*, p. 177. See also: Pound, *Vol. 3*, pp. 315-324. Pound, *Interpretations of Legal...*, pp. 143-145. Pound, *Spirit...*, pp. 110-111.

11. Pound, *Vol. 3*, p. 318. See also: Pound, "Theory...," p. 42. Pound, *Task...*, pp. 86-87. Pound, *The Ideal Element...Tagore*, pp. 194-195. Pound, *Spirit...*, pp. 182-183. Pound, *Social Control...*, pp. 101-103.

12. Pound, "A Comparison...," p. 17. See also: Pound, *Task...*, p. 21. Pound, *The Ideal Element...Tagore*, p. 222. Pound, *Social Control...*, pp. 25-26.

13. See Chapter Seven: Theory of Interests.

14. Pound, *Social Control...*, p. 65. See also: Pound, *Task...*, p. 12. Pound, *The Ideal Element...Tagore*, pp. 177-178.

15. Pound, *The Ideal Element...Tagore*, p. 50, 187, 191. See also: Pound, *Vol. 3*, pp. 8-11. Pound, *Social Control...*, pp. 81-83, 112-118.

16. Pound, *The Ideal Element...Tagore*, pp. 70-82. See also: Pound, *Vol. 3*, pp. 5-15, 327-352. Pound, *Introduction...*, pp. 54-71.

17. Pound, *Social Control...*, p. 65. See also: Pound, "Law and Christian...," p. 106. Pound, *History and System...Common...*, p. 2. Pound, *Justice...*, pp. 29-31.

18. Pound, *Development...Constitutional...*, pp. 2-3. See also: Pound, *Task...*, p. 32. Pound, *The Ideal Element...Tagore*, pp. 182-184. Pound, *Social Control...*, pp. 16-20, pp. 132-134. Roscoe Pound, "The Theory...," pp. 641-662.

19. Pound, *Social Control...*, p.102. See also: Pound, *Spirit...*, pp. 181-183. Pound, *Task...*, pp. 59-61. Pound, *Vol. 2*, pp. 9-18. Pound, *Justice According...*, pp. 90-91. Pound, "The Theory...," pp. 641-662.

20. Pound, *Task...*, pp. 36, 44-46. See also: Pound, *Justice According...*, pp. 54-56. Pound, *Spirit...*, pp. 181-183. Pound, *Vol. 2*, pp. 9-18. Pound, "The Theory...," pp. 641-662.

21. Pound, *Task...*, p. 35, 43. See also: Pound, *Justice According...*, pp. 50-51, 54. Pound, *Social Control...*, pp. 48-49, 130-132. Pound, *Vol. 2*, pp. 9-18.

22. Pound, *Social Control...*, p. 42. See also: Pound, *Vol. 3*, pp. 8-10. Pound, *The Ideal Element...Tagore*, pp. 76-77, 82-83, 184-192. Pound, *Spirit...*, p. 82. Pound, *Introduction...Philosophy...*, pp. 85-91, 105-109, 140, 159. See also Chapter 7, Theory of Interests.

23. Pound. *The Ideal Element...Tagore*, p. 237. See also: Pound, "The American Idea...," p. 497. Pound, "Place of the Judiciary...," p. 135.

24. Pound, *Vol. 2*, p. 371. See also: Pound, *The Ideal Element...Tagore*, 269, 270-283. Pound, "Administrative Agencies...," p. 26. Pound, "Administrative Law...Courts," p. 223.

25. Pound, Vol. 2, p. 280. See also: Pound, *The Ideal Element...Tagore*, p. 77. Pound, *Social Control...*, pp. 30-33. Pound, *Task...*, pp. 14-17, 36. Pound, *Justice According...*, pp. 34-36.

26. Pound, *Vol. 2*, p. 382. See also: Pound, *The Ideal Element...Tagore*, pp. 182-183. Pound, *Interpretations of Legal...*, p. 160. Pound, *Vol. 3*, p. 6.

27. Pound, Vol. 2, p. 381. See also: Pound, *The Ideal Element...Tagore*, p. 2. Pound, *Social Control...*, pp. 39-41. Pound, *Task...*, pp. 37-39. Pound, *Justice According...*, pp. 49-56. Roscoe Pound, "Justice According to Law II," Vol. 13 *Columbia Law Review*, January, 1914, pp. 103-121, (Hereinafter referred to as "Justice...II").

28. Pound, *Vol. 2*, pp. 384-385. See also: Pound, *Justice According...*, pp. 87-90. Pound, "The Theory of Judicial Decision I," Vol 36, *Harvard Law Review*, April, 1923, pp. 641-662. Vol. 1 PB 113, (Hereinafter referred to as "The Theory...Judicial...I"). Pound, "Justice...II," pp. 103-121. Pound, *The Ideal Element...Tagore*, pp. 218-226.

29. Roscoe Pound, "The Future of Law," Vol. 47 *Yale Law Journal*, November, 1937, p.13. Vol. 1 PB 227. (Hereinafter referred to as "Future..."). See also: Pound, "Twilight...," p. 47. Pound, *Development...Constitutional*, p. . Pound, *Justice According...*, pp. 62-91. Pound, "Administrative Agencies...," p. 26.

30. Pound, *Vol. 2*, p. 381, 447-448, 456-463. See also: Pound, *The Ideal Element...Tagore*, pp. 5-7, 94-98. Pound, *Social Control...*, pp. 42-44, 121-122. Pound, *Task...*, p. 43. Pound, *Justice According...*, pp. 54-56. Pound, "The Theory... Judicial...I," pp. 640-662.

31. Pound, *Vol. 1*, p. 385. See also: Roscoe Pound, "The Theory of Judicial Decision III," Vol. 36, *Harvard Law Review*, June, 1923, pp. 940-959. Vol. 1 PB 113, (Hereinafter Referred to as "The Theory Judicial...III"). Pound, *The Ideal Element...Tagore*, pp. 5-7, 94-98. Pound, *Social Control...*, pp. 42-44, 121-122. Pound, *Task...*, p. 43. Pound, *Justice According...*, pp. 54-56. Pound, "The Theory Judicial...I," pp. 640-662. Pound, *Vol. 2*, pp. 447-448, 456-463.

32. Pound, *Vol. 1*, p. 385. See also: Pound, "The Theory of Judicial...I," pp. 640-662. Pound, "The Theory of Judicial...III," pp. 940-959. Pound, *Justice According...*, pp. 62-91. Pound, *The Ideal Element...Tagore*, pp. 61-65. 218-234. Pound, "Justice...," pp. 103-121. Pound, *Vol. 2*, pp. 447-448, 456-463.

33. Pound, *Vol. 1*, p. 385. See also: Pound, "Justice...II," pp. 109-111. Pound, *Justice According...*, pp. 62-91. Pound, *Vol. 2,* pp. 447-448, 456-463. Pound, "Twilight...," p. 91.

34. Pound, *Vol. 1*, p. 381. See also: Pound, *Vol. 2*, pp. 447-448, 456-463. Pound, *Justice According...*, pp. 89-90. Pound, "Twilight...," p. 91.

35. Pound, *Vol. 1*, p. 386. See also: Pound, *Vol. 2*, pp. 111-112. Pound, "The Problems...," p. 84. Pound, *Social Control...*, pp. 8-9, 41-42. Pound, *Task...*, pp. 35, 43, 48. Pound, *Justice According...*, pp. 51-54. Pound, *The Ideal Element...Tagore*, pp. 21-26.

36. Pound, *Vol. 1*, p. 389. See also: Pound, *Vol. 2,* pp. 390-404, 406. Pound, *Justice According...*, pp. 65-70. Pound, "Justice...II," pp. 7-12.

37. Pound, *Vol. 1*, p. 397. See also: Pound, *Vol. 2*, pp. 390-404, 406. Pound, "Making Law...," pp. 298-300. Pound, *Justice According...*, pp. 65-70. Pound, "Justice...II," pp. 7-12.

38. Pound, *Vol. 1*, pp. 398-399. See also: Pound, *Vol. 2*, pp. 390-404, 406. Pound, "Making Law...," pp. 298-300. Pound, *Justice According...*, pp. 65-70. Pound, "Justice...II," pp. 7-12.

40. Pound, *Vol. 1*, p. 402. See also: Pound, *Vol. 2*, pp. 390-404, 406.Pound, "Making Law...," pp. 298-300. Pound, *Justice According...*, pp. 65-70. Pound, "Justice...II," pp. 7-12.

41. Pound, *Spirit...*, p. 279. See also: Pound, *Vol. 2*, pp. 390-404, 406. Pound, *Justice According...*, pp. 65-70. Pound, "Justice...II," pp. 7-12.

42. Pound, *Justice According...*, p. 67. See also: Pound, *Vol. 2*, pp. 390-404, 406. Pound, "Justice...II," pp. 7-12.

43. Pound, *Vol. 2*, p. 46. See also: Pound, *The Ideal Element...Tagore*, pp. 271-272. Pound, *Justice According...*, pp. 73-78. Pound, "Justice...II," pp. 12-26. See also Chapter Nine Administrative Law.

44. Pound, *Vol. 2*, p. 410. See also: Pound, *The Ideal Element...Tagore*, p. 225. Pound, *Task...*, pp. 52-54. Pound, *Justice According...*, pp. 78-80.

45. Pound, *Vol. 2*, pp. 425-428. See also: Pound, *The Ideal Element...Tagore*, Pound, "Justice...II," pp. 12-26. Pound, *Justice According...*, pp. 80-85. See also Chapter Eight Administrative Law.

46. Pound, *Vol. 2*, p. 433, 449-450. See also: Pound, *Justice According...*, pp. 84-88. Pound, "Justice...III," pp. 103-121.

47. Pound, *Vol. 2*, p. 435. See also: Pound, "Justice...II," pp. 12-26. Pound, *Justice According...*, pp. 73-78.

48. Pound, *Vol. 2*, p. 435. See also: Pound, "Justice...II," pp. 12-26. Pound, *Justice According...*, pp. 73-78. Chapter 4, Pound on the Law.

49. Pound, *Vol. 2*, pp. 273-275. See also: Pound, "Place of the Judiciary...," p. 135. Pound, "Recrudescence...," p. 25. Pound, "Twilight...," p. 42.

50. Pound, "Justice...," p. 107. See also: Pound, *Vol. 2*, pp. 390-406, 407-449, 455. Pound, *Justice According...*, pp. 63-78.

51. Pound, *Vol. 2*, pp. 380-388, 447-448. See also: Pound, "Making Law...," pp. 298-299. Pound, *Justice According...*, pp. 28-29, 91. Pound, *Task...*, p. 18. Pound, *The Ideal Element...Tagore*, pp. 60-62. Pound, "Justice...III," pp. 103-111. Pound, *Social Control...*, p. 112.

52. Pound, *Vol. 2*, pp. 380-388, 447-448. See also: Pound, *Social Control...*, p. 112. Pound, "Making Law...," pp. 298-299. Pound, *Justice According...*, pp. 28-29. Pound, *Task...*, p. 18. Pound, *The Ideal Element...Tagore*, pp. 60-62. Pound, "Justice...III," pp. 103-111.

53. Pound, *Spirit...*, pp. 111, 183. See also: Pound, *Task...*, p. 26. Pound, *The Ideal Element...Tagore*, p. 52. Pound, *Social Control...*, pp. 130-135.

54. Pound, *Vol. 2*, p. 456. See also: Pound, "Justice...III," p. 108. Pound, *Justice According...*, pp. 87-88.

55. Pound, *Vol. 2*, p. 456. See also: Pound, "Justice...III," p. 108. Pound, *Justice According...*, pp. 87-88. Pound, "Administrative Agencies...," p. 92.

56. Pound, *Spirit...*, p. 176. See also: Pound, "Justice...III," p. 108. Pound, *Justice According...*, pp. 87-88. Pound, "Administrative Agencies...," p. 92.

57. Pound, *Spirit...*, p. 182. See also: Pound, *Vol. 2*, p. 458. Pound, *Justice According...*, pp. 87-88. Pound, "Administrative Agencies...," p. 92.

58. Pound, *Vol. 2*, p. 452. See also: Pound, "Justice...III," pp. 104-105. Pound, *Justice According...*, p. 85.

59. Pound, *Vol. 2*, p. 456. See also: Pound, *Justice According...*, pp. 85-86. Pound, "Justice...III," pp. 104-105.

60. Pound, *Spirit...*, p. 182. See also: Pound, "Justice...III," pp. 105-106. Pound, *Justice According...*, pp. 85-87. Pound, *Vol. 2,* pp. 452-454.

61. Pound, *Vol. 2*, p. 372. See also: Pound, *Justice According...*, p. 71. Pound, *Spirit...*, pp. 60-61.

62. Pound, *Vol. 2*, p. 238. See also: Pound, *Justice According...*, pp. 88-89. Pound, "Justice...III," pp. 108-109. Pound, *Spirit...*, pp. 170-172.

63. Pound, *Vol. 2*, p. 238. See also: Pound, *Justice According...*, pp. 88-89. Pound, "Justice...III," pp. 108-109. Pound, *Spirit...*, pp. 170-172.

64. Pound, *Vol. 2*, p. 456. See also: Pound, *Justice According...*, pp. 88-89. Pound, "Justice...III," pp. 108-109. Pound, *Spirit...*, pp. 170-172.

65. Pound, *Vol. 5*, pp. 673-675. See also: Pound, *Social Control...*, p. 50. Roscoe Pound, "The Legal Profession and the Law," *Proceedings of the Eighteenth Annual Meeting of the Oklahoma Bar Association*, 1925, pp. 179-205, Vol. 1 PB 133, (Hereinafter referred to as "The Legal Profession...,"). Pound, "Justice...," pp. 108-109. Pound, *Justice According...*, pp. 88-90.

66. Pound, *Spirit...*, p. 165. See also: Pound, "The Theory...," pp. 641-662. Pound, *Social Control...*, pp. 2-3, 52-62. Pound, *Task...*, pp. 62, 72-79. Pound, *Justice According...*, pp. 41-43. Pound, *Vol. 2*, pp. 11-16. Pound, *Vol. 3*, pp. 354-355. Pound, *Interpretations of Legal...*, pp. 1-2.

67. Pound, *Vol. 2*, p. 456. See also: Pound, "The Theory...," pp. 641-662. Pound, "Justice...III," pp. 106-110.

68. Pound, *Vol. 5*, p. 657. See also: Pound, "The Theory...," pp. 641-662. Pound, "Justice...III," pp. 106-110. Pound, "The Legal Profession...," pp. 179-205.

69. Pound, *Task...*, p. 32. See also: Pound, "The Theory...," pp. 641-662. Pound, "Justice...III," pp. 106-110. Pound, *Social Control...*, p. 108. Pound, *Vol. 2*, pp. 382-386.

70. See: Chapter One: Pound on the Law; and Chapter Seven: The Theory of Interests.

71. Pound, *Vol. 5*, p. 676. See also: Pound, "The Legal Profession...," pp. 179-205. Pound, "The Theory...," pp. 641-662. Pound, "Justice...III," pp. 106-110. Roscoe Pound, "The Law School and the Professional Tradition," Vol. 24 *Michigan Law Review*, December, 1925, pp. 156-165. Vol. 1 PB 128. (Hereinafter referred to as "The Law School...,").

72. Pound, *Vol. 5*, p. 667. See also: Pound, "The Legal Profession...," pp. 179-205. Pound,"The Theory...," pp. 641-662. Pound, "Justice...III," pp. 103-121. Pound, "The Law School...," pp. 156-165.

73. Pound, *Vol. 2*, pp. 238, 457. See also: Pound, *Justice According...*, pp. 88-89. Pound, "Justice...III," pp. 108-109. Pound, *Spirit...*, pp. 170-172. Pound, *Social Control...*, p. 50. Pound, "The Legal Profession...," pp. 179-205.

74. Pound, *Vol. 2*, pp. 238, 457. See also: Pound, *Justice According...*, pp. 88-89. Pound, "Justice...III," pp. 108-109. Pound, "The Legal Profession...," pp. 179-205.

75. Pound, *Vol. 2*, pp. 238, 457, 459. See also: Pound, *Justice According...*, pp. 88-90. Pound, "Justice...III," pp. 108-110. Pound, "The Theory...," pp. 642-662. Pound, *Spirit...*, pp. 182-183.

76. Pound, *Vol. 2*, pp. 460-462. See also: Pound, *Justice According...*, pp. 88-90. Pound, "Justice...III," pp. 108-110. Pound, "The Theory...," pp. 642-662. Pound, *Spirit...*, pp. 182-183.

77. Pound, *Vol. 2*, p. 460. See also: Pound, *Justice According...*, pp. 88-90. Pound, "Justice...III," pp. 108-110. Pound, "The Theory...," pp. 642-662.

78. Pound, *Vol. 2*, p. 459. See also: Pound, *Justice According...*, pp. 88-90. Pound, "Justice...III," pp. 108-110. Pound, "The Theory...," pp. 642-662.

79. Pound, *Task...*, p. 17. See also: Pound, *Vol. 2*, pp. 458-462. Pound, Pound, *Justice According...*, pp. 88-90. Pound, "Justice...III," pp. 108-110. Pound, "The Theory...," pp. 642-662.

80. Pound, *The Ideal Element...Tagore*, p. 276. See also: Pound, "The American Idea...," p. 497. Pound, *Vol. 2*, pp. 374-388.

81. Pound, *Spirit...*, p. 183. See also: Pound, *Justice According...*, pp. 62-91. Pound, "Justice...III," pp. 103-121. Pound, "The Theory...," pp. pp. 641-662. Pound, *Vol. 2*, pp. 447-465.

CHAPTER TEN

CONCLUSION

This book outlines the major themes that appear in sixty years of Roscoe Pound's writing and scholarship. During his long career, Pound never deviated from certain basic values which influenced his theory of law. Richard Wigdor, I think, misapprehends Pound's theory by arguing that it is composed of an irreconcilable dualism between instrumentalism and organism. Wigdor says:

> The competition between instrumentalist and organic elements in Pound's thought created a crippling dualism, which undermined his attempt to erect a comprehensive theoretical system, and confined his mature jurisprudence to a collection of brilliant but inconclusive insights. The organic element in his thought made it impossible for him to develop the implications of instrumentation in a sustained fashion, and the expansive phrases of his progressive vocabulary obscured his fundamental caution, both for Pound and his contemporaries and for later readers.[1]

A fairer assessment of Pound compels one to recognize that there is a consistent philosophy in Pound's writings—from the earliest to the latest of them—which reflects certain principles regarding the nature, purpose, content, and use of the law from which he never deviated, and which constitute, in their totality, a philosophy of law which is comprehensive. Pound's theory of law is a splendid mixture of the requirements which law must serve if it is to be properly denominated as law. On one hand Pound rejects the development of legal philosophy which is unrelated to the practical necessities with which the law necessarily is concerned. To do so, in Pound's view, is to engage oneself in excessive moral concern which serves only minimally to assist in the development of the law in serving to maintain and further civilization. On the other hand, Pound rejects the whole school of legal realism, since it reduces the notion of law to nothing more significant that a contest between "wits" and "power," thus failing to realize that the vital force of the law is its role in controlling power. Pound believed that the law should reflect both realism and idealism, indeed, realism and idealism must exist in a symbiotic relationship in any desirable legal order or legal philosophy. Few legal philosophers have succeeded as well as Pound in fashioning a legal philosophy which effectively and helpfully blends realism with idealism. Pound is a very effective spokesman of the great western liberal tradition, who recognizes that the role of the ideals in this tradition are the guidelines within which legal development must occur.

In commenting on the American Constitution, for example, Pound points out that this great document was a product of both realism and idealism, and was designed to construct a government under law which would curb and control the exercise of power.[2] As Pound points out this fundamental instrument of governance in the United States developed from the idealism found in the philosophy of law dating from the ancients to the eighteenth century, and practical experiences men had had with the exercise of uncontrolled power. Thus, in constructing a philosophy of law Pound followed this prescription and what Pound fashioned, in the course of his long and productive career, was a philosophy of law which was realistic, in the sense that it provided the mechanisms and precepts to deal with problems and issues raised in a changing social, economic, and political environment, as well as providing guidelines to tailor these responses to values implicit and explicit in the history of western liberal civilization.

Probably no legal philosopher is as misused by those against whose views of law he protested and so studiously ignored by those who would find Pound to be a sympathetic colleague. The misuse to which sociological jurisprudence had been put, was considered by Pound to be a scandal. His counsel about law as a mode of controlling power has been altered by those who use his words to justify and endorse the expansion of governmental power into areas of life which Pound would never have felt proper, desirable, or necessary.

Pound viewed the development of the "service state" as almost necessary in the face of the changed circumstances following in the wake of industrialization, urbanization, and technological advancement. He makes a compelling case for his argument that the older strict theories of contract and tort, for example, which were so central to nineteenth century jurisprudence, were ill-equipped to fashion the response that should be made to the changes which followed the developments so characteristic of the twentieth century. However, he condemned the growth of this "service state" which grew from the use of power and not law. The consequence of law as a result of uncontrolled power is a self propelling development which expands control into all areas of a society's institutions and practices, and encourages the notion, ill founded and erroneous, in Pound's view, that all of men's expectations can be fulfilled and met by governmental action. The result of this changed perception of law has been the development of state power that is used to redistribute resources and to control individual liberty and enterprise. The notion of the service state has been transformed, according to Pound, into an authoritarian ideal of government which leads to greatly inflated and uncontrolled use of state power, and to a society governed by will and not law. The confused thinking underlying the proponents of this expanded service state is criticized by Pound, who shows that the argument that a service state in a democracy cannot be oppressive, is wrong in both principle and practice. Absolutism and unchecked power are as oppressive in a democracy as they are in a monarchy or a totalitarian state. Pound further condemns the idea that power can be employed in the pursuit of egalitarianism, for the mere use of such power for such purposes must, of necessity, result in the use of state power to deal with the citizens of the society in unequal ways. This changed perception of law is primarily the result of the vacuous theories of the legal positivists and realists, who have ignored the fact that law is the product of incremental and slow development over the centuries, and embodies ideals, technique, and precepts which, when followed, condition and limit the employment of political power. For Pound the realists and the positivists subscribe to the notion of "subordinating" law and have rejected the ideal of "coordinating" law. The difference between the two is startling. Subordinating law employs the coercive apparatus of the state to compel adherence to a prescribed set of values and practices favorable to those who sit in the seats of power. Because its source of authority is power, that power is expanded at every turn, and ultimately this view of law celebrates the "cult of force" and rejects totally the idea that law is to be used to protect human liberty and enterprise and to control power. The great western liberal tradition, of which Pound is an effective spokesman, is based on the idea of "coordinating" law, *i.e.*, the belief that law's role is to confine the power of the state, and in so doing to permit the state to use its power to create the conditions and circumstances in which human liberty can best flourish and enterprise can be encouraged. The twentieth century generally reflects a movement away from this civilizing role of law.

Pound's argument that legal development is a result of cyclical movements between rigidity of the law and periods of fluidity and looseness, deserves closer attention from both historians and legal philosophers. The general outlines of this theory advanced by Pound are successfully proven by his argument for the most part. Implicit in his thesis, however, is a far more profound and important issue that should be considered carefully by both the practitioner and theorist of law, *i.e.*, what are the indices that should be employed to measure the degree of flexibility that is needed in the face of changing circumstances, as opposed to the degree of certainty and fixity that must be retained. Certain developments in the field of contract law, for example, profoundly underscore this issue which Pound has raised. Should doctrines such as unconscionability play any role in the interpretation and enforcement of contracts? Most assuredly such notions when carried to their furthest development leave contracts uncertain and determination of their enforceability becomes a province of almost total judicial discretion. In such a case the development of enterprise is placed in jeopardy, for the growth of enterprise, as Pound has argued so cogently, depends on men being able to assume that their investment of time and resources is secured to them by the law, and yet, if the contracts, on which enterprise is necessarily based, are subject to revocation or revision at the will of the judge, then certainty is removed and the growth of enterprise is thwarted. These are the matters that are contained in Pound's theory on the stages in the development of the law. Although at one point he concluded that the stage of "socialization of the law" might have marked the end of this sequential development, much of his later writing implicitly was calling for a new stage of fixity and certainty to repair the damages that had come from the overexpansion of fluidity in the law. One need only read Pound's devastating critique of the growth and development of administrative law to conclude that he was calling for a tightening of the law to restrain and hold in check this development because it threatens the entire fabric of a legal order. Much could be done by legal research in carrying forward this interesting and important thesis of Pound in the face of the great flexibility and uncertainty that has characterized American legal development over the past few decades.[3]

Pound's thorough examination of the development of legal philosophy from antiquity to the modern era deserves closer attention by law schools and legal philosophers. The great wealth of material in legal scholarship and philosophy that he surveys is largely ignored in law school curricula while such a school as "critical legal studies" enjoys effervescent popularity. Pound, who had a most impressive understanding of the scope of legal philosophy as it has developed in the western world, would undoubtedly be astounded that such a pretentious and vacuous theory as "critical legal studies" could be taken seriously. This fashionable doctrine is merely repetitive of what had been examined by more profound theorists in the past, and does not provide much that is new over the previously discredited attempts to view law in such a one dimensional fashion. What Pound does emphasize as significant in the long history of legal philosophy is the general line of development, abandoned mainly by legal realists and positivists, which viewed legal philosophy as the most effective means to develop an understanding of the nature, origin, and purpose of law, considered as a major element in the maintenance and furtherance of civilization. His approach is properly critical and analytical. He gives credit for significance where credit is due and criticism where it is deserved. Law schools would do well to focus on the breadth of this type of scholarship in order to prepare attorneys for the practice of law understood as a *bona fide* profession, which has a definable content and purpose that makes it a profession; and which has a common heritage, a set of ideals, an identifiable technique, and classifiable precepts and doctrines which in their totality constitute the nature of the profession. When this is understood and transmitted the quality of the profession would be improved and elevated.[4]

As we have seen, Pound expressed great regret over the coloration that had been given to "sociological jurisprudence" by those who had corrupted it to become a tool for the expansion of the service state. In Pound's view sociological jurisprudence was a descriptive and analytical term, not a prescriptive one. To equate sociological jurisprudence with any variant of socialism would be to ignore the refined expression of this theory that was provided by Roscoe Pound. Pound viewed sociological jurisprudence as the articulation of the socialization of law. To understand these terms and concepts as he did requires that one understand that for Pound the emphasis on relation that comes in the wake of socialization of law is not a new concept. Rather it is the recapturing of what he calls the "feudal principle" that he feels is one of the two elements of the tradition of law in the western world.

This socialization includes, he says, "...the shifting from the individualist justice of the past century to a newer ideal of justice...."[5] What Pound is referring to is the legislative and judicial emphasis on the relationships in which men find themselves to determine the degree of legal right and duty that they have. This particular view of law dictated by relationship, is not new in the legal traditions of the west. Quite the contrary, it derives mainly from the developments in law most specifically associated with the feudal era and reflected in that time period by land relationships as well as familial and other relationships. Pound believed that in the modern era, in response to the impact and necessities stemming from industrialization, urbanization, and technological advancement, reconsideration of this notion of law is required in order to enable it to deal with men as they find themselves in relationship to others. This is a mark of the socialization of law. Thus, Pound points to the emergence of Workmen's Compensation Laws as reflective of this renewed emphasis on relation. However, what must be clearly and fully understood in Pound's description of these notions of socialization and relation, is not a plea for extended "social" or "socialistic" legislation or judicial interpretation. Rather, what Pound is describing is the necessity of law to fashion responses that enable it to deal with emerging new interests that were not found in the nineteenth century, and which, therefore, call for legislative, judicial, and administrative relief. Such relief is not predicated on the belief that the state should assume powers and responsibilities that are not called for, but only fashion conditions in which the newly emergent interests can be accommodated without sacrifice of other interests already in existence which must be preserved. For example, Pound cites the need for traffic legislation and regulations that followed in the wake of the introduction of the automobile in society, showing clearly and convincingly that such legislation and regulation would neither have made sense, nor would have been needed to handle the traffic problems of a society relying on horse carriages and wagons. Further, in his view there was no great mystery or problem in having the law move into other areas to accommodate problems that were unique to a newly created laboring class in the era of industrialization. Pound also felt that the development of such law would, could, and should be accommodated to the nature of the common law of tort and contract, and that no disservice would be done to them as a result of this legal development. Indeed he felt keenly that such developments in the law retained the vitality of the common law and reinforced its most beneficial effects, *i.e.*, a "living force for justice."[6] Clearly, Pound was not urging a prescription, or a formula that called for society to be fashioned along lines of some egalitarian ideology, nor was he urging the bestowal of advantageous rights upon some while imposing additional duties upon others. Rather, his conception of the socialization of law and sociological jurisprudence both were directed at using the law as a vital force for the resolution of conflicting claims in a society, which he felt, and quite properly, could not be done through the employment of some static and fixed notion of law which insisted that legal reality must be forced to conform to some Procrustean bed of legal philosophy.[7]

Because Pound felt that the law was the most effective mechanism available to modern man to achieve the social control necessary for maintaining and furthering civilization, he was concerned with fashioning an explanation of the process by which this task could be best achieved. For him one of the most identifiable realities of a society was the fact that there were interests which must be taken into account in the employment of social control. According to Pound these interests were not fictional creations, they were, rather, descriptive categories of what major issues had to be reconciled within a society in order to achieve order, security, predictability, and progress. Although Pound spends a great deal of effort in explaining the nature of individual interests of personality, domestic relations, and substance, he felt that in most instances reconciliation of competing claims should be done by balancing the social interests that were involved. In his theory no damage is done to the individual interests in doing this, since the individual interests were subsumed in the social interest in individual life. As conflicts of interests and aspirations arise in society, one should feel compelled to consider what the protection of such claims, if recognized, would do to the entire range of social interests that must be considered. Basic to this formulation was Pound's insistence that the protection accorded to any one of the social interests should not be done by destroying or severely damaging the other social interests which must be taken into account. His formulation of this concept of interests was not tied exclusively to economic concerns which it is fashionable to do when discussing interests today. Indeed the social interest in the general security, conservation of natural resources, general progress, general morals, and the security of social institutions are equally important in Pound's theory, and should not be slighted in consideration when evaluating what resolution will serve the society's needs at a particular point in time. In order to appreciate the constructive use to which this theory is to be directed one must remember Pound's insistence that reconciliation of conflict must also serve the criteria established by the jural postulates which, in effect, define a civilized order. These jural postulates embody, in succinct form, the major values that underlie western liberal society. Attempts to employ a "balancing of interests" test becomes a relatively sterile undertaking unless constant attention is given to the fact that the purpose of such reconciliation is to serve in the maintenance and furtherance of civilization. If this purpose does not lie at the heart of legislation and adjudication then law becomes only a tool in the exercise of power, no more moral than a gun, and no more justifiable. Law, to serve its purposes in fashioning social control, is an instrument of civilization, and as such is compelled to serve in the constraint and limitation of governmental power. Pound's theory of interests provides a workable method of measuring respective claims in the total context of what a civilized society requires, and enables the legislator and the judge to determine what resolution is consistent with the maintenance and furtherance of civilization.[8]

In the growing era of governmental absolutism Pound could easily see the destructive impact that administrative action was having on the role law must play in controlling governmental power. Both executive justice and legislative justice create distortions in the role that law should play. Indeed they corrupt law and in turn serve to dismantle civilization. Consequently, Pound places great reliance on the judiciary as the institutional system best designed to give effect to the proper purposes of law and to assure its employment in maintaining and furthering civilization. For Pound the courts are the only institutions capable of keeping in check the excesses that are bound to come from increased legislative and executive action. Such excesses in the demand for the use of governmental power for the achievement of particularized benefits is particularly pronounced in systems that are "democratically governed." The fatal flaw of democracies lies in the temptation to clothe in rightness that which has extensive popular support. Determination of solutions to conflict that are measured by the amount of power aligned behind one group of interests to the detriment of another group, is characteristic of all abusive governmental authority. What should prevail is the operation of the law in determining the legitimacy and propriety of the solution, and this can best be achieved by confining such decisions ultimately to the courts. The executive and legislative branches of government are susceptible to the corruption of numbers, passion, and power, while, in Pound's view, the courts are guided by the necessary dictates of the law which embody the ideals of the society, the technique that must be employed in their operation, and the precepts and conceptions which control their outcomes. It is the courts alone which are capable of recognizing and preserving the long term interests of the society against the demands that stem from popular passion and temporary majorities. Pound very clearly points to the correctness of this view when he urges the review of all administrative action by independent judicial bodies. Given the judicial activism of the past decades, however, one might be suspicious of Pound's reliance on the courts to achieve what he felt they would, *i.e.*, the control of the exercise of power. However, if one assumes, as Pound did, the continuation of proper legal education tailored to informing the practitioners of law of the proper nature, role, and purpose of law his argument holds together. Current developments in legal education, however, make one less optimistic than Pound about the capacity and ability of the judiciary to serve in restraining the excesses of power and the abandonment of law.

Pound's treatment of administrative law, surely is among the finest of his writing and most timely in its importance. The tempo of growth of administrative law in the United States is increasing and not decreasing.[9] The threats to a society under law that come from administrative law are extensive and very real. Little has been done to correct the abuses of administrative behavior about which Pound warns, and much more attention should be given to his writing in this area of law. Pound understood what impelled bureaucracies and warned of the great intrusions they would make into the daily lives of the citizens of a society subject to extended administrative law. The urgency of his message is not dated, and the outlines of the issue he presents are as germane today as when they were written, and practitioners and theorists of law would do well to inform themselves of Pound's writing in this area. The demands for growth of administrative law are even greater today than they were when Pound wrote, but the demand for judicial restraint of such action has diminished in turn. Pound's solution, while it cannot provide the ultimate answer to the problems created by administrative regulation and control, does provide a respite to the assault made by it on a society ruled by law.[10]

The closest Pound came to providing us with a comprehensive and thorough statement of his philosophy is in a series of lectures given late in his life at the University of Tagore, India, which have not been reproduced in the United States.[11] Much of Pound's writing is merely repetitious of earlier statements made by him. The Tagore lectures are a refreshing change from this pattern in Pound's scholarship. What stands out clearly in these lectures is a philosophy of the law, in which the role of the ideal element dominates and influences Pound's judgment of the law. The content of this ideal element, as we have seen, is in his earlier writings. Pound's philosophy of law is succinctly presented in his statement that "Civilization involves subjection of force to reason, and the agency of this subjection is law."[12] Much of Pound's writing was given over to tracing the evolution of law in practice, and a history of the development of the philosophy of law. One can be critical of Pound's historical writing on several grounds—primarily his oversimplification, and inadequate scholarship,—but Pound's purpose in fashioning this history was clear. To him, law was the major force which elevated man from bestiality to civilized conduct, and from primitive modes of social organization to refined civilization. Pound attempted to classify and order this progression of legal development and to account for the content and significance of legal philosophy in the centuries of law's development. He posed one of the most significant problems confronting both the legal historian and the legal philosopher—why, how, and when does law change and to what ends or purposes is law to be directed? Pound's answers should not be considered definitive by any means but at least they provide a necessary preliminary step to further inquiry into the problem. As Pound points out, that while each stage of legal history

> is taken to be self-sufficient such periods of legal development when stability is the norm require and rely upon analysis rather than philosophy. It is in periods of growth, periods in which the law is fluid, periods in which an infusion of ideas from without is making over the law, that philosophy has played a leading role in legal history.[13]

Thus, to Pound, the practice of law and the philosophy of law are inextricably bound, with both providing the two vital elements in law—stability and change. As Pound remarks:

> Law must be stable and yet it cannot stand still. Hence all thinking about law has struggled to reconcile the conflicting demands of the need of stability and of the need of change.[14]

It is no exaggeration to suggest that no more profound a question exists in legal philosophy than that of determining how, why, and for what reason law should alter to meet altered circumstances. Hayek and others suggest that the recordation of this vexing problem is evidenced in early Greek writing on the law and that the conflict between that view which considered law fixed and immutable and embodied in settled custom and values came into conflict early with that view of law as something "made" by the will of men. Such a conflict between ideas continues even today between legal positivists and natural law writers. Pound attempts to show that settled law's weakness is to be found in its inflexibility and therefore its inability to deal with what he calls newly-emerging interests. The historical changes in law are a consequence of the need for law to so reconstruct itself to meet such new conditions. In Pound's view, however, such response is not some mechanical operation of challenge and response which has as its consequence a rudderless and non-directed pattern of development. Rather, such changes are, or should be tailored, to effect justice, which he suggests involves the adjusting

> of relation and ordering of conduct...[that] will make the goods of existence, the means of satisfying human claims to have things and do things, go round as far as possible with the least friction and waste.[15]

One must be careful in evaluating Pound's formulation of justice, for it was conditioned by his ardent belief that law was governed by the ideal of liberating men in two senses. First, it enables man to restrict his capacity to let his passions rule his reason. Selfishness and the unrestrained drive for self-aggrandizement could be fatal to a civilized order. Thus law's purpose—in addition to the aid it receives from family training, religious instruction, and the moral principles of the society—is to aid man in restraining his selfish drives and fashion them to assist in the cooperative enterprise needed to maintain and further a civilized order. Second, law facilitates cooperative efforts which ultimately provide for the greatest comforts, maximum efficiency, and the progress of civilization.

Pound's formulation of law's role and the nature of justice is not a prescription for a redistributive fascist state. Rather, it is a wise formulation of what law must do in order to maintain and further a civilized order. To be sure, law must fashion the conditions in which order and security are preserved, for as Pound wisely observes men are averse to committing their energies, their talents, their time, and their substance if there is little guarantee they can profit from having done so.[16] Release of individual ability and talents in a civilized society is very desirable according to Pound, and limitations, when they occur, must be for rational purposes, and careful attention must be given to the consequences such limitations may have on the overall good of the society. His argument basically is a reflection of his belief that law is an agency of social control designed to serve those interests and values necessary for society's and civilization's maintenance and furtherance. In this respect his ideas are at some variance with much nineteenth century and early twentieth century thought which was tied to abstract notions of liberty as a supreme good to be served in all cases and without reservation. However, Pound does consider liberty to be a very significant value that is to be protected whenever possible unless its preservation threatens or harms other equally significant values. In Pound's writing this emphasis is bound up in his concept of the social interest in the individual life, which according to Pound, is on a par with other social interests such as those in the general progress, morals, etc. but not an interest subordinate to them. Pound's ideal of law is that it could and would employ reason and experience, on the one hand, to fashion accommodations within society to new needs and new interests; and, on the other hand, control and limit the exercise of state power so men could enjoy the fruits of a civilized order in which power is not law, but is controlled by law. As Pound notes:

> Law is the real foe of absolutism. It presupposes a life measured by reason, a legal order measured by reason, and a judicial process carried on by applying a reasoned technique to experience developed by reason and reason tested by experience.[17]

The method as we have seen[18] involved law's use of social engineering which was a primary facet of Pound's sociological jurisprudence. One must also note, however, that what Pound means by socialization of law is not what it has come to mean in modern terms, for as we have seen, Pound states, this newer conception reverses his formula. Pound rejected the use of this concept that endorses the idea of unfettered power by the state to fashion society as it sees fit, unchecked by law. Indeed, such a view he labelled authoritarian.[19]

It was beyond Pound's imagination at the early part of his career when he began to write about the socialization of law, to foresee the purposes to which it would be put and the values by which it would be guided. He was fairly convinced that those in the law—jurists, philosophers, teachers, practitioners—would understand the predicates of law as they developed in the western legal tradition—and more particularly within the Anglo-American tradition. That is to say, law would not be used as an implement of power by any class; that it would make only those adjustments dictated by necessity to face modern conditions following in the wake of industrialization and economic growth; and that it would always employ reason and experience in measuring its purposes and practices. As he approached the final years of his life he realized that such a faith was not well founded. Really society was captivated by notion of power and authority and seemed anxious to forget the bases that had made our legal order one in which individuals could flourish and be protected. As he writes:

> Nowadays, in a time of the cult of absolutism, reliance on force rather than reason, and of current philosophies which disparage liberty and rate satisfaction of material wants as the highest good and the end of government, those who write on the science of government are prone to speak lightly of...constitutional provisions [to limit government]. To some they are inconsistent with democracy. It is assumed that democracy must be an absolute rule of a majority for the time being, and the idea of limitations on those who exercise the powers of a politically organized society under a democracy is rejected. In the same way, under the Tudors and Stuarts many thought that monarchy must be the absolute rule of an autocratic king and that limitations on what his agents could do were obsolescent remnants from the feudal regime. But, as Mr. Justice Miller put it, the spirit of our government is opposed to the deposit of unlimited power anywhere. Democracy does not require that its agents have absolute power and be, like the Eastern Roman emperor, free from the laws. A generation which is willing to give up the legal inheritance of Americans and set up a regime of absolute rule of a majority may find that in that event it is under the absolute rule of a leader of the majority.[20]

Pound provides an eloquent defense of a rational and prudent conception of law understood as an instrument to serve free men and protect them from the abuses of power.

No finer summation of what lay at the base of Pound's whole notion of law is available than his summary of our Constitutional scheme of governance as he understood it. He writes:

> whether rule is borne by Rex or Demos, a ruler ruling reasonably under God and the law founds his kingdom on a rock.[21]

ENDNOTES

CHAPTER TEN

1. David Wigdor, *Roscoe Pound: Philosopher of Law*; Westport, Connecticut, Greenwood Press, 1974, p. 284.

2. Pound, *Development Constitutional Guarantees..., passim.*

3. See Chapter Two: Pound on Legal History.

4. See Chapters Three, Four, and Five.

5. Roscoe Pound, "A Feudal Principle in Modern Law," *The International Journal of Ethics*. October, 1914, Vol. 25, pp. 5-24. Vol. 1, PB 68 (Hereinafter referred to "Feudal Principle...").

6. Pound, "Feudal Principle...," p. 24.

7. See Chapter Six: Socialization of Law.

8. See Chapter Seven: Theory of Interests.

9. See Chapter Nine: Judicial Justice.

10. See Chapter Eight: Administrative Justice.

11. Pound, *The Ideal Element...Tagore*.

12. R. Pound, "The Future of Law," *Yale Law Journal*, Vol. 47, November, 1937, p. 19. Vol. 1, PB 227 (Hereinafter referred to as "Future...").

13. Pound, *Spirit...*, p. 149.

14. Pound, *Interpretations of Legal...*, p. 1.

15. Pound, *Social Control...*, p. 65.

16. Pound, *Vol. 2*, p. 380.

17. Pound, *The Ideal Element...Tagore*, p. 269.

18. See Chapter Seven: Theory of Interests.

19. Pound, *The Ideal Element...Tagore*, p. 268.

20. Pound, *Development...Constitutional*, p. 109.

21. Ibid., p. 111.

Selected Bibliography

These are sources referred to in the text of this book, and are arranged chronologically. The two volume set of Pound's writings are the most complete sources that compile Pound's writing. For the convenience of the reader, the number, following each entry refers to its citation in these two volumes of the Pound Bibliographies published at Harvard University. *A Bibliography of The Writings of Roscoe Pound.* Franklyn C. Setaro (ed). Cambridge, Massachusetts, Harvard University Press, 1942. (Vol. 1). A Bibliography of the Writings of Roscoe Pound: 1940-1960. George A. Strait (ed). Cambridge, Massachusetts, Harvard Law School Library, 1960. (Vol. 2).

Vol. I

1906

"The Causes of Popular Dissatisfaction with the Administration of Justice." *Report of the 29th Annual Meeting of the American Bar Association*, Vol. 29, 1906. pp. 395-417. #20.

1907

"Executive Justice," *American Law Register*, Vol. 55, March, 1907. pp. 137-146, #22.

"The Need of a Sociological Jurisprudence," *Green Bag*, Vol. 19, October, 1907. pp. 607-615, #24.

1908

"Enforcement of Law," *Green Bag*, Vol. 20, August, 1908. pp. 401-410. #28.

1909

"Liberty of Contract," *Yale Law Journal*, Vol. 18, May, 1909, pp. 454-487. #18.

1910

"Some Principles of Procedural Reform," *Illinois Law Review*, Vol. 4, January-February, 1910. pp. 388-407, 491-508. #35.

"A Practical Program of Procedural Reform," *Chicago Legal News*, Vol. 42, June, 1910, pp. 370-371. #36.

1911

"The Scope and Purpose of Sociological Jurisprudence," *Harvard Law Review*, Vol. 24. *Ibid.* Vol. 25. I June, 1911, pp. 591-619. II December, 1911, pp. 140-168. III April, 1912, pp. 489-516. #43.

1912

"Social Justice and Legal Justice," *Central Law Journal*, Vol. 75. December, 1912, pp. 455-463. #51.

"Theories of Law," *Yale Law Journal*, Vol. 22. December, 1912. pp. 114-150. #52.

1913

"The Administration of Justice in the Modern City." *Harvard Law Journal*, Vol. 26. February, 1913. pp. 302-328. #57.

"Political and Economic Interpretations of Jurisprudence," *Proceedings of the American Political Science Association*, Vol. 9, 1913, pp. 94-105. #63.

1914

"Justice According to Law," *Columbia Law Review*, Vol. 13, December, 1913, pp. 696-713; Vol. 14, January-February, 1914, pp. 1-26; pp. 103-121. #60

"The End of Law as Developed in Legal Rules and Doctrines." *Harvard Law Review*, Vol. 27. January, 1914, pp. 195-234. #64.

"The Socialization of the Common Law," *Green Bag*, Vol. 26, April, 1914. #65.

"The End of Law as Developed in Juristic Thought." *Harvard Law Review*. Vol. 27. May, 1914, pp. 605-628. *Ibid.* Vol. 30, January, 1917. pp. 201-225. #66.

"A Feudal Principle in Modern Law," *International Journal of Ethics*, Vol. 25, October, 1914, pp. 1-24. #68.

1915

"Interests of Personality," *Harvard Law Review*, Vol. 28, February-March, 1915, pp. 343-365, 445-456. #71.

"Making Law and Finding Law," *Ohio Law Reporter*, Vol. 13, August, 1915, pp. 283-300. #72.

1916

"Individual Interests in Domestic Relations." Michigan Law Review. Vol. 14. pp. 177-196. #78.

"Equitable Relief against Defamation and Injuries to Personality." *Harvard Law Review*. Vol. 29, April, 1916, pp. 640-682. #80.

"The Limits of Effective Legal Action," *American Bar Association Journal*, Vol. 3, January, 1917, pp. 55-70. #82.

1917

"The Revival of Personal Government," *Proceedings of the Nebraska State Bar Association*. Vol. 9, 1916. pp. 105-124. #89.

1918

"Juristic Science and Law." *Harvard Law Review*, Vol. 31, June, 1918, pp. 1047-1063. #91.

1921

The Spirit of the Common Law. Boston, Mass., Marshall Jones Co., 1931. #107.

"A Theory of Social Interests." *Papers and Proceedings of the American Sociological Society*, Vol. 15, 1921, pp. 16-45. #108.

1922

An Introduction to the Philosophy of Law. New Haven Conn., Yale University Press, 1937. #111.

1923

"The Theory of Judicial Decision, I & II," *Harvard Law Review*, Vol. 36, April, May, 1923, pp. 641-662, 802-825. # 113.

"Preventive Justice and Social Work." *Proceedings of the National Conference on Social Work.* May, 1923, pp. 151-163. #115.

"The Growth of Administrative Justice." *Proceedings of the Wisconsin State Bar Association.* Vol. 14, 1923, pp. 191-208. #117.

Interpretations of Legal History. Cambridge, England, The University Press, 1930. #118.

1924

Law and Morals. Chapel Hill, N. C., The University of North Carolina Press, 1924. #123. Reprinted New York: Augustus M. Kelly, 1969.

John C. H. Wu, "The Juristic Philosophy of Roscoe Pound," *Illinois Law Review*, Vol. 18, January, 1924, pp. 285-304. Appendix A, #A-3.

1925

"The Law School and the Legal Tradition," *Michigan Law Review*, Vol. 24, December, 1925, pp. 156-165. #128.

"The Legal Profession and the Law," *Proceedings of the 18th Meeting of the Oklahoma Bar Association*, 1925, pp. 179-205. #133

"The Problem of Law." *American Bar Association Journal*, Vol. 12, February, 1926. pp. 81-87. #134.

1926

"Law and the Christian Code." *In: An Outline of Christianity: The Story of Our Civilization. Vol. 5*. New York; Bethlehem Publishers, Inc., 1926. #144.

1927

"The Progress of the Law - Analytical Jurisprudence, 1914-1927." *Harvard Law Review*. vol. 41, December, 1927. pp. 174-199. #154.

1928

"The Future of the Common Law." *Nebraska Law Bulletin*, Vol. 7, July, 1928, pp. 107-122. #160.

1929

"Jurisprudence." *In: Research in the Social Sciences, Its Fundamental Methods and Objectives.*, 1929. pp. 181-206. #168.

1931

"The Call for a Realist Jurisprudence." *Harvard Law Review*. Vol. 44, March, 1931. pp. 697-771. #178.

1932

"The Problem of an Ordered Society," *Tennessee Law Review*, Vol. 11, December, 1932, pp. 1-13. #186.

1933

"What Use Can Be Made of Judicial Statistics." *Oregon Law Review*, Vol. 12, February, 1933, pp. 89-95. #191.

"A Comparison of Ideals Of Law." *Harvard Law Review*, Vol. 47, November, 1933, pp. 1-17. #195.

1934

"Law and The Science of Law in Recent Theories." *Yale Law Journal*, Vol. 43. February, 1934. pp. 525-536. #199.

"Law and Laws in the Twentieth Century." In: *Dedicatory Exercises of the Law Quadrangle, University of Michigan Law School*, June 15, 1934, pp. 25-46. (not in the bibliography.)

1936

"The Theory of Judicial Decision." *Harvard Law Review*. Vol. 36, April, 1923, pp. 641-662. #112.

1937

"Fifty Years of Jurisprudence I." *Harvard Law Review*. Vol. 50, February, 1937, pp. 557-582. *Ibid* II & III. Vol. 51, January-March, 1938, II pp. 444-472, III 777-812. #224.

"The Future of Law." *Yale Law Journal*, Vol. 47, November, 1937, pp. 1-13. #227.

1938

"Executive Justice," (See Bibliographic Entry 1907, Reprinted in: *Selected Essays on Selected Essays on Constitutional Law*, Chicago: Foundation Press, Inc., 1938, pp. 63-75.

1939

"The Recrudescence of Absolutism," *Sewanee Review*, Vol. 47, January-March, 1939, pp. 18-28. #236.

The History and System of the Common Law. New York, P. F. Collier & Son., 1939. #249.

"Modern Administrative Law," *Proceedings of the 50th Annual Meeting of the Virginia Bar Association*, 1939, p. 372-388. #251.

1940

"The Economic Interpretation and the Law of Torts," *Harvard Law Review*, Vol. 53, January, 1940, pp. 365-385. #252.

Contemporary Juristic Theory, Pomona College, Scripps College, Claremont College, 1940.

"The Twilight of Liberty," *Nation's Business*, Vol. 28, August, 1940, p. 8ff. #50.

Vol. II

1941

The Task of Law, Franklin and Marshall College, Pennsylvania, 1941. #2.

"Administrative Law; Its Growth, Procedure and Significance." *Pittsburgh Law Review*, Vol. 7, June, 1941, pp. 269-282. #4. Reprinted University of Pittsburgh Press, 1942, not in Pound Bibliography.

Social Control Through Law, New Haven, Connecticut, Yale University Press, 1942. #7.

"Place of the Judiciary in a Democratic Polity; an Examination of the Walter Logan Veto Message." *American Bar Association Journal*, Vol. 27, March, 1941, pp. 133-139. #58.

"Disappearance of the Law," *Alabama Lawyer*, Vol. 2, October, 1941, pp. 363-381. #62.

"Symposium, Administrative Procedural Legislation." For the "Minority Report." *American Bar Association Journal*, Vol. 27. November, 1941, pp. 664-678. #63.

1943

"Sociology of Law and Sociological Jurisprudence." *University of Toronto Law Journal*. Vol. 5, Lent Term, 1943. #10

"A Survey of Social Interests," *Harvard Law Review*, Vol. 57, October, 1943, pp. 1-39. #12.

1944

"The Legal Profession in England from the End of the Middle Ages to the Nineteenth Century." *Notre Dame Lawyer*. Vol. 19. pp. 315-333. #88.

"The Challenge of the Administrative Process." *American Bar Association Journal*. Vol. 30, March, 1944. pp. 121-126. #96.

"The American Idea of Government." *Vital Speeches*, Vol. 10, September, 1944, pp. 681-687. #98.

"Proposed Legislation as To Federal Administrative Procedures." *Indiana Law Journal*, Vol. 20, October, 1944, pp. 29-33. #100.

"Administrative Law and the Courts." *Boston University Law Review*, Vol. 24, November, 1944, pp. 201-223. #101.

1945

"A Survey of Public Interests," *Harvard Law Review*, Vol. 58. September, 1945. pp. 909-929. #70.

1946

"Administrative Agencies and the Law," *New York National Industrial Conference Board, Inc.*, 1946. #22. Reprinted in shorter form in *American Affairs*, Spring, 1946, under the title: "What is Happening to the Law?".

1951

Justice According to Law. New Haven, Connecticut, Yale University Press, 1951. #27.

1952

"Natural Natural Law and Positive Natural Law," *The Law Quarterly Review*. Vol. 68. July, 1952. pp. 330-336. #62.

1953

Introduction to the Philosophy of Law. (rev. ed.)New Haven, Connecticut, Yale University Press, 1954. #34.

1957

The Development of Constitutional Guarantees of Liberty. New Haven, Connecticut, Yale University Press, 1957. #39.

1958

The Ideal Element in Law, Calcutta, India, University Of Calcutta, 1958. #42.

1959

Jurisprudence. 5 Vols. St. Paul, Minnesota, West Publishing Co., 1959.

"Judicial Trial or Administrative Investigation," *NACAA Law Journal*, Vol. 24, November, 1959. pp. 290-302. #256.

1960

Law Finding Through Experience and Reason. Athens, Georgia, University of Georgia Press, 1960.